PLOUGHSHARES AND SWORDS

PLOUGHSHARES AND SWORDS

INDIA'S NUCLEAR PROGRAM IN THE GLOBAL COLD WAR

JAYITA SARKAR

CORNELL UNIVERSITY PRESS
Ithaca and London

Thanks to generous funding from the Swiss National
Science Foundation, the ebook editions of this book are
available as open-access volumes through the Cornell
Open initiative.

First published 2022 by Cornell University Press

Library of Congress Cataloging-in-Publication Data

Names: Sarkar, Jayita, 1986– author.
Title: Ploughshares and swords : India's nuclear program
    in the global Cold War / Jayita Sarkar.
Other titles: Plowshares and swords
Description: Ithaca [New York]: Cornell University Press,
    2022. | Includes bibliographical references and index. |
Identifiers: LCCN 2021054784 (print) | LCCN 2021054785
    (ebook) | ISBN 9781501764400 (hardcover) | ISBN
9781501764424 (pdf) | ISBN 9781501764417 (epub)
Subjects: LCSH: Nuclear energy—India—History—20th
    century. | Nuclear energy—Government policy—
    India—History—20th century. | Nuclear weapons—
    India—History—20th century. | Nuclear weapons—
    Government policy—India—History—20th century. |
    Technology and state—India—History—20th century. |
    India—Foreign relations—1947–1984.
Classification: LCC HD9698.I52 S27 2022 (print) |
    LCC HD9698.I52 (ebook) | DDC 333.792/40954—
    dc23/eng/20220112
LC record available at https://lccn.loc.gov/2021054784
LC ebook record available at https://lccn.loc.gov
    /2021054785

For Dadu, Ma, and Cheryl

CONTENTS

Maps and Illustrations

Maps

Illustrations

ACKNOWLEDGMENTS

Location matters for the writing of history. It mattered for writing this book. Having grown up in India, I have vivid memories of the eleven nuclear weapon tests that shook South Asia in May 1998. As a young adult, I read passionate editorials in favor and against the 2008 US-India civil nuclear agreement. But, when I saw the world from the shores of Lac Léman in Switzerland, where this project began, the Mont Blanc in the horizon offered much-needed emotional and intellectual distance. It influenced this book's conception, research, and writing.

The French role in India's nuclear program first caught my attention while chatting with Robert S. Anderson (or Bob da, as he likes to be called by his Bengali friends) at Crêperie des Pâquis in Geneva. Since then, Bob da's decade-long mentorship has been enormously fruitful for this book. Research support from 2010 to 2014 from the Graduate Institute Geneva's Department of International History, a 2011 visiting fellowship at the Institute for Defence Studies and Analyses in New Delhi, the 2013 Albert Gallatin predoctoral fellowship at Yale University's South Asian Studies Council, a 2013 junior visiting scholarship at the Woodrow Wilson Center's History and Public Policy Program, the 2013 Moody Research Grant from the Lyndon B. Johnson Presidential Library, a 2014 fellowship from the Norwegian Institute for Defence Studies, and a 2016 research grant from the Gerald R. Ford Presidential Library facilitated research and writing for this book. Travel grants from the History of Science Society, Peace History Society, Swiss Academy of Humanities and Social Sciences, and Society for Historians of American Foreign Relations facilitated my participation at major conferences, where this project benefited from helpful feedback. The Woodrow Wilson Center's Nuclear Proliferation International History Project was a tremendous source of support.

Many individuals provided feedback and asked insightful questions that helped me to improve this book over the years. My utmost gratitude goes to Jussi Hanhimäki for believing in me and to Francis J. Gavin for asking helpful questions in the early stages of this project. I am particularly grateful to Debjani Bhattacharyya, Matthew Bunn, William Burr, the late Stephen P. Cohen,

Alexandre Debs, David Engerman, Šumit Ganguly, Michael Graziano, Gabri-elle Hecht, David Holloway, Sheila Jasanoff, the late Robert Jervis, John Krige, Stuart W. Leslie, Michele Louro, Robert McMahon, Zia Mian, Steven E. Miller, Leopoldo Nuti, Christian Ostermann, Jean-Luc Racine, Srinath Raghavan, M. V. Ramana, Andrew Rotter, Asif Siddiqi, Fiona Smyth, Nina Tannen-wald, and Maurice Vaïsse. Or Rabinowitz and Mircea Raianu shared archival documents, for which I am indebted.

At Dartmouth College, where I held a residential fellowship and hosted a book workshop in 2019, the manuscript went through extensive rewriting. In Hanover, I benefited from the encouragement of Douglas Haynes, Stefan Link, Edward Miller, Jennifer Miller, Nicholas Miller, Daryl Press, Benjamin Valen-tino, and William Wohlforth. Ed Miller gave me the courage to invoke "techno-politics" more forcefully. I would like to especially thank Elisabeth Leake, Ed Miller, Jenni Miller, and Lydia Walker, for reading several revised drafts even after the workshop. Elaine Waterman, my landlady in Norwich, Vermont, kept me on my toes during the fellowship by regularly inquiring about "the book."

Feedback and help from the staff and editors at Cornell University Press and Westchester Publishing Services were significant. I am particularly thank-ful to my editors Sarah Grossman and Michael McGandy, production editors Susan Specter and Kristen Bettcher, and the two anonymous reviewers. Sec-tions of the book draw on research from previously published journal articles. I am grateful to MIT Press, Oxford University Press, Sage Publishing, and Tay-lor & Francis for permission to reprint some of this content.[1] An open-access book grant from the Swiss National Science Foundation made this book avail-able to all.

No part of this research would have been possible without the help of tire-less archivists in various parts of the globe. Research assistants Namara Burki and Sara Idris Hussein facilitated "second looks" at documents in archives in Paris and New Delhi, respectively. Jay Slagle, Angela Valente, and Tom Ware made some of the prose readable.

At Boston University, I benefited from great collegiality and support, not least from Houchang Chehabi, who shared from his personal collection a trove of 1970s newspaper clippings about India and Iran. Houchang even person-ally translated sections from Akbar Etemad's biographies from Persian to En-glish. Insightful questions from the students of IR377, IR315, and IR522 strengthened the book's arguments. The Global Decolonization Initiative's re-search interns were a source of much-needed inspiration during the COVID-19 pandemic, when I completed the book's final revisions.

My friends Rez Ahmed, Kranti Biswas, Pavel Chakraborty, and Smruthi Ram-mohan, stood by my side and made the slog bearable in Geneva, Switzerland.

My spouse, Cheryl, has been inspiring me since we first met in New Haven, Connecticut. My cats, Gorky and Grieg, have been reliable assistants in Boston, Massachusetts, as I completed this book. Ma and Baba's endless encouragement from Calcutta made everything possible. I remain in eternal gratitude to Dadu and Didu, my late grandparents, who taught me to stop and smell the roses, and to Cheryl, the rock of my life. To Dadu, Ma, and Cheryl, I dedicate this book.

Abbreviations

AECI	Atomic Energy Commission of India
AECL	Atomic Energy of Canada Limited
AEOI	Atomic Energy Organization of Iran
BARC	Bhabha Atomic Research Centre
BJP	Bharatiya Janata Party
CANDU	Canada Deuterium Uranium (a reactor type)
CEA	Commissariat à l'énergie atomique
CIA	Central Intelligence Agency
CIRUS	Canada-India Reactor with US heavy water
CISAC	Committee on International Studies of Arms Control (American Academy)
CSIR	Council of Scientific and Industrial Research
DAE	Department of Atomic Energy (India)
DRDO	Defence Research and Development Organisation
ENDC	Eighteen Nations Disarmament Committee
GOI	Government of India
IAEA	International Atomic Energy Agency
IISc	Indian Institute of Science
INR	Bureau of Intelligence and Research, US Department of State

ISRO	Indian Space Research Organisation
MEA	Ministry of External Affairs (India)
MIT	Massachusetts Institute of Technology
NASA	National Aeronautics and Space Administration
NATO	North Atlantic Treaty Organization
NPT	Nuclear Nonproliferation Treaty
NRC	Nuclear Regulatory Commission
NSC	National Security Council
OAPEC	Organization of Arab Petroleum Exporting Countries
OPEC	Organization of Petroleum Exporting Countries
PLA	People's Liberation Army
PNE	peaceful nuclear explosion
PURNIMA	Plutonium Reactor for Neutronic Investigations in Multiplying Assemblies
R&AW	Research & Analysis Wing
SLV	satellite launch vehicle
STR	Société de Produits Chimiques des Terres Rares
TIFR	Tata Institute of Fundamental Research
UKAEA	UK Atomic Energy Authority
UN	United Nations
UNCTAD	UN Conference on Trade and Development
USAEC	US Atomic Energy Commission
USAID	US Agency for International Development

PLOUGHSHARES AND SWORDS

Introduction

Freedom of Action

Jawaharlal Nehru spent most of the Second World War in prison. Along with most leaders of the Indian National Congress, he was incarcerated in 1942 after the party adopted the Quit India Resolution against British colonial rule. Nehru was released in June 1945 when the war ended in Europe but continued in much of Asia. After US B-29 bombers dropped "Little Boy" and "Fat Man" atomic bombs on Japan, the destructive potential of nuclear fission deeply moved the future prime minister of independent India. Opposing the Muslim League's calls to partition British India, Nehru emphatically declared at a rally in Lahore that "the talk about Pakistan sounds empty and meaningless in this age of atomic bombs."[1]

The dawn of the nuclear age was also the onset of the era of global decolonization. The Second World War weakened European colonialism, increasing anticolonial dissent in much of Asia, including British India. Anticolonial leaders—future statesmen of soon-to-be sovereign nation-states—recognized the vast potential of nuclear fission to develop and secure the *nation*. Their sociotechnical imaginaries of the nation influenced the organization, development, and pursuit of nuclear technologies.[2]

India's nuclear program embodied the hopes and anxieties of a postwar colony at the cusp of independence. Its leaders hoped that their new nation-state would leapfrog toward economic development through big science projects, in which nuclear fission would feature prominently. In January 1947, Nehru, then the vice president of the interim government, a position equivalent to prime minister, declared as president of the Indian Science Congress, "This great force—atomic energy—that has suddenly come through scientific research may be used for war or may be used for peace. We cannot neglect it because it might be used for war; obviously, in India, we want to develop it, and we will develop it to the fullest."[3]

Territoriality, or the attributes generated by the "control of bordered political space," was immanent in decolonization.[4] Territoriality in South Asia was manifest in hard borders but intermestic threats.[5] The internal-external, domestic-international, and inside-outside were closely intertwined with important implications for what geopolitical challenges meant to the nation-state. As British colonial rule ended, the boundaries of modern India were shaped and reshaped through the bloody partition of 1947 and violent contestations over princely states such as Kashmir, Junagadh, and Hyderabad.[6] The processes of territoriality then continued through wars with adversarial neighbors, disputes over French colonial territories, seizures of Portuguese enclaves like Goa, annexation of Himalayan borderlands such as Sikkim, spatial reorganization of fraught regions as in the northeast, and frequent suppression of secessionist and Maoist movements.

The leaders of the nuclear program saw in nuclear fission the possibility to augment geopolitical goals of the territorial state as well as the technopolitical goals of the developmentalist state, leading to a large dual-use enterprise, simultaneously serving military and civilian ends.[7] Technopolitics, or the use of technology to enact political goals, was not unique to India's nuclear program. Yet, nuclear technologies were "inherently political artifacts" associated with "particular institutionalized patterns of power and authority."[8] In India, a small group of elite scientists and engineers with access to political power, social capital, and global financial networks led the nuclear program. This powerful group with sophisticated technical expertise saw nuclear fission as intrinsically associated with the nation—both *developing* and *securing* it.

Freedom of action was a core element of the nuclear program, resulting from the sociotechnical imaginaries of political leaders like Nehru and scientific institution builders like Homi Jehangir Bhabha and Vikram Sarabhai. Freedom to act with autonomy meant to them the expansion of choices writ large in political, economic, social, and technological spheres—inside and outside the country.[9] They, therefore, kept multiple technological options open, leading to a vast undertaking that could serve geopolitical ends and developmentalist goals simultaneously. (See map 1 and key to map, which is in table format on the facing page.)

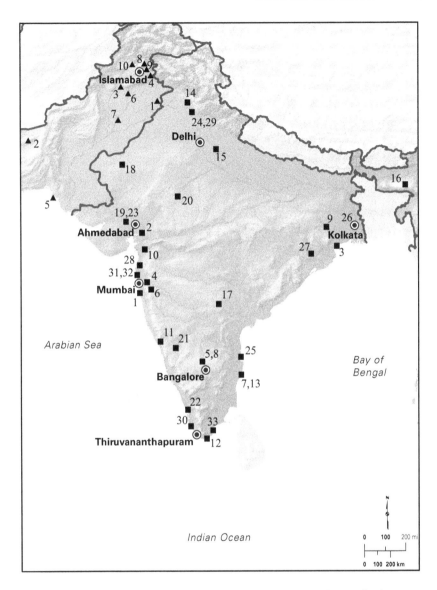

MAP 1. India's key nuclear and space sites. Credit: Scott Walker, Harvard Map Collection.

The pursuit of freedom of action led to deliberate technological ambiguity in the nuclear program: Which technological objects were "ploughshares" and which ones "swords"?[10] The ambiguity allowed its leaders to counter the regulation imposed by the nonproliferation regime as well as deflect criticism at home. In practice, the leaders of India's nuclear program adopted a strategy of hyperdiversification through partnerships with foreign atomic energy commissions

Key to map 1

KEY ID	INDIA FACILITY NAME (■)
1	Bhabha Atomic Research Centre, Trombay
2	Baroda Heavy Water Plant
3	Balasore Integrated Test Range
4	Department of Atomic Energy, Mumbai
5	Department of Space/Indian Space Research Organisation, Bangalore
6	High Energy Research Materials Laboratory (DRDO), Pune
7	Indira Gandhi Atomic Research Centre, Kalpakkam
8	Indian Institute of Science, Bangalore
9	Jaduguda Uranium Mine
10	Kakrapar Atomic Power Station
11	Kaiga Atomic Power Station
12	Kudankulam Nuclear Power Plant
13	Madras Atomic Power Station
14	Nangal Heavy Water Plant
15	Narora Atomic Power Station
16	Northeast Space Applications Centre, Shillong
17	Nuclear Fuel Complex, Hyderabad
18	Pokhran Test Site
19	Physical Research Laboratory, Ahmedabad
20	Rajasthan Atomic Power Station
21	Rattehalli Uranium Enrichment Plant
22	Rare Earths Division, Aluva
23	Space Applications Centre, Ahmedabad
24	Semiconductor Laboratory, Chandigarh
25	Satish Dhawan Space Centre, Sriharikota
26	Saha Institute of Nuclear Physics, Kolkata
27	Talcher Heavy Water Plant
28	Tarapur Atomic Power Station
29	Terminal Ballistic Research Laboratory (DRDO), Chandigarh
30	Thumba Equatorial Rocket Launching Station
31	Tata Institute of Fundamental Research, Mumbai
32	Tata Memorial Hospital, Mumbai
33	Tutikorin Heavy Water Plant

and private companies. They procured multiple types of research and power reactors. They pursued research and development of technologies of nuclear fission and outer space. They obtained technologies and materials from Europe and North America, including both superpowers. The large size of the nuclear program with a variety of technological artifacts that could concurrently serve civilian and military ends hid the program's deficiencies, flaws, and failures. The

KEY ID	PAKISTAN FACILITY NAME (▲)
1	Atomic Energy Minerals Centre, Lahore
2	Chagai Hills Test Site
3	Chashma Nuclear Power Complex
4	Khan Research Laboratories, Kahuta
5	Karachi Nuclear Power Plant
6	Khushab Nuclear Complex
7	Multan Heavy Water Production Facility
8	Pakistan Atomic Energy Commission, Islamabad
9	Pakistan Institute of Nuclear Science and Technology, Rawalpindi
10	Wah Weapon Complex

quest for freedom of action thus increased the leaders' choices abroad while reducing democratic accountability at home.

This book charts the history of India's nuclear program during its first forty years from the 1940s when it began until the 1980s when the program readapted to national, regional, and global pressures. It recounts why and how the leaders of the nuclear program prioritized certain kinds of technologies and technological systems over others. It is about the processes through which they pursued their freedom of action, the consequences of those pursuits, and their limitations. This book traces the global and local networks through which politically savvy scientists and engineers parlayed capital and political power to procure and redevelop myriad technological objects, which could concomitantly serve *national* goals of development and security.

The Nation and Fission

The first partnership between the future architects of India's nuclear program began while anticolonial leaders like Nehru and Gandhi were still in prison. In 1942, five years before India's independence, Homi J. Bhabha and Vikram Sarabhai met for the first time at the Indian Institute of Science (IISc) in Bangalore. The IISc was an eminent institution established in 1909 by the industrialist Tata family together with the king of Mysore. It was in wartime Bangalore that Bhabha and Sarabhai began their friendship and scientific collaboration, the fruits of which would earn them epithets as "fathers" of India's nuclear and space programs, respectively.

After completing his PhD in physics at the Cavendish Laboratory of the University of Cambridge, Bhabha had returned to India in 1939. The outbreak of the Second World War prevented him from returning to Europe to look for a permanent university position. He joined the IISc as a reader in theoretical physics with the support of C. V. Raman, who was a Nobel laureate in physics and the first Indian director of the IISc. Vikram Sarabhai had also returned to India following the outbreak of the war, after studying physics at the University of Cambridge. He began conducting research under Raman at the IISc.

Early institutional initiatives associated with India's nuclear program were informal and scattered. Funding was procured mainly through family connections and corporate philanthropy, though at times with the support of the colonial government. In March 1944, at the height of the Burma Campaign (1942–45), Bhabha approached Sir Dorabji Tata Trust with the goal to fund a "vigorous school of research in fundamental physics."[11] The late Sir Dorabji Tata was Bhabha's uncle, and his trust readily accepted the request, leading to the establishment of the Tata Institute of Fundamental Research (TIFR) on June 1, 1945.[12] Nehru was still in prison—he would be released on June 15.

In its first months, TIFR resided at the IISc because Bhabha was based there. In December 1945, the British governor of Bombay inaugurated TIFR at the Kenilworth Building on Pedder Road at Bhabha's family home. The location of Bombay (present-day Mumbai) was significant. Not only was it the home to Tatas and Bhabhas, but it was also nearly 900 miles from the capital of New Delhi. The location of TIFR and later of the nuclear program in and around Bombay would help to insulate the program from political influence as well as parliamentary oversight. Today, TIFR is located in Navy Nagar on the island of Colaba in Mumbai. The neighborhood derived its name from its past as an imperial military cantonment and a major site for British and US naval activities during the Second World War.

British India had a strong scientific knowledge base that had produced notable scientists like C. V. Raman, J. C. Ghosh, S. N. Bose, P. C. Ray, and many others.[13] Many Indian scientists were educated and trained at prestigious European universities such as Cambridge, Oxford, Edinburgh, Paris, and Göttingen. As independence neared, the role of science and technology in future India became a source of disagreement between Nehru, who would become India's first prime minister, and Mahatma Gandhi, the leader of nonviolent resistance against British colonial rule. Nehru's faith that science and technology would enable India to advance toward economic modernity stood in opposition to Gandhi's ideal of preindustrial village autarkies.[14] Nehru wrote to Gandhi in October 1945: "I do not think it is possible for India to be really independent unless she is a technically advanced country. I'm not thinking for the moment in terms of just armies but rather of scientific growth. In the present context of the world we can-

not even advance culturally without a strong background of scientific research in every department."[15]

Nehru's "pedagogical style of leadership," to quote historian Dipesh
Chakrabarty, placed great emphasis on the "scientific approach and temper"
as the "temper of a free man."[16] Developing a free nation thus meant cultivat-
ing a scientific-minded citizenry. In November 1945, Nehru declared at the
Royal Institute of Science in Bombay that "of all the big problems that face[d]
India today nothing is more important than the development of scientific research, both pure and applied, and scientific method."[17] Any "research Institute which has done pioneering work in this direction is, therefore, deserving
of support" of the interim government, and of the soon-to-be independent
Indian government.[18]

For Nehru, large-scale government investment in scientific institutions was
the way forward. His position aligned with the influential A. V. Hill Report of
1944 that had recommended government support for and control of industrial research in India, similar to the Department of Scientific and Industrial
Research in the United Kingdom, established during the First World War. Not
all Indian scientists supported the centralization and government control proposed by the Hill Report, but those who opposed such as astrophysicist Meghnad
Saha, director of Palit Laboratories at the University of Calcutta, were gradually
sidelined.[19]

From an institutional standpoint, the roots of India's nuclear program could
be traced to the Council of Scientific and Industrial Research (CSIR), formed
during the Second World War by the colonial government and modeled on
the British Department of Scientific and Industrial Research. The CSIR established the Atomic Energy Research Committee over a year before India's independence, which was on August 15, 1947. The committee initiated steps for
the organization of nuclear fission research in India in its first meeting held
on May 15, 1946, at Bombay House, the headquarters of Tata Industries. Homi
Bhabha, founding director of TIFR and relative of the Tata family, chaired the
meeting.[20]

The Tatas were a notable Parsi Zoroastrian family, who owned India's largest business conglomerate. Their "strategic philanthropy" cultivated a large
network of scientific and technical expertise in colonial India, and in years after
India's independence.[21] They significantly influenced India's nuclear program
through direct patronage of TIFR and the involvement of Jehangir Ratanji
Dadabhoy (J. R. D.) Tata, the chairman of Tata Sons, in the Board for Research
on Atomic Energy.

The majority of India's scientific elites supported early investment in a national nuclear program, an enthusiasm shared by Nehru. The 1947 partition

of British India into Hindu-majority, secular India and Muslim-majority Pakistan moved more scientific talent to India than to Pakistan. Regardless of their places of birth and origin, most Hindu, Parsi, and Sikh scientists settled within the territorial borders of India after independence. For instance, CSIR's director general Santi Swarup (S. S.) Bhatnagar was born and raised in the Shahpur district of Punjab, which became part of Pakistan. Meghnad Saha of the Palit Laboratories in Calcutta was born in East Bengal, which became East Pakistan after August 1947 and Bangladesh after December 1971.

Overlapping scientific, political, and social networks kept India's nuclear and space programs rooted within the CSIR, TIFR, and IISc from early on. The same individuals led multiple institutions, thereby consolidating their hold on authority and access to power and capital. After the Atomic Energy Act created the Atomic Energy Commission of India (AECI) in 1948, Homi Bhabha became the AECI chairman while remaining the director of TIFR. The AECI itself was a three-member body that reported directly to the prime minister. The other two AECI members, other than Bhabha, were CSIR's director general S. S. Bhatnagar and physicist K. S. Krishnan. Bhatnagar was also secretary to the Ministry of Natural Resources and Scientific Research of the Indian government and a TIFR council member from 1947.[22]

A large number of TIFR and IISc graduates went on to work in Trombay, just outside Bombay, where Bhabha set up India's premier nuclear research laboratory known as the Atomic Energy Establishment (renamed as the Bhabha Atomic Research Centre or BARC after his death). When Bhabha established the Indian National Committee for Space Research in 1962, Vikram Sarabhai led the committee, which was initially hosted at TIFR. When Sarabhai established the Indian Space Research Organisation (ISRO) in 1969, he headquartered it in Bangalore to ensure close coordination with the IISc, which was also close to the rocket and satellite launch sites in peninsular India.

An interconnected web of a small number of individuals and institutions thus steered the deeply intertwined nuclear and space programs of India. The individuals who led the institutions were transnationally connected and politically astute scientists, engineers, and technocrats who held proximity to local capital and state power. They circulated through global networks of multilateral institutions like the United Nations (UN) and the International Atomic Energy Agency (IAEA) and scientific gatherings like the Pugwash Conferences on Science and World Affairs. These scientific elite actors were not always policymakers in the exact sense of the word, but they enjoyed unwavering support from those at the helm of political and economic power. The AECI chairman, who was also the secretary of the Department of Atomic Energy (DAE) after 1954, worked directly under the prime minister's office.[23]

The eminent institutional positions of these elite scientists and engineers often resulted from social and economic privileges that preceded their involvement in India's nuclear and space programs. They were always men, who wore multiple hats of authority.

India's nuclear and space programs were manifestations of a heterodox postcolonial modernity. The "technicist nation-state" of India that emerged, to quote historian Gyan Prakash, was not a mimicry of the colonial state but one that would attain modernity through science on its own terms.[24] Like the "hybridized concept" of the nation, which was modern and archaic at the same time, India's pursuit of nuclear technologies represented a differentiated and pluralistic modernity.[25] The AECI/DAE imported technologies from industrially advanced foreign suppliers in France, Canada, the United Kingdom, and elsewhere. Indian scientists and engineers simultaneously improvised these technological objects by "fitting them" into Indian "society's peculiar circumstances," to quote political theorist Sudipta Kaviraj.[26]

The sequencing of development was such that it defied a linear transformation from traditional to modern. The nonlinear and contingent character of India's nuclear program could be found in its many contradictions. One such incongruity was visually captured in Henri Cartier-Bresson's 1966 photograph taken in Thumba, Kerala. The image showed a rocket engineer and a technician carrying the nose cone of a French Centaure rocket on a bicycle just before its launch. (See figure 4.1, chapter 4).

The Myth of Peaceful India

At the heart of the Indian nation-state lies the myth of a peaceful country built on Gandhian ideals of nonviolence. This myth ignores the territorial character of the Indian nation-state and its intrinsic intermestic violence. It plays into the self-serving ideology of the Hindu right that calls for a strong *Hindurashtra* (Hindu nation-state) to remedy the past of an emasculated, secular India led during its first fifty years by the Indian National Congress and its political successors. This myth partially explains the disparate memories of India's nuclear explosion of May 1974, on the one hand, and the series of five nuclear weapon tests of May 1998, on the other. The former is remembered as a domestic political act, while the latter is perceived solely through the lens of national security.[27]

The secular Congress government led by Indira Gandhi, the daughter of Jawaharlal Nehru, conducted the nuclear test of May 1974 in the midst of domestic political turmoil, calling it a "peaceful nuclear explosion." By contrast, the nuclear tests of 1998 remain entrenched in public memory and major works of scholarship as the moment when India actually "went nuclear," a policymaker's shorthand for the development of nuclear weapons.[28] The Hindu nationalist Bharatiya Janata Party (BJP)–led government of Atal Behari Vajpayee conducted those five nuclear tests. Within weeks, Pakistan's six nuclear tests made nuclear weapons an inescapable geopolitical reality in South Asia. Jaswant Singh from the Vajpayee government argued in a *Foreign Affairs* essay that the 1998 nuclear tests had inaugurated a brand-new era characterized by *realpolitik* in Indian foreign policy.[29] India had suffered, he claimed, under a half-century of "moralistic" stewardship of the secular Congress party, steeped in Nehruvian idealism.

The debate over India's "strategic culture" in political and intellectual circles and among scholars of South Asia, which transpired in the late 1990s and early 2000s, reinforced Singh's claim and reified the fiction of a peaceful India for much of its history after 1947.[30] In the debate, the 1998 nuclear tests were framed as militaristic actions that transformed India's strategic culture from pacifist Nehruvian idealism of the Cold War era into one characterized by Hindu nationalist militarism. The debate framed the discussion in terms of different geopolitical visions of India's two main political parties: the secular "peaceful" Congress and the Hindu nationalist "militaristic" BJP.

The myth of peaceful India does not hold against the reality of violence of partition and the wars that crafted India's borders with Pakistan and China. India's geopolitical threats remain intermestic, rooted in the emergence of the national space itself, which political scientist Sankaran Krishna has called "cartographic anxiety."[31] The 1947 partition led to nearly two million deaths and displaced almost fourteen million people through communal violence and forced population transfers. Princely states like Travancore that refused to join the Indian Union were threatened with airstrikes, while Kashmir, Hyderabad, and Junagadh saw military and paramilitary action. French colonial territories experienced economic blockades and political violence for years.[32] Militarism took the form of the annexation of Goa and Sikkim and the suppression of separatist movements in Kashmir, Mizoram, Nagaland, Punjab, and elsewhere.

The Hindu nationalists' ongoing assault on India's political history has increased in recent years.[33] The BJP government of Narendra Modi continues to resurrect the self-serving myth of a peaceful and weak India during the Cold War, when the secular Congress Party led the government. A closer look at India's foreign policy in the Cold War is, therefore, urgent. It can help reveal that the 1974 nuclear test was similar to the 1998 tests, differing only in rhetoric and political context. Both were in part geopolitical responses to China and Pakistan, and in part representative of India's anti-nonproliferation approach.

Anti-Nonproliferation and the Global Cold War

The term "proliferation" in biology refers to a rapid increase in the number of cells. It has a neutral medical status, but can also refer to cancerous growths. The term began to dominate the vocabulary of US defense intellectuals in the 1960s to indicate an increase in the number of countries with their own nuclear weapons or capabilities. Prior to that, "dissemination," "diffusion," "dispersal," and "spread" were interchangeably used with "proliferation" in the context of nuclear weapons.[34] With the 1968 Nuclear Nonproliferation Treaty (NPT), "proliferation" and "nonproliferation" became shorthand among US policymakers to indicate the perceived national security threat when foreign countries acquired their own nuclear weapons and US-led efforts to counter that threat, respectively.

The leaders of India's nuclear program publicly opposed nonproliferation in its various forms, such as the NPT, IAEA safeguards, and strengthened bilateral safeguards, as contraventions of their freedom of action. The AECI/ DAE argued that its anti-nonproliferation stance was to protect the sovereignty of the Indian nation-state. India never signed the NPT on grounds that the treaty discriminated against those without nuclear weapons or the "nuclear have-nots." This refusal has transformed the leaders of India's nuclear program into national heroes till this day.[35]

Policymakers and scientific elites leading the nuclear program have been portrayed in the mainstream political discourse in India as those fighting a righteous battle for the nation against an unequal nuclear order led by the United States. This was especially in the context of India's 1974 nuclear explosion, 1998 nuclear tests, and 2008 US-India civil nuclear agreement. Even though both superpowers were opposed to the acquisition of nuclear weapons by foreign countries, the United States has been far more proactive in formulating an expansive system of constraints that became the present-day global nonproliferation regime.

Ambassador V. C. Trivedi, India's representative at the negotiations in Geneva that drafted the NPT, famously criticized the biased nature of the treaty as "atomic apartheid."[36] He argued that the NPT would restrict India's free access to peaceful uses of nuclear energy by making technical assistance conditional upon joining the treaty. When historian Shane Maddock described US policies against nuclear weapons possession by other countries as "nuclear apartheid," he was referring to Trivedi's well-known remark. For Maddock, nuclear apartheid was based on the false presumption of "American moral and political guardianship over atomic technology."[37]

Even though the leaders of India's nuclear program preferred US nuclear assistance owing to the superiority of US technology, they also cooperated with the Soviet Union to retain political leverage. Since the US government was not inclined to transfer technology and know-how, scientific elites at the helm of India's nuclear program developed a robust relationship with France, a technologically advanced but recalcitrant US Cold War ally. They even explored nuclear aid to countries less technologically advanced than India, such as Brazil, Argentina, Libya, and Iran, irrespective of whether the countries had signed the NPT.

India's anti-nonproliferation practice and its emphasis on equality and fairness resembled its nonaligned position in the Cold War. The world's attention was first drawn to the soon-to-be independent Indian government and on Nehru in particular, with the 1947 Asian Relations Conference in New Delhi, held only months before India's independence.[38] This was followed by the 1949 New Delhi Conference that drew global attention to ongoing Dutch colonial violence in Indonesia. The Asian-African Conference of April 1955, held in Bandung in Indonesia itself, was a watershed in the history of solidarity among recently decolonized countries of Asia, Africa, and the Middle East. At Bandung, Nehru's speech to the political committee was a *tour de force*. He articulated his government's foreign policy against Cold War bloc rivalry, when he famously declared, "We will defend ourselves with whatever arms and strength we have, and if we have no arms we will defend ourselves without arms . . . if we rely upon others, whatever great powers they might be, if we look to them for sustenance, then we are weak indeed."[39]

To many observers, India's nonalignment was an ideological expression of the indignant pride of a postcolonial nation-state. Just as how the myth of peaceful India has led scholars to emphasize domestic politics as the driver of the country's nuclear program, an ideological interpretation of India's nonalignment and anti-nonproliferation stance has contributed to the prominence of a prestige-driven explanation of India's nuclear program.[40]

The anti-nonproliferation position of the leaders of the nuclear program was neither moralistic nor ideological. It resulted from their pursuit of freedom of action. It was above all a pragmatic path, in which legality was key. While publicly opposing the NPT, those at the helm of the nuclear program made sure that they did not violate India's legal obligations under the 1957 IAEA statute and the 1963 Partial Test Ban Treaty. They continuously adapted the nuclear program through technopolitical choices to maneuver around restrictions of the nonproliferation regime and global Cold War politics.

India's nonalignment and anti-nonproliferation stance were part of a pragmatic response to an asymmetrical world order. In a bipolar world divided between the communist East and the capitalist West, nonalignment brought new opportunities for Indian policymakers.[41] They could, for instance, seek development assistance from both superpowers, as historian David Engerman has masterfully shown.[42] By invoking nonalignment and Afro-Asian solidarity, Indian leaders reformulated the Cold War through the lenses of decolonization and economic disparity between the Global South and the Global North.

India's dual-use nuclear program that aimed to fulfil national development goals, together with its anti-nonproliferation approach, was readily compatible with the global discourse of economic rights in the 1970s. The calls for a New International Economic Order echoed at the UN General Assembly in May 1974. Weeks later, the DAE conducted its underground nuclear explosion in Pokhran, claiming it to be an experiment for natural gas exploration.

Argument and Book Structure

India's nuclear program has been the subject of several important historical studies, among which the contributions made by Itty Abraham, Robert Anderson, George Perkovich, and Jahnavi Phalkey have transformed our understanding of the subject matter.[43] Journalist Raj Chengappa's account has filled gaps in our knowledge at a time when archival documents were not available, while physicist M. V. Ramana has drawn our attention to the economics of India's nuclear energy enterprise.[44] The revitalization of political and diplomatic histories of South Asia over the past decade and the declassification of a vast amount of primary sources in India and elsewhere have made it possible to write a comprehensive global story of India's nuclear program during the Cold War.[45]

Social science accounts divide India's nuclear program into distinct peaceful and military phases.[46] The peaceful phase is said to have lasted from 1947 until the 1980s. The weaponization phase is said to have begun in the 1980s in response to Pakistan's nuclear weapons program and consolidated after the nuclear tests of May 1998. This has relegated the formative years of India's nuclear program (1940s–1980s) to a "prehistory" of the nuclear weapons project. Apart from Itty Abraham's pioneering work on ambivalence and secrecy, the implicit scholarly treatment of national development and national security as mutually exclusive spheres, has further impeded a clear understanding of the early decades of the program.[47] Furthermore, the nuclear program's close association with the space program remains largely neglected. Moreover, India's well-publicized anti-nonproliferation approach has led to numerous studies of its ideological opposition to the nonproliferation regime but occluded analyses of the nuclear program's global and transnational dimensions. [48]

This book fills a lacuna in the scholarship by making three main arguments. First, India's nuclear program was a dual-use endeavor, simultaneously serving civilian and military ends, not because of the nature of nuclear technologies, but owing to deliberate plans and decisions undertaken by the AECI/DAE. The energy program did not develop into a weapons program over time, but the nuclear program itself was conceived as both from the onset. The program's dual-use characteristics were manifest in its technologies, infrastructure, training, and, above all, foreign partnerships. The deliberate duality in the nuclear program was the outcome of the leaders' pursuit of freedom of action, which itself resulted from sociotechnical imaginaries of the nation and the role of fission in it. From the program's inception, ploughshares were swords, and swords were ploughshares.

In practice, the Janus-faced nuclear program functioned as a hyperdiversification device. The nuclear program, which was a collection of multifarious technological objects serving development and security goals, attracted multiple foreign partners. If one partner withdrew from cooperation, the AECI/DAE could easily turn to another. Inside the country, the polyvalent nuclear program enforced consensus among citizens and domestic political coalitions in support of the program. To oppose ploughshares was to oppose national development. To oppose swords was to oppose national security. Taking a stand against both was defying the nation itself. The intentional duality of the nuclear program thus checked dissent within the democratic polity by controlling the discourse on modernity. The result was the coproduction of a large dual-use nuclear program with little democratic accountability and a society that tolerated the risks, flaws, and failures of the program.[49]

Second, the Indian nuclear program's geopolitical dimensions were evident in the intermestic nature of territorial threats and their entanglements with the global Cold War. The fluidity of internal-external, domestic-international, and inside-outside spheres heightened Indian policymakers' geopolitical anxieties, resulting in frequent territorial violence either short of interstate wars or as limited wars. Intermestic territorial threats and Indian policymakers' responses to those threats illuminate the geopolitical dimensions of the nuclear program.[50] India's wars often resulted in stalemates, as in 1947 and 1965, or were kept deliberately brief, as in 1971. The 1971 war, for instance, ended in Indian military victory, but it increased geopolitical anxieties for the Indira Gandhi government about the war's medium- and long-term consequences in the politically unstable northeastern hills, Naxalite violence–affected West Bengal, and the Himalayan kingdom of Sikkim on the border with China. From a geopolitical standpoint, securing borderlands mattered to the territorial Indian nation-state just as much as protecting borders.

Third, the leaders of India's nuclear program pursued a dual-use space program, while keeping space research purposefully separate from the nuclear program and the defense laboratories. They did so to benefit from foreign cooperation in outer space technologies without arousing suspicion of the nonproliferation regime. The same individuals or groups of individuals led the nuclear and space programs. Overlapping technical personnel created shared knowledge in nuclear and space research. Indian scientists and engineers thus mastered the know-how for missiles through developing rockets and satellite launch vehicles while simultaneously working on underground nuclear explosions. The AECI/DAE's sequencing of nuclear weapons development was nonlinear—the manufacture of a nuclear device did not precede the development of delivery vehicles, but the two were concurrent and parallel—defying expectations of US policymakers and defense intellectuals, who based their anticipation of linearity on US and Soviet experiences.

This book is chronologically organized into three parts and seven chapters. Each chapter examines certain technological objects that the leaders of India's nuclear program pursued in a way that allowed them to preserve their freedom of action. The first two chapters constituting the first part of the book (1940s–1953) cover India's nuclear program prior to President Eisenhower's "Atoms for Peace" proposal, when the French atomic energy commission emerged as the AECI's key technology partner. The third, fourth, and fifth chapters that make up the second part of the book (1953–70) examine the institutional expansion of the nuclear and space programs in response to China's nuclear weapons and missile programs, the US-led nonproliferation regime, and domestic pressures to produce electricity from nuclear energy. The sixth and seventh chapters comprising the third part of the book (1970–1980s) discuss the geopolitical and technopolitical effects of the 1971 Bangladesh Liberation War, India's 1974 nuclear explosion, and the Reagan administration's "no-test bargain" with the Gandhi government, against the backdrop of Soviet occupation of Afghanistan.

Ploughshares and Swords is not about India alone. It is about how geopolitical and technopolitical visions influence decisions for an imagined modernity after decolonization. It is a provocative history that challenges conventional wisdom about nuclear proliferation and nonproliferation. Finally, it is a story of how politics influences technology and territoriality to shape and reshape history.

PART ONE

World War and Decolonization

CHAPTER 1

Atomic Earths and State-Making, 1940s–1948

A major corporate scandal broke out in London in 1916. It was over German control of monazite sands in the princely state of Tiruvitamkur, anglicized as Travancore, in British India. Travancore was home to one of the world's largest monazite deposits. Monazite was a major source of thorium nitrate used in incandescent gas mantles for street lighting—a cheap alternative to electric lights. The discovery at the height of the First World War that thorium nitrate shipped to Britain originating from Travancore's monazite was actually processed in Germany shook the British gas mantle industry.[1]

The German leader in incandescent lighting, *Auergesellschaft*, had invested huge sums of capital in the British firm Travancore Minerals Company. By the time German economic involvement in Travancore came to light, the *Auer* company already held "the whole of the preference shares and eleven thousand ordinary shares" of the British company in its trust.[2] The economic implication was that the British gas mantle industry was paying nearly nine times the price for Travancore's monazite than their German counterpart. The geopolitical repercussions of this wartime revelation convinced the India Office in London to cancel all of the British company's German contracts and hire only British-born directors.[3]

The intersection of capital, geology, and geopolitics in Travancore's monazite-rich sands reemerged during the Second World War with the need for thorium in nuclear fission. For the first forty years of the twentieth century, the chief commercial purpose of thorium was to light up gas mantles, but its radioactive properties were known to the scientific world owing to Marie Curie and Gerhard Carl Schmidt's research. In the 1940s, Glenn Seaborg and his team at the Metallurgical Laboratory in Chicago began to research thorium for the Manhattan Project. Seaborg found that uranium-233 bred from thorium was fissile, such that a nuclear fuel cycle using thorium could be used in breeder reactors.[4]

The breakthrough that thorium had applications in nuclear fission transformed thorium-bearing monazite sands into "atomic earths" and Travancore into a fraught turf of territorial claims and counterclaims.[5] The Anglo-American stockpiling of rare earths and minerals during and immediately after the Second World War brought multiple geopolitical actors to Travancore's coast. The monazite-rich sands metamorphosed from lucrative commodities into *strategic* materials. The kingdom of Travancore thus became the battleground where imperial and neoimperial forces, local elites, and new nation-states collided against each other.

Decolonization in the South Asian subcontinent influenced the strategies of local and national elites for controlling Travancore's monazite-bearing sands. Both the kingdom of Travancore and the soon-to-be independent Indian government stalled external access to monazite in their contestations for sovereign power. Sir C. P., the dewan of Travancore (a position equivalent to prime minister), used the monazite sands as the bargaining chip to keep the princely state independent of the Indian Union, *albeit* unsuccessfully.[6]

German and French Interests in Travancore's Monazite

German chemist and prospector C. W. Schomberg discovered monazite deposits in the sands of Travancore in 1909. According to records of the US Department of Interior, Schomberg was affiliated with the British company London Cosmopolitan Mining.[7] Soon after, he became the company's local agent in Travancore, holding two thousand of the company's shares.[8] In 1911, when Travancore Minerals Company was formed as a subsidiary of London Cosmopolitan, Schomberg became the local agent for the new company. Five years later, during the First World War, British colonial authorities arrested him as an "enemy agent," exposing the fact that Berlin-based *Auergesellschaft* owned the majority of shares in Travancore Minerals Company.[9]

German dominance of the world's gas mantle industry went back to the invention of the gas mantle itself. Austrian chemist Carl Auer von Welsbach invented the gas mantle and cofounded the *Deutsch Gasglühlicht AG* in 1892, the forerunner of *Auergesellschaft*. At the turn of the twentieth century, German companies owned a large number of patents in chemical extraction and processing of rare earths obtained from monazite, such as thorium and cerium. German capitalists invested large sums of money in the rare earths trade and industry such that the German Thorium Syndicate controlled global prices of thorium nitrate.[10]

Germany's defeat in the First World War created opportunities for the French rise in monazite extraction. Established in 1919 in Paris, *Société de Produits Chimiques des Terres Rares* (STR) emerged at its forefront. Joseph Blumenfeld, STR's founder, had started out as a doctoral student conducting research on rare earths under chemist Georges Urbain's direction, who appointed Blumenfeld as the trustee of a sequestered branch of *Auergesellschaft* in France. This led to the creation of STR. The French firm benefited from both Blumenfeld's training as a chemist as well as his familial connections. Blumenfeld's brother-in-law was Zionist leader and chemist Chaim Weizmann, who in the 1920s had taken out patents for extracting ilmenite and titanium oxide from monazite.[11] During the interwar years, STR's Serquigny plant in Normandy processed monazite from Travancore, Brazil, and elsewhere.[12]

Under the Nazi policy of "Aryanization," *Degussa* bought out *Auergesellschaft* in 1934 from its Jewish owner Alfred Koppel.[13] One of the premier companies for processing monazite was thus transformed into an economic enterprise for the German war machine. Among other things, the company began to produce gas masks using forced labor from the Sachsenhausen-Oranienburg concentration camp. In occupied France, in 1941, STR combined its capital with *Auergesellschaft* and supplied twice as much monazite for Germany than for France.[14] Despite Blumenfeld's Russian Jewish heritage, he remained STR's owner.

STR enjoyed a monopoly in monazite processing in occupied France while contributing to thorium research for the Nazi nuclear weapons program.[15] At its Oranienburg plant, about twenty miles north of Berlin, *Auergesellschaft* enriched uranium and purified thorium as part of the Third Reich's efforts to develop nuclear weapons.[16] The thorium at Oranienburg came from STR in Paris.[17] Travancore had imposed an embargo on its monazite exports during the Second World War. It was, therefore, unlikely, though not impossible, that Travancore's monazite had ended up in *Auergesselschaft*'s Oranienburg plant.[18]

Anglo-American Scramble for Atomic Earths

In 1939 the US Congress enacted the Strategic and Critical Materials Stockpiling Act, which became the legal premise for the US government to extract or buy up strategic raw materials across the world. The act stated that, "natural resources of the United States in certain strategic and critical materials being deficient or insufficiently developed," the US government would acquire "stocks of these materials" and "encourage the development of mines and deposits of these materials within the United States" to meet "industrial, military, and naval needs of the country for common defense."[19] These raw materials—metals and minerals hidden in the Earth's crust—were called "strategic" or "critical" to indicate their usefulness for national defense and economic development. Some of these materials were called "rare earths" to highlight their imagined scarcity, leading to US stockpiling efforts through public and public-private initiatives.[20]

Raw materials, particularly atomic earths, comprised the wartime economic backbone of the Anglo-American partnership. The Atlantic Charter signed in August 1941 explicitly stated trade and access to the world's raw materials.[21] Two years later, the Quebec Agreement formulated a two-fold policy in matters related to nuclear fission. The British and US governments agreed to stockpile atomic earths like uranium, thorium, and beryllium from around the world and to censor information regarding fission research. The goal was to prevent knowledge from flowing outside the three governments involved in the Manhattan Project—the United States, the United Kingdom, and Canada.[22]

Signed when the Manhattan Project was in full swing, the 1943 Quebec Agreement reflected the Anglo-American special relationship in matters of nuclear fission and projected US primacy in no uncertain terms. The agreement stated, "The Prime Minister expressly disclaims any interest in these industrial and commercial aspects beyond what may be considered by the President of the United States to be fair and just and in harmony with the economic welfare of the world."[23] The Quebec Agreement established the Common Policy Committee to coordinate information censorship in fission research among US, British, and Canadian governments.

The following year, in 1944, the Common Development Trust was formed in Washington, DC, as a subsidiary of the Common Policy Committee. The Common Development Trust's goal was to procure and stockpile atomic earths. During the war, it accumulated almost six thousand tons of uranium oxide ore, two-thirds of which came from the Katanga province of Belgian Congo, and about one-sixth from Canada.[24] By December 1945, General Leslie Groves, the military commander of the Manhattan Project, who spearheaded the procurement activities, confirmed that the Common Development Trust controlled 97 percent of the world's known uranium reserves.[25] Not everyone was pleased. Chalmers Jack Mackenzie, the president of Canada's National Research Council, lamented that "as far as Canada was concerned, it was a one-sided bargain that gave all our uranium away and did not provide much assurance of co-operation for our laboratories."[26]

The Anglo-American accumulation of atomic earths went hand in hand with preventing Axis and Communist countries from gaining access. Under the Common Development Trust, the British government was responsible for its colonies spanning from Africa and the Middle East to Asia up to Hong Kong, while the US government was free to procure atomic earths from everywhere else.[27] The division of the non-communist world into US and British extractive spheres placed British India within the United Kingdom's zone of influence. Travancore's vast monazite deposits, however, made it attractive to US policymakers, leading to significant Anglo-American competition.

The United States in Wartime South Asia

The Roosevelt administration's direct military involvement in the China-Burma-India theater of the Second World War set India apart from other British colonies. The war effort drew multiple US actors—government, corporate, individual, and those in between—to the South Asian subcontinent. British India was the Allied base to provide military and economic support for Chiang Kai-Shek's Chinese Nationalist troops that were fighting the Japanese and the Communists in the Chinese Civil War. Allied pilots routinely flew over the Himalayas, nicknamed "the Hump," to provide supplies to the Chinese Nationalists. By late 1941, India had raised three hundred thousand men to fight in the war. Indian troops were fighting in North and East Africa, and its men were garrisoned in the Far East.[28]

India's military significance further increased in the spring of 1942, when the Japanese invaded and occupied neighboring British Burma. Since defending India became vital to the war effort, the Roosevelt administration provided US economic and military assistance under the Lend-Lease arrangement. US interest in India worried Whitehall where there was much concern that Lend-Lease could upset "imperial preference"—the system of reciprocal preferential tariffs that operated within the British empire.[29]

The Roosevelt administration published war propaganda in vernacular languages justifying US troop presence in South Asia. As the Japanese bombed the city of Calcutta and its harbor in December 1942, a US front-page poster in the local newspaper *Jugantar* showed an oil lamp and a globe (see figure 1.1). Its flame lit up the Philippines. In bold Bengali letters were the words, "For the future of Asia." Adjacent to the star-spangled banner, the text reassured its

FIGURE 1.1. US government propaganda poster during the Second World War in Bengali. "For the Future of Asia," *Jugantar* 6, no. 85 (December 17, 1942), courtesy of Centre for Studies in Social Sciences, Calcutta, and the Endangered Archives Programme of the British Library, EAP262/1/2 /1369, https://eap.bl.uk/archive-file/EAP262-1-2-1369.

readers that "the US military is present today in India to save it from a 'Japanese Asia.'" The poster sloganeered, "This American war is a war for freedom."[30]

American businessman and self-taught aviator William Douglas Pawley, the president of the Intercontinental Aviation Corporation, assisted Chiang Kai-Shek's Chinese Nationalist forces through airpower. In the early 1930s, Pawley founded the China National Aviation Corporation and the Central Aircraft Manufacturing Company, both based in China, to supply fighter planes to the Chinese Nationalist forces. Frequent Japanese destruction of his aircraft manufacturing units in China led Pawley to convince the Roosevelt administration and Generalissimo Chiang Kai-Shek to allow him to form the "American Volunteer Group," better known as the "Flying Tigers." Formed in 1940, it was "a special arrangement whereby trained American pilots were permitted to 'resign' from the US Army Air Corps without losing rank."[31] The group conducted aerial raids on Japanese forces in China prior to the official US entry into the Second World War.

In British India, Pawley and Gujarati industrialist Walchand Hirachand Doshi, along with the support of the princely state of Mysore, cofounded a light aircraft factory, Hindustan Aircraft Limited, in Bangalore also in 1940.[32] The British colonial government invited Pawley to construct the factory to help the war effort. Hirachand Doshi's chance encounter with Pawley on a clipper trip to China stoked his own interest in investing in the factory. In order to foster operational expertise needed for air support during the war, Pawley, Doshi, the kingdom of Mysore, and the British colonial government provided financial support to set up the Department of Aeronautical Engineering at the IISc in Bangalore in 1942. The department was the first of its kind to be established in South Asia. Homi Bhabha and Vikram Sarabhai were based at the Department of Physics at the time.

By September 1943, as the Allied forces engaged in direct combat with the Japanese in Burma, Hindustan Aircraft Limited produced planes solely for the US Army Air Forces. After India's independence in August 1947, when the kingdom of Mysore signed the treaty of accession to join the Indian Union, the Indian government became the owner of the aircraft factory. Renamed as the Hindustan Aeronautics Limited, it became the government's premier aircraft production facility.[33]

The Tatas and Atomic Energy Research

The Tatas' philanthropic support to promote scientific research in British India and their global commercial networks set the family a class apart from the locally oriented Parsi Zoroastrian business community in Bombay.[34] Jamsetji Nusserwanji Tata, the founder of Tata Group, spearheaded the establishment of the IISc in Bangalore on land donated by the princely state of Mysore. IISc was formally established in 1911, seven years after Jamsetji's death. His chance encounter in 1893 with Bengali Vedantic monk Swami Vivekananda, when both were en route to Chicago aboard a steamship, is said to have infused in him the vision to establish such an institution.

The idea was to provide world-class science education to Indians without them having to study in Great Britain or elsewhere.[35] At the time the anticolonial *Swadeshi* movement was gaining traction in British India. The movement emphasized self-sufficiency by curtailing dependence on British goods and preventing brain drain. Retaining talent at least in part guided the Tatas' support first for the IISc and, later, for the TIFR.

Homi Bhabha solicited philanthropic support from Sir Dorabji Tata Trust in March 1944 to establish what became the TIFR. He reassured the trust's chairman, Sir Sorab Saklatvala, that any future "financial support from Government, need not, however, entail Government control."[36] This was a reference to A. V. Hill's lecture at the Science Congress in Delhi. The British Indian government had invited Hill, Nobel laureate physiologist and senior secretary of the Royal Society London, to advise the government on the organization of scientific and industrial research once the war was over. Hill's recommendation was in favor of significant state support for scientific research in India. The A. V. Hill Report of April 1944 influenced Nehru's thinking on the role of the state in promoting big science–driven nation-building projects. It also informed the Tatas' philanthropy in supporting atomic energy research.

"What distinguishes a Trust is not its ability to give or the extent and range of its giving but the character of its giving," wrote Professor Rustum D. Choksi, director and trustee of Dorabji Tata Trust.[37] It was "important for a Trust to maintain its 'pioneering' character," he wrote, which was only possible when "from time to time a Trust initiates and fosters new institutions and new types of service to society."[38] Choksi recommended that his fellow trustees support Bhabha's proposal to establish a school of physics, citing the "considered opinion of Prof. A. V. Hill that much of scientific work in England has been built around an individual."[39]

Bhabha was going to be that pioneering individual. The trust granted Bhabha's request to provide what Choksi called "moderate support in sponsoring the initial stages of this project." In its April 1944 meeting, the trust agreed to provide one lac rupees annually (~US$30,370) to establish a school of physics in Bombay.[40] J. R. D. Tata, the chairman of Tata Sons and himself a trustee of

Dorabji Tata Trust, avidly supported the initiative. Indeed, he had encouraged Bhabha to formally solicit the trust's financial support to create a world-class institution in order to retain scientific talent in India after the war.[41]

Wartime philanthropy of Dorabji Tata Trust charted the institutional genealogy of India's nuclear and space programs. It included the Tata Memorial Hospital in Bombay in 1941, the Cosmic Ray Research Unit at the IISc in 1942 led by Bhabha, and the TIFR in 1944. Institutions that were "pioneered" through funding from the Tatas expanded with the colonial government's support to help the war effort. For example, the IISc experienced institutional growth directly as a result of the Second World War, like its Department of Aeronautical Engineering. Its Department of Physics attracted returning scientific talent such as Bhabha and Sarabhai, who took up academic positions there during the war. As India's independence neared, Bhabha tapped into the Tata Industries' global commercial networks to serve the TIFR, the Tata Memorial Hospital, and India's nuclear program simultaneously.

The early phase of India's nuclear program was a unique business-government partnership. The Tatas' philanthropy for scientific research at the dawn of decolonization was not in competition with the state. It was collaborative. In January 1947, while the Indian Science Congress met in Delhi, Sir Dorab Tata Trust decided to jointly provide funding for TIFR with the Government of Bombay. The Trust agreed to provide an annual grant of 45,000 rupees (~US$13,613) for the Institute's maintenance and to furnish up to a maximum of four lacs rupees (~US$121,000) for a site for the Institute, the construction of its building, and provision of its equipment. The government of Bombay agreed to provide an annual block grant-in-aid of 25,000 rupees (~US$7,563) for three years, and a nonrecurring grant-in-aid of a maximum of two lacs rupees (~US$60,500) for the costs of a site, building, and equipment for the institute.[42] Thus began the process to move the TIFR to the island of Colaba in Bombay, where it is located still today.

The global commercial networks of the Tata House and the family's Bombay-based philanthropy created opportunities for Bhabha to forge foreign partnerships that would benefit India's nuclear program. An early example is Bhabha's search for a radium worker from Paris to work in Bombay. In April 1947, Bhabha wrote to French chemist and Nobel laureate Irène Joliot-Curie, who was the director of the Radium Institute in Paris. He was seeking a French physicist who could work with radium at the Tata Memorial Hospital in Bombay. Specifically, he was looking for a physicist who could "deal with two grammes of radium, the extraction of radon, its dosage and calibration, and the physics of X'ray calibration."[43] The post was for two or three years to work on cancer research as part of the nuclear medicine unit at the hospital. Bhabha added that should the French expert be so inclined, they could also use the "facilities for research in this Institute" (namely, TIFR).

Irène Joliot-Curie enthusiastically recommended an experienced engineer from the Radium Institute, who was a graduate of the prestigious *Ecole supérieure de Physique et de Chimie industrielles* like both her parents, Marie and Pierre Curie, and her husband, Frédéric Joliot-Curie.[44] The engineer, Monsieur Gandy, had a successful interview with the leadership of the hospital, after which Bhabha offered him a two-year position. Once the recruitment was completed in November, Bhabha wrote to Sir Frederick James at the London office of Tata Limited informing him that "Tata Limited will have to deal with the matter in due course."[45] After all, Bhabha had grown interested in several scientific apparatus related to radium that Irène Joliot-Curie had recommended to him—instruments that could create "an absolute standard of radium measurement such as does not exist in India at the moment."[46] The price tag of the equipment was 160,000 French francs (~US$134,800), which could only be afforded with the support of the Tatas.[47]

Through supporting Bhabha's work at the TIFR and the Tata Memorial Hospital, the House of Tatas thus cast a significant influence on India's nuclear program from early on. The business-government partnership propelled the program forward at a pace and scale that would have been otherwise impossible during the formal decolonization of South Asia.

Decolonization and Monazite

At the dawn of decolonization, there were over five hundred princely states of varying territorial sizes in South Asia.[48] Travancore was one of them. The kingdom had signed a treaty accepting British "paramountcy" in 1723. Paramountcy involved British control of princely states' foreign affairs, succession, and various political and economic matters, established through unequal treaties.[49] The "native states" or "princely states" were indirectly ruled by the British Crown while being directly ruled by their own hereditary rulers. The transfer of power in British India, as spelled out in the memorandum of the Cabinet Mission on May 12, 1946, involved the end to paramountcy of the British Crown. This meant that these kingdoms could, at least in theory, become sovereign territorial units.

The Cabinet Mission memorandum stated that "the British Government could not and will not in any circumstances transfer paramountcy to an Indian Government."[50] As a result, "the rights of the [princely] States which flow from their relationship to the Crown will no longer exist" but "the rights surrendered by the[se] States to the paramount power will return" to the princely states themselves.[51] The "void will have to be filled" by the princely states through a "federal relationship" or "particular political arrangements" with "successor Government or Governments in British India."[52] This implied that the princely states would have to negotiate their political futures with the independent governments of India and Pakistan.

The production of national space in South Asia thus proceeded through territorial contestations over sovereign power.[53] Not every leader of a princely state wanted to choose between Hindu-majority India or Muslim-majority Pakistan. Many wanted to retain their quasi-independent status or even become fully sovereign. Not every kingdom ultimately made choices that the leaders of India and Pakistan peacefully accepted. When Muslim-majority Hyderabad and Junagadh wanted to join Pakistan, the Indian Union responded with military action.[54] Kashmir's Hindu king Hari Singh's decision to merge his Muslim-majority kingdom with the Indian Union led Pakistan to invade Kashmir, leading to the first India-Pakistan War from 1947 to 1948.

In the first half of the twentieth century, Travancore had emerged as one of the most socially progressive monarchical bastions in British India. Its revenues from rare earth mining increased its economic wealth and boosted industrialization. In the 1930s, the kingdom had established the first public transport and telecommunications systems, invested in a large public sector particularly in heavy industry, and opened Hindu temples to members of all castes, which until then had been limited to only upper-caste Hindus. Chithira Thirunal Balarama Varma was Travancore's monarch. Sir Chetpat Pattabhirama (C. P.) Ramaswami Aiyar was initially the legal adviser to the young monarch and, from 1936 onward, the dewan.[55] As dewan, he oversaw the kingdom's large industrial projects and single-handedly took political and economic decisions for the princely state. Prior to becoming Travancore's dewan, Sir C. P. had been at the forefront of anticolonial politics through the Indian National Congress. A lawyer by training, he was also a veteran diplomat, having served as the Indian delegate to the League of Nations in 1926 and 1927.[56]

Sir C. P. staunchly opposed Hindu-majority Travancore's merger with the Indian Union.[57] He suggested that Travancore should become a sovereign nation-state and a UN member. According to him, as a sea-facing trading kingdom with vast mineral resources of its own, Travancore could realistically remain independent, unlike the landlocked princely states of Kashmir and Hyderabad. His objective was to transform the quasi-independence of his kingdom under British colonial rule into complete independence in decolonized South Asia. To attain that goal, Sir C. P. used his kingdom's monazite-rich sand deposits as the bargaining chip.

US mining presence in Travancore preceded its wartime military involvement in the subcontinent. Since the interwar years, Chicago-based Lindsay Light and Chemical Company mined monazite in the kingdom along with British companies, Travancore Minerals Company and Hopkin and Williams Limited.[58] Lindsay Light processed Travancore's monazite to produce thorium at its Rare Earths Facility in West Chicago. After the discovery that thorium could be used in nuclear fission, Lindsay Light began supplying thorium metal for the Manhattan Project.[59]

During the Second World War, impressed by William Pawley's successful entrepreneurship in cofounding Hindustan Aircraft Limited in Bangalore, Sir C. P. reached out to him to seek support for the construction of an ammonia-sulphate fertilizer plant. Travancore, which heavily depended on rice imports from Burma, was experiencing a devastating famine. It was caused first by crop failure in coastal Arakan in 1941 and then exacerbated by the 1942 Japanese invasion and occupation of Burma.[60] Against the backdrop of war and famine, the dewan hoped that the fertilizer plant could increase his kingdom's agricultural output and reduce its dependence on food imports from elsewhere.

The British Indian government in New Delhi did not easily grant its approval for US investment and construction of the fertilizer plant. Providing famine relief was not a priority for the British colonial government.[61] Nor were British officials interested in supporting long-term solutions to local food production. More importantly, US commercial involvement in the princely state made British authorities suspicious and uncomfortable. William Pawley expressed his own vexation with British fence-sitting to the *Miami Daily News* in February 1945:

> We found it was not easy for the Government of India to okay the construction of a plant for the state of Travancore to be built by an American firm and to be financed with United States dollars allocated by the London Control Board. Travancore had ample funds in sterling and in rupees, but she is not a free agent in the use of United States dollars, even though that state may have received millions of United States dollars for its products sold to the United States.[62]

Pawley eventually built the plant in Travancore, which later became India's first large-scale fertilizer plant. Sir C. P.'s ruthless repression of communists within Travancore earned him the trust of US actors, like Pawley. By the end of the war, the dewan leveraged his US and British contacts to solicit support for Travancore's political sovereignty or at least quasi-independence in exchange for access to monazite.

During the Second World War, the Travancore government had placed an embargo on its export of monazite and other rare earths at the behest of British authorities.[63] The embargo's underlying reason for the British was to prevent enemy access to Travancore's monazite, not least to avoid a reoccurrence of the 1916 scandal involving *Auergesellschaft*. After the war ended, Sir C. P. declared that he would maintain the kingdom's embargo on monazite and rare earths like ilmenite. He announced at the Travancore legislature in 1945, "No mineral sands will be exported hereafter and no licenses issued hereafter. If firms which operated in the country want to operate further, they will come into contact with the government of Tiruvitamkur and enter into association with them . . ."[64]

Sir C. P. hoped to use the export embargo to obtain a monazite processing plant from US or British companies that had been mining the kingdom's rare earths for decades. His broader political goal was to solicit support for Travancore's full or limited sovereignty from British and US governments to ensure their own security of supply. Travancore's export embargo directly affected Lindsay Light and Chemical as well as British firms Travancore Minerals and Hopkin and Williams Limited. Yet, none of the firms were interested in entering into an agreement with the Travancore government to obtain access to monazite in return for constructing a processing plant.

For British and US companies, extracting monazite from Travancore and processing it in Amersham or West Chicago was far more lucrative. For Travancore, if it could process its own monazite without dependence on foreign mining companies, then it itself could sell thorium nitrate and other profitable industrial products obtained from the monazite. Sir C. P. even asked William Pawley to pressure Thomas Lindsay III of Lindsay Light to build the plant but to no avail.

In the face of British and US disinterest in building a monazite processing plant while nurturing hopes for a French offer, Sir C. P. granted STR an exemption to its export embargo. STR began processing Travancore's monazite in its factory in Thann, Alsace, in 1946. By then the French firm had emerged as "the most important company in the Rare Earth field," and was even "appointed by French government to handle Atomic Energy Projects."[65] In 1946 alone, STR procured two hundred tons of monazite from Travancore, which it processed in Alsace, close to the French border with Germany and Switzerland.

On May 15, 1946, CSIR's Atomic Energy Research Committee and its adjunct Board for Research on Atomic Energy held their first meeting at the headquarters of Tata Industries in Bombay.[66] The CSIR had established the committee in April. The board included J. R. D. Tata, the chairman of Tata Sons, which depicted the close ties of India's largest business conglomerate to atomic energy research from early on. At the meeting, which Homi Bhabha chaired, the future leaders of India's nuclear program discussed institutional arrangements and funding for atomic energy research in soon-to-be independent India. They decided at the meeting that the pursuit of atomic energy research was going to be centralized under a single institution—namely, the TIFR. Although there were other prominent research institutions in nuclear physics at the time, such as the Palit Laboratory and the Bose Institute (both in Calcutta), from that moment on, TIFR became the nerve center of research on all things nuclear.[67]

The acquisition of raw materials for nuclear fission became a priority for the future Indian government. The Atomic Energy Research Committee and the Board included on their list the procurement of monazite from Travancore and beryllium from Udaipur, both princely states. Jawaharlal Nehru, the future prime minister of India, was in agreement. In his presidential address at the Indian Science Congress in January 1947, not only did he declare that India would develop atomic energy "to the fullest," but at the same session, the scientific body also adopted a special resolution on state ownership and control of "those minerals which are necessary for the production of atomic energy."[68]

Travancore's monazite, however, was far from becoming "Indian." At a time when atomic energy was becoming a priority for the imminently independent Indian government, Sir C. P. became determined to keep Travancore outside of the Indian Union.[69] His goal was to keep the Hindu princely state with one of the largest deposits of thorium-bearing monazite sands as a sovereign entity. After Thomas Lindsay of Lindsay Light refused to build a monazite processing plant despite Pawley's efforts and a French offer was not forthcoming, Sir C. P. turned once again to the British. In April–May 1947, he signed an agreement with the British government granting them an exemption from the export embargo on monazite for three years in return for the British government's commitment to encourage Thorium Limited to build a monazite processing plant in Travancore. Thorium Limited worked in association with the aforementioned Hopkin and Williams Limited. The British Indian government shared information of the agreement with S. S. Bhatnagar, the director general of the CSIR, and Homi Bhabha, the chair of the Atomic Energy Research Committee. This prompted Bhatnagar and Bhabha to visit Travancore to discuss with Sir C. P. and Travancore's king how the future Indian government could access the monazite sands.

Territorial claims and counterclaims of Travancore and the future Indian Union came head to head in June 1947. On June 3, the viceroy of India, Lord

Louis Mountbatten, announced on All India Radio that Great Britain would transfer power and grant independence to two sovereign entities, India and Pakistan, on August 15 of that year. The hasty British exit and the partition of British India into India and Pakistan caused much confusion and concern. The borders of the new nation nation-states were already in flux. The diverse territorial landscape of the subcontinent, comprising directly ruled provinces, indirectly ruled princely states, Himalayan kingdoms with unequal treaties, and non-British colonial enclaves, suddenly experienced an uncertain future.

On June 11, Sir C. P. publicly stated that as soon as power was transferred from Great Britain to India and Pakistan, Travancore would become an independent nation-state.[70] According to him, the end to British paramountcy implied territorial sovereignty for his kingdom. Even though Travancore's population was primarily Hindu, he saw no reason to join Hindu-majority India. The king of Travancore supported his dewan's decision, leading Sir C. P. to appoint Travancore's representative to the dominion of Pakistan. He even began negotiations to buy rice from Pakistan's Sindh province to reduce dependence on the territories of the Indian Union that surrounded Travancore.[71] This greatly upset Jawaharlal Nehru, who in retaliation threatened an economic blockade of Travancore and even aerial bombing by the Royal Indian Air Force if the kingdom did not reverse its decision.[72]

The same month, CSIR announced the establishment of the Travancore-India Joint Committee for the extraction of monazite for atomic energy production. The committee gave more power to the imminently independent Indian government. As a nine-member body, it had only three members appointed by Travancore and six by CSIR. The committee was the institutional outcome of Bhatnagar and Bhabha's efforts to secure the Atomic Energy Research Committee's access to Travancore's monazite. Although Sir C. P. participated in the joint endeavor, it was far from a sign of his capitulation.

On July 25, 1947, even after a communist activist tried to assassinate him, Sir C. P. adhered to his original position that Travancore would not join the Indian Union.[73] Unfortunately for him, Travancore's monarch had changed his mind by then, likely under pressure from the soon-to-be independent Indian government led by Nehru. Five days after the assassination attempt on Sir C. P., the king of Travancore declared that his kingdom would join the Indian Union unconditionally, "though not without hesitation."[74]

Travancore's decision to accede to India and the Travancore-India Joint Committee did not completely end British hopes of access to Travancore's monazite. In April 1948, after the independent Indian government adopted its Atomic Energy Act, the UK Commonwealth Relations Office wondered whether the Indian legislation affected Travancore. The British official searched for legal loopholes: "Under the present constitution, the Indian [princely] States are not included in the Provinces of India. . . . It remains to be seen how the government of India will arrange to bring the development of the Travancore minerals under control."[75]

The Indian government's decisions that accompanied the act quelled all doubts. Travancore's monazite had indeed become India's monazite. The act established the Atomic Energy Commission of India or AECI under the direct authority of the central government in New Delhi. It assigned to the AECI control over all industry and raw materials for the use, production, and research in atomic energy. More importantly, the AECI identified monazite and beryllium as priority raw materials for atomic energy and retained the embargo on their exports.[76]

Over the next months, the AECI would be in quest of a monazite processing plant to be constructed in Travancore in return for access to *Indian* monazite. The independent Indian government would adopt a similar strategy to that of the dewan of Travancore—namely, to make the sale of atomic earths conditional upon the construction of a processing plant. To those at the helm of India's nuclear program, exporting raw materials and importing processed products reeked of the economic exploitation that had characterized British colonialism.[77] As they would soon find out, as Sir C. P. already had, very few foreign companies would show interest.

Conclusion

While contestations over Travancore's monazite represented the geopolitical ambitions of the territorial Indian nation-state, the Tatas' philanthropic support marked the business-government partnership that characterized the developmentalist state in atomic energy research. Territoriality and technopolitics seemed to inhabit parallel worlds. Bhabha's transnational procurement of technologies and personnel transpired at a time of communal violence between Hindus and Muslims over partition and independence. Bhabha's note to Sir Frederick James in November 1947 arrived from Mexico City where he was part of the Indian delegation at the UNESCO General Conference. At the time, troops from India and Pakistan battled over Kashmir.

In reality, the seemingly parallel universes of the territorial and the developmentalist state were deeply entangled. Crafting borders by swallowing contiguous lands brought new territories within the folds of the Indian nation-state. Such territories had resources like monazite, beryllium, and other minerals that could be exploited and harnessed to bring about economic development. As we shall see in the next chapter, the entanglements of geopolitics and technopolitics would resurface through tensions over French colonial territories between postcolonial India and postwar France at a time when their atomic energy commissions would consider jointly developing power reactors.

CHAPTER 2

Radium to Reactors, 1948–1953

Marie Curie in her Nobel lecture had called radium "an entirely separate kind of chemistry . . . the chemistry of the imponderable."[1] After the Curies isolated radium from pitchblende, the new self-luminous element became a source of public fascination. It found itself in everyday items such as watch dials, lipsticks, and water fountains. It was even hailed as a wondrous cure for cancer.[2] Radium's use in cancer treatment attracted the philanthropic attention of Dorabji Tata Trust that had been considering plans to establish a cancer hospital in Bombay.[3]

Radium's arrival in Bombay traced itself directly to Madame Curie, when the trust recruited Pattipati Ramaiah Naidu, her former doctoral student, as the first chief physicist at the Tata Memorial Hospital. Inaugurated in 1941, Naidu set up the first facility to separate radon from radium for cancer treatment.[4] Six years later, when Bhabha wrote to Irène Joliot-Curie seeking a French expert from the Radium Institute in Paris to work in Bombay, he was seeking someone to replace Naidu, who had fallen ill due to radiation exposure.[5] Radium thus already connected Bombay with Paris. Over the following years, new forms of cooperation with French physicists, chemists, engineers, and technical personnel would advance India's fledgling nuclear program.

The relative openness surrounding nuclear fission research in postwar France was in sharp contrast to the information censorship in the United States. US policymakers feared communist subversion and Soviet espionage, contributing to the expansion of secrecy in research and know-how involving nuclear fission.[6] In the summer of 1946, the US Congress had passed the Atomic Energy Act that declared most information related to nuclear fission as "born secret" and hence "restricted data."[7] Commonly known as the McMahon Act, named after its legislative sponsor, Brien McMahon, Democratic senator from Connecticut, the legislation retained practices of secrecy in the postwar years that were originally intended as temporary wartime measures.[8] The Vannevar Bush Report and the Henry D. Smyth Report had recommended that the Truman administration keep the US public informed and "lift the lid" on nuclear fission research. Nevertheless, the executive and legislative branches of the US government favored more secrecy, not less.[9] Together with the revised 1946 Critical and Strategic Materials Stockpiling Act, the McMahon Act extended wartime control of nuclear fission into peacetime.

Against the backdrop of US-led information censorship and stockpiling of atomic earths, France emerged as the first technology partner of India's nuclear program. The partnership first took the form of French company STR's 1949 decision to construct a monazite processing plant in Travancore. This was followed by a power reactor development initiative in 1951 between the AECI and its French counterpart, *Commissariat à l'énergie atomique* (CEA). During the Second World War, the Joliot-Curies had remained in Paris. Frédéric Joliot-Curie had continued his research at Collège de France, becoming the CEA's first *haut-commissaire* (high commissioner or chairman) after Charles de Gaulle's Provisional Government had established the body by ordinance in October 1945.

On the face of it, technological cooperation between nuclear programs of the two countries seemed unlikely. India was a recently decolonized country. France was a European power that had reclaimed its colonial territories in Asia and Africa immediately after its liberation from Nazi occupation. The implausibility was not least because the political future of French colonial enclaves or *établissements* in peninsular India remained largely uncertain. Nevertheless, Bhabha, Nehru, and Joliot-Curie forged ahead with plans for long-term institutional cooperation in fission research.

Two systemic factors influenced the choices made by the leaders of India's nuclear program in these early years. First was the US-led system of controls on nuclear fission research. The second factor was the East-West divide of the Cold War. Through cooperation with French commercial and scientific institutions, those at the helm of India's nuclear program preserved their freedom of action. Indian scientific elites who led the nuclear program found in the French a similar streak of discontentment with respect to US-led information censorship and secrecy in nuclear fission. The CEA offered to jointly develop beryllium-moderated power reactors with the AECI at a time when no other technologically advanced foreign country was coming forward to cooperate. As this chapter will also show, the AECI would later subvert Cold War divisions through policy choices that were solely possible because of technologies and materials obtained from the CEA and STR.

Processing Monazite

On August 20, 1948, the AECI held its very first meeting, during which it devised its general policy.[10] Presided over by Prime Minister Nehru himself, the meeting charted an ambitious plan for nuclear fission research. The AECI's policy included technologies and materials that could be useful for the production of nuclear energy as well as weapons. As part of its policy, the AECI aimed to set up a small reactor to produce radioactive elements for biological, chemical, and metallurgical research, to test materials such as beryllium and graphite for use in a larger reactor, and to train Indian technical personnel in atomic energy. The AECI wanted to process monazite to produce thorium nitrate and thorium, and even extract uranium from monazite. They sought to investigate the possibilities of "making heavy water, beryllium metal, and pure graphite."[11] For the rest of the year 1948, the AECI embarked on its mission to find a foreign firm that would build a monazite processing plant in Travancore, India.

Retaining Travancore's export embargo on monazite, the AECI's quest took Bhabha and Bhatnagar to Berlin and Paris, not Washington, DC, or London. The *modus vivendi* of January 1948 extended the secrecy regime of the McMahon Act to the other two Manhattan Project partners, Britain and Canada. Its Article 7 elicited formal commitment of US, British and Canadian governments "in the interest of mutual security" to not disclose "classified information in the field of atomic energy" to "other governments or authorities or persons in other countries without due prior consultation."[12] Like the 1943 Quebec Agreement that had prevented dissemination of fission-related information outside of the three countries, the 1948 *modus vivendi* did the same in peacetime.

US-imposed secrecy in nuclear fission research was not the only stumbling block in the AECI's quest for a monazite processing plant from US and British firms. Firms like Lindsay Light and Thorium Limited wanted to continue to benefit from the capitalist structures and imperial networks of the colonial era even after formal decolonization. For them, the construction of a monazite processing plant in Travancore would have rendered their processing facilities in the United States and the United Kingdom redundant. Moreover, their role as intermediaries that extracted and processed cheap raw materials to sell back processed chemical compounds at high prices would have been no longer necessary.

In the fall of 1948, Bhabha and Bhatnagar shortlisted three firms: Paris-based STR, Berlin-based *Auergesellschaft*, and London-based New Metals and Chemicals Limited.[13] Unlike STR and *Auergesellschaft*, the British firm had no prior experience in extracting Travancore's monazite. It was surprising that the AECI even considered the German company given the partition of Germany and Berlin after 1945. Bhatnagar met Dr. Egon Ihwe of the Oranienburg plant of *Auergesellschaft* after preliminary contact was established through the Indian Military Mission in Berlin.[14] The German company's past experience in processing Travancore's monazite during the first decades of the twentieth century and its accomplishments in thorium-based fission research for the Nazi nuclear weapons program made it attractive to the AECI.

Although it was going to be impossible for the AECI to actually sign an agreement with *Auergesellschaft* because of what Bhabha called "political reasons," he enthusiastically wrote to Nehru that the information Bhatnagar had "brought back from Berlin was of great value."[15] The *Auer* company, then located in Soviet-occupied East Berlin, had provided Bhatnagar with a list of "finished products which can be obtained by suitably treating the raw materials and rare earths" from monazite and "the extent to which it will be possible in the future to develop this industry."[16] Bhabha provided Nehru with a clear-eyed assessment of *Auergesellschaft*'s goals:

> It appears that the German firm was willing to part with this information because under the present conditions they have been prohibited from undertaking any research or manufacture in the radioactive and atomic fields. Moreover, they are quite willing that their experts should be absorbed in similar industries abroad so that they may keep their knowledge of the subject up-to-date in order to be of use to the German industry when it is allowed to develop in future.[17]

Despite his interest in what *Auergesellschaft* could informally offer, Bhabha was most enthusiastic about a partnership with STR. When Bhabha wrote to Nehru in December 1948, negotiations had already been concluded between the AECI and the French firm, and a draft agreement had been produced. The AECI had directly negotiated with STR's owner Joseph Blumenfeld. The company had recently set up a factory for the CEA for the purification of uranium oxide in Boucher and was keen on signing an agreement with the AECI on monazite processing.

J. R .D. Tata played a key role in the negotiations with STR. J. R. D. had French connections of his own. He was born in Paris to a French mother, spoke fluent

French, and had even completed mandatory military service in the French Army. He had relinquished his French citizenship in 1929 to remain in India and serve on the board of Tata Sons, eventually becoming its chairman in 1938. Bhabha informed Nehru that J. R. D. provided "very great help" in the "financial part of the negotiations" so much so that "his efforts throughout the period of negotiations covering several weeks reduced the financial terms of the agreement to the very favorable ones."[18] The direct involvement of J. R. D. Tata in one of the first foreign partnerships of the AECI represented the business-government partnership that was taking shape in India's nuclear program.

According to the initial terms of the agreement, STR agreed to construct the monazite processing plant in Aluva, anglicized as Alwaye, in Travancore within two years. Once completed, the plant would process 1,500 tons of monazite annually and would have a total initial capital cost of two million rupees (~US$716,600).[19] The plant would separate thorium nitrate and sulphate, various kinds of "extremely valuable rare earth and phosphates in a commercially usable form," and over time "turn these intermediate products into more and more finished products thus increasing the profits which will accrue to the Government." It was also agreed that 50% of the payment to STR would be in either US dollars or Swiss francs and the remaining 50% in either unblocked sterling pounds or rupees.[20]

In February 1949, Joseph Blumenfeld visited India to finalize STR's agreement with AECI. It was decided that the monazite plant would be run by "an independent Government owned company under the auspices of the Atomic Energy Commission [of India]."[21] This led to the creation of the Indian Rare Earths Limited, a public sector undertaking, which still exists today. *Banque Marocaine de Crédit*, a subsidiary of Paris-based *Crédit Agricole*, undertook the financing of the project. Under the terms of the agreement, STR would train chemists from India in its factories and laboratories in France, for which one hundred tons of monazite were to be sent by the Indian government. It was also decided that "the thorium and uranium extracted from the monazite sands will remain the property of the Government of India and will have to be returned," by STR.[22]

With its 1949 agreement with the AECI, STR acquired a monopoly access to India's monazite at a time when British and US companies continued to experience India's export embargo. While the factory was being built in Alwaye, STR processed Travancore's monazite at its factories in Thann, Serquigny, and La Rochelle, sending back thorium nitrate, cerium, and other rare earths, to meet India's needs. The STR contract laid the groundwork for a reactor cooperation agreement between the AECI and the CEA—the first such contract outside the Manhattan Project two years prior to the US Atoms for Peace program.

French Colonial Possessions in South Asia

The decolonization of British India itself did not cause political uncertainty for French colonial possessions in South Asia. The attitudes of the leaders of the Indian National Congress and of Nehru in particular, however, raised questions about the political future of French India. Comprising five noncontiguous territories of a total of 196 square miles, French India included the land-locked enclave of Chandernagore surrounded by the state of West Bengal and the four coastal territories of Pondichéry, Karikal, Yanaon, and Mahé in peninsular India (see map 2). A French governor-general based in Pondichéry administered these five noncontiguous French enclaves.

The inhabitants of French India regularly crossed into British India. They spoke multiple languages. They were ethnically close to the inhabitants of the neighboring British Indian territories. With the Nazi invasion and occupation of France, these French colonial possessions expressed allegiance to Free French Forces led by Charles de Gaulle. Their territories were used in the Allied war effort. After the war, when France reclaimed its empire in Africa, Indochina, and South Asia, the five enclaves became fully French colonial territories once again.

The Jaipur session of the Indian National Congress in December 1948 attended by around three thousand party delegates alarmed the French colonial administration in Pondichéry and the French government in Paris. At the session, Nehru's political party adopted a resolution declaring that all colonial possessions in the subcontinent belonged to the Indian Union and that no other solution was possible.[23] Through negotiations between Indian and French governments, referenda were called in the French enclaves to allow the inhabitants to decide their own fate—whether to join the Indian or the French Union.

In January 1949, Nehru stated at the Indian Parliament, "We believe that for a variety of reasons it is natural and proper that all foreign possessions in India should be united with India. We propose to give effect to this policy through friendly discussions with the powers concerned."[24] Prime minister Nehru's statement represented the official Indian position toward French and Portuguese colonial territories scattered across South Asia. In June of that year, the inhabitants of Chandernagore voted overwhelmingly in favor of joining the Indian Union. The four other enclaves were far less inclined to merge with India. A tense episode began between the Indian government newly freed from colonialism and the French Fourth Republic recently liberated from Nazi occupation and Vichy rule.

Decolonization of French India was "negotiated between a subservient imperial power and a post-colonial nation-state," wrote historian Akhila Yechury.[25]

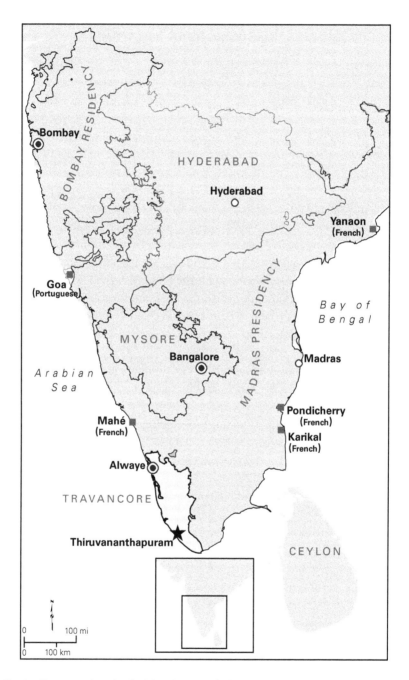

MAP 2. Travancore, French colonial territories, and other territorial configurations in peninsular India prior to their merger with the Indian Union. Credit: Scott Walker, Harvard Map Collection.

Communal tensions, political violence, and communist activities affected order in the four territories. The French colonial authorities brutally suppressed rallies and demonstrations that supported a merger with India, as in the case of Mahé. Antimerger protests were attacked by activists and criminals close to the Indian National Congress.[26] As a result of partition, communal violence between Hindus and Muslims and the arrival in the French territories of Muslim refugees fleeing riots further increased political instability in the enclaves.

In the fall of 1952, Nehru declared that India could not accept referenda in the four French territories. He added that the French and Indian governments ought to work toward the direct transfer of those territories to the Indian Union. The dispute between the two governments was exacerbated in light of the Nehru government's claims of French voter fraud and smuggling and its economic blockade of the French territories. It would not be until October 1954 that an indirect vote by elected representatives in Pondichéry would determine the outcome. They would vote in favor of a merger with India by 170 to 8.

The French exit from Indochina would thus be followed by its departure from South Asia. The India-France bilateral accord for the *de facto* transfer of the French possessions to the Indian Republic would be finalized soon after. The French Senate, however, would not ratify the 1956 final treaty of *de jure* cession until 1962, after the French were compelled to bow out of Algeria.[27]

The geopolitics of intermestic territorial violence was entangled in the technopolitics of atomic earths. Against the tense political backdrop of French India, STR conducted its negotiations with AECI in 1948, signed the agreement in February 1949, and constructed the monazite processing plant by 1952. The monazite plant in Alwaye was only one hundred and forty miles away from the disputed French territory of Mahé. There promerger groups rioted, and their demonstrations were violently suppressed by French colonial authorities.

Beryllium-Moderated Power Reactors from France

Newly independent India and recently liberated France were not "cosubalterns."[28] Yet, in the context of US-led controls and censorship in nuclear matters, their atomic energy commissions sensed camaraderie. France as a country could not participate in the Manhattan Project due to Nazi occupation, despite being one of the leaders in fission research before the Second World War.[29] Five French physicists took part in the Manhattan Project in their individual capacity: Bertrand Goldschmidt, Jules Guéron, Pierre Auger, Hans Halban, and Lew Kowarski. Frédéric Joliot-Curie had decided to stay in Paris to continue to work at Collège de France. As a result, on the one hand, the postwar French government was not subject to the information censorship and controls of the 1943 Quebec Agreement and the 1948 *modus vivendi*. On the other hand, France did not have ready access to the raw materials for nuclear fission unlike the United States, the United Kingdom, and Canada.

France's "Manhattan Complex," as I have called it elsewhere, led French scientists and policymakers to perceive the US-led wartime atomic bomb project as an Anglo-Saxon endeavor.[30] Bertrand Goldschmidt looked back on his participation in the Manhattan Project with some regret. He wrote in the *Atomic Complex*, "Although the total French contribution was important and out of proportion to our tiny number, it could never represent a real political asset for France for we were not grouped in a coherent unit with a recognised leader who could have negotiated with the British on our behalf. Had Joliot-Curie gone to England, he would have naturally assumed this role."[31]

The CEA's interest in reactor cooperation with the AECI was driven by the possibility of accessing India's atomic earths. Most of the known atomic earths were under the control of the Common Development Trust.[32] Uranium was still believed to be a scarce commodity, which made thorium as a raw material for nuclear fission an attractive option for the French nuclear program. Bhabha and Bhatnagar were fully aware of the CEA's interest in India's atomic earths. After the AECI's contract with STR was finalized in 1949, Bhatnagar wrote to CEA high commissioner Joliot-Curie offering him "a certain percentage of this material" (monazite) to be used "for experimental purposes with a view to developing further co-operative scientific work in the field of atomic energy" between the CEA and the AECI.[33] The CEA was the only institution outside of the Manhattan Project that had succeeded in constructing a functioning nuclear reactor, the ZOÉ, in December 1948 within three years of the establishment of the CEA.[34]

Apart from thorium-bearing monazite, the CEA was also attracted to India's beryl ore deposits in Udaipur and the Deccan peninsula. The metal beryllium had been used as a moderator and a source of neutrons when Lise Meitner, Otto Frisch, Otto Hahn, and Fritz Strassmann discovered nuclear fission in December 1938. Scientists later also found out that beryllium could reduce the critical mass of weapon-grade uranium and plutonium needed in nuclear weapons. India's reserves of beryl were deemed to be "self-sustaining for present needs and those of the immediate future," according to a 1946 report prepared by the Department of Works, Mines, and Power of the British Indian government.[35] Nevertheless, the Nehru government had imposed an export embargo on beryl, like they had for monazite, in order to obtain processing technologies from abroad.

Over the course of two secret meetings on January 16 and 17, 1950, in New Delhi, the AECI and the CEA reached their initial understanding regarding their agreement for reactor cooperation.[36] This was the first bilateral power reactor cooperation for both the French and the Indian atomic energy commissions. During this period, British and US governments' efforts to access India's atomic earths remained unsuccessful. London insisted that the Indian government release at least commercial quantities of cerium, obtained from monazite, to meet British needs.[37] Washington tried to access thorium salts produced from Indian monazite.[38] The AECI with full support of the Nehru government maintained its refusal.

Joliot-Curie's remark at the meeting of January 16 that "every great nation should take its place in developing and using atomic energy and not leave it to a few highly industrialized nations" was in stark contrast to the position of the United States and the effects of US policies on British and Canadian potential for nuclear cooperation with third parties.[39] The French chemist's position on atomic earths even echoed the AECI and the Nehru government's policy. Joliot-Curie said, "[T]he thorium should be kept by India for her own use and not sold abroad on a commercial basis except in limited quantities in return for special concessions in the field of atomic energy," and that it "applied equally to all materials of importance in atomic energy, such as uranium, beryllium, etc."[40] Prime Minister Nehru, who hosted the meeting at the Ministry of External Affairs (MEA), wanted to know from his French guest the general scientific possibilities of harnessing atomic energy for power generation, its timeframe, and costs. Joliot-Curie estimated that "within five to ten years a central production plant for atomic energy with a uranium reactor would be possible."[41] The AECI shared with Frédéric Joliot-Curie its general policy agreed to at its first meeting held in August 1948 to facilitate cooperation in areas of mutual interest.

At the meeting of January 17, held at Bhatnagar's home in New Delhi, Joliot-Curie proposed a bilateral cooperation agreement between the CEA and the AECI. His offer was in alignment with the priorities set by the leaders of India's nuclear program two years ago. He offered to share technical information with India on the purification of uranium, graphite reprocessing, and the designs of a low-power reactor in return for India's export of beryllium, thorium, mineral oil, and uranium (if it were discovered in large quantities in India in the future).[42] The proposal from the CEA high commissioner was for joint research, development, and construction of two beryllium-moderated power reactors to be built in India and France. The initial contract was drawn up in March 1950, and the final agreement was concluded in August 1951.[43] Soon after, the French foreign ministry informed the British and US embassies in Paris about the AECI-CEA bilateral cooperation agreement.[44]

Beryllium-moderated natural uranium reactors were under research and development also in the United Kingdom and the United States. Bhabha had even concurrently explored the possibility of a similar kind of reactor cooperation with Sir John D. Cockcroft, then director of the UK Atomic Energy Research Establishment. The news of the AECI-CEA agreement, therefore, displeased the British.[45] They were anxious about the increasing French involvement in India's nascent nuclear program and considered it "was desirable to wean them [AECI] away" from the CEA.[46] Officials at the UK Foreign Office bemoaned that the 1948 *modus vivendi* curtailed opportunities to collaborate with Commonwealth countries, including former colonies like India and mineral-rich dominions like Australia and South Africa.

The AECI-CEA reactor cooperation agreement had two stages.[47] First, the two organizations would conduct joint theoretical studies on a beryllium-moderated power reactor (one thousand to ten thousand kilowatts) that would use natural uranium as its fuel.[48] The natural uranium would be furnished by France and the beryllium by India. The theoretical studies would take place in France involving both Indian and French technical personnel. The CEA would also process beryllium for the AECI during this stage. Second, once the theoretical studies were concluded, such a power reactor would be constructed first in India over a period of five years. During this five-year period, India would supply beryllium to France for the construction of a similar reactor in France. At the end of five years, the reactor constructed in India would become the property of the AECI. Construction costs for the reactor in India would be covered by the AECI through direct payments or reimbursements.

The reactor cooperation agreement with the CEA through the selective offering of atomic earths allowed the leaders of India's nuclear program to pursue its freedom of action. Yet, the cooperation also had its shortcomings. This was not least because beryllium-moderated reactors were untested, and therefore, the viability of the final product was far from certain. The construction of the first reactor was to be in India, which meant that test runs and their trials and tribulations would have to be dealt with by the technologically less-advanced partner, namely, the AECI, which was also going to become the eventual owner of that first reactor. If the first reactor had technical flaws, as was often the case for untested reactor technologies, those were to be dealt with by the AECI. Moreover, the CEA bore half of the total costs (approximately, £250,000 in 1950), procured access for the French firm *Pechiney* to India's beryl that was otherwise embargoed, and could gather technical knowledge at no extra cost from the first five years of operation of the first reactor in India.[49] In other words, the actual benefits to the AECI were modest.

The political advantages were manifold, as noted by British ambassador Sir Oliver Harvey in Paris: "For their part, the Indians will have the benefit of much existing French experience and will have another country interested in their beryl, which may help them in bargaining with the Americans, who already have some claim to their ore."[50] The AECI had begun its search for a beryl processing plant since it had imposed the embargo on its export in 1946–47. In the United States, beryl, like monazite, was a strategic material under the 1946 Strategic and Critical Materials Stockpiling Act.[51] The US government aimed to accumulate raw materials like beryl and monazite so that Communist countries were denied access to them. India's export embargo on atomic earths thus directly affected US stockpiling efforts.

In early 1949, the AECI had offered to relax the beryl embargo for the US government in exchange of a beryl processing plant. The AECI's attempt to use its embargo as a bargaining chip had met with resistance from the US Atomic Energy Commission (USAEC), just like Lindsay Light and Chemical had resisted the ask for a monazite processing plant in Travancore. This time, however, the USAEC was made to reconsider its position by the State Department on grounds of national security.[52]

In May 1949, two USAEC officials in charge of raw materials, Gustafson and Wells, had visited New Delhi to discuss matters concerning beryl and took the opportunity "at the same time to obtain more information on monazite and thorium position" of the Nehru government.[53] A draft agreement on a beryl processing plant for India was initialed by the AECI and the USAEC in October 1949, only months after the AECI's contract with STR for the monazite processing plant. Nevertheless, institutional differences had remained over the details of the agreement.

Under the 1951 AECI-CEA agreement for beryllium-moderated reactors, even though French firm *Pechiney* would process India's beryl, its services would be tied to the reactor development project. The AECI would receive beryllium oxide processed from its own beryl by the French firm, just like Travancore had received thorium nitrate processed from its own monazite through British and US firms. The AECI, therefore, began in earnest "exploring the possibilities of setting up a plant in India for processing beryl ore and producing beryllium compounds and ultimately beryllium metal."[54] Meanwhile, the US Congress also searched for new ways to compel India to relax its export embargo on atomic earths.

US Food Aid for Atomic Earths

Atomic earths entered the domain of US Cold War–era development assistance through the Truman administration's Point Four Program. President Truman had stated in the fourth point of his 1949 inaugural address that his government would share the benefits of US "scientific advances and industrial progress" for the "improvement and growth of underdeveloped areas" of the world.[55] Under the program, several thousand technical experts were unleashed on the developing world through the State Department's Technical Cooperation Administration, with strategic materials configuring prominently on their agenda.[56]

With the outbreak of the Korean War in June 1950, within months of the Point Four Program being launched, the extraction of raw materials became further integrated into US foreign and military policies.[57] The Defense Production Act reorganized resource procurement and management within the federal government. The formation of the International Materials Policy Commission in January 1951 chaired by William S. Paley of the Columbia Broadcasting System was a watershed moment. Commonly known as the Paley Commission, the *ad hoc* body in its report predicted that the United States would experience a major shortage of raw materials by the 1970s and recommended that the Point Four Program be steered in ways to meet future US mineral needs.[58] The Paley Commission's influential report titled *Resources for Freedom* proclaimed the use of US development aid as a means to procure raw materials worldwide. Procuring beryl and monazite from India therefore aligned with the priorities of US foreign policy, as the Paley Commission envisioned it.[59]

Food scarcity in northern India in the middle of 1950 provided an opportune moment for US policymakers to make economic assistance and minerals extraction converge. On the one hand, the Cold Warriors in the Truman administration worried that a famine in India could mean "losing" the country to communism. In light of Communist victory in the Chinese Civil War and the establishment of the People's Republic of China, US policymakers were particularly sensitive to losing another large Asian country to the specter of communism.[60] On the other hand, Nehru's neutral position at the United Nations on the Korean War aggravated lawmakers on Capitol Hill.

In the first half of 1951, US legislators attempted to make food aid to India conditional upon India's supply of atomic earths like monazite and beryl.[61] Charles Lindsay III and James S. Murray of the Lindsay Light and Chemical Company testified at the US Congress arguing that in order to receive US wheat, the Indian government must terminate its export embargo on monazite.[62] Congressional deliberations on the India Emergency Food Aid Bill provided Lindsay Light and Chemical the perfect opportunity to put pressure on the Indian government.

A Herblock cartoon published in the *Washington Post* in April 1951 aptly captured the mood on Capitol Hill on food aid for India. It showed the eighty-second Congress delivering its "sermon on the mount" atop heaps of US grain. To a starving emaciated mother and child representing famine-stricken India, a cigar-smoking US lawmaker held the sign, "You don't get anything for nothing in this world, pal" (figure 2.1).[63] As the Soviet Union and Communist China made barter offers of food to the Nehru government—Soviet wheat and Chinese rice and corn for Indian jute—the Truman administration grew anxious.[64] The State Department was worried about the geopolitical consequences of food aid from communist countries reaching India. Yet, the food aid bill remained "held up in the House Rules Committee by members who hold that this country [United States] should get critical materials from India in return for the grain."[65]

William Pawley, who since his wartime experience in India had grown close to the Truman administration, recommended to US policymakers that direct references to India's atomic earths be dropped from the food aid bill. By then, Pawley had already served as the US ambassador to Peru and Brazil, also a major monazite producer. Given his close ties to India during the Second World War, Pawley was called upon to help the Truman administration resolve what seemed to be an intractable problem between US and Indian governments. Pawley believed that offering US food aid tied to Indian monazite and beryl was counterproductive to immediate US interests and even detrimental to US long-term relationship with the largest noncommunist democracy in Asia. Brien McMahon, the chairman of the Joint Committee on Atomic Energy, agreed with Pawley that direct references to monazite or thorium would make it difficult for the Nehru government to accept US food aid.

In May 1951, Soviet grain shipments arrived in India with much political and media fanfare. The public relations effect of Soviet grain rescuing poor Indians jolted the US Congress, convincing lawmakers that US food aid for India was necessary for US national security.[66] The India Emergency Food Aid Act was signed by Truman in June 1951. It used "strategic or critical materials" in a deliberately vague way, making the US wheat loan to India partially payable in terms of strategic materials like monazite, beryl, and manganese. The State Department accepted Pawley's suggestion that he be allowed to negotiate separately with the Indian government and the AECI to elicit their commitment to supply atomic earths to the US government.

From 1951 to 1952, US-Indian negotiations to secure Indian atomic earths for the US government and firms were led by Pawley on the US side and Bhatnagar

FIGURE 2.1. "Sermon on the Mount" by Herblock published in the *Washington Post*, April 5, 1951. Published with permission from the Herb Block Foundation.

on the Indian side. In these talks, Bhatnagar asked Pawley for a second monazite processing plant to be built by a US firm, in addition to the one that STR was already constructing in Alwaye. Given the flurry of activities surrounding India's atomic earths—US interest in India's monazite and beryl, and French-Indian power reactor cooperation, Roger Makins at the UK Foreign Office repented that the British were "running a bad third to the French and the Americans."[67]

The AECI released some monazite for the US government and private companies to cultivate interest in constructing a second monazite processing factory, but in vain. Pawley could not successfully convince Union Carbide to build such a plant in India. Lindsay Light and Chemical had already refused, informing the State Department that it would not purchase "semiprocessed" monazite from the Alwaye plant. US ambassador Chester Bowles, an advocate for technical assistance to India, could do little to resolve the impasse.[68] In response, the Nehru government informed the Truman administration that it would look for potential buyers for its thorium products elsewhere, including communist countries.

By April 1952, the USAEC had become resistant to the idea of importing India's monazite. Thorium itself was becoming less attractive as a raw material for nuclear fission, and cheaper sources of monazite with fewer conditions were becoming available from Brazil and South Africa.[69] The US government sought Indian monazite as part of its stockpiling efforts in the Cold War with the goal to prevent access of the atomic earths by the communist world. The CIA estimated in July 1952 that if there were a communist takeover of the Indian subcontinent, the "USSR would probably hasten to exploit India's thorium-bearing monazite for atomic energy purposes."[70]

By the fall of 1952, the US Department of Defense stepped in. They feared that Indian atomic earths could end up in the Communist bloc. Secretary of Defense Robert Lovett directed William Pawley to visit India to continue negotiations with the Indian government. New Delhi still sought a US construction of a monazite processing plant in India in exchange for lifting its export embargo for the US government to allow the purchase of Indian thorium oxide, monazite sands, and rare earth compounds. Lovett directed Pawley to obtain commitment from the Nehru government to "prevent ores and compounds of uranium and thorium from reaching Iron Curtain countries."[71] For this purpose, the Department of Defense offered up to US$1.4 million to be used at Pawley's discretion.

Bhatnagar and Pawley met several times in October 1952 to discuss the construction and operation of a joint Indo-American monazite-processing plant in India.[72] Pawley summarized the US position as follows: although the "monazite supply position for the United States had become substantially easier in the months intervening since the monazite problem was first broached," the US government was willing "to cooperate with the Government of India in the establishment of a second Indian monazite processing plant provided it was found to be in the common interest." In exchange for this US technical assistance, India would provide between 1,500 and 2,500 tons of unprocessed monazite annually to the United States.[73]

Bhatnagar informed Pawley that it would "require consideration at the top level."[74] More importantly, "a favorable decision could not be looked for unless the Prime Minister could be convinced that the proposal was an economically attractive one" to India. In December 1952, when Prime Minister Nehru officially dedicated the STR-built monazite processing plant in Alwaye to the nation, Indian newspapers reported heavily on the vast export potential that the plant had created for India.[75] The leaders of India's nuclear program were well aware that US policymakers' Cold War anxieties would be stoked through any export of thorium products to the Communist bloc.

On July 17, 1953, ten days before the armistice agreement for the Korean war was signed in Panmunjom, the US embassy in New Delhi learned that a shipment of 2,248 pounds of thorium nitrate had left the Bombay harbor in the Polish freighter *SS Mickiewicz*. It was bound for the Chinese port of Tianjin, close to the Korean peninsula.[76] The thorium nitrate was being shipped from the Indian Rare Earths Limited factory in Alwaye. Information arrived to the US embassy that several shipments of thorium nitrate had already left harbors in Bombay and Cochin in India for Chinese ports that July. The thorium nitrate shipments were too small to be useful in atomic energy experiments, but they certainly alarmed policymakers within the Eisenhower administration.

The 1951 US Mutual Defense Assistance Control Act, also known as the Battle Act after its sponsor Laurie Battle of Alabama, required US military, economic, or financial assistance to be automatically terminated if an aid recipient country was found to be trading in embargoed items with the Soviet Union, the Soviet bloc, and/or China.[77] US ambassador George Allen in New Delhi feared that the AECI's sale of thorium nitrate with the knowledge and encouragement of Prime Minister Nehru was going to lead to a "crisis in Indo-American relations and afford encouragement to American isolationists."[78]

The MEA's secretary general, Narayan Raghavan Pillai, who had accompanied Bhatnagar in his earlier talks with Pawley, summarized the position of the Nehru government as follows: "If United States would purchase entire output of this material from factory of Indian Rare Earths Ltd, they would not supply anymore to China."[79] Pillai added that "the sale of thorium nitrate to China was on all fours with Ceylon's sale of rubber to China," thereby, playing down the strategic significance of atomic earths.[80] The British, who had been keeping a close eye on US-India negotiations, noted that India's thorium nitrate shipments to China were "in practical terms insignificant," despite their implications for US law.[81]

By exporting thorium nitrate to Communist China, the AECI and the Nehru government skillfully employed their atomic earths to preserve their freedom of action against the backdrop of Cold War rivalry between the East and West and US stockpiling of strategic materials. The State Department was against terminating economic assistance to India because US foreign policy officials feared that such a measure could push the Indian government further toward trading with the Communist bloc. The Nehru government thus succeeded in drawing the Eisenhower administration back to the bargaining table by playing on US policymakers' Cold War anxieties.

US ambassador Allen met Prime Minister Nehru to discuss the matter at the end of August 1953. Nehru casually told Allen that approving the export licenses for thorium nitrate shipments to China was "merely one of dozens of matters he had to handle in course of one day, that he had attached no particular significance to it and was greatly surprised at the consequences that it had engendered."[82] When pressed for an assurance that such incidents would not recur, Nehru remained noncommittal. Allen wrote to Secretary of State John Foster Dulles about Nehru's response: "As regards future, he said GOI did not operate secretly or in vacuum and was always glad to consult with other powers on matters of mutual concern. He could not say that India could undertake to consult with us re[garding] every export application among hundreds which might bear in some way on items named in embracive provisions of Battle Act."[83]

The Eisenhower administration thus began quiet negotiations with the Nehru government to avoid Congressional meddling. Allen recommended that the US government buy AECI's surplus thorium nitrate to prevent its export to the Communist bloc. He had earlier written to Dulles: "[W]e shall find it increasingly difficult to sustain position on denying trade with iron curtain countries unless we show some willingness to purchase ourselves."[84] Dulles accepted Allen's recommendation.

With the US government back at the negotiating table for Indian atomic earths, the AECI began to disagree with the USAEC over the price of the thorium nitrate. When the USAEC suggested the price of US$2.75 per pound, the AECI asked for US$3.05 per pound—the price that India had paid to the United States for thorium nitrate before the Alwaye plant was built. The USAEC remained unwilling to pay a high price for a commodity it did not require and could procure at a lower rate from South Africa. In October 1953, New Delhi raised the price to US$3.50 per pound.

While AECI and USAEC bickered over the price of thorium nitrate, the Eisenhower administration discovered in November 1953 that the Nehru government had shipped 3,328 pounds of thorium nitrate to Poland, in the Eastern bloc.[85] The Chinese-Polish shipping company *Chipolbrok* handled the shipment from India. The Chinese government had established the company in January 1951 to avoid US trade sanctions.[86] In response, the Eisenhower administration swiftly accepted the final price set by the AECI.[87]

A memorandum was finalized by the terms of which the USAEC would import 230 tons of thorium nitrate from the AECI, while the AECI would be permitted to sell small amounts of the material to a specific list of noncommunist European and Asian countries mutually agreed upon by the two governments.[88] When President Eisenhower approved funds amounting to US$2.2 million for the purchase of Indian thorium nitrate, he underlined that it was "important for the security of United States."[89]

Conclusion

Foreign competition for raw materials without offers of processing technologies represented to the leaders of India's nuclear program the persistence of extractive colonial relationships even after formal decolonization. Skillful diplomacy around monazite led by Bhatnagar, Bhabha, and Nehru embodied their pursuit of freedom of action. Unlike the USAEC, the AECI found in the CEA a near-equal technology partner. The French interest in procuring Indian atomic earths was not through the "stick" of emergency food aid, but joint reactor development. Atomic earths thus became the technopolitical tool through which the AECI articulated its opposition to US policies of stockpiling, control, and censorship in the realm of nuclear fission.

PART TWO

Cold and Hot Wars

CHAPTER 3

Nuclear Marketplace Opens for Business, 1953–1962

President Eisenhower's "Atoms for Peace" speech at the UN General Assembly on December 8, 1953, caught most members of his administration off guard. Outside of a small group of close advisors that included USAEC chairman Lewis Strauss, Secretary of State John Foster Dulles, and his special assistant and confidante Charles Douglas Jackson, the majority of officials in his administration did not know in advance about the proposal. At the UN, the US president declared, "The United States knows that if the fearful trend of atomic military buildup can be reversed, this greatest of destructive forces can be developed into a great boon, for the benefit of all mankind."[1] The "peaceful power from atomic energy . . . would rapidly be transformed into universal, efficient, and economic usage," he announced.[2] It was the dawn of a new era. The global atomic marketplace was about to open for business.

The US proposal was music to the ears of the leaders of India's nuclear program. They had been swimming against the tide of US censorship and controls in their attempt to procure nuclear technologies. Partly owing to anticipated policy shifts as a result of the US Atoms for Peace initiative, and partly as a culmination of Bhabha, Bhatnagar, and Nehru's earlier decisions, India's nuclear program expanded several folds over the next years. From 1954 onward, the program's institutional growth went hand in hand with its consolidation under Bhabha's leadership. The spatial concentration of nuclear research facilities around Bombay resulted in the nuclear program being based geographically far from the central government in New Delhi, but close to its key source of private capital, the Tata Group.

In the year 1954, a flurry of public activities and official events surrounded India's nuclear program. The TIFR's foundation stone was laid with much fanfare on January 1, 1954 (see figure 3.1). Two days later, Prime Minister Nehru declared the development of the Atomic Energy Research Establishment in Trombay, less than fifteen miles from TIFR in Bombay, under Bhabha's leadership. On August 3 of the same year, the Nehru government established by presidential order, thus circumventing parliamentary scrutiny, the Department of Atomic Energy (DAE), with Bhabha as its secretary—answerable solely to the prime minister.[3] Through a government resolution in March 1958, the DAE secretary became the ex-officio chairman of the AECI, while the AECI became officially located within the institutional machinery of the DAE. Bhabha would remain as the AECI chairman and the DAE secretary until his death.

The centralization of nuclear research around Bombay and the role of the Tatas in the nuclear program were resented not least by Calcutta-based leftist astrophysicist Meghnad Saha. He complained to Nehru that the "concentra-

FIGURE 3.1.   J. R. D. Tata receiving Prime Minister Jawaharlal Nehru on the occasion of the foundation stone-laying ceremony of TIFR on January 1, 1954. Others in the picture are Mr. Handoo (left) and CSIR's director general and AECI member S. S. Bhatnagar (right). Disclaimer: Tata Institute of Fundamental Research (TIFR)/TIFR Archives has only provided the above images. The opinion expressed in the said text/article are author's own and does not reflect the opinion of TIFR, including TIFR Archives.

tion of all power and distribution of patronage in a few hands" made the AECI a "the pocket bureau of a particular Indian commercial firm."[4] In response, Bhatnagar defended the Nehru government's policies at the TIFR's foundation stone-laying ceremony. He boldly stated in his speech, "We have been blamed for connections with the Tatas. . . . I am of the opinion that the Tata Organization can be considered capitalistic only because it gives large capital sums to all good causes, in the world."[5] The business-government partnership through the Tatas' philanthropy in India's nuclear program would become more entrenched over the years.

As the nuclear marketplace opened for business, most sellers' attention was focused on India's nuclear program, which was one of the most advanced in the newly decolonized world. Nehru's leadership of nonaligned countries in Bandung in 1955 placed India in the global limelight. Similarly, Bhabha's presidency of the 1955 UN Conference on Peaceful Uses of Atomic Energy in Geneva and his prominent role at the negotiation of the IAEA statute made India's nuclear program a class apart from that of its peers. Immediately after Eisenhower's Atoms for Peace proposal, the DAE signed reactor cooperation agreements with the United Kingdom and Canada. In August 1956, when the British-supplied APSARA reached criticality, the DAE became the first atomic energy organization in Asia to have an operational research reactor.

US Eagerness to Sell Power Reactors

Atoms for Peace is often understood as part of the Eisenhower administration's classic psychological warfare in the Cold War to win the hearts and minds of the free world.[6] It portrayed a peaceful image of the United States at a time of the heightened US-Soviet arms race and the administration's policy of massive retaliation with nuclear weapons against adversaries. It emerged as part of "Project Candor," the administration's public relations strategy of providing national security reports to the US people in the "age of peril" posed by communism.[7] While the administration promoted the peaceful atom, the US nuclear arsenal increased from 841 warheads in 1952 to 18,638 in 1960.[8] Although Atoms for Peace was at least partly an instrument in the US Cold War against the Soviet Union, in order to implement it key legislative changes inside the United States and new multilateral initiatives outside were needed.[9]

In the summer of 1954, William Sterling Cole, Republican senator from New York, introduced the bill to amend the 1946 US Atomic Energy Act. It sailed through Capitol Hill and was signed into act by President Eisenhower on August 30 that year.[10] The 1954 US Atomic Energy Act ended the era of government-imposed controls and censorship in matters concerning nuclear fission. It paved the way for declassification of extensive information related to fission.[11] Private firms like Westinghouse and General Electric could thus begin to sell nuclear technologies and information in the nuclear marketplace. Inside the United States, probusiness actors within the government like Lewis Strauss tried to spur the interest of utility companies by claiming that the electricity produced from nuclear power would be "too cheap to meter."[12]

Light water reactors became the preferred US model for domestic and foreign consumption owing to the wartime development of naval reactors by Westinghouse under the stewardship of naval officer Hyman Rickover. Rickover wanted portable reactors that could power submarines and ships for the US Navy. In early 1953, when the National Security Council (NSC) decided to develop a nuclear energy program for domestic consumption and foreign export, Strauss decided to reorient Rickover's project of naval reactors to produce commercial power reactors. He commissioned Westinghouse to build a small prototype reactor, which the company did in Shippingport, Pennsylvania.[13]

Under NSC 5507/2 of March 1955, the Eisenhower administration decided that the "national resource represented by US atomic facilities and technology can be a great asset in the effort to promote a peaceful world compatible with a free and dynamic American society."[14] Exporting nuclear technologies could "generate free world respect and support for the constructive purposes of US foreign policy." To that end, the administration began signing bilateral nuclear cooperation agreements under section 123 of the 1954 US Atomic Energy Act, also called 123 agreements.

The source of funding for nuclear energy projects initially remained unclear. An earlier NSC draft had emphasized that nuclear power was to be promoted "through private, not government financing."[15] After all, the Republican Party that controlled both houses of the Congress as well as the presidency was wary of any effort to increase the government's role in industrial activities. However, US firms were not keen to participate in the new form of energy unless major financial risks were underwritten by the government. Similarly, US utility companies preferred coal and hydroelectricity and were not enthusiastic about nuclear power unless there were attractive government subsidies.

The final NSC document, therefore, adopted a more capacious language on funding. It encouraged "private financing wherever possible."[16] The new language opened up the possibility for federal agencies like the US Export-Import Bank and USAID to provide financial incentives to ensure that private companies partake in this new tool of US foreign policy, namely, civilian nuclear assistance.

India's Nuclear Program Expands

The institutional expansion of India's nuclear program from the AECI to the DAE in August 1954 as President Eisenhower signed the US Atomic Energy Act was not coincidental. President Eisenhower in his Atoms for Peace speech had called for cooperation among countries "principally involved" in matters of nuclear fission and "encourage[d] the world-wide investigation into the most effective peacetime uses of fissionable material."[17] This generated great anticipation in those at the helm of India's nuclear program.[18] Nuclear technologies for electricity generation held the promise of large-scale industrialization and economic development of the country. In his address to the Pan-Indian Ocean Science Association in October 1954, Bhabha declared, "Adequate industrial power—and this means atomic power—is the only means by which the standards of living of the most under-developed, under-industrialized, heaviest-populated countries can be raised to the highest standards known in the Western world today."[19]

Meghnad Saha's public criticism of the AECI's "do-nothingness" as a member of the Rajya Sabha or the upper house of the Indian Parliament and on the pages of his journal, *Science and Culture*, had created pressure on Bhabha to deliver on his promises.[20] Saha had questioned why, even years after its creation in 1948, the AECI had very little to show for in terms of actual output, while monopolizing resources for science and technology in India.[21] Against the bristling critique of Saha, Bhabha's global nuclear diplomacy at the 1955 Atoms for Peace conference became a resounding political victory.

Officially known as the First UN Conference on Peaceful Uses of Atomic Energy held at the Palais des Nations in Geneva, Switzerland in August 1955, it was a twelve-day meeting that was both a scientific conference and an industrial fair promoting peaceful nuclear technologies.[22] It was attended by over 1,400 delegates from seventy-three countries and by more than nine hundred journalists.[23] US firm Union Carbide and Carbon Corporation even showcased a swimming pool–type reactor, which was in and of itself a "masterpiece of marketing" as historian John Krige had remarked.[24]

Homi Bhabha was the president of that conference. In his opening speech, he made a strong case for civilian nuclear programs, when he stated that for the underdeveloped countries, "atomic energy is not merely an aid; it is an absolute necessity."[25] Bhabha, who was chosen to preside over the conference as a scientific representative from a nonaligned country, impressed many with his charming and powerful personality. Four months after the Bandung conference, where Nehru had emerged as one of the leaders of the nonaligned nations of Africa and Asia, Bhabha rose as the global spokesperson for India's nuclear program and those of other developing countries. He reminded his audience in Geneva that the nuclear power industry would soon "put into the hands of many nations quantities of fissile material, from which the making of atomic bombs is but a relatively small step."[26] Safeguards, or external measures to prevent diversion of nuclear materials and technologies from civilian to military purposes, thus could not be permanently effective.

Bhabha settled scores at home through his global endeavors. For instance, he refused to include anyone from Saha's Institute of Nuclear Physics in the Indian delegation to the 1955 UN conference in Geneva. Saha was upset to find that a "fine distinction drawn by Dr. Bhabha between nuclear scientists and technologists" was the official reason behind the decision.[27] Bhabha justified his distinction in the following words: "[W]e have tried to concentrate the work of this UN Conference on the technology of atomic power, rather than fundamental physics. There would be no point in including the two people from the Institute of Nuclear Physics in our delegation, and I may add that we have included none from the TIFR either."[28] Even after Prime Minister Nehru recommended that some well-known physicists from Saha's institution, like Basanti Dulal Nagchaudhuri, be included, Bhabha refused and made logistical excuses. Nagchaudhuri himself was greatly accomplished. He had completed his PhD at the University of California, Berkeley, under the supervision of Nobel laureate physicist Ernest O. Lawrence, the inventor of the cyclotron.

While Bhabha prepared for the Geneva conference, Saha attended the Moscow Conference on the Peaceful Use of Atomic Energy organized by the Soviet Academy of the Sciences in July 1955. The Moscow event was organized by the Soviet government as a response to the US-led Atoms for Peace conference in Geneva. While Bhabha sought out reactor technologies from the Western countries, Saha's affinity lay with the Soviet Union. Upon his return from Moscow, Saha attempted to dissuade Nehru from entering into reactor contracts with the United States. He wrote, "My belief is that if we purchase a power reactor in this fashion we shall have to depend on this American company, not only for the maintenance of the plant, but also for the nuclear materials (uranium, natural or enriched), as well as for processing of these materials. We thus subject ourselves to the atomic imperialism of USA."[29]

Like Frédéric Joliot-Curie of the CEA, Saha was a communist, whose political sympathies for the Soviet Union were well known. Like Joliot-Curie, who was abruptly removed from his position as the high commissioner of the CEA in April 1950, because of his communist affiliations, Saha too was gradually sidelined from India's nuclear program and the central government.[30] His critiques of the DAE grew harsher. His postgraduate students despite studying nuclear physics failed to obtain gainful employment at the DAE, while Bhabha and Bhatnagar complained that there were inadequate university courses on atomic energy in India.[31]

British and Canadian Research Reactors for India

In the wake of Atoms for Peace, the UK Atomic Energy Authority (UKAEA) and the Atomic Energy of Canada Limited (AECL) looked for markets for reactor technologies that they had developed during the Manhattan Project. The era of US-led postwar information censorship was over, and the atomic marketplace was open for business. India's nuclear program became "the first battlefield of Western nuclear competition in the Third World," to quote French scientist Bertrand Goldschmidt.[32] Bhabha's Cambridge connections facilitated the DAE's negotiations for buying its first reactors. He personally knew John D. Cockcroft, the founding director of Harwell, the main center for British atomic energy research and development, and Wilfrid B. Lewis, the director of atomic energy research in Canada's National Research Council and head of the Chalk River research facility in Ontario. The DAE purchased one reactor from the UKAEA and another from the AECL. Both research reactors offered numerous learning opportunities for the DAE. Unlike the beryllium-moderated reactor development project with the French, the British and the Canadians were offering reactors that were already proven to work.

In late 1954, the UKAEA provided the DAE with engineering drawings and technical data for a swimming pool–type research reactor along with six kilograms of enriched uranium fuel rods for the reactor. Engineers at the DAE began constructing the reactor based on British technical know-how, using imported fuel rods, valves, and associated components. The CEA also provided enriched uranium for reactor fuel. This one-megawatt research reactor called the APSARA reached criticality in the August of 1956.[33] It would be the first reactor to become operational in Asia outside of the Soviet Union.

Sudipta Kaviraj's notion of "multiple modernities" is pertinent in this context. It can help us to understand "a kind of writing upon writing" that took place as the DAE used foreign assistance to develop its own reactors, plants, and various technological artifacts that made up India's nuclear program.[34] Although the APSARA reactor was constructed through foreign assistance, Indian personnel gained valuable technical experience as they constructed the reactor themselves. French humanist photographer Henri Cartier-Bresson's image of Trombay, which shows local construction workers digging loose earth against the backdrop of the round façade of the APSARA and the symmetrical architecture of

BARC, appositely captures Kaviraj's idea of "multiple modernities" (see figure 3.2). The technology of the reactor was foreign, but its implementation was irrefutably Indian.

Nehru's speech at the inauguration of the APSARA reactor in January 1957 encapsulated the pluralistic and self-differentiated modernity in the Indian nuclear program. He declared: "We are not reluctant in the slightest degree to take advice and help from other countries. We are grateful to them for the help which they have given—and which we hope to get in future—because of their long experience. But it is to be remembered that the Swimming Pool reactor in front of you is the work, almost entirely, of our young Indian scientists and builders."[35] The day after Nehru inaugurated the APSARA reactor, R. K. Laxman published his "Wheel of Progress" cartoon in the *Times of India* (see figure 3.3). It showed a smiling Nehru eagerly driving the metaphorical bullock cart of the nation, powered with atomic wheels. Aboard the cart was one bemused passenger—Laxman's iconic "common man."

The DAE's search for a heavy water reactor was met by the AECL, funded through the development assistance of the Colombo Plan. Launched in 1951, the Colombo Plan was a cooperative arrangement to promote economic development in countries of the British Commonwealth through economic and technical assistance. The AECL desired a foothold in India's reactor market. After all, the DAE led the most advanced atomic energy enterprise in the developing world. The DAE-AECL negotiations began in late 1954, and in April 1956, the governments of India and Canada signed the agreement on the "Canada-India Colombo Plan atomic reactor project." The industrial supplier, Canadian General Electric, was tasked to construct the experimental research reactor of forty megawatts in Trombay. The reactor became known as the Canada-India Reactor or "CIR." Since the USAEC provided the heavy water to run the reactor, it came to be known as the "CIRUS," in which the "US" stood for the heavy water supplier.

The CIRUS was based on reactor designs developed by French physicists Hans Halban and Lew Kowarski, who worked for the Manhattan Project in Montreal, but their patent claims remained unresolved for years afterward. Bertrand Goldschmidt regretfully wrote in the *Atomic Complex*, "Without Halban, Kowarski, and their heavy water, it is certain that the Montréal project could not have been born, and that the Canadian program, true descendent and heir of the work at the Collège de France, could never have achieved today's leadership in the development of heavy-water power reactors."[36]

The involvement of Canadian General Electric in developing and exporting the pressurized heavy water reactor worried some AECL officials because its US parent company had already developed a separate reactor design—the boiling water–type light water reactor—to rival Westinghouse's pressurized water

Figure 3.2.   Henri Cartier-Bresson's 1966 photograph of BARC showing laborers toiling the grounds of Trombay with the APSARA and CIRUS reactors in the background. APSARA is the round structure in the front. CIRUS is the large dome structure behind. Cartier-Bresson's caption: "INDIA. Maharashtra. Trombay near Bombay. 1966. Atomic energy plant." Media identifier: PAR49558. Copyright: Fondation Henri Cartier-Bresson/Magnum Photos. Published with permission.

FIGURE 3.3.   R. K. Laxman's "Wheel of Progress" in the *Times of India* on January 21, 1957. It was published the day after Prime Minister Jawaharlal Nehru inaugurated the swimming pool–type APSARA reactor in Trombay. Published with permission with the accompanying text, "A Tribute to R. K. Laxman on His One Hundredth Birth Anniversary."

reactor model.[37] However, when the Canadian General Electric offered two million Canadian dollars to the AECL for the research and development of the heavy water reactor design, the AECL put aside its concerns and got on board.[38]

The CIRUS, which was a pressurized heavy water research reactor, produced plutonium as its by-product. Plutonium was a fissile material needed to develop nuclear weapons.[39] The CIRUS that produced nuclear energy and fissile material was a "ploughshare" and a "sword" by virtue of the nature of its technology. What the DAE now needed for its *deliberate* pursuit of national development and security goals was a reprocessing plant to chemically separate, or reprocess, the plutonium from the spent fuel of the CIRUS. The reprocessed plutonium could be used as the core in an implosion-type nuclear device, like the one used in the Nagasaki bomb. It could also be used to fuel breeder reactors. Thus began Project Phoenix—the DAE's endeavor to indigenously build a plutonium reprocessing plant.

Plutonium Reprocessing Designs from US Firm

The declassification of "restricted data" under the 1954 US Atomic Energy Act created a permissive environment for US companies that had participated in the Manhattan Project. Such companies could finally begin to sell the nuclear know-how that they had produced during the Second World War. One such firm was the Kellex Corporation, the wartime subsidiary of M. W. Kellogg Company, formed solely for participation in the Manhattan Project.[40] Kellex had participated in gaseous diffusion for enriching uranium to build nuclear weapons and in the construction of plutonium reprocessing plants such as those at Hanford and Oak Ridge. In 1952, Kellex had reconstituted itself as the Vitro Corporation and obtained a USAEC contract to design and construct a new plutonium reprocessing plant at the Hanford site's 200 Area.[41] This Plutonium Uranium Extraction Plant or "PUREX" was the fifth and final reprocessing facility at the Hanford site, which went into operation in 1956.[42]

Vitro Corporation's strong record in constructing plutonium reprocessing plants in the United States impressed Bhabha, who signed a contract to purchase the designs of a PUREX plant in 1959. Edward Durell Stone, the Arkansas-born architect who had designed the recently completed US embassy building in New Delhi, connected the DAE secretary to Vitro International, the company's external subsidiary. Stone then went on to design the façade of India's plutonium reprocessing plant in Trombay, that the DAE built using Vitro International's engineering designs.[43]

What Sudipta Kaviraj calls the "logic of self-differentiation" through improvisation in the postcolonial context reemerges as a theme here.[44] Similar to the APSARA reactor built using British designs obtained from the UKAEA, the plutonium reprocessing plant was constructed using US designs bought from Vitro International. In the process of constructing the reprocessing plant, Indian engineers and scientists gathered know-how and learned new skills that would steer the DAE over time toward self-sufficiency. As Indian technical personnel constructed the plant in Trombay based on designs for the PUREX plant in the Hanford site in Washington, they improvised and adjusted the engineering to meet the needs of their surroundings. At the inauguration of the reprocessing plant, Bhabha declared "that so complicated and difficult a plant has been designed and built entirely by our own scientists and engineers is a credit to their skill."[45]

The CIRUS was under bilateral safeguards under the DAE-AECL agreement, but since the plutonium reprocessing plant was indigenously built, it was not subject to any safeguards. When the DAE and the AECL finalized their agreement for the CIRUS, the system of IAEA safeguards was not yet in place, and the IAEA's statute itself was under negotiation. The bilateral safeguards on CIRUS required the DAE to commit to use the CIRUS for solely peaceful purposes. Plutonium reprocessing plants did not ring alarm bells of proliferation in the late 1950s as they would do much later. The transfer of blueprints from Vitro International to the DAE was, therefore, both legitimate and uncontroversial at the time.

Safeguards and Atomic Earths

Bhabha's staunch opposition to safeguards worried USAEC chairman Lewis Strauss. While he gushed to President Eisenhower about the thirty-nine bilateral or 123 agreements that the US government had signed within two years of the 1954 US Atomic Energy Act, he considered the DAE's opposition to safeguards a major problem for any US nuclear cooperation with India. Strauss wrote to Eisenhower: "The Commission has learned, through Department of State channels, that the Government of India strongly objects to the safeguards and control provisions which are a necessary part of our bilateral agreements. . . . This may prevent the conclusion of an agreement with that Government, and have an adverse effect with respect to agreements with countries subject to Indian influence."[46]

Strauss had earlier directed the USAEC to provide nuclear materials to the DAE outside of a bilateral agreement. The USAEC had provided to the DAE ten and twenty tons of heavy water in 1955 and 1956, respectively, for a research reactor under construction, the ZERLINA. This reactor was also not subject to safeguards on grounds that it was indigenously built.[47] Strauss had thought that the heavy water sales would be "only a first important step in a broader collaboration in this field," but his hopes were dashed by Bhabha's public criticisms of safeguards at the negotiation of the IAEA statute held at the UN headquarters in New York.[48]

Bhabha physicist claimed that the IAEA's safeguards system would jeopardize national sovereignty of developing countries that would seek its technical assistance. He protested: "[W]ith the safeguard provisions as they are at present framed, any aid given by the Agency then leads to an infinite chain of control provided any fissionable material produced in the project is used again. We think that this clearly is not in accordance with any requirements of equity or common sense. . . . This particular type of control will apply to countries which come to the Agency for aid and not to those which do not."[49]

Bhabha found a willing compatriot against IAEA safeguards in Bertrand Goldschmidt, the French representative and director of the CEA's international relations.[50] The two of them adopted similar positions in deliberations over Article XII of the IAEA statute on "Agency Safeguards." His professional relationship with Goldschmidt went back to the early 1950s when the CEA had signed its agreement on beryllium-moderated reactors with the AECI/DAE. Bhabha and Goldschmidt jointly opposed IAEA safeguards on "source materials," namely, atomic earths such as natural uranium and thorium.

The Indian and French representatives argued that IAEA safeguards should apply only after chemical processing of IAEA-supplied source materials or atomic earths had taken place. Goldschmidt reminded the delegates that uranium and thorium were far more abundant in nature than was estimated during and immediately after the Second World War. Imposing the same controls on "source materials" as on "special fissionable materials" (enriched uranium and plutonium that were direct pathways to nuclear weapons production), would amount to "abuses of control."[51] Goldschmidt added, "Controls are rather like certain drugs—efficient in certain doses, but becoming harmful if the dose is increased."[52]

The reality was that atomic earths or source materials influenced power distribution within the IAEA. Major uranium producers that were US allies received preference. Yet, not all atomic earths were created equal, which meant that the DAE was at a disadvantage. A thorium-producing nonaligned country was not an "atomic earth equal" to a uranium-producing US ally like apartheid South Africa or a colonial power such as Belgium with access to Congolese uranium.[53]

Outside of the IAEA, India's atomic earths were still worth bartering for. In his quest for research and power reactors, Bhabha was already offering atomic earths as *quid pro quo* to potential foreign suppliers. In the summer of 1954, he had written to Edwin Plowden, then the chairman of the UKAEA, that the DAE could sell to the British government ten tons of thorium nitrate by the end of September 1955 and supply another ninety tons of the same material in 1956. In the same letter, Bhabha had added: "As I informed Sir John D. Cockcroft last year, our aim is to construct a medium powered heavy water reactor, say of 5000 kW and we would appreciate any technical advice or assistance that your organization may be able to give in this project."[54] Even though Plowden had not been eager to offer the DAE a British reactor of those specifications, US officials were still eyeing India's thorium resources.

USAEC chairman John McCone, who had succeeded Lewis Strauss, drew President Eisenhower's attention just before the US president's trip to New Delhi: "India has a great resource of thorium, and he has the AEC people looking into this to see whether we could make some substantial offer to be helpful to the Indians."[55] Bhabha himself during his November 1959 visit to the United States had "told Mr. McCone that India really needs power reactors," leading USAEC officials to see if they "can help them [DAE] in any way."[56]

To US officials, those countries that had supplied atomic earths to the United States were more deserving of US power reactors than others, under the Atoms for Peace program. For instance, in the spring and summer of 1954, the Operations Coordinating Board and the State Department had toyed with the idea of exporting a power reactor to West Berlin for Cold War gains, but Lewis Strauss had reminded them that the United States had other responsibilities. He succinctly put them in terms of atomic earths: "In view of the clear and unmistakable obligation incurred by this country in connection with the ore procurement program, the Commission believes that assistance should be given (to) Belgium in the construction of a power reactor before similar projects are undertaken elsewhere. Such assistance may be essential in assuring continued deliveries of ore."[57] A US power reactor was indeed offered to Belgium. The BR-3 in Mol, sold by Westinghouse, became the first pressurized water reactor built outside the United States. The USAEC also signed a reactor contract with uranium-producing South Africa, leading to the construction of the Safari-I research reactor in Pelindaba.[58]

Through the DAE's grand plans to develop breeder reactors that would use thorium-based fuel, Bhabha used futuristic claims to raise the value of India's atomic earths. In his paper at the Second UN Conference on Peaceful Uses of Atomic Energy in Geneva in 1958, Bhabha had laid out the three-stage program for attaining nuclear energy sufficiency for India.[59] The three-stage reactor program involved primary reactors using natural uranium-based fuel, secondary breeder reactors using plutonium-based fuel, and tertiary slow neutron breeder reactors that would use thorium-based fuel.

Bhabha's vision of thorium-based reactor fuel was also the epitome of the concurrent and deliberate pursuit of national development and security. It crafted an official peaceful-use rationale for the plutonium from the CIRUS. At the same time, the plutonium from the CIRUS when reprocessed could become the fissile material for nuclear weapons. As geopolitical tensions between India and China would rise, US policymakers would begin to take note of the significance of the DAE's opposition to safeguards and the dual-use character of its nuclear program.

In response to Chinese repression of Tibetan nationalists, the Dalai Lama fled to India in March 1959 with the help of the CIA. The Nehru government granted him refuge, which infuriated the Chinese leadership. Prior to this, US overtures to India to permit US-led covert support to Tibetan guerillas against Beijing had met with resistance from Nehru on grounds of nonalignment.[60] The Sino-Indian rift was out in the open in 1959, creating an opportune moment for the Eisenhower administration to draw the Nehru government geopolitically closer to the United States.

President Eisenhower became the first serving US president to visit India when he arrived on a five-day tour of the country on December 9, 1959. During their meeting on the evening of December 13, Nehru broached the subject of India's atomic energy development with Eisenhower. Earlier that day, the two leaders had visited the Taj Mahal in Agra with great fanfare (see figure 3.4). The Indian prime minister told the US president that India was a "very promis-

FIGURE 3.4. "India's Prime Minister Jawaharlal Nehru accompanied President Dwight D. Eisenhower as the party left the famed Taj Mahal at Agra, India on Dec. 13, 1959, after a tour of the Indian Shrine. Ike, en route by cruiser, Dec. 15 from Athens to Tunis, told his Indian hosts that the visit to the Taj Mahal fulfilled a boyhood dream." Caption by Associated Press. Photo identifier: 5912130126. Published with permission.

ing place for atomic power development because of the cost of fuel, and the fact that the cheaper sources of water power have already been exploited."[61] Nehru added that he was "anxious to carry out a major program in this field and said he would like to get at least one plant of 50,000 to 100,000 kw capacity to start the program." Eisenhower promised to direct USAEC chairman Mc-Cone to look into it. Within two months of his visit, a fact-finding technical mission arrived in India to "provide the USAEC with first-hand information on the technical and economic potential of the Indian nuclear power program."[62]

To US policymakers, democratic noncommunist India could function as a geopolitical counterweight to authoritarian communist China in the Cold War struggle between the East and the West. Eisenhower wanted "something spectacular" to demonstrate US commitment to nonaligned India.[63] Nehru's interest in expanding India's atomic energy program with US nuclear assistance was therefore attractive to the US president. His Atoms for Peace program could break new ground in US relations with India. At the end of his presidential tour, President Eisenhower and Prime Minister Nehru released a joint statement committing their respective governments to "ensure the maintenance and development of the strong ties of friendship between the two countries."[64]

Consequences of Chinese Nuclear Weapons Capability

In December 1960, the CIA noted that "there was no longer a question as to whether communist China was engaged in a nuclear weapons program but when a detonation might be expected."[65] The document concluded that China would be able to detonate a device sometime between 1962 and 1964. Within two or more years after that, it "would probably have a limited number of small bombs available to it."[66] The prospect of a nuclear Red China would cause significant consternation for the Kennedy administration that would take office the following month.

Ted Clifton, retired major general and military aide to President Kennedy, thought that a Chinese nuclear detonation "could hit the [Kennedy] Administration almost as hard as Sputnik" had struck the Eisenhower administration.[67] In the minds of the US public, a successful Chinese nuclear weapon test was incompatible with the image of China as a poor, pastoral nonwhite country. A successful nuclear test by Beijing could radically challenge US popular perception as Sputnik had done when the Soviet Union launched the world's first Earth satellite in 1957.[68] US policymakers therefore spent substantial time and energy reflecting on the "psychological impact" of a Chinese nuclear weapons detonation.

Officials within the Kennedy administration worried about the impact of a Chinese nuclear weapon test on Communist, non-Communist, and neutral countries of the world. What if awestruck non-Communist and neutral countries were attracted to communism as a result? Top policymakers within the administration, therefore, decided that a propaganda campaign was necessary to "blunt the impact of a successful ChiCom test."[69] Such a propaganda campaign involved multiple US agencies—the Department of State, the Department of Defense, the CIA, and the United States Information Agency—to conduct psychological warfare on a global scale. The US propaganda strategy explained in a March 1961 memo to NSC staffer Bob Komer read as follows:

The main goal would be to get across the idea that . . . the Chinese capability is actually a "paper tiger" which need not be feared. We should point out that they are striving desperately to pull off one or more "show" bomb tests to enhance their prestige but that this has little or no relation to a real nuclear weapons capability. . . . We should explain that, these days, it is quite simple to put together a few atomic bombs; but getting enough plutonium and engineering know-how to produce significant numbers of warheads and developing delivery vehicles (planes and missiles which the Chinese lack) is another matter entirely.[70]

The Kennedy administration officials, thus, aimed to play down the significance of Chinese nuclear weapons development through the prisms of prestige and technological backwardness. Johnson administration officials would espouse a similar strategy toward India when they would offer technical assistance to satisfy India's supposed quest for status and prestige in the face of an advanced Chinese nuclear weapons program. India's perception of geopolitical threat vis-à-vis China would not be as prominent in the minds of US policymakers.

By June 1961, the US Joint Chiefs of Staff sent an analytical paper to Secretary of Defense Robert McNamara titled "A Strategic Analysis of the Impact of the Acquisition of Communist China of a Nuclear Capability."[71] The paper recommended, as a medium-term goal, that the US government "provide certain selected Asian allies in the area with a potential nuclear delivery capability" with US control. In the short run, the paper called for immediate US peaceful nuclear cooperation with Asian countries, India and Japan, which would be most directly affected by a Chinese nuclear explosion. The underlying logic was that peaceful nuclear programs of New Delhi and Tokyo would provide the "additional proof of the technological advancement of non-Communist Asian countries," offsetting the psychological effects of a Chinese nuclear test.[72]

In September 1961, George McGhee, the director of the State Department's Policy Planning Council, even proposed that the United States assist India to test a nuclear device. He argued that such a measure could alleviate the psychological impact of the Chinese nuclear test because a non-Communist Asian state would "pull the first punch" instead of a Communist one. McGhee's proposal gathered nominal support at the State Department but was eventually shot down by Secretary of State Dean Rusk. Such a policy would be a departure from US commitment against nuclear proliferation, Rusk noted. [73]

US policymakers' continued emphasis on the psychological fallout of an imminent Chinese nuclear detonation on India indicated that they considered prestige to be the most important driver behind India's potential nuclear weapons development. The Sino-Indian War of October 1962 would change that perception at least temporarily.

Fraught Geographies and Anti-Democratic Technopolitics

While the Sino-Indian border dispute over the McMahon Line was a legacy of British colonialism, the Nehru government was also managing it ineptly. Since the 1950s, there have been several clashes between the Indian Army and the People's Liberation Army (PLA) along the disputed border. Poor communications and lack of military insight plagued the situation on the Indian side. Prime Minister Nehru and his defense minister V.K. Krishna Menon, though concerned about the military tensions, believed that India would have the upper hand in case of an open conflict with China. In November 1961, the Nehru government adopted the "forward policy," which aimed to prevent the PLA's incursions by installing military posts and patrolling "forward" of the disputed Sino-Indian border.[74] The idea behind the policy was to convince the PLA that any advancement by its troops would be repelled by the Indian Army.

The Sino-Indian border dispute took place under the shadow of Chinese nuclear weapons capability. US embassy officials in New Delhi suspected that DAE secretary Bhabha and defense minister Menon wanted to develop nuclear weapons and were "maybe working towards that end."[75] The embassy had telegrammed the State Department in June 1961, reminding the Kennedy administration that the Nehru government was "clearly aware of and apprehensive about [the] probability of communist China developing nuclear military capability within the next few years."[76] The telegram had added that Prime Minister Nehru himself had "voiced his concern" to Ambassador Ellsworth Bunker that "such [a] development would change [the] whole power relationship in Asia." Menon's science advisor had even expressed concerns to US embassy officials that "Chinese Communists would not only develop atomic weapons in two or three years but would also probably not hesitate to use them" against India.[77]

While the Himalayan border was becoming increasingly precarious with the Nehru government's "forward policy," the Indian Army prepared for "police action" in the three Portuguese enclaves of Goa, Daman, and Diu along the Arabian Sea. At the Goan Political Convention held in Bombay in November 1961, top-ranking members from Nehru's political party such as M. C. Chagla, Vijaya Laxmi Pandit, and others, publicly came out in support of the "liberation of Goa."[78] They hailed freeing Goa from the shackles of Portuguese colonialism as the unfinished business of the Indian anticolonial struggle itself. The three 400-year Portuguese colonial possessions were already suffering from economic blockade since 1955, a year after the French government had agreed to *de facto* transfer of the French colonial enclaves to the Indian Union. The Nehru government wanted the Portuguese to follow the French example, but in vain. Like many inhabitants of the French territories, those living in Goa, Daman, and Diu were often ambivalent about joining the India Union. The Nehru government had already annexed in 1954 the landlocked Portuguese colonial possessions of Dadra and Nagar Haveli.

On December 18, 1961, following a thirty-six-hour battle on land, sea, and air between Indian and Portuguese militaries, the three enclaves joined the Indian Union. The following day, upon Portugal's complaint of Indian aggression, the UN Security Council drafted a resolution against India. It failed to pass because of a Soviet veto, but generated loud criticisms of Indian military action at the United Nations from US and West European representatives. Indian representative C. S. Jha defended India's seizure of the territories as the rightful course of action against colonialism. He was referring to the UN General Assembly Resolution 1514 of December 1960, on "Declaration on the Granting of Independence to Colonial Countries and Peoples."[79] To Jha, "the end of eliminating colonialism justified the means used."[80] Decolonization thus became the alibi for armed invasion by the Indian Union.

While Portuguese colonial possessions were being made "Indian" through military force of the Indian Army, Bhabha was overseeing the transfer of the Tata Memorial Hospital and the Indian Cancer Research Centre from the Ministry of Health to the DAE. Bhabha in his letter assured the trustees of the Dorab Tata Trust that the transfer from health to atomic energy would "not however alter in any way the scope of the work" of the two institutions.[81] The immediate administrative implication was reduced financial oversight from New Delhi. The representative from the Ministry of Finance, who was otherwise part of the hospital's governing board, was replaced by a DAE nominee based in Bombay. The formal justification was that the DAE's "financial arrangements are different from those of other administrative Ministries."[82] Bhabha's unofficial involvement with the workings of the Tata Memorial Hospital thus became more formalized, increasing the DAE's prospects for foreign cooperation in peaceful uses of nuclear technologies, such as health physics and nuclear medicine. After all, Atoms for Peace was not just about reactors. It involved the entire gamut of nuclear technologies that could be used for civilian ends. It included everything from desalination to food security to cancer treatment.

Concurrent with heightened Sino-Indian border tensions and diplomatic deadlock between New Delhi and Beijing in 1962, India's nuclear program rapidly expanded through institutional reorganization, new technological projects, further centralization, and increased secrecy. In 1962, the Nehru government took a series of important decisions for India's nuclear program. At a time of rising Sino-Indian tensions, the TIFR was inaugurated in January of that year. J. R. D. Tata, the chairman of the TIFR's council, reminded his audience of the significance of the institute in his inauguration speech. He stated, "[T]he foundations of the new atomic age in which we shall soon live happily—unless we are all blown up before that—the major part of the work done in India has been centred in this Institute."[83] In February 1962, Prime Minister Nehru formed the Indian National Committee for Space Research within the DAE to pursue a space program. Led by Vikram Sarabhai and located at the TIFR, the committee would engage with foreign space agencies like those of the United States, the Soviet Union, and France, among others. The first NASA equipment had already arrived in India in September 1961 in the form of an astronomy satellite that used a telemetry-receiving equipment.[84] The leaders of India's nuclear program were thus preparing for a more expansive and expensive pursuit of technologies of outer space.

By March 1962, the transfer of the Tata Memorial Hospital to the DAE and the reconfiguration of its governing board were completed.[85] That month, Bhabha reconstituted the AECI to include J. R. D. Tata as one of its members.[86] The deaths of S. S. Bhatnagar and K. S. Krishnan in 1955 and 1961, respectively, meant that new members were needed to fill their positions in the AECI. The inclusion of J. R. D. Tata was still noteworthy. It depicted the persistence of business-government partnership in India's nuclear program through the unique influence of the Tatas and of J. R. D. in particular. The Nehru government also allocated US$2.5 million for the plutonium reprocessing plant in Trombay, which was expected to be completed in 1965.[87]

One of the most far-reaching changes to the nuclear program was the new Atomic Energy Act of India that entered into force on September 21, 1962, replacing its 1948 predecessor. The 1962 legislation expanded the DAE's powers and those of the central government in New Delhi. The government could mine atomic earths, like uranium, wherever it pleased. It could restrict information on nuclear matters at its will. It could also take possession of land and premises for the production of atomic energy with little to no compensation.

Much like the 1946 US Atomic Energy Act that had created the new legal classification of "restricted data" for information related to nuclear fission, the 1962 Indian Atomic Energy Act created categories such as "restricted information" and "prohibited areas" to prevent citizens' access to nuclear things managed by the state machinery. The legislation was repressive towards indigenous populations. Since most uranium mining sites were in *adivasi* (native or indigenous) lands, the act became the legislative driver for the expropriation of mining lands through the disenfranchisement of indigenous people. The geographies of atomic earths thus uprooted *adivasis* in the name of the nation, whether it was uranium mining in Jaduguda in present-day Jharkhand, Meghalaya, in the northeast, or elsewhere.

The act even prevented legal recourse by citizens. Under section 29 of the act, no legal proceedings could be undertaken against the central government, any person, or authority "in respect of anything done by it or him in good faith in pursuance of this Act or of any rule or order made thereunder."[88] The Nehru government passed the 1962 Atomic Energy Bill into act in great haste, disrupting regular democratic debate in the Indian Parliament.[89] Thus, as the Indian nuclear program expanded and became more centralized, it grew less transparent, more ambiguous, and more anti-democratic.

There were multiple clashes between Indian and Chinese troops throughout the spring and summer of 1962. The hostilities finally exploded into open war that fall, when the PLA launched its military offensive on October 20.[90] The Chinese military had the upper hand in the war, which ended in their unilateral proclamation of ceasefire on November 21. Chinese troops did not just occupy. They built new roads in the difficult terrain of the eastern Himalayas, as a "dress rehearsal," to quote historian Bérénice Guyot-Réchard, "experimenting and projecting a version of the future" for the people living there.[91] Chinese territorial gains in Aksai Chin in western Himalayas and their conventional military superiority on the inhospitable eastern border not only demonstrated India's military and intelligence failures, but also raised questions about the long-term allegiance of the "borderlanders" to the Indian nation-state.

During the Sino-Indian War, Prime Minister Nehru wrote to President Kennedy requesting air support against Chinese troops. Nehru asked for twelve squadrons of supersonic aircraft, radar installations, and two squadrons of B-47 bombers, all manned by US personnel.[92] The request for US manpower was because the Indian Air Force did not have the requisite training to operate the military equipment that Nehru was requesting. The Congress Party and the Indian Parliament were not aware of Nehru's request, because it could have led to public controversy given India's nonaligned status in the Cold War. The Kennedy administration did not reject Nehru's plea for help, but US military assistance arrived quite late. The Cuban Missile Crisis was on top of the policy agenda in Washington, DC.

Prior to the beginning of the war, the Soviet leader Nikita Khrushchev—keen on getting Mao's support for Soviet actions in Cuba—opposed India's stance on the border dispute. At the presidium meeting of October 14, 1962, Khrushchev decided to hold back on the delivery of previously negotiated MiG fighter jets to India and even offered the MiGs to China.[93] Khrushchev called China's actions in Tibet "rational" and India's demands "humiliating" for Beijing.[94] On October 20, on the day the war broke out and two days prior to President Kennedy's address to the nation about Soviet missiles in Cuba, the Soviet ambassador in New Delhi handed a note to Prime Minister Nehru that contained propagandist references against the United States.[95] The note warned against those "interested in intensifying world tension, who wish to line their coats by military clash between India and China."[96]

Unlike the disappointment it experienced from Moscow, the Sino-Indian War of October 1962 brought the Nehru government unprecedentedly close to the Kennedy administration. Nehru's request for military assistance and Kennedy's positive response improved their countries' bilateral relations.[97] Over the next year, in the face of a fast-advancing Chinese nuclear weapons program, Kennedy administration officials would look to finalize the USAEC-DAE agreement on power reactors and expand bilateral cooperation in space technologies. US policymakers would hope to stall a potential Indian decision to develop nuclear weapons through providing US technologies that could boost India's prestige.

Immediately after the 1962 war, Prime Minister Nehru formed the National Defence Council comprising former chiefs of army staff, generals K. S. Thimayya and Rajindrasinhji Jadeja, key cabinet ministers, leaders of the opposition, and the DAE secretary Homi Bhabha.[98] The council met for the first time at Rashtrapati Bhavan, or the president's house, on November 25, 1962.[99] In March of the following year, the Nehru government increased the DAE's budget several folds. According to a CIA brief, for fiscal years 1963 to 1964, the Indian Parliament approved US$48.3 million (230 million rupees) as DAE's budget. This was a nearly 76 percent increase from its 1962–63 number of $27.5 million.[100]

From this time onward, Bhabha publicly made exaggerated claims that India could explode a nuclear device within twelve to eighteen months of a decision to do so. Nehru retained his formal stance against nuclear weapons. Yet, the inclusion of Bhabha in the National Defence Council within weeks of the Chinese military offensive, the massive DAE budget, and increased secrecy and control under the 1962 Atomic Energy Act were telltale signs that the Nehru government was keeping the nuclear weapons option open while intentionally maintaining ambiguity.

Conclusion

With the US Atoms for Peace initiative, the leaders of India's nuclear program procured technologies that concurrently served their goals of national security and development. The program's growth was spurred by the needs of the developmentalist state to use nuclear energy for large-scale industrialization, as well as the goals of the territorial state to control a fraught geography characterized by intermestic geopolitical threats. China and the Eastern Himalayan borderlands emerged as a space of vulnerability in the minds of Indian policymakers, which would influence their decisions about that region over the ensuing decades. The deliberate ambiguity afforded by the expansion of the nuclear program allowed its leaders plausible deniability. They continued to make polyvalent technopolitical choices to keep the nuclear weapons option perpetually open.

CHAPTER 4

Plutonium, Power Reactors, and Space Projects, 1962–1964

After India's military defeat in the Sino-Indian War of October 1962, the Kennedy administration officials looked for a way to both play down the global significance of an imminent Chinese nuclear test as well as prevent India from developing its own nuclear weapons in response. US intelligence agencies had interpreted the 1962 Indian Atomic Energy Act as the DAE's inclination toward developing nuclear weapons. The CIA reported that the Indian "government's broad programs ranging from ore extraction to plutonium separation could, when completed, be converted into a small nuclear weapons program at only moderate cost."[1] Against this backdrop, the DAE's ongoing search for a foreign supplier to build two power reactors in Tarapur offered a possible way to exert US influence on India's nuclear program.

John Kenneth Galbraith, Harvard economist and then US Ambassador to India, had been imploring the Kennedy administration even before the Sino-Indian War. He wanted the USAEC to push ahead with its negotiations with the DAE to build two light water reactors in Tarapur. At a State Department meeting in May 1962, Galbraith had succinctly summarized the significance of US power reactors for India. He remarked that when Beijing would detonate its first nuclear bomb the question would be, "What is India doing in the nuclear field? It will be useful if the GOI could point to its own nuclear power plant."[2]

The DAE's plans to develop the full nuclear fuel cycle from uranium mining and uranium fuel fabrication to plutonium reprocessing worried Kennedy administration officials. Of particular concern was the DAE's access to plutonium, an artificial metallic element that can be chemically separated for use in a Nagasaki-type implosion bomb. By 1961, the DAE had built three research reactors: APSARA built with British assistance, ZERLINA built with US cooperation, and the CIRUS built with Canadian technologies and running on US-supplied heavy water. All three reactors could produce various quantities of plutonium. A secret NSC study from September 1961 had concluded that "[w]hile APSARA and ZERLINA are capable of producing only small, research quantities of plutonium, the CIR[US] could produce a significant amount of plutonium if it is operated for such production."[3] As a result, the study warned that "should the nuclear power reactors [in Tarapur] be provided by a country which does not require safeguards, a considerable amount of weapons grade plutonium could be produced" by the DAE.[4]

The main stumbling block for USAEC-DAE negotiations was Bhabha's well-known opposition to accepting safeguards. Time was running out for the USAEC. Homi Bhabha was expressing great interest in the CEA's offer to build two gas-cooled reactors in Tarapur without safeguards.[5]

US Power Reactors in Tarapur

The DAE had originally requested international bids in October 1960 for the construction of a nuclear power plant in Tarapur, north of Bombay, comprising two power reactors of a total installed electric power capacity of around three hundred megawatts electrical. The DAE preferred natural uranium-fueled reactors like the CIRUS but was open to other kinds of reactors. By August 1961, the DAE had received seven bids, out of which three were from the USAEC, two from the UKAEA, one from the CEA, and one from the AECL.

For US policymakers, to prevent India from developing nuclear weapons, it was necessary to curtail the DAE's future sources of plutonium. It was in US interest to ensure that the reactors the DAE bought were not natural uranium reactors like the AECL's CANDU, which produced plutonium as a byproduct. The power reactors sold to the DAE also had to be with safeguards, unlike what the CEA was offering. The US reactor model—light water reactors that ran on low-enriched uranium fuel—was a "better" option from the US perspective because it did not produce plutonium. More importantly, light water reactors would keep the DAE dependent on the USAEC for reactor fuel, thereby increasing opportunities for US control and oversight. Last but not least, in order to buy US power reactors, the DAE would have to accept the

USAEC's bilateral safeguards and eventually subject the reactors to IAEA safe-guards when a multilateral system would be put in place.

The DAE expressed interest in the USAEC's offer, sending its team to the United States in June 1962 to begin negotiations with the State Department, USAEC, and USAID. While the Indian team visited Washington, DC, to dis-cuss reactors for Tarapur, Ambassador Galbraith reminded NSC staffer Bob Komer about the geopolitical importance of US power reactors for India: "[T]o the extent that India can make a splash in peaceful atomic development, it will help counter the impact of a ChiCom [Chinese Communist] nuclear test."[6] The DAE issued a letter of intent to General Electric International in Septem-ber 1962 in which Bhabha stated that he would accept the US firm's bid pro-vided there was satisfactory mutual understanding between the Nehru government and the Kennedy administration on questions of financing the project, reactor fuel, and safeguards.[7]

The State Department, USAEC, and USAID expressed their favorable dis-position to undertake the reactor construction in Tarapur provided some con-ditions were met. First, the Indian government had to include the Tarapur nuclear power plant in its Third Five-Year Plan (1961–66) and, thereby, express serious government intent in favor of the project. Second, technical studies had to demonstrate that nuclear energy was competitive vis-à-vis thermal power, which Homi Bhabha was publicly claiming. Third and finally, the DAE had to accept "reasonable safeguards" on the power reactors—this last one be-came the bone of contention.[8]

Bhabha informed Galbraith that if the Tarapur agreement were to be placed at the IAEA, "the whole thing will fall through."[9] He suggested that the In-dian government would have "no objection, to a clause to the effect that both parties will consult together to see whether and in what way the services of the IAEA can be utilized by mutual agreement."[10] In other words, the DAE wanted to keep their commitment on safeguards as flexible and nonbinding as possible.

With USAEC-DAE negotiations stalled over Bhabha's objection to safe-guards, Ambassador Galbraith reached out to Secretary of State Dean Rusk. In his January 1963 telegram, he reaffirmed the gravity of the situation for US geopolitical interest in Asia. Galbraith wrote to Rusk that "[a]t some time [sic] in the foreseeable future, probably sometime in the next year, China will set off a nuclear explosion and probably in the desert to the north of India."[11] In anticipation of the imminent Chinese nuclear explosion, "India's self-esteem and her prestige in Asia requires that she be doing something of comparable magnitude in the field of peaceful atomic energy . . . This plant provides them the opportunity."[12]

After neither the Kennedy administration nor the USAEC budged on the question of safeguards, Bhabha wrote to Henry D. Smyth, author of the famed 1945 Smyth Report and then US ambassador to the IAEA. The DAE secretary warned that the delays in DAE-USAEC talks on Tarapur could "cause a serious setback to the prospects for American nuclear power stations in India and elsewhere."[13] He cautioned Smyth that "the Government of India may be forced to make alternative arrangements for the supply of power in this region" because "officers of the central and state governments engaged in planning are quite likely to take the view that if nuclear power plants are so difficult to negotiate for political reasons that it would be better to rely on conventional sources of power."[14]

The Planning Commission of India was unamenable to Bhabha's requests to increase DAE funding under the government's Third Five-Year Plan. Owing to the DAE's budgetary battles with the Planning Commission, the USAEC's reactor offer that came with USAID funding was particularly attractive to Bhabha. The bid from General Electric was priced at US$101 million, out of which approximately 70 percent of the cost was expected to be funded by US economic assistance.[15] Few foreign governments could provide what the DAE secretary looked for, namely, power reactors that came with its own financial aid package separate from other forms of economic assistance that the Indian government was receiving at the time.[16]

Concurrent with the Tarapur negotiations, the Indian government through its Ambassador Braj Kumar (B. K.) Nehru, cousin of Prime Minister Jawaharlal Nehru, requested increased US military and economic aid, citing Chinese military threat. In response, President Kennedy requested the State Department for a prompt appraisal whether China could attack India once again.[17] He wanted the study to find out: "(A)re we doing enough to help India? If we are doing enough, are we doing it soon enough?"[18] The State Department's study concluded that it saw little likelihood of a renewed Chinese attack because China was satisfied with acquiring its limited military objectives in the 1962 war. It added that Beijing saw no reason to cause further military aggression in South Asia because it feared triggering an Anglo-American intervention. According to the State Department, US aid to India was "at about the right pace."[19] President Kennedy, however, was not fully convinced.

As the Lok Sabha or lower house of the Indian Parliament approved nearly US$48.3 million for the DAE's budget in the fiscal year 1963–64, an increase of about 76 percent from the previous year, the Kennedy administration grew apprehensive about possible "alternative arrangements" that the DAE might make for Tarapur. A confidential research memo by the State Department's Bureau of Intelligence and Research had already concluded that the United

States need not worry about the Soviet Union poaching the Tarapur deal.[20] The Soviets faced difficulties in managing large power reactor projects of the kind envisaged for Tarapur. Moscow's own economic retrenchment and perceived meager political gains from nuclear cooperation with India contributed to low Soviet interest. Moreover, the Soviet government's aid commitments to India were already high with large projects such as the steel plant in Bhillai in present-day Chattisgarh. Last but not least, the Soviet Union sought safeguards on its nuclear exports because it did not want to "be identified as contributing to the spread of nuclear weapons capabilities," which would have made a Soviet reactor offer far less attractive to the DAE.[21] With respect to the French reactor offer, there was far more uncertainty among US officials.[22]

Homi Bhabha and the CEA's Bertrand Goldschmidt had both adopted common positions against safeguards at the IAEA meetings in Vienna. Both called safeguards as contraventions of their national sovereignty. The CEA's reactor offer for the Tarapur site without safeguards thus posed a challenge to the US offer. NSC staffer Charles Johnson wrote to Carl Kaysen, deputy special assistant to the president for national security affairs, in April 1963 that the "French bid will be considered by the GOI if we are unable to reach agreement with them on safeguards" because "[a]ll of the nations that are in a position to supply either reactor equipment or uranium, except France, are enforcing effective safeguards."[23] Johnson added that "applying safeguards under a bilateral agreement as a fallback position" might help move the USAEC-DAE negotiations forward given Bhabha's continued opposition to any involvement of the IAEA. The CEA's offer even fitted better with the DAE's own technological plans. The original Indian tender had sought natural uranium-fueled reactors while the US reactors used low-enriched uranium as reactor fuel.

The DAE's own budget constraints and the USAID's generous aid offer ultimately influenced Bhabha's choices. When comparing the CEA's natural uranium-fueled gas-graphite reactor with the US light water reactor, Bhabha admitted to French minister for atomic energy Pierre Guillaumat that he preferred whichever he "did not have to pay for."[24] The Kennedy administration's fears of an Indian decision to develop nuclear weapons in response to a Chinese nuclear weapon test ultimately gave the Tarapur negotiations their final impetus. In June 1963, the two negotiating sides reached consensus that the DAE would accept US bilateral safeguards on Tarapur and give "sympathetic consideration" to IAEA safeguards on the reactors at a later date.[25]

US officials were well aware that the Limited Test Ban Treaty that was being negotiated at the time could not prevent a Chinese nuclear weapon test. China would not join the treaty, even if it were to be invited. They also knew that a Chinese nuclear test would definitely increase pressures on the Nehru government to develop nuclear weapons. In June 1963, an internal NSC memo claimed that India's nuclear program would depend on safeguarded materials until 1965, after which the DAE could explode its first nuclear device in 1967–68, and the Indian government could have a limited nuclear weapons delivery capability by 1970.[26]

The US-India agreement was signed on August 8, 1963, for the construction of two reactors in Tarapur, which would become the DAE's first power reactors.[27] The agreement was signed at the US State Department in Washington, DC, by Indian ambassador B. K. Nehru and Assistant Secretary of State Phillips Talbot. It was a turnkey project for two boiling water–type light water reactors of 190 megawatts electrical each to be sold by General Electric International and constructed by Bechtel.[28] The USAEC was responsible for providing the low-enriched uranium reactor fuel for a thirty-year period.

The final contract demonstrated two main compromises on the US side. First, the agreement only included bilateral safeguards. It provided for a future trilateral agreement involving the IAEA after that multilateral agency adopted a safeguards system consistent with the US-India bilateral safeguards agreement. Second, USAID agreed to provide a loan on generous terms from the US Export-Import Bank for the construction of the reactors. The loan was going to be for US$80 million, which was US$20 million more than what the Kennedy administration intended to offer in 1961.[29] Under the terms of the loan agreement for Tarapur that was signed in New Delhi in December that year, the USAEC also agreed to furnish low-enriched uranium for reactor fuel worth US$15 million, while the Indian government was to "provide the rupee equivalent of $34 million to cover domestic costs of the projects."[30] The final loan figure was adjusted to US$71.8 million at 7.5% interest that did not require any principal repayment until after ten years.

The signing of the Tarapur agreement went largely unnoticed in mainstream US media because the signing of the Limited Test Ban Treaty in Moscow on August 5, 1963, grabbed all the headlines.[31] Negotiated in the wake of the Cuban Missile Crisis that brought the two Cold War superpowers close to a nuclear war, the treaty banned nuclear tests everywhere except underground. The Nehru government became one of the first countries outside of the three negotiating parties (the United States, United Kingdom, and Soviet Union) to sign the treaty on August 8, the same day as the Tarapur agreement. After all, Prime Minister Nehru himself had held the distinction of being the first national leader to call for a halt to nuclear weapons testing with his proposal for a "standstill agreement" in April 1954.[32]

Nonproliferation and Tarapur

The idea that US national security interests were best served by preventing other countries from developing their own nuclear weapons went back to the beginning of the nuclear age. In the minds of US policymakers, the ideal number of nuclear-armed countries was one.[33] Yet, the terms "nonproliferation" and "proliferation" did not enter the lexicon of US policymakers until the mid-1960s. Policymakers in the United States and the United Kingdom interchangeably used "nuclear spread," "nuclear diffusion," and "nuclear dissemination" to mean an increase in the number of countries that possessed indigenous nuclear weapons programs. In the late 1950s and early 1960s, two other related expressions appeared in English-language archives. Those were the "fourth power problem" and the "n+1 country," both coined in the context of the French nuclear weapons program.[34]

The causal relationship between nonproliferation and Tarapur remains largely neglected, if not misunderstood in the extant scholarship on India's nuclear program. George Perkovich and Itty Abraham claim that economics and technological development dominated US-India discussions on Tarapur. According to Perkovich, US proliferation "concerns did not particularly affect the Tarapur negotiations," but that it was rather the "desire to promote nuclear power that overcame all doubts."[35] For Abraham, the US government's eagerness to sell power reactors to India was to enable US firms to enter the Indian reactor market.[36] David Engerman, who examines Homi Bhabha's role in playing the United States against the Soviet Union during the negotiations, mentions US government's proliferation concerns only in passing.[37]

It is well known that after India's 1974 nuclear explosion, Tarapur became synonymous with US nonproliferation policy toward India. However, the role of US nonproliferation efforts toward India in the earlier period has remained largely unaccounted for. A closer look at the Kennedy administration's policies reveals that nonproliferation concerns drove the very decision to sell the two power reactors to the DAE. Fears of a nuclear domino in South Asia preoccupied US policymakers, who believed that such a domino would begin with India developing nuclear weapons in response to Chinese nuclear weapons, which in turn would lead to reactive proliferation by Pakistan.[38]

Exporting power reactors to the DAE was only one element in the Kennedy administration's multipronged nonproliferation approach in Asia. While his administration negotiated the Limited Test Ban Treaty with the Soviet Union and the United Kingdom, President Kennedy considered a preemptive air strike to destroy Chinese nuclear weapons installations in Lop Nor.[39] The administration even discussed US nuclear security guarantees to counter the psychological and geopolitical effects of a Chinese nuclear weapon test on non-aligned India and US allies in Asia.

In a secret Policy Planning Council memo from October 1963, Kennedy administration officials decided to adopt a dual strategy to counter the impact of the imminent Chinese nuclear detonation.[40] On the one hand, the administration agreed to offer a general assurance to Asian countries that felt threatened by China without entering into "more formal clear-cut US commitments." The paper suggested that, if needed, the US government could consider the "emplacement on an ad hoc basis of nuclear weapons under US control on Asian territory or nearby" without any joint control of the "emplaced" weapons.[41] On the other hand, US policymakers agreed to increase safeguards on India's nuclear program to delay India's technological capability to develop nuclear weapons. They noted that among Asian countries, India was most likely to take a decision in favor of nuclear weapons as a result of a Chinese nuclear test. According to US estimates, if the Nehru government decided to develop a nuclear device in 1964, it could do so by 1969–70.

Lyndon Baines Johnson inherited the Chinese nuclear weapons problem in November 1963, when he was sworn in as the US president aboard Air Force One in the wake of Kennedy's assassination. Given the continuity in key personnel in national security affairs from the Kennedy to the Johnson administration, the thinking on US nonproliferation policy remained largely similar. The most notable difference in the Johnson administration would be the escalation of the US war in Vietnam and President Johnson's tendency to link India's opposition to the war with everything else in US-India relations, including food aid and nonproliferation.

India's Plutonium Plant before the Chinese Nuclear Test

In February 1964, the DAE's plutonium reprocessing plant codenamed, "Phoenix," was completed in Trombay.[42] The plant that was built by Indian personnel based on designs from US firm Vitro International raised fresh proliferation concerns for US policymakers. The State Department's Bureau of Intelligence and Research (INR) reported that with the successful construction and operation of the reprocessing plant, the DAE had met most of the capital costs needed for a small nuclear weapons program.[43] Eight months before the first Chinese nuclear test, the DAE therefore had the indigenous capability to produce weapon-grade plutonium—the fissile material needed to build a Nagasaki-type implosion bomb. The INR note estimated that it was "unlikely that the

Indians would test a weapon barring further changes in its internal political or international position—for example a Chinese communist nuclear test."[44] The first active load of plutonium was reprocessed in May 1964, only weeks before Jawaharlal Nehru's death.[45]

India's first prime minister, who had led the country for seventeen years, died of coronary thrombosis on May 27 after weakened health since a paralytic stroke that January. The *New York Times* reported that 1.5 million people lined the streets of New Delhi the following day to pay their last respects as sixty men of the Indian Army, Navy, and Air Force drew his body in a gun carriage.[46] Nehru had announced his imminent retirement from national politics but was yet to pick his successor when he died. In June, the Congress Party unanimously elected Lal Bahadur Shastri, an advocate of nonviolence and nonalignment but a largely unknown figure in public life, as the next Indian leader.[47]

The INR note on the Phoenix reprocessing plant reported that the DAE was changing the reactor core of the CIRUS every six months, which was too short for that kind of reactor.[48] Although research and training could explain the short cycle, the high frequency of the change of the reactor core was appropriate for the production of weapon-grade plutonium. The note raised concerns within the Johnson administration that the DAE was probably reprocessing plutonium from the CIRUS without any immediate justification for its civilian use. The DAE thus crossed the first threshold of nuclear weapons development, namely, "to have available on demand, unsafeguarded weapons grade plutonium, or at least the capacity to produce it."[49]

Neither the reprocessing plant nor the reactor fuel of the CIRUS was subject to safeguards. The DAE's reprocessing plant was indigenously built and, hence, not subject to safeguards. By the middle of 1964, the DAE had replaced the Canadian-supplied natural uranium fuel in the CIRUS, which was subject to Canada's bilateral safeguards, with indigenously produced natural uranium fuel. As a result, according to Bhabha, the reactor fuel was no longer subject to safeguards. As for the USAEC-supplied heavy water for the CIRUS, it "was sold outright without controls."[50]

Bhabha had reiterated his opposition to safeguards earlier that year at the Twelfth Pugwash Conference held in Udaipur, India, where he called them both ineffective and unfair.[51] It was likely motivated to also publicly signal that his position was unchanged since the Tarapur agreement. After all, the *New York Times* had reported that "India has agreed conditionally to accept international inspection" in Tarapur "under considerable prodding from the United States."[52]

The official DAE justification for reprocessing plutonium was experimental research for its breeder reactor program. Breeder reactors fueled by plutonium formed the second stage in Bhabha's "three-stage program." The indigenous capability to reprocess plutonium and the steady dissolution of safeguards on the CIRUS provided the DAE with the ability to preserve their freedom of action. Indigenously reprocessed plutonium with no safeguards was both a "ploughshare" and a "sword." It could become both reactor fuel as well as fissile material for a nuclear device.

The Johnson administration took to playing down the Chinese nuclear weapons threat to the Shastri government. In September 1964, the CIA's signals intelligence picked up significant movement around Chinese nuclear weapons installations in Lop Nor in its Xinjiang province. US intelligence officials concluded that a Chinese nuclear test could take place any day. US ambassador Chester Bowles, who had succeeded Galbraith in New Delhi, urged the Johnson administration to share accurate intelligence estimates about Chinese nuclear weapons capabilities with the Shastri government. Bowles thought that if the Johnson administration continued to play down Chinese nuclear weapons capabilities, as they were at the time, the Indian government would eventually find out "very possibly from the Russians," which would hurt US credibility in New Delhi.

Bowles wrote to McGeorge Bundy, special assistant to President Johnson, that "[t]he more opportunity we have to talk to the Indians about this situation the more likely we are to persuade them that the nuclear deterrent that could provide a real threat to Chinese cities was beyond her capacity and that the ultimate solution maybe some kind of understanding with us."[53] The US ambassador recommended the sharing of unclassified intelligence on the Chinese nuclear weapons program with the Indian government and dissuading an Indian decision to develop nuclear weapons through a cost-driven argument. Bowles, second-time US ambassador to India, lacked a forthcoming audience in Washington, DC. Bundy never considered his suggestions seriously. Johnson administration officials such as McGeorge Bundy and Bob Komer considered his correspondence from New Delhi too verbose and empathetic for his host country than the administration wanted.

Days before the first Chinese nuclear weapon test, the State Department's Committee on Nuclear Weapons considered a report from its subcommittee that Turner Cameron of the Bureau of Near Eastern Affairs had chaired.[54] The report, entitled "The Indian Nuclear Problem: Proposed Course of Action," recommended that the Johnson administration reinforce the peaceful dimension of the Indian nuclear weapons program by "developing one or more dramatic projects" that "could capture the imagination of Indians."[55] The USAEC's assistance to the DAE for building power reactors in Tarapur and NASA's ongoing cooperation with the DAE and its Indian National Committee for Space Research fitted well with this approach.

The Turner Cameron Report, however, was skeptical that US technical assistance alone could work. Hence, it also called for "continuing efforts to achieve international arrangements designed to inhibit further proliferation."[56] As far as US security assurances for India were concerned, the report reinforced the position of the Kennedy administration that the language of assurances should be kept deliberately vague and that assurance to India should be provided only in private. However, the report added that if the Soviet Union were willing to provide public assurance to India, then the United States could consider making its private assurances public.[57]

There was not much time between October 9, 1964, when the Committee on Nuclear Weapons met to discuss the Turner Cameron Report, and October 16, when China conducted its first nuclear weapon test. Nevertheless, the report would become a blueprint for US nonproliferation policy toward India during the Johnson years. The administration would engage the DAE in nuclear and space technology projects, on the one hand, and begin negotiations for a multilateral nonproliferation treaty, on the other. President Johnson would also appoint the Committee on Nuclear Proliferation under the chairmanship of Roswell Gilpatric, deputy secretary of defense during the Cuban Missile Crisis, to devise US policy in the wake of the first Chinese nuclear test.

Outer Space Projects

Since the Soviet Union had launched Sputnik I, the first artificial Earth satellite, in October 1957, outer space had become a key technological terrain of Cold War rivalry between the superpowers. Soviet ability to launch satellites into space indicated that Soviet scientists possessed the know-how to develop missiles that could carry nuclear weapons to US territories and those of US allies. The nuclear arms race and space race thus became deeply intertwined. Like nuclear technologies, space technologies were complex, highly sophisticated, and expensive. Foreign cooperation was often needed to make progress. Both could concurrently serve goals of national development and national security.

India's space program began with research in cosmic ray physics involving balloon experiments led by Homi Bhabha and Vikram Sarabhai at the IISc in Bangalore. Bhabha's own specialization was in cosmic ray physics while Sarabhai had always been interested in technologies of outer space. Their camaraderie and scientific partnership had a lasting influence on India's nuclear and space programs. After his stint at the IISc, Sarabhai founded the Physical Research Laboratory in his hometown of Ahmedabad in November 1947, only months after India's independence. It was a private laboratory to conduct research on cosmic rays and space technologies. Prime Minister Nehru inaugurated the Physical Research Laboratory in April 1954, only months after he laid the foundation stone of TIFR. The laboratory was established with Sarabhai's personal funds and the money he raised from the affluent Gujarati business community from which he hailed. Like Bhabha, Sarabhai was a physicist trained in Cambridge at the Cavendish Laboratory, who returned to India during the war. Both were wealthy and cosmopolitan elite members of Indian society.

As India's nuclear program expanded in response to the Chinese nuclear weapons program, the leaders of India's nuclear program pursued space technologies that could serve both development and security goals of the nation-state. The DAE's cooperation with NASA was significant for the growth of the Indian space program. Vikram Sarabhai had first expressed the DAE's interest in possible space cooperation with NASA in the spring of 1961 during his stay at MIT.[58] He was a visiting senior scientist at the Laboratory of Nuclear Science under the sponsorship of Italian physicist Bruno Rossi in the 1960s. At the time, Sarabhai was working on space experiments at his Physical Research Laboratory with the DAE secretary Bhabha.

Walt Rostow's modernization theory had a strong influence on India's scientific elites who led the country's nuclear and space programs, such as Sarabhai, who believed that science and technology would enable the agrarian economy of India to leapfrog to its takeoff phase, particularly when supported by appropriate US economic aid.[59] At MIT, Sarabhai interacted with both cutting-edge research in space technologies as well as imbibed the Rostovian view of a linear trajectory of development of underdeveloped countries through foreign aid and technical assistance. He believed that large institutions with vast infrastructure would enable his country to swiftly reach the phase of a Rostovian takeoff.[60] His institution-building was not limited to the space program. Sarabhai also spearheaded the establishment of the Indian Institute of Management in Ahmedabad with the help of the Ford Foundation, which was modeled on the Harvard Business School.[61]

The first telemetry-receiving equipment loaned from NASA that had arrived in India on September 6, 1961, was for recording data from NASA's Explorer 11 astronomy satellite launched into space earlier that April. [62] The Explorer 11 was NASA's first fully dedicated gamma ray satellite, which carried an MIT-built gamma ray telescope to "view" the universe.[63] Even though the astronomy satellite lost power by September that same year, the telemetry equipment from NASA to the DAE symbolized new possibilities for India's space program. In February 1962, Prime Minister Nehru established the Indian National Committee for Space Research under the DAE to be led by Sarabhai and overseen by Bhabha.

The DAE established its rocket launch site in 1963 in Thumba, a coastal village outside Thiruvananthapuram, the capital of the state of Kerala and that of erstwhile Travancore. Thumba's geographical proximity to the magnetic equator of the Earth (0°24' S) made it a desirable location for a launching station for sounding rockets to conduct geophysical studies of the Earth's magnetic field.[64] Sounding rockets or research rockets are those that carry various kinds of instruments to undertake scientific experiments and gather research data.[65] In November 1963, at the Thumba Equatorial Rocket Launching Station, the DAE launched its first sounding rocket, the Nike Apache, donated by NASA.

The Thumba site was initially conceived as a US-India bilateral rocket launching station. It eventually became a global site as the DAE increased cooperation with the UN Committee on the Peaceful Uses of Outer Space, established in 1959.[66] The Nehru government offered the Thumba site to the UN as an equatorial rocket launching facility to spacefaring nation-states. A UN team visited in January 1964 to assess the launching site's suitability and approved it. Against the backdrop of an imminent Chinese nuclear explosion, the Nehru government's global rocket launching facility portrayed India's emerging technological strengths in outer space. Around 105 rocket experiments were launched from the Thumba site between 1963 and 1971 by various countries, including the United States, the Soviet Union, France, West Germany, Japan, and the United Kingdom.[67]

The leaders of India's nuclear program, who were also the leaders of the space program, preferred to diversify their technology partners instead of remaining confined to NASA. The DAE's quest for freedom of action converged with NASA's own Cold War agenda. Arnold W. Frutkin, NASA's assistant administrator of international affairs, believed that a global rocket launching facility in a nonaligned country where the Soviets also participated could make more information available on the Soviet space program to the US government.[68]

Historian Asif Siddiqi's four tropes of the "master narrative of the history of space exploration" readily applied to India's space program, namely, "the myth of the founding father, the claim of indigenous creation, the connection between spaceflight and national identity, and the essential need to justify space activities."[69] India's space program, like its nuclear program, was also an embodiment of Sudipta Kaviraj's notion of a revisionist postcolonial modernity through a "logic of self-differentiation" and improvisation. India's space program held the distinction of having rocket cones being carried on bicycles

FIGURE 4.1.   Henri Cartier-Bresson's 1966 photograph of a French Centaure sounding rocket at the Thumba Equatorial Rocket Launching Station. Cartier-Bresson's caption: "INDIA, Kerala, Near Trivandrum. 1966." Media identifier: PAR145194. Copyright: Fondation Henri Cartier-Bresson/ Magnum Photos. Published with permission.

and the first sounding rocket from NASA being launched from a church in 1963 (see figure 4.1).[70] Through the launches of foreign rockets in which the DAE's scientific personnel also learned the technologies involving those rockets. Soon they began building rockets themselves, and forayed into the development of satellite launch vehicles, whose technological makeup was similar to that of ballistic missiles.[71]

Underground Nuclear Explosions Program

At the second Conference of Nonaligned Nations in Cairo held from October 5 to 10, 1964, Prime Minister Lal Bahadur Shastri tried to elicit a conference-wide effort to "persuade China to desist from developing nuclear weapons."[72] He failed. Six days after the Cairo conference, the Chinese government conducted its first nuclear test in Lop Nor in the southeastern part of its Xinjiang province. A week after the Chinese nuclear explosion, Bhabha delivered a speech on October 24 on the occasion of UN Day on All-India Radio in which he announced, "The explosion of a nuclear device by China is a signal that there is no time to be lost. Neither the United Nations nor the great powers have yet succeeded in creating a climate favourable to countries which have the capability of making atomic weapons, but have voluntarily refrained from doing so."[73] Bhabha's radio address stirred great controversy because he furnished very low-cost estimates of developing nuclear weapons: "a stockpile of 50 atomic bombs would cost under Rs. 10 crores [~US$21 million] and a stockpile of 50 two-megaton hydrogen bombs something of the order of Rs. 15 crores [~US$31 million]."[74] He added that such "expenditures are small compared with military budgets of many countries."[75]

At the All-India Congress Committee meeting in Guntur held during the first week of November 1964, pressures within Shastri's own political party to build nuclear weapons was on full display. During the debate to adopt the Congress party's foreign policy resolution, the "majority of the speakers came out strongly and frankly in favour of India manufacturing atom bombs."[76] Claiming that India's foreign policy appeared feeble, party members such as Bibhuti Mishra suggested that the Shastri government ask the Indian people whether the government should build the "atom bomb." Mishra asserted, "You will find that they want India to have it."[77] Another party delegate and member of the Parliament Kamal Nath Tewari warned Shastri that "the people will lose confidence in you if you do not develop the bomb."[78]

In the face of pro-bomb pressures emerging from within its own party, the All-India Congress Committee in Guntur adopted by acclamation its foreign policy resolution that declared that "advances in science should be exploited only for peaceful development."[79] Prime Minister Shastri's position against India developing its own nuclear weapons was on moral and economic grounds. He declared unequivocally, "[T]he talk of making bombs has no place in the deliberations of the Congress party, with pictures of Gandhi and Nehru, apostles of peace, looking down on us."[80]

The matter was far from settled. Later that month, pro-bomb advocates within the Congress Party and beyond attacked Shastri's position at the foreign policy debate held in the Lok Sabha or the lower house of the Indian Parliament. On November 27, 1964, the right-wing Jana Sangh Party introduced a motion in favor of the "Manufacture of Nuclear Weapons" by the government of India.[81] During the debate, Bhabha's cost estimates provided in his radio address became a bone of contention. Prime Minister Shastri went on the defensive as pro-bomb members of the Parliament used Bhabha's numbers to openly contest Shastri's economic argument that India was too poor to develop nuclear weapons.[82] The tension between Bhabha and Shastri's stance was best represented in R. K. Laxman's cartoon, "Atom for Peace," dated November 29, 1964, that showed Shastri as an angel of peace and Bhabha with an atom at his fingertip (see figure 4.2).

At the Lok Sabha debate, members of the Parliament from left parties seemed to oppose India's development of nuclear weapons while those from the right were in favor. Right-centrist Swatantra Party member Kapur Singh argued that if security assurances from the United States and the Soviet Union were not forthcoming or that "in the national interests it is not desirable to get this umbrella protection," then "we must not sit silent but must take some action."[83] Singh declared emotively, "[W]e should, even if we have to go with one meal a day, have our own nuclear weapons . . . for slavery is always worse than hunger."[84]

Others called for more realistic expectations in terms of what was achievable, such as K. A. Nambiar from the Communist Party of India, who had visited the DAE's Trombay facilities. He stated that "what we are actually producing in our country as [sic] a few kilograms of plutonium," with which "we can produce two atom bombs of the smallest type ever produced in any part of the world."[85] Nambiar asked rhetorically that at a time when India was importing food to meet its needs and paying with "hard-earned foreign exchange and incurring debts," would "our venturing into the production of a nuclear bomb add to our strength?"

Shastri maintained that his position was that of nonviolence. He argued that Bhabha's numbers about the costs of nuclear weapons were estimates based on US numbers, which did not readily apply to the Indian context. This led some members of the Parliament to complain about Bhabha himself. Hirendranath Mukherjee also from the Communist Party of India retorted: "Will the Prime Minister please ensure that eminent people like Dr. Bhabha, who happens to be an Official of his Ministry are not encouraged to make statements which unnecessarily give rise to complications and unpleasant misunderstandings?"[86] N. G. Ranga of the Swatantra Party added, "We sincerely hope that hereafter the Prime Minister and his Government will take sufficient care to see that not only Dr. Bhabha but other scientists also are approached with

FIGURE 4.2. "Atom for Peace" by R. K. Laxman depicting Homi J. Bhabha with an atom at its fingertip and Prime Minister Lal Bahadur Shastri as the angel of peace. Laxman gifted the cartoon to Homi Bhabha's brother, Jamshed J. Bhabha. The cartoon was dated November 29, 1964, which was two days after the Lok Sabha debate on whether India should develop its own nuclear weapons. Published with permission with the accompanying text: "A Tribute to R. K. Laxman on His One Hundredth Birth Anniversary."

the national request that whatever they have to say in regard to these very delicate matters should better be communicated to the Government first before they go to the radio or they go to the press."[87]

Notwithstanding the uproar, the Shastri government was able to defeat the motion of November 27, but the prime minister's position was no longer a staunch stance against nuclear weapons, but a nuanced one about nuclear devices. Shastri declared at the debate that DAE secretary Bhabha's position was that "we ought to augment the development of nuclear devices as far as possible so that we can use them for peaceful purposes."[88] The prime minister did not clarify whether the DAE would begin an underground nuclear explosions program, or whether such an endeavor was already underway. The remainder of his intervention in the Lok Sabha debate was about the importance of Gandhian principles of nonviolence in guiding India's foreign policy. Indian newspapers such as the *Times of India* reported the next day that the prime minister had remained steadfast in his anti-bomb position in the Lok Sabha debate.[89]

The DAE's underground nuclear explosions program believed to have started around this time aimed to produce nuclear devices for civilian purposes, like mining and constructing harbors, like the US Plowshare Program. The USAEC had launched the Plowshare Program in June 1957 to investigate the technical and economic feasibility of underground nuclear explosions. Bhabha in his radio address had discussed costs of a nuclear weapons program based on what he claimed was a US paper on underground nuclear explosions presented at the Third UN Conference on the Peaceful Uses of Atomic Energy in Geneva in September 1964.[90]

According to the CIA, the DAE's underground nuclear explosions project was a political compromise: "Opponents of a weapons program can claim to have maintained India's public position against nuclear proliferation, while those who advocate building a bomb presumably feel they have assurance that the coming year will not be 'lost' in terms of weapons development."[91] The significance of the underground nuclear explosions project was that it kept the Indian nuclear weapons option open by encouraging research and development in nuclear explosive devices that could be "ploughshares" as well as "swords." There was after all little technological distinction between a nuclear device used to build harbors and mine ores and that used as a weapon. From this time onward, Johnson administration officials began to suspect what they termed, the "Plowshare loophole," namely, India's potential development of nuclear weapons under the guise of an underground nuclear explosions program for civilian uses.

After the first Chinese nuclear test of October 1964, Bhabha and Sarabhai discussed with NASA the possibility of building a satellite launch vehicle through procuring technologies of the US four-stage, all-solid Scout rocket.[92] A launch vehicle is a rocket that can place an artificial satellite or a spacecraft into space. Hence, it is technologically more sophisticated than sounding rockets carrying telemetry equipment. Arnold Frutkin at NASA was disinclined to transfer technology of the Scout rockets to the DAE on geopolitical grounds. Technologies of outer space fitted the recommendations of the Turner Cameron Report to develop "dramatic technology projects" with the DAE to prevent an Indian decision to develop nuclear weapons.[93] However, rockets were technologically closer to missiles, unlike satellites. India was not a US Cold War ally, which meant that NASA also needed the approval of the State Department and the Munitions Board of the Defense Department. After months of wrangling, the DAE could not obtain the rocket technologies it sought from NASA.

As a result, the DAE initiated its own indigenous program to develop rockets, their related subsystems, and launch vehicles. At Thumba, the DAE established a rocket propellant plant and a rocket fabrication facility. It did so by seeking out technology partners like France. The French space agency was far more willing to share technologies with the DAE than their US counterpart, just like the CEA had done in the domain of nuclear technologies. In 1964, the DAE signed an agreement with a French company, *Sud Aviation*, to produce under license the Centaure sounding rocket systems in India.[94] Personal friendship between Vikram Sarabhai and Jacques Blamont, the founding director of the French space agency *Centre National d'Études Spatiales*, played a crucial role in facilitating space cooperation between India and France.[95]

Despite NASA's refusal to transfer technology involving the Scout rockets to the DAE, space cooperation between the two agencies did not end, but it continued in other domains, notably communication satellites. Cooperation in space technologies with India made sense to US policymakers for a variety of reasons. First, both the Kennedy and the Johnson administrations offered "dramatic technology projects" to the DAE in order to attain US nonproliferation objectives. Their underlying logic was that if India's quest for status and prestige was met through spectacular technological artifacts, such as power reactors in Tarapur and sounding rockets and communication satellites in Thumba, then perhaps India would not develop nuclear weapons to counter China. Second, US policymakers sought to meet their Cold War objectives through space technologies. They hoped to draw India, a nonaligned, noncommunist democracy, into the US sphere of influence through cooperating in technologies of outer space. Third and finally, they also believed that if a poor country like India allocated substantial resources in space technologies that were prestigious but peaceful, then its scarce resources in the forms of funds, institutions, and personnel could be diverted away from potential use in nuclear weapons development.[96] This practice of "positive disarmament" or using technology to delay, divert, and disarm a potential proliferating country, influenced US policy during the Kennedy-Johnson years, as historian John Krige has masterfully shown.[97]

Nevertheless, US policymakers rarely took into account India's national security interests. Instead, the US emphasis remained on India's status and prestige in Asia and the world. The view from New Delhi was, however, more often geopolitical. That view was influenced by the anxieties of a postcolonial nation-state with disputed territorial borders, a history of military conflict with adversaries China and Pakistan, and insurgencies in the borderlands.

Conclusion

While the Chinese nuclear weapons program accelerated, the DAE earned laurels in peaceful uses of nuclear and space technologies in Asia. These included the first reactor to become critical in Asia with the APSARA in 1956, the first boiling water reactors in Asia with Tarapur, and the first global rocket launching facility in Asia with Thumba. The Tarapur reactors were not only India's first power reactors, but their sheer capacity was also impressive. At 380 megawatts electrical, Tarapur was slated to become the world's second largest nuclear power plant after Britain's Hinkley Point.[98]

On the face of it, the leaders of India's nuclear program seemed to have capitulated to US pressure and at least partially compromised on their freedom of action by signing the contract on Tarapur. The turnkey nature of US reactor assistance provided limited learning opportunities for the DAE. It also made India's first power reactors dependent on the USAEC for low-enriched uranium for reactor fuel and subjected the DAE to bilateral safeguards and eventually IAEA safeguards. In reality, the DAE manufactured several pieces of engineering hardware for the Tarapur plant. Moreover, the freedom of action that the DAE lost through cooperating with the USAEC, it regained through its contract with the AECL, also signed in 1963.

The DAE-AECL contract was for the construction of a CANDU-type pressurized heavy water power reactor in Kota, Rajasthan. Unlike the Tarapur reactors, the Canadian reactor project for the Rajasthan Atomic Power Station was not a turnkey project. The AECL provided the designs and Montreal Engineering built the conventional plant, while a large portion of the technical equipment was manufactured in India.[99] Through the 1963 DAE-AECL contract for Kota, the DAE got the opportunity to learn more about its CIRUS reactor, which was also supplied by AECL and a predecessor of the CANDU-type reactor. Moreover, the reactor in Kota would also produce plutonium as a by-product, thereby theoretically adding to the DAE's source of plutonium.

The Tarapur reactors embodied the unintended consequences of the DAE's freedom of action. As we shall see in the next chapters, from construction of the reactors to their fueling, refueling, and repair, US policymakers would employ their technical assistance as both a carrot and a stick to attain nonproliferation goals with respect to India.

CHAPTER 5

The Plowshare Loophole, 1964–1970

In December 1964, a high-ranking MEA official leaked to the US embassy in New Delhi a paper titled "India and the Chinese Bomb."[1] C. V. Ranganathan, deputy secretary of the MEA's China Division, shared the eleven-page document allegedly "without the knowledge or consent of his colleagues in the Division."[2] It was "loaned, therefore, on the condition that it would be held in the strictest confidence," such that its contents were not even to be "discussed in conversation with any other Indian official."[3] Dated November 25, 1964—two days before Prime Minister Shastri faced the debate in the Indian Parliament that strongly favored nuclear weapons development—the MEA paper agreed with pro-bomb advocates within the government. The only option for India, it argued, was "some kind of a counterblast to the Chinese bomb."[4]

Ranganathan reassured L. Douglas Heck, a US embassy official, that the document was a working paper "prepared primarily to stimulate debate within MEA on the subject."[5] Although the document's arguments for building nuclear weapons had "won many adherents at lower and middle levels in the Ministry," it had "been rejected at the top," reported the Indian official.[6] Despite that reassurance, the US embassy promptly wired the MEA paper to the State Department, and from there it made its way to the Johnson administration's National Security Council. After all, it offered US actors a window into the minds of Indian foreign policy officials, particularly the MEA's China experts in the aftermath of China's first nuclear test in October 1964.

The MEA document expressed great concern that "[t]he practical possibilities of organizing Asian opinion against China on the question of the nuclear test are very limited."[7] Furthermore, the majority of nonaligned leaders were full of "admiration for this scientific feat by a non-white country who until 15 years ago was at the very bottom of the scale of nations."[8] The Algerian Foreign Office had even expressed to the Indian ambassador in Algiers that "while they regretted the Chinese test they cannot condemn it because they appreciated China's reasons in making the bomb."[9]

The MEA paper opposed nuclear security guarantees or a nuclear umbrella for India, just like Prime Minister Shastri had. At the All-India Congress Committee meeting in Guntur in early November 1964, Shastri had publicly cautioned that "alignment with those who also have the bomb, against China" would result in India's loss of "economic and political independence."[10] Adopting a similar line of reasoning, the MEA paper warned that a joint nuclear umbrella by the United States and the Soviet Union was not only infeasible but that it "would produce a psychology of dependence and uncertainty in India and encroach upon our basic independence and freedom of action."[11] For the MEA's China Division, the reasoning was unmistakable: "India is too great a nation to dwindle by consent into an international protectorate."[12]

The discussion of nuclear security guarantees in the MEA paper and the Indian prime minister's speech took place in the context of the US president's statement immediately after the Chinese nuclear test on October 16, 1964. President Lyndon Johnson had stated that the United States would "help the nations of Asia to defend themselves."[13] Johnson had delivered a similar message in his radio and television address two days later on October 18, in which he proclaimed that nonnuclear countries "that do not seek national nuclear weapons can be sure that if they need our strong support against some threat of nuclear blackmail, then they will have it."[14]

Shastri's objections to nuclear security guarantees were nuanced. During his visit to London to meet British prime minister Harold Wilson in early December 1964, Shastri called for nuclear security guarantees from countries with nuclear weapons to *all countries* without nuclear weapons, including India.[15] His position in London was not a U-turn from his earlier stance in Guntur. Rather, it was an effort to square the circle—specifically, to make nuclear security guarantees compatible with India's stated policy of nonalignment and its leaders' persistent quest for freedom of action.

Despite Indian political leaders' and foreign policy officials' ambivalence toward nuclear security guarantees, such guarantees became prominent in the context of the negotiation of the NPT (1965–68) and India's relationship with the global nonproliferation regime.[16] The leaders of India's nuclear program, including Bhabha's successor as DAE secretary Vikram Sarabhai, would later argue that unclear and unreliable mechanisms of nuclear security guarantees from the superpowers resulted in India not signing the NPT. As this chapter shows, the Johnson administration rightly worried about the DAE exploiting the aforementioned "Plowshare Loophole," because Indian scientists and engineers at the helm of the nation's nuclear program most certainly gravitated toward that option. Concurrently, Indian policymakers continued to publicly cite inadequate nuclear security guarantees when discussing India's policy choices in the nuclear realm.

While the Johnson administration was introducing a draft treaty on nonproliferation at the Eighteen Nations Disarmament Committee (ENDC) meeting in Geneva, Switzerland, on August 17, 1965, Indian and Pakistani troops were facing off against each other in Kashmir and Kutch.[17] Geopolitical anxieties spiked within the Shastri government when China announced its support for Pakistan during the military conflict, stoking fears in New Delhi of yet another Chinese invasion along India's border with Tibet. Domestic political pressures for the bomb and multilateral negotiations for a nonproliferation treaty were not the only forces at play for the Indian government at this time. Geopolitics was front and center.

India's Second War with Pakistan

War began in April 1965, when Indian and Pakistani troops clashed in the Rann of Kutch, a vast desert salt marsh along India's western border. The 1965 war had far-reaching geopolitical consequences because it exacerbated Pakistan-Indian, Sino-Indian, US-Indian, and US-Pakistan tensions.[18] As fighting between Indian and Pakistani forces intensified, China conducted its second nuclear weapon test on May 14. In June, Indian ambassador B. K. Nehru informed US secretary of state Dean Rusk that the Indian government was running out of patience in the face of military provocations by Pakistan president Ayub Khan and inaction by the Johnson administration to rein in its military ally in South Asia.

Pakistan's military launched Operation Gibraltar on August 5 to 6, 1965, when Pakistan troops entered Indian-controlled Kashmir following their early military successes in the Rann of Kutch. In response, Prime Minister Shastri authorized the Indian military to take the war into Pakistan-controlled Kashmir.[19] The Indian military began advancing on three fronts from Kargil, Tithwal, and the Poonch-Uri bulge. When this in turn led Pakistan to retaliate with Operation Grand Slam in the Chhamb valley of Kashmir on September 1, Prime Minister Shastri held two emergency committee meetings in which the unanimous decision was made to launch a diversionary offensive on West Pakistan's Punjab province.[20] On September 6, 1965, Indian troops pushed far enough into Pakistan's Punjab such that they came within a short distance of the Pakistani cities of Lahore and Sialkot and were capable of disrupting the communication and transport links that could have effectively divided West Pakistan in half.[21] Against this backdrop, the first Chinese note of formal protest against Indian military action arrived at the MEA in New Delhi on September 8. A second note followed on September 16, which Beijing claimed was an ultimatum that would result in a war between China and India on the Tibet-Sikkim border in the east, if the Indian troops did not stop their offensive in the west.[22]

The 1965 war in South Asia finally ended through a UN-mediated ceasefire. The Johnson administration placed an embargo on its military assistance to the subcontinent, thereby earning the ire of both the Ayub Khan and Lal Bahadur Shastri governments. The Indian government blamed the US government for the conflict arguing that US-supplied arms were used by Pakistan against India's military.[23] In reality, the US-Pakistan bilateral relationship had already become strained before the 1965 war. The Kennedy and Johnson administrations opposed the Pakistan government's tilt toward China.[24] In 1964, Ayub Khan had publicly protested US military and economic assistance to India in his article published in *Foreign Affairs*.[25] Tensions between the two countries exacerbated so much that the Ayub government threatened to pull out of US-led multilateral security arrangements in Asia.[26] The once "most allied ally" of the United States even refused to send a token contingent of troops to participate in the US war effort in Vietnam.[27] The Shastri government's support for China's seat in the United Nations despite Sino-Indian tensions, on the one hand, and the Ayub government's friendship with Mao Zedong's government, on the other, worried the Johnson administration. Frustrated NSC staffer Bob Komer wrote to then national security advisor McGeorge Bundy, "We have got to convince them (the Indians and the Pakistanis) that they can't have their American cake and eat it with chopsticks too."[28]

The Special National Intelligence Estimate 31–1–65 produced by the CIA in October 1965 was yet another indicator that the "Plowshare Loophole" might be the DAE's way to develop nuclear weapons under the guise of nuclear devices for peaceful civilian uses. The document stated: "If India decided to proceed to construct a device and test it underground, it might claim that it was merely exploring the potentialities of nuclear explosions for peaceful purposes—an Indian Plowshare program. By this means it could obtain the prestige of having produced a nuclear device while maintaining it had neither proliferated nuclear weapons nor violated its agreement with Canada" on bilateral safeguards on the CIRUS reactor.[29] US intelligence officials concluded that the "pace and scope of the Chinese nuclear program" would have a massive influence on India, in particular, if there were multiple Chinese nuclear tests, and another war in the subcontinent. They predicted that India would not accede to a multilateral treaty that did not restrict Chinese nuclear weapons development.

India was not the only country in South Asia that was considering developing its own nuclear weapons. Within months of the 1965 war, Pakistan foreign minister Zulfikar Ali Bhutto stated in a widely quoted interview to the *Manchester Guardian*: "If India builds the bomb, we will eat grass or leaves, even go hungry, but we will get one of our own. We have no alternative."[30] The nuclear dominoes seemed to have finally started falling.

Chinese Nuclear Weapons and Pakistan's Actions

Within a year of the Chinese ultimatum to India during the 1965 India-Pakistan War, China acquired nuclear delivery vehicles that were capable of reaching India from Tibet and western Xinjiang. As Indian policymakers reeled from the untimely deaths of Prime Minister Shastri and Homi Bhabha—both died within a span of less than two weeks in January 1966—they confronted a harsh two-pronged reality. There was a military adversary on their east that had the capability to drop nuclear weapons on Indian territory across the Himalayas, and whose nuclear weapons program would not be contained by the imminent NPT.

The odds were stacked against Indira Gandhi. The old guard of the Congress Party or the "Syndicate" supported her to succeed Shastri as the Indian prime minister in hopes of manipulating her. The Syndicate even dubbed her as the *gungi gudiya* (or dumb puppet). When she made her first speech as the prime minister at the All-India Jaipur Congress in February 1966, she was largely isolated within her own party. Henri Cartier-Bresson's photograph of her at the Jaipur meeting was poignant. Against the backdrop of a large poster of her father, Jawaharlal Nehru smelling a rose with a wide smile, she appeared deeply reflective. Her furrowed eyebrows and askance glance made her seem aloof and perhaps even a bit lost (see figure 5.1).

As the Cultural Revolution disrupted Chinese society, the Chinese government conducted three nuclear weapon tests in May, October, and December 1966. That summer, its first nuclear-tipped, medium-range ballistic missile—the DF-2A—became fully operational. On October 27, 1966, Chinese scientists successfully conducted a nuclear weapon test of a 1,290-kg device that was

FIGURE 5.1.   Henri Cartier-Bresson's photograph of Prime Minister Indira Gandhi at the All-India Congress Committee meeting in Jaipur in February 1966. Cartier-Bresson's caption: "INDIA. Rajasthan. Jaipur. 1966. Congress sessions. Indira GANDHI, Congress' president." Media identifier: PAR93674. Copyright: Fondation Henri Cartier-Bresson/Magnum Photos. Published with permission.

delivered by a DF-2A missile.[31] China's ballistic missile capability indicated that it had the requisite delivery vehicles to target Indian cities with its nuclear weapons.

In July and August 1966, public allegations surfaced that India was on its way to explode an underground nuclear device. The head of Pakistan's delegation at the IAEA, Dr. Ishrat Hussain Usmani, initiated the allegations that caused an uproar in the Canadian media and raised serious questions in the Indian Parliament. Pakistan's delegation at the United Nations also circulated a note to the UN secretary-general to that effect. The furor compelled a spokesperson from the Canadian Ministry of External Affairs to go on record as saying that "Canada had no evidence of an atomic explosion by India" that was imminent. The Office of the Indian High Commissioner in Ottawa criticized Pakistan's claims as "baseless" and a "piece of imagination."[32] Usmani's allegations exasperated Sarabhai, who even dismissed them in his meeting with his US counterpart, USAEC chairman Glenn Seaborg.

Sarabhai said that he was "personally very disturbed by the ridiculous Pakistani charges that India would explode an atomic weapon in a few days" and it was "particularly unfortunate coming at the very time that Professor Salaam had been in Peking negotiating some sort of atomic cooperation."[33] The "some sort of atomic cooperation" that had raised eyebrows among the Indian policymakers was the China-Pakistan negotiations for a nuclear reactor in Ruppur in East Pakistan, barely fifty miles from the border with India. Pakistani physicist and the government's science advisor Abdus Salam was conducting the negotiations on behalf of the Pakistan Atomic Energy Commission. However, political differences between East Pakistan and West Pakistan in the late 1960s that would eventually lead to the 1971 Bangladesh Liberation War would remove any possibility of a Sino-Pakistan reactor construction project in Ruppur.

In the Rajya Sabha or upper house of the Indian Parliament, Banka Behari Das asked Minister of External Affairs Swaran Singh what steps the government had taken to "counter this Pakistani propaganda against India" at the United Nations.[34] Singh responded that the Indian government had informed the UN secretary-general and other concerned governments that Pakistan's allegations were "baseless." Pakistan's permanent UN representative had originally requested on July 19, 1966, that the secretary-general circulate to all ENDC members Pakistan's note about an imminent Indian underground nuclear explosion. In response, the Indian representative protested that in 1965 Pakistan had brought similar allegations to the First Committee of the UN General Assembly. Furthermore, the Indian representative argued that those were allegations made by one country against another that a multilateral UN committee like the ENDC ought not to be concerned with. As a result of Indian efforts, Pakistan's note was circulated neither as an official ENDC document nor as an official UN record.[35]

Unlike India, Pakistan was not a member of the ENDC. Its public allegations at the United Nations and the IAEA were along the lines of what US actors had known for some time: India's plutonium reprocessing plant gave it the technical capability to produce fissile material for nuclear weapons; the Canada-India bilateral safeguards on the CIRUS were not enough to prevent the DAE from reprocessing plutonium from the CIRUS; and the Limited Test Ban Treaty permitted underground nuclear explosions, which the DAE had been studying since the first Chinese nuclear test in 1964.

It was unclear what had triggered Pakistan's efforts at the UN and the IAEA in the summer of 1966, but generating public outcry through India's primary adversary may have been one way for US officials to stave off an Indian nuclear explosion at a time when their available policy options toward India were limited.

British and US Assessments of India's Nuclear Program

The spring and summer of 1966 witnessed a flurry of activities in British and US policy circles to assess India's nuclear weapons potential. In May 1966, Lord Chalfont, the British ENDC representative and minister of state for foreign affairs, appointed a panel to study "India, the Bomb and Nonproliferation."[36] The panel's goal was to assess the "internal pressure in India to develop nuclear weapons or to resist a non-proliferation treaty, her potential ability to develop them and the economic and political cost of doing so." John D. Cockcroft was asked to provide his analysis of Lord Chalfont's panel report because of his long-standing knowledge of the DAE's workings.

Lord Chalfont's panel report was a remarkably accurate assessment of the DAE's technological capability to develop nuclear weapons. It noted that "India has almost all the essential requirements for embarking on a nuclear warhead program, at least in the low kiloton range." The panel also observed that, under the provisions of the Limited Test Ban Treaty, any Indian nuclear test would have to be carried out underground. More importantly, it stated that "[a]n underground test might have the advantage of facilitating disguise as a nuclear device for peaceful purposes, which would at the same time circumvent any possibility of being charged with breaking the safeguards agreement with Canada." Such a test—"a short-term 'one-off' nuclear test, in the kiloton range"—would cost the government of India "a negligible sum in cash terms, compared to the total nuclear investment already made."[37]

Regarding delivery vehicles, Lord Chalfont's panel report assessed that the Indian government would be using "an aircraft/plutonium combination" because it had the capability to reprocess plutonium and possessed British-supplied Canberra bomber aircraft that could reach Chinese cities when accompanied by air-refueling tankers. According to the report, India's balance-of-payments deficit was so high (£553 million or ~US$1.5 billion in 1965–66) that it could not afford to invest in long-range bombers and missile systems immediately or in the near term. Such a nuclear force, the report noted, would be like "when the French had plutonium but not enriched uranium and aircraft but not a missile industry."[38] Interestingly, Lord Chalfont's panel claimed that the DAE could conduct a nuclear test for a fraction of the price that Bhabha had claimed in early 1965. In its report, the panel estimated that the DAE could conduct such a nuclear test for about £1 million (~US$2.8 million). Bhabha's price tag was £3 to £6 million (~US$8.4 to $16.7 million), within eighteen months of a political decision to do so.[39]

Since the first Chinese nuclear test, Bhabha had publicly provided wildly low-cost estimates for a nuclear explosion in hopes of garnering political support. He had once stated that the DAE could conduct a two-megaton nuclear explosion for US$600,000, based on estimates from a USAEC report on the US Plowshare Program presented in Geneva.[40] In January 1965, he had told Jerome Wiesner, the dean of the School of Science at MIT and former science advisor to President Kennedy, that "he could make and test a crude nuclear device for approximately ten million dollars."[41] Wiesner was visiting New Delhi and Bombay upon the request of the Johnson administration to ascertain India's technological capabilities and political intent for nuclear weapons. He was struck by the fact that a nuclear explosion was not the only goal for several Indian policymakers, but that "there was some desire for a deterrent against China and some vague feeling that if a nuclear minefield makes sense in Europe it could be useful in India-China border."[42] Wiesner would hear about this rudimentary deterrent plan from his Indian interlocutors once again upon his return to India as part of the American Academy of Arts and Sciences delegation in June 1966.

The US delegation of scientists and technical experts in India was part of the Committee on International Studies of Arms Control (CISAC), formed by Harvard biochemistry professor Paul Doty.[43] CISAC was based at the American Academy of Arts and Sciences in Massachusetts. The delegation was visiting India to informally discuss nuclear policy with high-level members of Indira Gandhi's government and top scientists at the DAE, TIFR, and IISc. Its visit was funded by the Ford Foundation.[44] Officially called the "Indo-US Study Group Meeting on Problems of Economic Growth, Arms Control and Disarmament," held on June 3 to 6, 1966, in New Delhi, it was jointly sponsored by the Nehru Foundation for Development and the American Academy of Arts and Sciences.[45] The gathering was the first of its kind between Indian and US scientific experts to discuss "nonproliferation," although the term itself was not mentioned.

The delegation's goal was to sound out their Indian hosts on the ongoing ENDC negotiations for an NPT. US-Soviet tensions over a multilateral nuclear force for western Europe had brought those negotiations to a standstill.[46] However, the US Congress' Joint Committee on Atomic Energy was bringing pressure to bear on the Johnson administration to respond to what the lawmakers perceived as a global nonproliferation problem. Earlier that year in May, the US Senate had approved the Pastore Resolution with a vote of 84–0, calling on the US president to undertake "serious and urgent efforts to negotiate international agreements limiting the spread of nuclear weapons."[47]

The star-studded team of US experts met with the scientific and diplomatic elites who represented India's nuclear program—Vikram Sarabhai and V. C. Trivedi, among them—and stressed to their hosts the expensive and intricate nature of an effective Indian nuclear deterrent against China's military superiority. The timing of the meeting and the probing nature of the Americans' inquiry indicated that their high-profile visit had a dual purpose as both a fact-finding and dissuading mission. The CISAC team was in India just before the Johnson administration expected to make key decisions on India's nuclear program, on the one hand, and decisive rounds of multilateral negotiations in Geneva to formulate the NPT, on the other. Their discussions had the same tone as that of Chester Bowles's suggestion to McGeorge Bundy two years earlier. Bowles had written to Bundy that the best chance of stalling India's nuclear weapons development was to convey to its leaders that an Indian nuclear deterrent that could actually hurt China was "beyond her capacity."[48]

At the meeting, Jerome Wiesner opened the discussion by emphasizing the prohibitive costs of India developing an effective Indian nuclear deterrent against China. Wiesner remarked that India was at a geographical disadvantage vis-à-vis its nuclear-armed adversary to the east because of the Himalayas. With the world's loftiest mountain range standing as a formidable natural barrier between the two countries, the leaders of India's nuclear program needed to decide whether to adopt the "aircraft route," a "missile force," or a "converted version of the supersonic transport" as delivery vehicles for their nuclear weapons against China. Morton Halperin from the Pentagon reminded his Indian hosts that a potent nuclear deterrent required command-and-control systems, intelligence, and early warning mechanisms that were "all terribly expensive."[49]

Vikram Sarabhai responded by wondering out aloud about the "possibility of mining the Himalayan passes with radioactive waste" to counter the Chinese military.[50] George Kistiakowsky, the Harvard chemistry professor and former science advisor to President Eisenhower, pointed out that the major drawback to Sarabhai's idea was that the passes in the Himalayas along the India-China border were topographically inclined toward India, meaning that any radioactive material deposited in the passes could contaminate Indian rivers and the streams when the snow melted. Sarabhai's response was pragmatic. He "pointed out that the British have developed a way of incorporating radioactive waste into ceramics," which perhaps could mitigate the risks.[51]

The CISAC delegation's cost-driven approach to discourage Indian nuclear weapons development was reminiscent of the Kennedy administration's propaganda campaign to minimize the psychological effect of a Chinese nuclear weapon test. The message the US administration had disseminated both at home and abroad was that "the Chinese capability is actually a 'paper tiger' which need not be feared. . . . [I]t is quite simple to put together a few atomic bombs; but getting enough plutonium and engineering know-how to produce significant numbers of warheads and developing delivery vehicles (planes and missiles which the Chinese lack) is another matter entirely."[52]

As India's nuclear program crossed the threshold of fissile material production and research in nuclear explosions, US actors adopted a similar strategy. They played down the significance of the milestones that the DAE had already attained and played up the importance of the anticipated next steps in an imagined linear trajectory of nuclear weapons development: fissile material to nuclear device, to testing of the device, to miniaturization, and then to delivery vehicles. Those at the helm of India's nuclear program, however, defied the US actors' teleological assumptions and expectations—and the established conventional wisdom—in order to preserve their own freedom of action. They procured technologies associated with delivery vehicles prior to testing a nuclear device.

At the June 1966 Indo-US meeting, India's representative to the ENDC, V. C. Trivedi, said that while national prestige and security were the two drivers of nuclear proliferation, the prestige factor was easier to deal with: "[o]ne could get around it by making a distinction between 'nuclear power' and 'nuclear weapons power'. It was the security factor that was far more difficult."[53] DAE secretary Vikram Sarabhai did not mince his words. He bluntly stated that national security was his main concern. Sarabhai said that "[t]he big powers have to say what they are willing to do for us," because "[i]t is callous of them to stay aloof from disputes in which countries like India have national interests at stake."[54] He emphasized that "India cannot sign away its inherent right to defend its own security, though its national policy is at present against development of nuclear weapons."[55]

When Jerome Wiesner asked "whether an escape clause would not be enough" for the Indian government to sign the imminent NPT, Sarabhai "replied with a categorical no." Carl Kaysen, a Harvard professor of political economy and former deputy national security advisor to President Kennedy, reminded Sarabhai that a "total security guarantee" was hardly feasible. It had already been difficult to "make the US guarantee to the NATO powers credible." So then, what "concrete steps could be taken" to convey the credibility of a nuclear security guarantee to the Indian government? Sarabhai promptly "asked for an automatic UN presence" but one backed by the "combined might of the two big nuclear powers."[56] Trivedi summarized India's official position to the US visitors: the NPT "was not urgent" because it would not change the status quo in anyway, and India "would not sign a treaty that would primarily benefit China."[57] In other words, what the American Academy visitors learned in New Delhi in the hot summer of June 1966 was a reaffirmation of the US intelligence assessment from October 1965, and it was essentially what Lord Chalfont's panel would conclude in July 1966 in its report.

As the American Academy meeting ended in India, Walt Rostow, then national security advisor to President Johnson, called for an interagency study "in great depth" to devise a "strict cost-benefit analysis" of US options in discouraging India's nuclear weapons development under National Security Action Memorandum 351.[58] The results of the study concluded that the Johnson administration had been "unable to devise anything dramatic which would not cost us more than any anticipated gain."[59] Consequently, the Rostovian decision, as stated in National Security Action Memorandum 355, was to *do nothing* about India's nuclear weapons ambitions but buy time and hope that the Indian government signed the NPT.[60]

In July and August 1966, two high-level decisions in Washington, DC, charted the course of what would become the Johnson administration's nuclear legacy. The first decision was that the administration would accept the inevitability of India's nuclear weapons development. The second one was that they would discard the multilateral force proposal for NATO allies and push ahead with closed-door negotiations with the Soviet government to formulate a nonproliferation treaty that would be mutually acceptable to both superpowers.[61] That the Johnson administration considered its negotiations with the Soviet government such a high priority was arguably attributable to the successful influence of the Gilpatric Committee.[62]

Formally known as the President's Task Force on the Spread of Nuclear Weapons, the committee is better known after its chairman, Roswell Gilpatric, former US deputy secretary of defense. Immediately after the first Chinese nuclear test, President Johnson had formed the committee to reevaluate US nonproliferation policy and the impact of the Chinese nuclear explosion on world politics. In its report to President Johnson submitted on January 21, 1965, the Gilpatric Committee had called for the intensification of US global nonproliferation efforts by raising the specter of nuclear dominoes in South Asia, East Asia, the Middle East, and Europe. It had recommended "energetic and comprehensive steps" in collaboration with the Soviet Union to prevent reactive nuclear proliferation in the world.[63]

The Carrot and Stick of US Technical and Food Aid

When the Johnson administration had sent Jerome Wiesner to assess India's nuclear weapons capabilities in early January 1965, Homi Bhabha was the DAE secretary. Wiesner's visit was followed by USAEC official John Palfrey's visit. Bhabha had invited Palfrey to attend the inauguration ceremony of India's plutonium reprocessing plant in Trombay held on January 22, 1965. From the US government's perspective, Wiesner's visit was intended to further two major objectives. The first was "to help India demonstrate that its scientific and technological capabilities are at least equal to those of Chicoms" through exploring "certain scientific projects which might have [the] result of demonstrating Indian scientific prowess." The second objective was to communicate to Indian policymakers the serious dangers of nuclear proliferation and its high costs in order to dissuade them from developing nuclear weapons.[64] Upon his return, Wiesner had sent a somber status report to President Johnson about India:

> The Chinese invasion and nuclear explosion have badly shaken their self-confidence, and they are seriously questioning the wisdom of their decision not to make nuclear weapons. The government is under considerable pressure, both from within and from outside, to undertake the development of a nuclear device. . . . I believe that pressure to develop a bomb will become too great to resist when the Chinese have carried out a few more explosions, and the Indian government has not.[65]

While admitting that he could not find a "simple technical spectacular, which would have sufficient psychological advantage" for India, Wiesner recommended that the Johnson administration explore options for US-Indian scientific and technological cooperation together with the State Department, USAEC, and NASA. Wiesner's report proposed a series of technological projects: space cooperation (satellites, sounding rockets, and optical and radio tracking facilities), population control, the sharing of satellite data for monsoon predictions, desalination efforts, joint studies on waterlogging problems, and even underground nuclear explosions "in connection with large water catchment areas and harbors" like Project Plowshare in the United States.

According to Wiesner, Bhabha was particularly "interested in the possibility of making harbors and water reservoirs" through underground nuclear explosions.[66] Wiesner's suggestion to offer US assistance to India to conduct such nuclear explosions was entertained by John Palfrey but outright rejected by arms control experts such as Spurgeon M. Keeny Jr. because of proliferation concerns. Nevertheless, the basic premise of Wiesner's recommendations was accepted—namely, to engage in technological collaboration with India across multiple sectors, and particularly in space technologies, in order to dissuade the DAE from developing nuclear weapons and diverting its resources elsewhere.[67] Wiesner, like other US actors, also emphasized the importance of technological collaboration for stroking India's national prestige vis-à-vis China.

NSC aide Robert Komer and then national security advisor McGeorge Bundy adopted a different approach from late 1965 to April 1966. Combining the two issues of India's nuclear weapons development and its need for US economic and technical assistance, the US officials "held up for a couple of months the actual signing of a contract for nuclear fuel for the Tarapur power plant."[68] Komer believed that "holding off might help soften up the Indians" on nonproliferation.[69] Even when the USAEC and General Electric wished to move ahead, Komer and Bundy instructed the State Department to hold off on signing the reactor fuel contract. The resultant delays led to unofficial complaints from the DAE.[70]

The Johnson administration seemed to have adopted a stick-and-stick approach, with little carrot to offer. About a week before Prime Minister Gandhi's March 1966 visit to the United States, Komer wrote to President Johnson: "One of your trickiest jobs with Mrs. Gandhi will be to stiffen her intention not to go nuclear without promising too much."[71] Komer advised the US president to encourage the Indian prime minister "to limit India's nuclear energy development to peaceful uses and to concentrate on economic development." More importantly, "without threatening to cut off aid," he advised Johnson to make "it clear how hard it would be for [him] through economic aid to underwrite an Indian nuclear weapons program."[72] President Johnson did exactly that when he met Prime Minister Gandhi later that month.

The relationship between Indira Gandhi's government and the Johnson administration was strained, not least on the question of economic aid and reforms.[73] Following the advice of the World Bank and in response to India's balance-of-payments deficit exacerbated by drought and famine, the Gandhi government devalued the Indian rupee by 36.7 percent on June 6, 1966.[74] Overnight, the rupee fell from 4.76 to 7.50 to the US dollar, a fall of 57.5 percent. Devaluation proved to be deeply unpopular. It weakened Indira Gandhi's already debilitated political position, just months after becoming the Indian prime minister in January 1966. The Johnson administration had insisted upon currency devaluation, deregulation, structural agrarian reforms (that became known as the Green Revolution), and trade liberalization as conditions for continued economic assistance through USAID and the Aid India Consortium of the World Bank. However, when the Aid India Consortium failed to provide the promised US$900 million in nonproject aid to India to help cushion the impact of devaluation, Indian policymakers' misgivings about the World Bank and the US government only increased.[75]

In the summer of 1966, National Security Advisor Walt Rostow insisted that US aid recipients needed to demonstrate improved economic performance if they were to receive continued US economic assistance. Yet, the politics over India's opposition to the US war in Vietnam and its support for Chinese entry into the UN interfered with President Johnson's actions on food aid.[76] The US president held back wheat shipments to India under Public Law–480 (PL–480) even when US ambassador Chester Bowles, USAID, and the State Department judged India's efforts to be "generally satisfactory."[77]

Johnson adopted the so-called "short tether" policy under which food aid to India was provided on a month-to-month basis and only upon presidential approval. During food shortages and famine in northern India, the president's policy led to a "ship-to-mouth" situation. A *New York Times* article from November 1966 expressed frustration that "[t]he White House statement that the new drought required a new survey is unconvincing," because it did "not explain why shipments are being held up while the study is made."[78] The article added that "[t]he situation leads Indians to suspect that the hold-up may be partially due to President Johnson's displeasure with Prime Minister Gandhi's recent call for a halt in the bombing of North Vietnam."[79]

Safeguards and Security Guarantees

In December 1966, Vikram Sarabhai agreed to accept IAEA safeguards on the CANDU-type power reactor that the DAE has been constructing in Rajasthan with Canadian help as a result of a 1963 DAE-AECL agreement.[80] When news of the DAE's acceptance of IAEA safeguards broke in India in January 1967, Sarabhai found himself in the eye of a political and media storm. Newspaper articles criticized Sarabhai for making the Indian government "resile from its previous position" against IAEA safeguards. S. A. Dange, leader of the Communist Party of India, even demanded Sarabhai's immediate resignation for "agreeing with Canada to have inspection by an outside agency."[81] A headline in the *Indian Express* demanded, "Dr. Sarabhai must go," and questioned his commitment to India's "nuclear self-reliance."[82]

Indian media and political leaders criticized Sarabhai for overturning Bhabha's practice of opposing multilateral safeguards and thereby presumably compromising India's national sovereignty. In reality, Bhabha had already committed the DAE to accepting IAEA safeguards, as in the case of the Tarapur reactors (discussed in chapter 4). The IAEA's first complete safeguards system was formulated only in December 1965, a month before Bhabha's death.[83]

Amidst the media furor against Sarabhai in January 1967, USAEC chairman Glenn Seaborg arrived in India. The Johnson administration had sent Seaborg on a tour of Asia and the Asia-Pacific region to discuss US allies' positions on the imminent NPT. India, neither a US ally in the Cold War nor an adversary, but technologically close to developing nuclear weapons, was one of Seaborg's stops. His other state visits during this tour were to Pakistan, Thailand, and Australia. In his meeting with Sarabhai, Seaborg unequivocally communicated to the DAE secretary that the US government considered the development of peaceful nuclear explosions (PNEs) as equivalent to the development of nuclear weapons. Sarabhai responded that the NPT ought not to legally prevent countries from developing PNEs. Seaborg then conceded that countries indeed retained that legal right under the imminent treaty.[84]

The Sarabhai-Seaborg exchange was indicative of the basic tenor of disagreement between the US and Indian policymakers. The US officials, driven by their nonproliferation objectives, wanted to dissuade other countries from carrying out underground nuclear explosions even though those were legally permissible under the 1963 Limited Test Ban Treaty and would likewise be legal under the future NPT. The Indian leaders, determined to retain their nation's freedom of action, emphasized their legal right to conduct subterranean nuclear explosions without conceding that those were technologically indistinguishable from nuclear weapons.

Within months of Seaborg's visit, Prime Minister Indira Gandhi sent her secretary L. K. Jha and DAE secretary Vikram Sarabhai to the capitals of the four nuclear-armed countries other than China—Washington, Moscow, Paris, and London. The Jha-Sarabhai team aimed to discuss the Gandhi government's position on the NPT and the question of nuclear security guarantees. Together, Jha and Sarabhai possessed the political and technological expertise to tackle the most intractable questions concerning the country's nuclear program and the policies associated with it.

On April 19, 1967, they met with President Johnson to discuss the Soviet draft text on nuclear security guarantees for nonnuclear countries. The Indian delegation wanted to know what the US president thought of the Soviet suggestion of a blanket nuclear security guarantee offered by both superpowers to all countries that did not possess nuclear weapons. On the advice of his national security advisor, Walt Rostow, the US president remarked to Sarabhai and Jha that the Soviet text was "very interesting" but he remained noncommittal.[85] Rostow had advised Johnson in a memo prior to the meeting to do nothing about the Soviet text. Rostow's position was that although the draft did not "look too onerous, at first glance," it precluded a US first-use policy of nuclear weapons against adversaries, which could become militarily and politically disadvantageous when applied to countries where US forces were directly involved, such as against North Korea and North Vietnam.[86] At the meeting, however, President Johnson did not miss a beat as he reminded his Indian visitors that he would very much appreciate if Prime Minister Gandhi were to support the US war in Vietnam.

That very same day, April 19, the Indian prime minister sent a letter to the French president through the Indian embassy in Paris. In the letter, Indira Gandhi told Charles de Gaulle that India's national security concerns with respect to China's military might were too substantial to forsake the development of nuclear weapons—the key commitment that accession to the NPT would require.[87] Prime Minister Gandhi had maintained good terms with President de Gaulle since becoming the Indian prime minister and had consulted the French leader from time to time on foreign policy questions. In addition, her government aides even closely observed the disputes between the French and the US governments over NATO to assess the credibility of US nuclear security assurances. In De Gaulle's response to Gandhi about a month later, he stated that he completely understood India's decision. He reaffirmed the French decision to also not sign the NPT on grounds that the treaty did not promote the ultimate goal of genuine disarmament.[88]

Upon his return to New Delhi, L. K. Jha prepared a note for the prime minister's secretariat in which he concluded that "a political guarantee is possible, but a legal guarantee is impossible."[89] "What would be negotiable," he wrote, "is a guarantee in a language which politically implies a firm commitment to help, but is not as water-tight as a Treaty of Alliance." Jha added that the French foreign minister Maurice Couve de Murville had drawn his attention to the fact that "even Article 5 of the NATO Alliance merely contains a promise of help and not of full-fledged counter-attack."[90]

According to Jha, a legal guarantee meant little because "[i]n a crisis, the guaranteeing powers can always, if they so wish, wriggle out of even a formal Treaty, leave alone a unilateral Declaration." In other words, given India's nonaligned status in the Cold War, nuclear security guarantees obtained outside of alliances were the only politically feasible option. More importantly, nuclear security guarantees were considered to be so unreliable that even an alliance treaty did not make them adequately credible. Jha was convinced that India's national security depended on the persistence of the Sino-Soviet and Sino-US rivalries. So long as the United States and the Soviet Union continued to oppose "Chinese domination," wrote Jha, India could "count on these two Powers acting" to provide military support to India in times of crisis.[91]

Jha's recommendations encapsulated in his note from May 3, 1967, charted India's policy toward the NPT specifically and the global nonproliferation regime more generally. Jha proposed that regardless of a suitable nuclear security guarantee for India, the Gandhi government must not permanently relinquish its right to develop nuclear weapons. He wrote: "We should make it clear that we are not prepared to tie our hands in perpetuity against making nuclear weapons—guarantee or no guarantee."[92] At the same time, he recommended that the Indian government not change its official policy against producing nuclear weapons. He advised that while the government "should not abandon our policy of not developing nuclear weapons for the present," its efforts "should concentrate a little more on developing our missile capacity which, incidentally, is not affected by the Treaty on non-proliferation."

Indeed, the NPT was overwhelmingly aimed at preventing more countries from developing their own nuclear weapons rather than regulating the arsenals of those nations that had already conducted their nuclear weapons tests. The treaty defined no mechanism for controlling the development of delivery vehicles for nuclear weapons, whether they be airplanes, missiles, or submarines. Until the Missile Technology Control Regime was formed in 1987, there were no multilateral instruments in place to prevent countries from acquiring missile capabilities, although restrictions were sometimes imposed by the US government on a case-by-case basis. For example, the DAE requested that NASA provide technologies for Scout rockets, but the US space agency refused on grounds that those rockets had military uses. The leaders of India's nuclear and space programs thus preserved their freedom of action by procuring—from a variety of technology partners—technologies that were proverbial "ploughshares" (rockets and satellite launch vehicles) but could be easily transformed into "swords" (missiles).

Chinese Hydrogen Bomb and Sikkim Clashes

When China successfully tested its first thermonuclear weapon on June 17, 1967, the Gandhi government's geopolitical anxieties increased several folds. The weapon could be either dropped from an aircraft or by a missile.[93] The Chinese government accomplished this technologically sophisticated and militarily impressive feat within thirty-two months of its first nuclear weapon test. By contrast, the United States took eighty-six months and the Soviet Union took seventy-five months to reach that same milestone. This was China's sixth nuclear test. It placed the Chinese nuclear program ahead of that of France, which by then had conducted several unsuccessful thermonuclear tests.[94] Coming on the heels of the Jha-Sarabhai tour discussing nuclear security guarantees, the affirmation of Chinese thermonuclear weapons capability further raised the stakes for the Indian government. China's pariah status in the world at the time meant that it was not going to sign the NPT, just like it had not been part of the Limited Test Ban Treaty. To Indian policymakers, it mattered that the NPT would not limit Chinese nuclear weapons capability in any way.

Sino-Indian military tensions increased in the fall of 1967 at the Sikkim-Tibet border along the geopolitically vulnerable Chumbi Valley of Tibet. There were three Himalayan passes—Jelep La, Nathu La, and Cho La—in northeastern Sikkim along Chumbi Valley, allowing easy access to Lhasa and major towns of southern Tibet (see map 3). In September and October 1967, the Indian Army and the PLA clashed at the Nathu and Cho La.[95] The Sino-Indian skirmish at Nathu La in September 1967 led to nearly a hundred Indian casualties, and the Cho La clash on October 1 lasted for the entire day.

Sikkim was a small Himalayan kingdom between Nepal and Bhutan with Tibet to the north and the Indian state of West Bengal to the south. It was ruled by its hereditary monarch or Chogyal of the Namgyal dynasty. The Namgyals were of the Bhutia ethnic group, originally hailing from Tibet. They practiced Tibetan Buddhism like the Lepchas, the original inhabitants of Sikkim. Under the 1817 and 1861 treaties with the British East India Company and the British Crown, respectively, the Chogyal of Sikkim accepted British control over its foreign relations, trade, and defense. With decolonization imminent and British paramountcy about to end, Palden Thondup Namgyal, the crown prince of Sikkim, lobbied hard with the British to not be reduced to an Indian "princely state," like Travancore or Kashmir on grounds that Sikkim had never been part of India "geographically, ethnically, or racially."[96] The monarchy wanted to maintain the status quo by continuing its treaty relations with the independent Indian government.

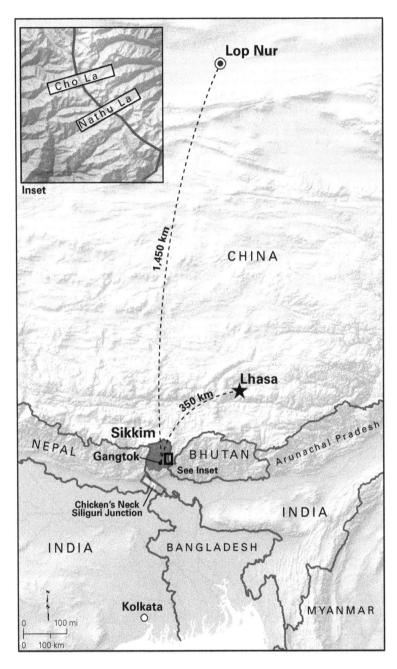

MAP 3. Sikkim's geopolitical significance. Credit: Scott Walker, Harvard Map Collection.

In December 1947, the prodemocracy Sikkim State Congress, made up of the Hindu Nepali ethnic majority, had called for a "merger" with India—a plea that Prime Minister Nehru rejected. Nehru preferred to retain Sikkim's status as a geographical buffer between Tibet and India, as had been the case during British colonial rule.[97] The Nepali population had settled in Sikkim to work in British tea plantations and copper mines, gradually increasing more in size than the traditional ethnic group of the Bhutia-Lepchas. The Nepali majority felt politically and economically disenfranchised in Sikkim. In May 1949, the Sikkim State Congress had violently agitated against Chogyal Tashi Namgyal and besieged the royal palace such that he had to be protected by the Indian Army. The Nehru government sent in more troops to Gangtok, Sikkim's capital, to restore the political authority of the monarch.

The Communist victory in the Chinese Civil War in October 1949, and Chinese entry into Tibet the following year, set the geopolitical stage in which Sikkim became a vassal state between two major powers, yet again. Under the terms of the India-Sikkim Treaty of 1950, the Indian government became responsible for the kingdom's foreign policy, defense, and strategic communications, just like the British colonial government had been prior to India's independence. The treaty retained the kingdom's status as a "protectorate," with the Indian government replacing the British colonial authority. The Chogyal was permitted a small group of decorated bodyguards, called the Sikkim Guards, but no military. He was forbidden from buying weaponry and developing any official contact, informal or formal, with foreign powers.[98] The dewan of Sikkim became responsible for Sikkim's internal matters, jointly nominated by the Chogyal and the Indian government, while an Indian political officer, usually a high-level MEA official, became the Indian government's highest representative in Sikkim.[99]

Since the 1950s, Chinese foreign policy propaganda had claimed Sikkim to be one of the "five fingers of China" along with Bhutan, Nepal, North-East Frontier Agency (later, Arunachal Pradesh), and Tibet. With Chinese repression in Tibet, Sikkim and particularly the town of Kalimpong in northern West Bengal became home to a significant body of elite Tibetans, including members of the Dalai Lama's family.[100] Mao Zedong and Zhou Enlai grew suspicious of the sizable Tibetan presence in the kingdom, even though the Nehru government continued to curb Tibetan activities in Sikkim and India. In December 1959, as Sino-Indian tensions had soared in the wake of the fourteenth Dalai Lama being offered refuge in India, the Sikkimese government agreed to permanently host an Indian military battalion in Gangtok, Sikkim's capital. Baleshwar Prasad, the dewan of Sikkim, and the crown prince "agreed that under the present circumstances which would continue indefinitely, there was a definite need for stationing permanently an army unit in Gangtok."[101]

Months prior to the 1962 war, the Chinese government had even made a full-fledged policy proposal to Sikkim, Bhutan, Nepal, North-East Frontier Agency, and Nagaland (the site of a violent secessionist movement against India) to become part of the Confederation of Himalayan States.[102] Throughout the 1960s, broadcasts from Radio Lhasa made references to "Sino-Sikkim" relations, negating the 1950 India-Sikkim treaty that had transformed Sikkim into an Indian protectorate. The 1962 Sino-India War transformed Sikkim from a geopolitical buffer zone into a long-term battlefield. The situation led to gradual discontent in the Sikkim Durbar or the royal court. Sikkim, though not fully sovereign, began to protest actions by the Indian Army on its territory.

Protests from the Sikkim Durbar began before the war and continued thereafter. Crown Prince Palden Namgyal was at the forefront of those complaints. In January to March 1962, the Indian Army sought to build a mortar firing range in Monmoi Chhu, a "sacred place" with a lake that was used for grazing by the locals and visits by the royal family. Crown Prince Namgyal suggested that the Indian authorities locate their mortar ranges in "other areas near Bhutan," bemoaning that Indian military was "asking for an area more than 20 times what we had committed."[103] In December 1962, Sikkim's forest ranger filed a report against the Indian Army for unauthorized deforestation of private land. The report noted that Indian military officers were "cutting trees and poles mercilessly" at Fourth Mile in northern Sikkim.[104] The Indian Army were felling trees to emplace canons targeting the PLA on Sikkim's border with Tibet. In response, the Indian government informed its Sikkimese counterpart that "in view of the emergency" since the 1962 war, the Indian government expected a Sikkimese representative to "mark the trees at the spot and make them available expeditiously."[105] By 1964, the Indian Army was routinely vacating the kingdom's inhabitants and livestock in eastern Sikkim for its artillery firing practice, leading to frequent objections from the Sikkim Durbar.[106]

Crown Prince Palden Thondup Namgyal's accession to the throne in December 1963 and the arrival in Gangtok of his wife, US socialite Hope Cooke, as the queen consort or Gyalmo, attracted international attention to the otherwise quiet kingdom. Cooke's uncle was US diplomat Selden Chapin. As Indo-Sikkimese relations grew more strained in the latter half of the 1960s, Cooke became a publicly controversial figure. She even penned a bulletin for Gangtok's Institute of Tibetology calling upon the Indian government to return Darjeeling (in the Indian state of West Bengal) to Sikkim, which was originally leased to the British in 1835.[107] The Bombay-based tabloid newspaper *Blitz* called Cooke a CIA agent, who "was aiming to put up US Bomber and Rocket bases in Sikkim and driving a wedge between India and Sikkim," leading the Chogyal to write directly to Prime Minister Gandhi to complain.[108] The Chogyal's letter to Gandhi dated June 30, 1967, arrived at a time when the Gandhi government was reeling from the Chinese thermonuclear weapon test. As Sino-Indian border tensions in Sikkim soared in the fall of 1967, Indian foreign secretary T. N. Kaul reassured the Chogyal through the Indian political officer N. B. Menon: "We are glad morale of our troops and people of Sikkim is high. You can rest assured that we shall not allow Chinese to cross the border. It seems they have realised our determination to defend the border and are refraining from attempting any further violations in spite of their radio propaganda. We have to live with this situation for some time to come until the Chinese realise the folly of their ways."[109]

From the point of view of Indian military operations, Sikkim occupied one of the most strategic and exposed geographical regions on the eastern China-India border.[110] The geopolitical significance of this small Himalayan kingdom had already been driven home for the Indian government during the 1962 Sino-India War when anxieties were stoked about a potential Chinese military takeover of the Siliguri corridor, also known as the "chicken's neck." During the 1965 India-Pakistan War, these fears were resurrected with the Chinese threat to open a second front on India's eastern border. The Sino-Indian military clashes at Nathu La and Cho La in 1967, combined with the stark reality of China's thermonuclear and missile capabilities, only served to exacerbate the Gandhi government's geopolitical insecurities.

Journalist Raj Chengappa claimed that the Chinese hydrogen bomb test gave renewed impetus to the underground nuclear explosions project at BARC, which Homi Bhabha had launched a month after the first Chinese nuclear test.[111] The Gandhi government might have come close to conducting an underground nuclear test in 1967. Dwarka Nath Chatterjee would make this claim to French officials during his term as the Indian ambassador in Paris (1969–76). In a June 1974 meeting with Geoffroy Chodron de Courcel, the secretary general of the French Ministry of Foreign Affairs, Chatterjee would claim that the Gandhi government was "ready for an underground nuclear explosion since 1967" but delayed it "owing to circumstances."[112]

India's Official Response to the NPT

In April 1968, just before the draft NPT was going to be debated at the UN General Assembly's Political Committee in New York, Prime Minister Gandhi's secretary Parmeshwar Narayan (P. N.) Haksar instructed the Indian representative to the United Nations, G. Parthasarathy, to "abstain on the resolution as whole."[113] Haksar's instructions were intended for the Indian government to maintain a low profile at UN General Assembly debate. The Gandhi government had decided to not sign the NPT, which was "based on coincidence of interest between USSR and USA" but that "will not lead to what we all desire, namely, some tangible steps toward disarmament, both nuclear and conventional."[114]

Haksar recommended a series of measured responses to the Indian representative. He was to state the Gandhi government's official position against the NPT but "avoid a polemical tone against the nuclear powers." While he might "comment on the special position of India vis-à-vis Chinese nuclear threat," the guidance was to "neither overplay that threat nor underplay it." Haksar even advised to "not mention Pakistan."[115] While recommending that Parthasarathy urge nuclear security assurances be delinked from the NPT, Haksar recommended that he neither criticize the nature of assurances nor propose any specific amendments to the draft resolution. More importantly, the Indian representative "should not spearhead any move for delay and postponement" of the timetable for the conclusion of the treaty. He should instead "go along with the Afro-Asian group" of countries and take care "not to be singled out in this process."[116] When, after six weeks of debate, the draft NPT was put to vote at the UN General Assembly, it received ninety-two votes in favor, four against (Albania, Cuba, Tanzania, and Zambia), and twenty-two abstentions. India was one of those twenty-two countries—not singled out, as Haksar had instructed Parthasarathy.[117]

When the NPT was formally opened for signature on July 1, 1968, the Gandhi government had already refused to sign it. They characterized the treaty as being discriminatory against countries that did not possess nuclear weapons because it established two categories of signatories—"nuclear weapon states" and "non-nuclear weapon states." The former were those countries that had already conducted tests of a nuclear explosive device by January 1, 1967. In other words, China would become a nuclear weapon state under the NPT, but India would not qualify as a nuclear weapon state even if it conducted a nuclear explosion in the future. To not accede to the treaty, therefore, was necessary for the Gandhi government to retain its freedom of action.

With the Gandhi government's refusal to accede to the NPT, the DAE attracted the world's attention with its technological capability to produce a nuclear weapon, long-standing opposition to safeguards, and multidecade experience in nuclear technologies. Even though the global nonproliferation regime was in its formative stages, the Indian government publicly presented itself as an opponent and an outlier through its vocal criticism of the regime. Against this backdrop, technologies related to outer space offered opportunities for freedom of action to the leaders of India's nuclear and space programs because of the absence of multilateral regulation of space technologies and their close association with delivery vehicles for nuclear weapons.

India's Technopolitical Responses to the NPT

In August 1968, when the United Nations hosted an international conference in Vienna on the "Exploration and Peaceful Uses of Outer Space," Vikram Sarabhai was appointed as the conference's chairman. Space technologies were still new to most developing countries that, unlike India, had not invested vast financial and political resources in that area of research and development. In his address at the conference, Sarabhai touted in typical Rostovian fashion how technologies of spaceflight could enable underdeveloped countries to "leapfrog from a state of backwardness and poverty" to a hypothetical state of development.[118] That same year, the Indian Ministry of Defence formed a "missile panel" at the Defence Research and Development Organisation (DRDO) in New Delhi. A. P. J. Abdul Kalam, an eminent aeronautical engineer, was a member of the missile panel while he worked on space technologies under Sarabhai. Kalam had visited NASA's Langley Research Center, Goddard Space Flight Center, and Wallops Island launch facility in 1962–63 as part of a DAE-NASA collaboration on developing sounding rockets, or research rockets that carry scientific instruments into space.[119] Also in 1968, Sarabhai tasked Kalam and fellow aerospace engineer Nambi Narayanan with developing rocket-assisted takeoff systems for military aircrafts based on the hardware of a Soviet engine.[120]

The Indian Air Force needed the rocket-assisted systems for the Soviet-supplied Sukhoi-22 and the Kurt Tank–designed HF-24 jetfighters in order to take off from high-altitude airfields in the Himalayas. Kalam and his colleagues succeeded in delivering these systems to the Indian Air Force. In other words, this was further evidence that Sarabhai, while publicly pushing space technologies as peaceful means to attain national development goals, was not shy about using these technologies for military purposes. There was intentional overlap in expertise and projects in space and defense in order for India to retain freedom of action—a situation made possible largely because Sarabhai wore many official hats and was popular in India's corridors of power.

In August 1969, Sarabhai established the Indian Space Research Organisation (ISRO) as an independent government body under the DAE. He remained the DAE secretary and became the chairman of ISRO. Thus, the scientific elites at the helm of India's nuclear enterprise wove a veil of false distinction between their peaceful and military pursuits of high technology by means of the institutional separation of the space program from the nuclear program. The former was thereby portrayed as unambiguously peaceful and distinct from the latter. Soon afterward, Sarabhai appointed Kalam to ISRO to work on satellite launch vehicles. Kalam would later work on ballistic missile development at the DRDO based on satellite launch vehicle technologies at ISRO.

As the NPT reduced the openness of the global atomic marketplace, the leaders of India's nuclear and space programs adopted a series of steps to keep multiple technological options open. First, the DAE signed a protocol with the Soviet Union in April 1968 for scientific cooperation in mathematics, physics, astrophysics, and nuclear physics. Although very broad in its scope, this protocol was the basis for the commencement and subsequent expansion of nuclear and space cooperation between the DAE and its Soviet counterpart. The second step was the DAE obtaining rockets and breeder reactor technologies from France. The Centaure rocket technologies arrived from the French space agency, the *Centre National d'Etudes Spatiales*, at a time when NASA was refusing to share the technology for its Scout rockets. Ultimately, the timely French space assistance boosted the DAE's indigenous rocket development efforts. The acquisition of breeder reactor technologies from the CEA enabled the DAE to develop a credible civilian-use justification for reprocessing plutonium from the CIRUS. The third step was the DAE signing nuclear cooperation agreements with Brazil and Argentina as a supplier of nuclear technologies to those countries. In anticipation of an NPT Exporters' Committee being formed, the DAE took on the mantle of "nuclear exporter" outside the treaty. The fourth step was the quiet continuation of the research being carried out by the underground nuclear explosions group at BARC, while Sarabhai's space-related endeavors received public attention both in India and abroad. This meant that while the DAE pursued sounding rocket and satellite launch vehicle technologies, it also kept moving ahead with its efforts to develop a testable nuclear device.

As the following sections will demonstrate, the leaders of India's nuclear and space program concurrently pursued nuclear and space technologies that could serve both national security and national development goals, through diversifying both technologies and suppliers. Notwithstanding national security concerns with respect to Chinese military might, there was no mad rush to develop nuclear weapons because the security dangers were not existential threats to the Indian nation-state. The 1967 border skirmishes on the Sikkim-Tibet border, though serious, did not imperil India's survival.

The leaders of India's nuclear and space programs had worked on missile technologies since at least 1968, but those initial efforts were unsuccessful because of technological barriers. Likewise, US policymakers were concerned about India's capability to produce nuclear weapons, but by July and August 1966, they were also convinced that they had exhausted most of the policy options that might actually work. US officials intended to attain their nonproliferation objectives vis-à-vis the DAE, but the nature of procured technologies made them difficult to control. Both sides encountered obstacles to attaining their respective objectives, but not for any dearth of effort.

Fast Neutron Reactor from the Soviet Union

In April 1968, Dr. Igor Dmitrievich Morokhov, the first deputy chairman of the State Committee on the Utilization of Atomic Energy of the Soviet Union, led his country's delegation during its two-week visit to India. The Soviet delegation visited BARC in Trombay and various DAE facilities in Bombay and Tarapur, the uranium mine in Jaduguda, the heavy water plant in Nangal, the reactor site in Madras, and the Atomic Minerals Directorate in Hyderabad. At the end of the visit, Morokhov and Sarabhai signed a protocol for bilateral cooperation "covering a wide range of activities in the application of the peaceful uses of atomic energy."[121]

When Sarabhai had visited Moscow in February 1967, he had discussed the possibility of cooperation between the DAE and its Soviet counterpart.[122] Since then, two DAE teams had visited the Soviet Union—one to hold talks on "reactors and generation of power using atomic energy" and the other one to deal with the "production and use of radioisotopes in industry, agriculture, and medicine." The Indo-Soviet protocol of April 1968 was the first such collaboration between the two countries. It laid the foundation for further bilateral cooperation between their nuclear and space programs. Coming at a time of closer geopolitical ties between the governments of Indira Gandhi and Soviet leader Leonid Brezhnev, and coinciding with India's opposition to the NPT, the 1968 Indo-Soviet protocol was a significant milestone.

When Dr. V. Ranganathan, chief of the science division within India's Planning Commission, discovered in October 1968 that the DAE had deputed a TIFR Physics Group to the Soviet Union to discuss experimental high-energy physics under the Indo-Soviet protocol, he sought the involvement of the Ministry of Education. The argument furthered by Planning Commission officials like Ranganathan was that if the purpose of the Physics Group was education and research, then the appropriate government ministry needed to be involved, namely, the Ministry of Education. In response, the DAE informed the Planning Commission that "proposals for collaboration between India and USSR in the peaceful uses of atomic energy will be considered by the Department of Atomic Energy who would take necessary action and that the Ministry of Education or any other ministry is not concerned."[123] M. A. Vellodi, joint secretary of the DAE, bluntly stated in his note to Ranganathan that "proposals for collaboration" as well as "all necessary action in the implementation of these proposals will be taken by this Department."[124] Thus unfolded the institutional cold wars within India.

To US actors who closely observed the Soviet visit, those at the helm of India's nuclear program played down the significance of the Indo-Soviet protocol. BARC director Homi Sethna dismissed it as "seventeen pages of crap."[125] Sethna told US policymakers that in light of Soviet obsession with secrecy in nuclear matters, very little substantive cooperation was anticipated between the DAE and its Soviet counterpart. This, however, would prove to be far from true. Sethna was either deliberately understating the significance of the protocol or could not foresee the eventual benefits that the DAE—particularly BARC—would gain from cooperation with Soviet scientists and engineers. Indo-Soviet collaboration in experimental high-energy physics would directly benefit the BARC explosions group through its cooperation with the high-energy physics laboratory at Dubna. The TIFR report produced by its Physics Group noted that the attitude of Dubna's scientists "was extremely cooperative and positive" and that "Dubna being an international institute would welcome our participation and collaboration."[126]

In late 1968, DAE secretary Vikram Sarabhai approved of the construction of a fast neutron reactor, PURNIMA, to be built based on the designs of the Soviet IBR-30 reactor of Dubna.[127] PURNIMA stood for "Plutonium Reactor for Neutronic Investigations in Multiplying Assemblies," and it belonged to the family of fast reactors that were being developed in the Soviet Union, France, and the United States at the time. DAE teams visited Dubna as part of Indo-Soviet cooperation in experimental high-energy physics while BARC physicist P. K. Iyengar was PURNIMA's chief designer. The fast neutron reactor was constructed in Trombay, where the nuclear explosions project was based, and it satisfied the DAE's multifaceted technological goals.

It was an experimental research reactor that created learning opportunities for BARC scientists and engineers in both breeder reactor technologies and nuclear explosions. The PURNIMA stoked Sarabhai's interest because it was technologically associated with the breeder reactor project that he was developing in Kalpakkam in cooperation with the French CEA. Although PURNIMA was based on Soviet reactor designs, it was built "as a mockup of the proposed air-cooled 30-kW Kalpakkam Pulsed Fast Reactor" that was going to be built based on French designs.[128] To explain the reactor's proliferation potential, the physicist M. V. Ramana wrote that "[w]hat was learnt from the Purnima reactor was physical details like, how long a neutron could survive before it was absorbed by plutonium, and how effective different materials would be in reflecting neutrons."[129] He added that those details "were useful both in building fast neutron reactors and in designing a nuclear weapon with a plutonium core."[130]

In 1969, Sino-Soviet military tensions increased leading to border clashes along the Ussuri River. During the conflict, the Soviet government threatened to use its nuclear weapons against China. In response, Mao Zedong ordered the Chinese Communist leadership to evacuate Beijing that October, and Chinese defense minister Lin Bao raised the country's military to the highest alert level.[131] As the Sino-Soviet border clashes continued, Soviet leader Leonid Brezhnev delivered a speech at the Communist International Conference in June 1969. At this conference, which was boycotted by China, the Soviet government first floated the idea of a collective security arrangement in Asia.[132] The following month, several Soviet officials made direct overtures to Indian officials emphasizing "the central role they assign to India in their plan for collective security."[133]

In separate conversations in New Delhi—the Soviet ambassador to the Indian foreign secretary, the Soviet chargé d'affaires to the Indian joint secretary, and again the Soviet ambassador to the Indian foreign minister—Soviet representatives assured Indian officials that Brezhnev's suggestions for a collective security arrangement were "not a military proposal, and that it was open to all countries of Asia regardless of ideology to join."[134] The Soviet representatives claimed that the proposals were "for security but not through military methods" and that they were not particularly directed "against any country," even though Soviet-Chinese military and political hostilities were widely known.[135]

In July 1969, the MEA prepared a secret note expressing interest in the trade-related components of the Brezhnev proposals and suggested efforts that could serve the Indian government's geopolitical interests. The note suggested that "we could perhaps propose to the USSR that they could build on the existing Afghan-Iran tentative ideas for building major trade routes from Afghanistan to Iran," even though "obduracy of Pakistan in opposing [such] cooperation" could be a stumbling block. The proposal put forth in the MEA's note was imaginative. It suggested that "[if] the Soviet Union can create a grouping independently of Pakistan which Pakistan will find beneficial to join, it is a policy in which China cannot compete and in which America cannot do much damage to Soviet influence."[136] The MEA note went on to claim that, as a result, "America would hesitate to restart an arms policy which would alienate India and would not benefit Pakistan," while "China cannot compete in this policy of building bridges between India and Pakistan."[137]

From July 31 to August 1, 1969, President Richard Nixon and his national security advisor Henry Kissinger were on a state visit to New Delhi—their one stop among visits to many world capitals—during which they held two meetings with Prime Minister Indira Gandhi and key members of her cabinet. Change was in the air in US foreign policy. It was manifest in Nixon and Kissinger's nonchalance about Chinese nuclear weapons and missile capabilities and their indifference toward Brezhnev's proposals for collective security arrangements in Asia. The Indian government representatives noted that the "American side indicated that they had no desire to take part in any anti-Chinese campaign or policy" and that "they would like to improve relations with that country and had recently made small gestures of relaxation which had not so far been reciprocated."[138]

With respect to the Brezhnev proposals, "the Americans felt this was formulated by the Soviet Government for its own purposes" but that it was "vague and not very clear." Repeating the tone from the Guam Doctrine (also known as the Nixon Doctrine), which had been proclaimed in July, the US visitors said that collective security initiatives for Asia "should be from Asians."[139] While discussing the military threat posed by China to nonnuclear countries with Indian foreign secretary Triloki Nath (T. N.) Kaul and the defense secretary H. C. Sarrin, Kissinger stated unequivocally that "the US reaction depends on what the US interests are" in Asia.[140] President Nixon and Kissinger then left for Pakistan for a meeting with President Yahya Khan and continued on to Romania to meet with General Nicolae Ceausescu. The die was cast for Sino-US rapprochement.

In October 1969, D. P. Dhar, the Indian ambassador in Moscow, urged T. N. Kaul to move fast on finalizing the draft of the Indo-Soviet treaty: "How long can we delay its finalization without risking to create suspicion in the Soviet mind? . . . Fast changes are taking place in Sino-Soviet relations, Pakistan-Soviet relations, and if we are wide awake, we can convert the course of these changes to our advantage."[141] As negotiations progressed over the next year between Prime Minister Indira Gandhi and Soviet premier Alexei Kosygin, the Indian ambassador noted a "new warmth in the Soviet attitude" and observed that the "old terseness and calculated irritation in their behavior [had] disappeared."[142] Before the 1969 Sino-Soviet conflict had completely petered out, China conducted its first underground nuclear weapon test and an airdropped nuclear weapon test both in September 1969.

Breeder Reactors and Rockets from France

Breeder reactors had occupied an important place in the DAE's reactor program ever since Homi Bhabha announced his futuristic "three-stage plan" to attain self-sufficiency for India in nuclear energy production. Breeders were to be used as second-stage reactors before the DAE could use thorium-based fuel for third-stage reactors. The underlying idea was to eventually make use of India's abundantly available monazite that contains that radioactive metal thorium. France's CEA was one of the western European leaders in breeder reactor technologies, and it was willing to share reactor designs with the DAE. Sarabhai had visited Paris in July 1966 to begin discussions with the CEA about purchasing designs for the French fast breeder reactor, Rapsodie, which was built in Cadarache—the first of its kind. Sarabhai also sought the CEA's commitment for the construction of heavy water plants in India. This was followed by two separate visits to France in January 1968, the first by Sarabhai and the second by BARC director Homi Sethna. The DAE wanted to conduct joint research with the CEA on fast breeder reactor technologies with the eventual goal being Indian construction of such a reactor for experimental purposes in Kalpakkam, India. The first contract for this joint project was signed on April 11, 1969.

Under the terms of the contract, the DAE would acquire designs for both the Rapsodie and Phénix reactors, the latter of which was still under construction at the time. Additionally, a team of Indian engineers would receive technical training in breeder technologies in Cadarache. The 1969 contract was followed by further agreements in 1971, 1972, 1973, and 1974. Since breeder reactors were plutonium fueled and plutonium producing, the DAE was able to justify the stockpiling of plutonium for civilian purposes.[143]

Between 1965 and 1969, the DAE sent a group of Indian scientists and engineers headed by M. R. Kurup to France for training in solid-propellant rocket fuel and production of Centaur rockets. The Centaur contract thus provided significant learning opportunities for the DAE / ISRO personnel and enabled them to successfully develop the Rohini sounding rocket.[144] The DAE launched its first indigenously built sounding rocket, the Rohini-75, from its Thumba launching facility in November 1967.

India as a Nuclear Supplier

In 1969, the DAE signed two bilateral cooperation agreements—one with Brazil and the other with Argentina—in peaceful uses of atomic energy. The two documents were identical. Both were five-year agreements involving the exchange of information on peaceful uses of nuclear energy, the lease of materials and equipment when necessary, and the training of scientific personnel.[145] The agreements were quite vague but they made it clear that the exchange of information would exclude "information of a classified nature or any information which either party is not free to exchange because it has been obtained from or developed in collaboration with a third party."[146] The Brazilian government ratified the India-Brazil agreement on April 10, 1969. About a month later, Vikram Sarabhai wrote to Oscar Armando Quihillalt, the president of the *Commission Nacional de Energia Atomica* in Buenos Aires, Argentina, expressing that he was "extremely happy" to receive Quihillalt's suggestion that "we might consider the possibility of signing an agreement for collaboration between our two countries in the peaceful uses of atomic energy."[147]

Like India, neither of those two Latin American countries had signed the NPT.[148] The treaty's so-called grand bargain was that its members would be guaranteed access to nuclear technologies, equipment, and materials for peaceful purposes. Access to the global marketplace had thus become conditional, based on accession to the treaty. The DAE's nuclear cooperation with the two Latin American countries thus flew in the face of the global nonproliferation regime. The meetings of the Western Suppliers Group, or the Ottawa Group—a multilateral export control arrangement—had been suspended after 1967, but a new multilateral export control body had not been formed.[149] As a result, there was a window of opportunity for non-NPT countries to create supply chains among themselves. Such supply mechanisms were perhaps subversive from the point of view of the global nonproliferation regime, but they did not violate established international law. US and Canadian actors pursued efforts throughout 1969 to either reactivate the Western Suppliers Group or establish a similar platform to regulate the "supply side" of the global atomic marketplace. This eventually took the form of the NPT Exporters Committee, also known as the Zangger Committee. It informally met in Vienna in July 1970 for the first time, chaired by the Swiss professor Claude Zangger, to discuss detailed mechanisms of safeguards and export controls under Article III of the NPT.[150]

BARC Explosions Group and the Sarabhai Profile

The scholarship on India's nuclear and space programs often portrays Vikram Sarabhai as someone who did not share Homi Bhabha's eagerness for the DAE's nuclear weapons development.[151] This is because, as the DAE secretary, Sarabhai prioritized the space program over the "Study of Nuclear Explosions for Peaceful Purposes" that had been underway at BARC since November 1964 (see chapter 4). This drove a wedge between him and BARC scientists Raja

Ramanna, Homi Sethna, P. K. Iyengar, and R. Chidambaram, who had been working on nuclear explosions under Bhabha's stewardship.[152] The underground nuclear explosions program, however, continued quietly while Sarabhai expanded ISRO's technological partnerships with the United States, the Soviet Union, and France, among other nations.

After Vikram Sarabhai approved the construction of the fast neutron PURNIMA reactor to be built based on designs for the Soviet reactor in Dubna, the BARC explosions group informally funded the reactor. They facilitated its funding to ensure that the reactor did not factor into the formal DAE budget, thereby avoiding the Planning Commission's financial oversight, fending off foreign intelligence, and possibly keeping Sarabhai from actively meddling in the project.[153] P. K. Iyengar would later publicly claim that the PURNIMA reactor "gave considerable experience and helped to benchmark calculations regarding the behavior of a chain-reacting system made out of plutonium."[154] The reactor, Iyengar stated, gave "[v]ery clever physicists" the opportunity to "calculate the time behavior of the core of a bomb on isotropic compression." The calculations allowed the scientists at BARC to investigate "[w]hat the critical parameters would be, how to achieve optimum explosive power, and its dependence on the first self-sustaining neutron trigger."[155] In other words, through PURNIMA, Indian scientists learned to develop the trigger mechanism that sets off a fission reaction in a plutonium-core implosion device.

In his ambitious ten-year plan for 1970–80, announced in May 1970, Sarabhai mapped out the development of an indigenously built satellite, its launch vehicle, and a launch site, as well as the development of advanced satellites. The plan, which was officially titled "Atomic Energy and Space Research: A Profile for the Decade," became known simply as the "Sarabhai Profile." In the plan, Sarabhai stressed the importance of research and development in both civilian and military domains of high technologies, with a dual emphasis on economic development and national defense: "I suggest it is necessary for us to develop competence in all advanced technologies useful for our development and defence, and to deploy them for the solution of our own particular problems, not for prestige, but based on sound technical and economic evaluation as well as political decision-making for a commitment of real resources."[156]

Sarabhai's ten-year plan explicitly mentioned ISRO's plans for the indigenous construction of a satellite launch vehicle for the purposes of communications, meteorology, and remote sensing. He and his subordinates at the DAE had already conducted a thorough cost analysis for achieving an indigenous satellite launch capability by 1968. The analysis had favored modeling the indigenous launch vehicle on the US Scout rocket. Even though NASA had refused to share its Scout rocket technology, Sarabhai and his team of aeronautical experts were hopeful that the solid-propellant, four-stage US rocket's designs could be successfully adapted to serve the DAE / ISRO's purposes. By 1971, its launch vehicle designs were completed, and Sarabhai chose the third of six designs that were presented to him. The first indigenous satellite launch vehicle (SLV) thus would be known as "SLV-3," and the project would be pursued by Sarabhai's successors.[157]

The Sarabhai Profile, which was publicly silent on the subject of nuclear explosions, was launched two months after the NPT entered into force on March 5, 1970. Sarabhai, however, continued to openly defend India's legal right to conduct PNEs in his conversations with US and Soviet officials. In a February 1968 meeting in New Delhi with the Soviet atomic energy chief V. S. Emelyanov, Sarabhai said that it was "dangerous to have certain technological advantages to be denied to some countries such as the use of atomic explosions but available for exploitation to the nuclear club."[158] He had also made a similar remark to the USAEC chairman Glenn Seaborg in January 1967 when Seaborg was visiting India.

In April 1970, the Chinese launch of a satellite into orbit ignited acute political criticism of the Gandhi government from leaders of the opposition parties in the Indian Parliament. George Fernandes, one of the foremost critics of Prime Minister Gandhi, called a motion in the Lok Sabha of the Indian Parliament demanding that the matter to be urgently discussed. The prime minister promptly sought Sarabhai's expertise. M. A. Vellodi, joint secretary of the DAE, prepared the response note that Sarabhai proofread and corrected before sending it back to the prime minister's secretariat. Sarabhai had known Vellodi from their time in IISc Bangalore, and it was at Sarabhai's invitation that Vellodi had joined the DAE to oversee government matters related to nuclear and space technologies.

Sarabhai instructed Vellodi to omit key technical details from the note prepared in response to Fernandes's motion in the Indian Parliament. These details concerned India's indigenous multistage rocket satellites, space electronics, and the DAE's cooperation with NASA on satellites. Sarabhai recommended that the details be replaced with a neutral statement: "The development by China was anticipated and demonstrates the high level of capability of that country in rocket technology."[159] This revision of Vellodi's response note played down the significance of the Chinese satellite test by calling it "anticipated." Sarabhai's decision to omit some of the details about India's space program from the note thus skillfully averted further parliamentary scrutiny. Indeed, this is a prime example of how the specialized expertise possessed by the leaders of India's nuclear program enabled them to dodge probing questions from politicians and bureaucrats, who were more generalists than specialists.

The DAE's cooperation with NASA on satellites, which Sarabhai had removed from Vellodi's note was a joint study with MIT's Lincoln Laboratories on a communication satellite, the designs of which were based on the laboratory's ongoing satellite development program for the US Air Force.[160] By the summer of 1970, Sarabhai had procured funding from the Ford Foundation for the project, thanks to the support of Jerome Wiesner and because of the DAE's long-standing cooperation with NASA. The joint study was completed by March 1971, and the satellite system was expected to be launched in India in 1975 as a large network of multipurpose geostationary satellites for telecommunications.[161] The DAE-NASA project would pave the way for the Indian National Satellite system for television broadcasting, launched in 1982.[162]

In September 1970, the Indian Planning Commission's Power Division made a cost-benefit analysis of the DAE's proposal for a "Nuclear-Powered Agro-Industrial Complex" in the Indian states of Gujarat and western Uttar Pradesh. Not only did the commission find flaws with the cost calculations for the project, but they actively advocated for hydroelectricity and coal rather than nuclear power plants.[163] The Planning Commission even questioned the methodology of the DAE's cost calculation to determine the viability of the project. It chided the DAE for not determining the cost of actual power production from nuclear reactors but instead focusing on the "indirect benefits accruing from the usage of power." The commission remarked that "if the same approach is adopted and sale proceeds of agricultural output in each State is accounted as return on investments on power development programs in each State, perhaps all the State Electricity Boards could be declared viable undertakings" for nuclear power, which was not clearly the case.[164]

Sarabhai had succeeded Bhabha as the chairman of the Electronics Committee. Under Sarabhai, the committee pursued the "ploughshares and swords" approach in both the nuclear and space technology domains but often encountered opposition from Planning Commission officials, who sought more transparency and accountability. At a meeting with the Planning Commission members, Vikram Sarabhai complained about what he called the "wrong policy" of the commission to levy excise duties on imported electronics components.[165] He said that it was unfair to impose such duties because "[t]he country still depended on imported equipment for a wide variety of things not only in defence but also in other areas like communication and broadcasting." Pitambar Pant of the Planning Commission replied that "a lot of things are being produced which are not important" and that the development of electronics was not progressing along "healthy lines." Pant advised an indignant Sarabhai to draw "a set of priorities for safe guarding [sic] our vital interests" and that the Electronics Committee "should have a policy" after all.

USAEC's Aide-Mémoire to the DAE

Vikram Sarabhai's relentless insistence that the NPT ought not to preclude the right of countries to conduct their own PNEs worried US actors. After being elected president of the IAEA General Conference held in September 1970, Sarabhai reaffirmed in Vienna the DAE's interest in PNEs. Two months later, on November 16, the USAEC sent an aide-mémoire to the DAE in which it formally stated what Glenn Seaborg had personally told Vikram Sarabhai in January 1967: the US government did not distinguish between nuclear explosions conducted for peaceful purposes from those for military purposes. The document added that US-supplied materials must not be used in Indian nuclear explosions.[166] The DAE never responded to the USAEC's aide-mémoire. What is known is that the CEA had invited Sarabhai to visit the Mururoa atolls in the Pacific Ocean in 1972 to witness the French nuclear weapons tests, and he had accepted their invitation.[167] In other words, Sarabhai's aversion to nuclear weapons based on the Gandhian philosophy of nonviolence was, therefore, more hagiographic than real.

Sarabhai's opposition to the nuclear explosions project at BARC in Trombay possibly stemmed from budgetary concerns inside the country, on the one hand, and the nonproliferation regime, on the other. As long as the nuclear and space programs remained under the DAE, the funds needed for BARC's nuclear explosions project would have encroached on the overall DAE budget and therefore, by extension, the budget for the space program. The Planning Commission officials, who determined the budget, were already seeking to expand their oversight of the financial implications of the DAE's activities.[168] Sarabhai also worried that foreign partners might halt technological cooperation in space technologies—space was both his passion and the perceived means for developing nuclear delivery vehicles—if they suspected the DAE's proliferation intent.

In fact, the separation of the space program from the nuclear program through the creation of ISRO thereby generated an artificial distinction between unambiguously peaceful space pursuits and ambiguous nuclear ambitions. Satish Dhawan, who would succeed Sarabhai to lead the newly formed Department of Space in 1972, would remain tepid about collaboration between the country's space program and the DRDO.[169] Technologies of spaceflight, nuclear fission, and defense were after all interrelated. On the subject of rockets, launch vehicles, and missiles, Dhawan once remarked, "What's the damn difference? Only the software! You make a few minor changes, and the damn thing goes differently."[170]

Conclusion

When US officials worried about the "Plowshare Loophole," they were predominantly concerned about India's development of a nuclear explosive device for supposedly civilian purposes. US officials such as Ambassador Chester Bowles and experts associated with the American Academy of Arts and Sciences therefore adopted a cost-based argument to dissuade India's leaders from developing nuclear weapons. They made the case that an effective nuclear deterrent against a country like China, which was militarily stronger and protected by the topography of the Himalayas and the Tibetan Plateau, was beyond India's economic means. The leaders of India's nuclear program largely ignored such economic arguments. They pursued rocket technologies to develop delivery vehicles before they had produced and tested an actual nuclear device. Concurrently, they kept rudimentary deterrent options theoretically open, such as mining the Himalayas with nuclear waste to prevent the PLA from a full-scale military invasion like they had done in October 1962.

This subversion of the perceived linear trajectory of nuclear proliferation by the DAE was noteworthy for several reasons. First, it defied US expectations and the conventional wisdom regarding the process of nuclear proliferation. The idea of this linear trajectory, which was based on the experiences of the superpowers and conjured in the minds of defense intellectuals at institutions such as the RAND Corporation, was premised on the following sequence of events: the production of fissile material, the development of nuclear explosive devices, tests of those devices (or nuclear weapons), the miniaturization of those weapons, and, finally, the acquisition of delivery vehicles such as airplanes and missiles to drop the miniaturized nuclear weapons on targets in adversarial countries. By developing rocket technologies related to ballistic missiles concurrently with nuclear explosive devices, the leaders of India's nuclear program overturned the received wisdom about how countries could or should develop their own nuclear weapons.

Second, Indian leaders' quest for freedom of action and legitimacy drove their subversion of the teleology of nuclear weapons development. Both Cold War superpowers were becoming more vigilant about the technologies, materials, and equipment that circulated within the atomic marketplace. India's nuclear program, which was dual use by design, thus struggled to remain legitimate in the face of the changing international rules of procurement and supply. The architects of India's nuclear program were determined to ensure that they were perceived as "innovators," who were playing by the rules, not "proliferators" violating them.[171] In other words, India's pursuit of space technologies (related to missiles) and its subversion of the conventional wisdom about nuclear weapons development were associated with its own goals of legitimacy.

Third, while the atomic marketplace was contracting with new rules set forth in the NPT and by the Zangger Committee, the domain of outer space technologies remained open. Although partially regulated, space technologies were not controlled through multilateral agreements to the same degree as nuclear technologies. The scientific and technical elites steering India's nuclear program thus attempted to preserve the program's legitimacy and freedom of action through an expanded space program. They formed technological collaboration with multiple reputable foreign institutions on both sides of the Cold War.

PART THREE

Unmaking and Making of India

CHAPTER 6

Fractured Worlds, 1970–1974

On November 12–13, 1970, tropical cyclone Bhola made landfall on the densely populated Bengal Delta of what was then East Pakistan.[1] The tidal wave "rose an estimated 25 feet above normal" with "winds of 100 or 150 miles per hour."[2] It submerged hundreds of low-lying islands, washing away homes, humans, and animals into the Bay of Bengal. The *New York Times* called the storm "the greatest disaster of the 20th century" in which more than five hundred thousand lives were lost and millions were left homeless.[3] Cholera and typhoid broke out in many areas. Communication and transportation breakdowns made relief work difficult.[4] Despite the unfolding tragedy in East Pakistan, the military administration of General Agha Mohammad Yahya Khan of Pakistan went ahead with the national and provincial elections, scheduled for December 7. For the first time since Pakistan's independence in 1947, its citizens were going to elect members of the National Assembly by popular vote.[5]

Ahead of the elections, President Nixon pledged US$10 million for disaster relief while the World Bank offered a comprehensive reconstruction plan worth US$185 million to the Pakistan government.[6] General Yahya's delayed and inadequate disaster relief, however, came under attack from several quarters, not least from Sheikh Mujibur Rahman, the firebrand leader of the Awami League, East Pakistan's dominant political party. Yahya's foot dragging in sending timely relief to cyclone-affected areas reignited anger in East Pakistan's people.[7] Many of them felt that the neglect resulted from Punjabi-majority West Pakistan's general apathy toward Bengali-speaking East Pakistan, already geographically separated by thousands of square miles of Indian territory. In response, leftist parties in East Pakistan called for independence and boycotted the elections, which only helped the Awami League.[8]

When the votes were counted on December 17, 1970, the Awami League won 160 seats in Pakistan's three hundred–member National Assembly and the majority of seats in the Provincial Assembly.[9] The election results meant that Mujibur Rahman would become the prime minister of Pakistan. He would lead an all–Awami League government and draft the country's first democratic constitution. In West Pakistan, none of the established political parties made substantial electoral gains, but former foreign minister Zulfikar Ali Bhutto's newly formed Pakistan People's Party won the majority of seats.[10]

West Pakistan's military and bureaucratic establishment could not imagine being subservient to East Pakistan's politicians. General Yahya's nightmare took a new turn on January 3, 1971. At a rally of two million people in Dhaka, East Pakistan's capital city, Mujibur Rahman called for the implementation of his 1966 Six Points, which had called for full provincial autonomy including a separate militia.[11] The lack of military protection of the eastern province during the 1965 India-Pakistan War had shocked the people of East Pakistan, who had felt vulnerable to an Indian military attack. Even though India did not invade, the press and the politicians in Dhaka had claimed that West Pakistan elites took the security of the east for granted, fueling demands for autonomy.

The election outcome in December 1970 precipitated a humanitarian and geopolitical crisis whose reverberations of violent territoriality would be felt in South Asia for decades. The crisis itself would first lead to Pakistan's military repression of Awami League members and their sympathizers, a civil war against Bengali-speaking Muslims and Hindus, and a refugee crisis. It would then spiral into a thirteen-day war between India and Pakistan in December 1971, with the Cold War superpowers and China taking sides in the conflict. Finally, it would lead to the independence of East Pakistan as Bangladesh (literally, nation of Bengalis) after nearly ten million people had been displaced and between five hundred thousand and three million had been killed over a period of nine months.[12]

The 1970s World

The world in the 1970s was becoming fractured on many fronts. Nationalist and communist insurgencies challenged nation-states in South Asia that had attained independence from British colonialism less than twenty-five years earlier. These violent nonstate actors demanded autonomy and even independence, and the state lashed out at them with unprecedented force. The fragilities of the newly independent states of South Asia and fissiparous tendencies along their borderlands and contested territories made the 1970s a decade of widespread political and geopolitical turbulence. This was not limited to East Pakistan. Violent unrest sprang up throughout the region: the Naxalite movement that took root in the Indian state of West Bengal, the secessionist movements in the northeastern hills of India, and demands for greater autonomy by the monarch of the Himalayan kingdom of Sikkim.[13]

If decolonization is understood as a "specific world-historical moment," then the 1970s was its third and final wave, during which several newly sovereign nation-states joined the United Nations such as Angola, Bangladesh, Bhutan, Guinea-Bissau, Mozambique, and Vietnam, among others.[14] If decolonization is a "multi-faceted process" and a "counterproject to imperialism" characterized by global solidarity, then the 1970s saw its last gasp before it completely faded away from the international scene.[15] This included the quest among countries of the Global South for increased economic cooperation among themselves at the fourth Conference of Nonaligned Nations in Algiers in September 1973, the oil price hike by the Organization of the Petroleum Exporting Countries (OPEC) and the concurrent embargo of the Organization of Arab Petroleum Exporting Countries (OAPEC) on shipments of crude oil to the countries that supported Israel in the Yom Kippur War leading to the oil shock of 1973–74, and the 1974 call for a New International Economic Order at the UN General Assembly.[16]

Conventional tenets of East-West bloc rivalry and communist/capitalist tensions could not explain Cold War diplomacy and high politics during the 1970s. Superpower détente and Sino-US rapprochement added a new layer of complexity. Pakistan's direct involvement in the Nixon administration's rapprochement with China made South Asia the ground zero of the transformation of the global Cold War. This would have important ramifications for the war and insurgencies that led to the creation of Bangladesh. Not only would the US government support General Yahya in his repression of the Bengalis in East Pakistan, but China would also cast its first veto as a UN Security Council member to bar Bangladesh from becoming a UN member.[17]

The Gandhi government would embark on a multipronged response that would be partly geopolitical and partly technopolitical. By 1972, it would begin preparing for an underground nuclear explosion. It would curtail Sikkim's autonomy, paving the way for the tiny kingdom's absorption into the Indian Union. The government would even entertain requests for nuclear technologies from oil-rich countries in the Middle East in hopes of repositioning itself as a leader of nonaligned countries.

Gandhi's Wars at Home

The day before cyclone Bhola struck, Prime Minister Gandhi declared in the lower house of the Indian Parliament that her government was enacting a new law to curb violent far left activities in the state of West Bengal, bordering East Pakistan.[18] Called "Naxalites" after the 1967 peasant uprising in Naxalbari, West Bengal, these far-left, anti-state, and often pro-Chinese groups comprised the Communist Party of India (Marxist-Leninist) and its splinter groups.[19] On November 22, 1970, the West Bengal Prevention of Violent Activities Act was enacted into law by the Indian president, V. V. Giri, at the instruction of Prime Minister Gandhi. The legislation equipped the state government with wide-ranging powers, including limited detention and arrests without a warrant, in the name of the "security of the State or the maintenance of public order."[20] The swiftness with which the law was passed and its draconian nature exemplified the character of Gandhi's leadership toward challenges to state authority from both the political left and the right. More importantly, the nature of the challenges and her responses diluted the distinction between internal and external security over time.

Since the late 1960s, Gandhi had adopted a series of measures that, as historian Gyan Prakash noted, were efforts to "project herself as a radical reformer, outflank rivals in the Congress, and cut the opposition parties down to size."[21] She removed pro-business finance minister Morarji Desai, who was also the deputy prime minister, from her cabinet and nationalized fourteen of India's private banks that controlled 70 percent of the country's monetary deposits.[22] Her government also curtailed the financial powers of large industrial firms, foreign companies, and their subsidiaries through the 1969 Monopolies and Restrictive Trade Practices Act. In November 1969, she formed her own political party, Congress (R), after the Syndicate, old guards of the Congress Party, expelled her for "indiscipline."

Gandhi frequently invoked Article 356 of the Indian Constitution, which allowed the president (a titular head in India's parliamentary system) to govern a particular state on the advice of the prime minister. She thus rendered state governments powerless when they opposed the central government in New Delhi. Between 1967 and 1974, she imposed "state emergency" or "President's Rule" under Article 356 a total of twenty-six times.[23] This hypercentralization of her political authority in the executive branch of the central government and her overreliance on close advisors like P. N. Haksar, P. N. Dhar, and Siddhartha Shankar Ray had lasting consequences on India's foreign policy and democracy.

While West Pakistan's military and bureaucratic elites were reeling from their election results, Gandhi instructed President Giri to dissolve the Indian

Parliament and order new elections. On December 27, 1970, for the first time in the history of independent India, the national legislature was dissolved before it had served its full term. Gandhi blamed the probusiness right-wing parties and individuals for preventing her government from implementing social and economic reforms to "keep our pledges to our people."[24] In reality, she was just as wary of sharing power with various communist parties in the Parliament.

Campaigning on the slogan of *Garibi hatao* (or abolish poverty), which became wildly popular, Indira Gandhi won a landslide victory in the general elections of March 1971.[25] Her party won a two-thirds majority with 352 out of 521 seats in the Lok Sabha, the lower house of the Indian Parliament. She would no longer have to depend on the support of a multiparty coalition. Prime Minister Gandhi thus reached the apex of her political power just as the crisis in East Pakistan was taking a turn for the worse.

The War for Bangladesh

After Sheikh Mujibur Rahman had refused a power-sharing arrangement with Zulfikar Ali Bhutto, General Yahya postponed the first session of the National Assembly, which was scheduled for March 3, 1971. This spurred demonstrations in Dhaka and elsewhere, leading to clashes between protestors and armed forces.[26] In mid-March, Yahya and Bhutto arrived in Dhaka to broker a political solution with Mujibur Rahman and other Awami League leaders. None of the proposed arrangements were acceptable to the parties concerned. As deadlock set in, General Yahya secretly flew more military troops into East Pakistan. On March 23, the Awami League presented a draft proclamation of provincial autonomy to Yahya with the warning that if autonomy were not granted within forty-eight hours, East Pakistan would spiral out of control.[27] By then, however, the general mood in East Pakistan had shifted toward independence, not autonomy.

On March 25, while talks continued with the Awami League, General Yahya departed East Pakistan instructing General Tikka Khan to conduct a full-blown armed assault on East Pakistan's citizens.[28] The goal was to reassert West Pakistan's dominance over its eastern province. Yahya's regime proclaimed martial law while tanks and armored vehicles rumbled through the streets of Dhaka, crushing everything and killing everyone in their way. Pakistan's army attacked Dhaka University, executing students and professors. Tikka Khan would later become known as the "Butcher of Bengal" due to his ruthless campaign of violence during the crisis. On March 26, in Dhaka, Mujibur Rahman declared independence of Bangladesh from Pakistan. In Chittagong, the following day, General Ziaur Rahman of the East Bengal Regiment declared Bangladesh's independence over the radio.[29] In response, Pakistan's military arrested Sheikh Mujibur Rahman, accusing him of treason. The Yahya regime banned all political activities as open rebellion broke out, with growing demands for an independent Bangladesh.

On March 27, at the opening session of the newly elected Fifth Lok Sabha, Prime Minister Gandhi declared that her government was "deeply conscious of the historic moment" and that "something new has happened" in East Pakistan.[30] Political pressures were increasing within the Parliament and the media for a decisive Indian military intervention in support of East Pakistan. At the request of Prime Minister Gandhi, on March 31, the Parliament adopted a resolution to state "its profound conviction that the historic upsurge of the 75 million people of East Bengal will triumph" and "to assure them that their struggle and sacrifices will receive the wholehearted sympathy and support of the people of India."[31] In the language of the resolution, crafted by P. N. Haksar, the Gandhi government avoided a pledge of official support, which would have amounted to meddling in Pakistan's internal affairs, and adopted the less formal "sympathy and support of the people of India."[32] The choice of "East Bengal" over "East Pakistan" was strategic, reflecting the Indian government's acknowledgment of Bengali nationalism.

East Pakistan's proximity to northeastern hills, where various armed groups such as the Mizos and the Nagas demanded secession from the Indian nation-state, was good reason for the Gandhi government to adopt a cautious approach toward the crisis. Moreover, Indian troops remained stationed in Sikkim to prevent a Chinese military incursion through the Himalayan passes to the "chicken neck" or the Siliguri Corridor, which could potentially cut off India's access to its northeastern corner. An additional concern was that far-left groups—particularly in the Indian state of West Bengal—could exploit the crisis in East Pakistan to further destabilize the region in their efforts to inspire communist revolutions throughout the Bengal Delta.[33]

Bengal was first divided along the lines of religion into east and west in 1905 under British colonial rule. After a brief period of being reunited (1911–47), it was repartitioned in 1947, with the Muslim-majority East Bengal joining Pakistan and the Hindu-majority West Bengal becoming a part of India. As news poured in of Pakistan's military attacking unarmed Bengalis, the flames of Bengali nationalism were reignited in West Bengal, leading to overwhelming support for East Pakistan's independence. Local groups in West Bengal collected money, food, and medical supplies to help those who were fleeing the violence in East Pakistan. Given the outpouring of emotional support and the political implications, the Gandhi government did not seal the long porous border along West Bengal, even as large numbers of refugees began pouring in.[34]

The silence of the Nixon administration on the atrocities in East Pakistan led to strong criticism from the US consulate in Dhaka via the State Department's Dissent Channel. Confidential telegram 1138 of April 6, 1971—also known as the "Blood telegram" after Archer Blood, the US consul general in Dhaka who sent it—objected to what it called the US government's failure to denounce the "suppression of democracy" and its "bending over backwards to placate the West Pak dominated government."[35] The telegram noted "ironically" that the Soviet Union had "sent President Yahya a message defending democracy." The signatories of the dissent cable requested a redirection of US policies regarding the "Awami conflict, in which unfortunately the overworked term genocide is applicable."[36] President Nixon remained unfazed. On April 28, 1971, while signing an action memorandum from Kissinger on Pakistan, he scribbled, "To all hands. Don't Squeeze Yahya at this time—RMN."[37]

The Indian foreign intelligence agency, Research & Analysis Wing (R&AW), and the Indian Army began covertly training the *Mukti Bahini* or "freedom fighters," who had regrouped on Indian territory.[38] These rebels were not all hardened fighters (see figure 6.1). Some were civilians who had taken up arms in what they saw as the rightful battle for their independence. Some were volunteers from the Bengali-speaking Indian states of West Bengal and Tripura.[39] Many were Bengali troops in Pakistan's army who had mutinied and defected to fight a guerilla war for Bangladesh. On April 10, 1971, the Provisional Government of Bangladesh proclaimed independence from Mujibnogor (or Mujib's town), only miles from the border with West Bengal, India.[40] Seven days later, its cabinet took their oaths. Recognized by India, the Provisional Government of Bangladesh was headquartered in Calcutta, the capital of West Bengal.

That month, Yahya's regime flew in a group of eight journalists from West Pakistan on a ten-day tour of the eastern province in hopes of constructing a favorable public image of the crisis. Foreign journalists were already expelled when martial law was proclaimed in March. Anthony Mascarenhas was one such journalist. He immediately returned back to Karachi, moved his family to London, and published his story in the *Sunday Times* on June 13, 1971. It was through Mascarenhas's article, titled "Genocide," that the world learned about the extent of violence perpetrated by the military in East Pakistan.[41]

Two days later, when Prime Minister Gandhi addressed the Indian Parliament, she declared that a political settlement was "becoming more remote" with each passing day.[42] Millions of refugees fleeing the violence were arriving in India while fears of a cholera epidemic were on the rise in the congested refugee

FIGURE 6.1.   Raghu Rai's photograph of the 1971 war. The photo shows an Indian Army tank on the left and a group of armed *Mukti Bahini* members on the right riding a tricycle or van-rickshaw. Media identifier: NYC133766. Copyright: Raghu Rai/Magnum Photos. Published with permission.

camps along the 1,378-mile border between East Pakistan and West Bengal.[43] According to official Indian estimates at the time, three million Bengali refugees had already arrived in India by May 1971, and hundreds and thousands were arriving with each passing day.[44] Prime Minister Gandhi told the Parliament that her government was looking after the refugees only on a temporary basis, but also that she could not ask "them to go back merely to be butchered." During the four-hour debate, some members of the Indian Parliament asked the Gandhi government to send Indian troops to support the *Mukti Bahini*. While Gandhi did not directly address that request, she unequivocally supported East Pakistan in her parliamentary statement: "We shall not for a moment stand for a political settlement that means the death of Bangla Desh and the ending of democracy and of the people who are fighting for their rights."[45]

On July 7, 1971, when Kissinger was visiting New Delhi, he had reassured the Indian defense minister Jagjivan Ram that the "US would take a grave view of any Chinese move against India."[46] By July 17, Kissinger's earlier reassurance was no longer standing when he met the Indian ambassador L. K. Jha. Kissinger had just concluded his secret trip to Beijing through Islamabad from July 9 to 11, laying the foundation for Sino-US rapprochement. Indian policymakers were surprised to learn that the Nixon administration would provide "no support to India, either military or political" in the context of "any Chinese invasion of India in response to any Indian action in the Bangla Desh."[47] That month, with refugee numbers reaching seven million, Prime Minister Gandhi wrote a letter to Chinese premier Zhou Enlai about the crisis in East Pakistan.[48] The letter, sent on July 18, did not generate a Chinese response.[49] The Chinese government did not want to alienate the governments of Pakistan and the United States and was likely aware that Gandhi and her advisors were closely studying Brezhnev's proposals for an Indo-Soviet treaty.

The transformation of the Cold War in 1971 through rapprochement between the US and Chinese governments facilitated by Yahya's regime, and the Indo-Soviet Treaty of Peace, Friendship, and Cooperation of August 1971, had important ramifications for the humanitarian and geopolitical crisis in East Pakistan. Signed by the Indian minister of external affairs Swaran Singh and his Soviet counterpart, Andrei Gromyko, the Indo-Soviet treaty included the provision that in the face of an attack or the threat thereof, there would be "mutual consultations in order to remove such threat" by its two contracting parties.[50]

The thirteen-day war between Indian and Pakistan troops began on December 3, 1971, after the Pakistan Air Force attacked multiple airfields in north and west India from West Pakistan. Pakistan's military aircraft struck Amritsar, Pathankot, Srinagar, Avantipur, Utterlai, Jodhpur, Ambala, and Agra in India while their infantry shelled Indian military posts in Sulemankhi, Khemkaran, Poonch, and elsewhere. Prime Minister Gandhi declared in her radio address to the nation that "the war in Bangla Desh has become a war on India," which "imposes upon me, my Government, and the people of India an awesome responsibility."[51] The Indian government had "no other option but to put our country on a war footing." Thus began the third India-Pakistan War, or the Bangladesh Liberation War.

During the war, the Nixon administration sent the *USS Enterprise*, the world's first nuclear-powered aircraft carrier, from the Gulf of Tonkin off the coast of North Vietnam to the Bay of Bengal to threaten the Gandhi government. Despite Kissinger's encouragement, the Chinese military did not open a second front against India in Sikkim during the 1971 war, as the Chinese government had threatened during the 1965 war.[52] The Indo-Soviet treaty of 1971 discouraged China and the United States from openly intervening in the war. As Indian foreign secretary T. N. Kaul wrote years later: "It was the US Administration that sent the Seventh Fleet into the Bay of Bengal but dared not land it in India or East Pakistan. India had already sunk a US submarine 'GHAZI' given to Pakistan and Soviet sub-marines were floating under the Seventh Fleet. China made warlike noises but refrained from intervening militarily in the subcontinent."[53]

The Nixon administration's dispatch of the US Seventh Fleet's Task Force 74, led by the *USS Enterprise*, into the Bay of Bengal had a significant psychological impact on the Indian policymakers. Prime Minister Gandhi made this point in her 1972 *Foreign Affairs* article in which she wrote emphatically in the first person: "I do not wish to analyze the US role at that time or go into the misrepresentations which were circulated. But it is necessary to take note of the dispatch of the warship *Enterprise* to support a ruthless military dictatorship and to intimidate a democracy, and the extraordinary similarity of the attitudes adopted by the United States and China. Imagine our feelings."[54] The *USS Enterprise* in the Bay of Bengal epitomized both the Cold War character of the 1971 war and the US administration's overt support for Pakistan against India.

The war for Bangladesh, which ended with Pakistan signing the instrument of surrender on December 16, 1971, severely damaged US-India bilateral relations.[55] It generated acute mistrust of the United States in the Indian media, the general populace, and above all, the Gandhi government. This was in sharp contrast to Soviet support for India in the war. A note from the MEA's Americas Division bluntly stated that "[b]efore 1971, the United States had far more admirers in India than the USSR" but "[m]ost of them have seen that the Soviet Union's role during the crisis was in marked contrast to that of the United States and highly constructive."[56]

With the transformation of the global Cold War, MEA officials wondered what a "Sino-American collusion" meant for Indian interests in the region and around the world. The Gandhi government elevated its diplomatic relations with North Vietnam to the ambassadorial level in January 1972, leading to protests from South Vietnam.[57] Anxious MEA officials worried that both the United States and China "are likely to cooperate in the UN and other Agencies in order to undermine India's prestige and power."[58] Their fears were borne out when China vetoed Bangladesh's entry into the UN in August 1972.

The War's Aftermath

The year 1971, beginning with Indira Gandhi's electoral victory and ending with India's military victory, bolstered Indira Gandhi's political position. This enabled her to make radical moves against her political opponents. The dividing line between internal and external security, which was already blurry, became even less distinct that year. In July 1971, as millions of refugees from East Pakistan arrived in politically destabilized regions of eastern and northeastern India, the Parliament passed the Maintenance of Internal Security Act. The new legislation, which replaced the Preventive Detention Act that had expired in 1969, would become an infamous tool during the Emergency (1975–77). It would be amended multiple times and used against anyone who opposed Prime Minister Gandhi's authority.

That same month, the Gandhi government introduced a bill to end privy purses and special privileges for former princely states on grounds that those entitlements were "incompatible with an egalitarian social order."[59] On December 28, 1971, only weeks after Pakistan's surrender, the Indian Parliament finally passed the Twenty-Sixth Amendment to the Indian Constitution, thus ending privy purses. With former princes becoming involved in state- and national-level politics as a reactionary force, Prime Minister Gandhi had been trying for some time to end privy purses.[60] This played a part in her decision to dissolve the Parliament and call for fresh elections in December 1970.[61] After the 1971 war, her party, Congress (R), won the 1972 state assembly elections by even greater margins.[62] Armed with a strong electoral mandate, the Gandhi government introduced numerous amendments to the Indian Constitution that limited the role of the judiciary, which at the time was upholding the rights of the landowning classes.[63]

More important, the Gandhi government territorially reconfigured the northeastern region of India affected by secessionist movements. The Northeastern Areas (Reorganization) Act of December 30, 1971, created the centrally administered "union territories" of Arunachal Pradesh and Mizoram and the states of Meghalaya, Tripura, and Manipur.[64] When Prime Minister Gandhi announced union territory status of Arunachal Pradesh, she made the hierarchies between the borderlands and the nation-state clear, promising "all assistance to the people of Arunachal so that they could march forward, keeping pace with the people in the rest of the country."[65] China had occupied Arunachal Pradesh (formerly, the North-East Frontier Agency) during the 1962 Sino-India War, and it still claims that territory as part of South Tibet.[66]

The 1971 war had witnessed the military deployment of ethnic minorities at an unprecedented scale. Tibetan exiles trained by India's R&AW fought the Pakistan military while Mizo rebels from India's northeastern region provided intelligence and guerilla support to Pakistan's troops.[67] Pakistan's government also deployed "Razakars"—non-Bengali Muslim militias—to perpetrate violence against Bengalis, leading to retributive violence against them after the war.[68] The tactical use of insurgents and militias along ethnic lines in a geopolitically fraught region made already intermestic geopolitical threats further entrenched, with the domestic and the international spheres becoming deeply intertwined.[69] For instance, in March 1972, the Indian military supported the Bangladesh government in suppressing an insurgency in the Chittagong Hill

Tracts. The renowned Indian diplomat K. P. S. Menon justified it in an MEA memo in the following words: "Bangladesh asked for help in combating armed and hostile Mizos. We responded."[70]

New Institutional Leaders

On December 30, 1971, two weeks after Pakistan's surrender in the war, the DAE secretary and ISRO chairman Vikram Sarabhai suddenly passed away (likely from a heart attack) at the rocket launching facility in Thumba.[71] Earlier that night, he had witnessed the launch of a Soviet rocket and then retired to his hotel room in Halcyon Castle, the former royal family retreat in Travancore. Under a May 1970 agreement between ISRO and the Soviet Academy of Sciences, the two institutions had agreed to launch Soviet weather rockets from Thumba.[72] Sarabhai was attending one of those rocket launches. The cause of his death remains a mystery, feeding conspiratorial speculations, as with Homi Bhabha's death in 1966 in a plane crash on Mont Blanc.[73]

Sarabhai's death untethered the BARC explosions group of Homi Sethna, Raja Ramanna, P. K. Iyengar, and R. Chidambaram. The group had had been quietly working on underground nuclear explosions since November 1964 (see chapter 5). Sarabhai had not actively encouraged the BARC group during his tenure (1966–71), but neither did he end the program. Sarabhai treaded carefully because he was facing a new world in which the global nonproliferation regime was increasingly constraining the DAE's freedom of action, and the Planning Commission was holding the DAE accountable.

In 1972, Homi Sethna, who was then the director of BARC, became the new DAE secretary and the AECI chairman. Raja Ramana succeeded Sethna as the director of BARC. It was the first time that India's nuclear program was led by an engineer, rather than a physicist. Unlike the two previous leaders of the DAE/AECI, who were both Cambridge-trained physicists, Sethna had studied chemical engineering at the University of Michigan at Ann Arbor. Yet there were also similarities and connections. Sethna was a Parsi from Bombay, like Bhabha. He had been close to Bhabha, who had put him in charge of the DAE's French-built monazite plant in Alwaye (see chapter 2).[74] Sethna was thus initiated into the DAE's foremost atomic earths project at the dawn of India's independence. He had also been the director of the DAE's Engineering Group under Bhabha's leadership, where he had led the construction of both the uranium metal plant in the late 1950s and the plutonium reprocessing plant in the early 1960s. He had been part of Bhabha's core research group at BARC for underground nuclear explosions and had accompanied Bhabha to

IAEA meetings from early on.[75] In other words, Sethna was very much an insider, although under Sarabhai he had felt that the DAE's focus on spaceflight came at the expense of the nuclear program.[76]

Within days of Sarabhai's death, Prime Minister Gandhi invited key scientists for a meeting with the prime minister's secretariat to discuss the institutional reorganization of the country's space program. The memo for the meeting noted: "Assuming that there would be a separate Space Agency or Commission, P.M. may invite a discussion on the kind of considerations which should weigh in structuring the Space Commission and the kind of person who should head it."[77] The prime minister had been considering the establishment of an independent space commission for some time, but Sarabhai had wanted to keep the space program under the DAE.[78]

Gandhi directed M. G. K. Menon, the TIFR director and the interim ISRO chairman, to explore possibilities for associating the space program with the defense laboratories of the DRDO. She wrote to Menon on January 14, 1972: "I think there should be some linkage between our Space Program and defence needs," and she directed him to find out "in a preliminary way the best manner to achieve this."[79] On Haksar's advice, Gandhi also sent a personal letter to Satish Dhawan, the IISc director who at the time was on a visiting professorship at his alma mater, the California Institute of Technology. She instructed Dhawan to take over the stewardship of the country's space program—the soon-to-be-established Department of Space.

The prime minister's encouragement of greater cooperation between the space and defense research programs did not bear fruit, owing to Dhawan's opposition. As secretary of the Department of Space, Dhawan opposed it on the same grounds as Sarabhai had—namely, to keep claims of proliferation at bay. Space technologies' association with missiles to deliver nuclear warheads meant that a space-defense collaboration would cause alarm at home and abroad. Technology partners like France could even withdraw from cooperation, as Dhawan explained to Gandhi.[80] Even though India's space program continued its pursuit of rockets and satellite launch vehicles, whose technologies were closely associated with those of missiles, the Department of Space steered clear of institutional collaboration with the Defence Research & Development Laboratory, DRDO's dedicated missile development body.

To be clear, this separation was not the result of moral opposition to delivery vehicles for nuclear weapons among personnel and leaders involved in space research in India. M. G. K. Menon, a key figure in nuclear and space research, admitted years later in an interview with journalist Raj Chengappa that "peaceful uses of space was [sic] legitimate for both our public image as well as to tap the benefits of such research for communications, remote sensing,

FIGURE 6.2.   Prime Minister Indira Gandhi (right center) with M. G. K. Menon (left) and Vikram Sarabhai (right corner) at TIFR in November 1968 at the inauguration of the Homi Bhabha Auditorium. Disclaimer: Tata Institute of Fundamental Research (TIFR)/TIFR Archives has only provided the above Images. The opinion expressed in the said text/article are author's own and does not reflect the opinion of TIFR, including TIFR Archives.

and weather prediction," while it "helped us develop all the capability needed for rocketry and therefore the option to make powerful missiles."[81] Scientific personnel also moved between institutions associated with space and defense. In July 1972, when Dhawan initiated the indigenous satellite launch vehicle (SLV) program, SLV-3, he chose A. P. J. Abdul Kalam to lead it. Kalam had originally begun his career at the DRDO before being recruited by Sarabhai for ISRO. After SLV-3's success with the 1980 launch of the Rohini satellite, Kalam would rejoin the DRDO to lead India's ballistic missile development program in 1983.[82]

In 1970, Prime Minister Gandhi had assigned the responsibility for building a short-range surface-to-air missile based on the Soviet SA-2 (Project Devil) and a long-range ballistic missile for delivering nuclear warheads (Project Valiant) to physicist Basanti Dulal Nagchaudhuri, the scientific advisor to the Ministry of Defence and the DRDO director general. In June 1972, when Nagchaudhuri requested 160 million rupees (~US$21.3 million) for Project Valiant, Gandhi's cabinet turned down the request, but the prime minister granted it through her discretionary funds.[83] To stay under the radar of oversight of the Planning Commission and the cabinet, Project Valiant's budget was divided into smaller five hundred thousand–rupee chunks (~US$66,500) that the DRDO could authorize itself.[84] Based at the Defence Research & Development Laboratory in Hyderabad, the project would eventually fail because of inadequate infrastructure and personnel skills. Nevertheless, by the summer of 1972, the Gandhi government had two potential institutional pathways to develop nuclear-capable missiles—SLV-3 and Valiant. The separation of the two projects enabled Indian policymakers and institutional leaders to maintain plausible deniability when faced with allegations of nuclear proliferation.

In the fall of 1972, Prime Minister Gandhi is believed to have given the formal approval to conduct an underground nuclear explosion.[85] Even though a paper trail of her 1972 decision has remained elusive in the archives—those documents either remain classified or do not exist—it is possible to say it was not the first time that she had considered such an action.[86] In November 1970, Nagchaudhuri had directed a small group of DRDO scientists and engineers to prepare a proposal for a long-range ballistic missile within four years because "Mrs. Gandhi wanted it."[87] He added that the prime minister believed that "we should prepare for it [nuclear explosion] in such a way that all the pieces fell in line." In September 1971, Sarabhai had shared at the Fourth International Conference on the Peaceful Uses of Atomic Energy in Vienna that the DAE was developing the engineering associated with PNE devices. This had triggered a reaction from Canadian prime minister Pierre Trudeau who warned Prime Minister Gandhi against the use of Canadian-supplied materials in a future Indian nuclear explosion.[88]

Unlike in the mid-1960s, when the Johnson administration first worried about a Plowshare loophole as India's potential pathway toward nuclear weapons, the circumstances in 1972 were unique. For the first time in India, there was an alignment in political will, institutional leadership, and technological capabilities for an underground nuclear explosion. With Sarabhai's death, the BARC Explosions Group had begun to enjoy political support. From 1972 onward, BARC cooperated with the Terminal Ballistic Research Laboratory in Chandigarh to determine the amount and structure of highly explosive materials that would surround the plutonium core in an implosion-type nuclear device.[89] It also collaborated with the Explosive Research and Development Laboratory in Pune to develop high-speed detonators for the nuclear device.[90] The support of these two DRDO laboratories would be key to BARC's overall success in conducting the nuclear explosion.

Pakistan embarked on its own nuclear weapons program in the wake of its military defeat in the 1971 war. Zulfi kar Ali Bhutto became Pakistan's president in late December 1971. It was he who had once made the famous remark about the people of Pakistan "eating grass" to get their own nuclear weapons if India was also developing them.[91] In January 1972, Bhutto appointed Munir Ahmed Khan as the chairman of the Pakistan Atomic Energy Commission, tasking him with developing nuclear weapons through reprocessing pluto- nium.[92] Although the Indian government was predominantly concerned with Chinese nuclear weapons, the MEA paper from November 1964 (discussed in chapter 5) had cautioned that "Pakistan, especially, may well go in for the bomb, if she can make it, even if India does not make it, in order to nullify the over- all superiority of India in the sub-continent."[93] As a result, with Bhutto in power, the Gandhi government worried about Pakistan's bomb, in addition to its geopolitical concerns stemming from US and Chinese political support for Islamabad.

Throughout 1972, British, Canadian, and US officials worried about the pos- sibility of an Indian underground nuclear explosion. There was a lack of con- sensus, however, about how imminent that explosion was. By the spring of 1972, the Canadian government and atomic energy officials were certain that "the Indians interpret existing safeguards with both Canada and the United States as permitting India to mount a PNE program if it decides to do so."[94] During this period, Japanese and Pakistan delegations raised concerns with US officials at the United Nations in Geneva claiming that their "informants" knew that the Gandhi government had decided to conduct a nuclear test in the Ra- jasthan desert. US officials dismissed those concerns as rumors motivated by the Pakistan delegation.[95]

At the Nixon White House, Richard T. Kennedy, an NSC staffer and later President Reagan's ambassador-at-large for nonproliferation, wrote to Kiss- inger in the summer of 1972 to authorize "the most careful analysis possible of U.S. interests," in light of "an Indian test in the not-too-distant future."[96] This became the National Security Study Memorandum 156, titled "India's Nuclear Developments."[97] It resulted in the Special National Intelligence Esti- mate 31–72 in August 1972 in which US intelligence officials could not find clear evidence of a political decision to conduct a nuclear explosion.[98] The fol- lowing month, an interagency memo admitted that "US ability to influence events is marginal" because of "the poor state of Indo-US relations" such that "an overly visible US effort could hasten, rather than delay, the day India ex- plodes a nuclear device."[99] In other words, US officials could do little but wait and watch. That was exactly what they did.

Technological Overtures of Explosion

Political differences between the US and Indian governments over the 1971 crisis and war diminished bilateral cooperation in specialized areas like space technologies. Consequently, the Soviet Academy of Sciences replaced NASA as ISRO's key partner in the war's immediate aftermath. Fresh discussions for space cooperation between the Soviet and Indian space agencies had already begun in the second week of August 1971. ISRO had agreed to launch a one hundred–kilogram Indian satellite from a Soviet range using a Soviet vehicle and to launch a similar satellite (carrying indigenous experiments) from an Indian site, using a Soviet Inter-Cosmos vehicle.[100]

After multiple rounds of negotiations, M. G. K. Menon from ISRO visited Moscow during May 4 to 10, 1972, to finalize "the proposal to launch a satellite wholly designed and manufactured in India with the help of a Soviet rocket carrier and from Soviet territory."[101] The agreement was signed on May 10, 1972, during Menon's visit.[102] A Soviet team from Dnipropetrovsk—the industrial Ukrainian city where Stalin constructed the largest missile factory in the Soviet Union—helped select the core design of the satellite, collected thermal calculations, and provided the gas jet system for stabilizing the satellite.[103] Satish Dhawan, then ISRO chairman at the time, later told a top-ranking British scientist that India had "nothing whatever to do with the rocket and the Russians have nothing whatever to do with the satellite, and therefore the latter is being built entirely within India with Indian resources."[104]

The PURNIMA reactor in Trombay, which was built to serve the dual purposes of gaining technical experience in both fast neutron reactors and plutonium-core implosion devices, reached criticality in mid-1972.[105] In December of that year, P. K. Iyengar, head of the BARC Physics Group, presented a paper on the PURNIMA to a visiting group of Soviet nuclear experts.[106] The reactor, after all, was based on the designs of the Soviet IBR-30 reactor built in Dubna. The Soviet delegation visited multiple DAE facilities: the fast breeder reactor site in Kalpakkam, the Nuclear Fuel Complex and the Electronics Corporation in Hyderabad, and the CANDU-type power reactor site in Rajasthan.[107] What was noteworthy, however, was that no official visit was scheduled to Trombay, the site of the PURNIMA, the CIRUS, and the plutonium reprocessing plant—all key facilities for preparations for the nuclear explosion. During this time, USAEC representative John J. Pinajian from Oak Ridge also found it impossible to visit BARC to undertake experimental research. His attempts were allegedly "rebuffed" by BARC director Raja Ramanna and TIFR director M. G. K. Menon. The US consulate in Bombay reported to the US embassy in

New Delhi and the State Department that "GOI could very well be working on nuclear device to demonstrate peaceful applications."[108]

The DAE embarked on a proactive quest for heavy water plants during this period. Its earlier policy had been to import heavy water from the United States, the United Kingdom, Norway, and elsewhere. Heavy water, or deuterium oxide, was useful as a moderator in nuclear reactors like the CIRUS.[109] Political tensions between the United States and India, and demands by the AECL to renegotiate fuel contracts to safeguard the CANDU reactor in Rajasthan, signaled to the DAE that procurement from its preexisting suppliers was unstable.

Against this backdrop, the DAE sought out new sources of heavy water that would not be subject to Zangger Committee restrictions. Heavy water was a controlled item on the Zangger Committee's trigger list, but heavy water plants were not. As a result, such plants constructed by foreign companies based in countries not subject to the NPT fit the DAE's bill. In 1972–73, construction began on four large heavy water plants in Baroda, Kota, Tuticorin, and Talcher by firms from France, Switzerland, and West Germany. Two of these plants were built in Kota and Talcher by West German firm *Friedrich Uhde GmbH*. The other two were constructed in Baroda and Tuticorin by Franco-Swiss consortium *Gelpra*, a subsidiary of the Sulzer Brothers of Switzerland.

The DAE's skillful choice of private firms reflected the hyperdiversification strategy that was central to its quest for freedom of action. France was not an NPT signatory at the time and hence not part of the Zangger Committee negotiations. Switzerland and West Germany had both signed the NPT in 1969, but neither had ratified it at the time. This made the *Gelpra* consortium and the *Friedrich Uhde GmbH* attractive to the DAE. The pressure that US and Canadian officials put on the West German representative at the Zangger Committee negotiations failed to curtail the construction of heavy water plants in India.[110] The DAE also obtained eighty tons of heavy water from the Soviet government in 1972, when the latter was not a full member of the Zangger Committee.[111]

In September 1972, the American Academy of Arts and Sciences invited M. G. K. Menon to Cambridge, Massachusetts, to discuss how Indian and American scientists could develop scientific exchanges. Despite the decline in bilateral relations between the two countries, Paul Doty wanted to host a meeting between CISAC and Indian scientists on India's nuclear policy similar to the one held in June 1966 (discussed in chapter 5). Doty pointed out to Menon that the "hiatus in Indian-US relationships may be an opportunity to place scientific cooperation between the two countries on a new level," removed from the "tradition and mentality" of US development aid.[112] Menon was receptive, but he wanted to avoid US-India workshops funded by USAID and the National Academy of Sciences because "US government funds had political implications" in India.

Tensions between the Gandhi government and the Nixon administration over aid had only exacerbated over the course of 1971, which historian David Engerman has credited to the financialization of US aid and the geopolitical crisis in the subcontinent.[113] Under Kissinger's direction and in response to the 1971 war, USAID had halted all forms of economic aid to India as well as the US$87 million that had already been authorized. It prompted public protests from Indian policymakers as well industrialists such as J. R. D. Tata. In response, the Gandhi government expelled USAID from India in May 1972. When Menon met the CISAC members in September 1972, it was already clear to both US and Indian scientific personnel that more informal mechanisms of meeting and cooperation would have to be adopted. The CISAC group therefore decided that US participation would be "under the aegis of Pugwash which would sound neutral to the Indians" with the American Academy of Arts and Sciences shouldering the primary organizational responsibility.

From the US point of view, the 1966 CISAC gathering in India was successful as "Doty & Co. were able to talk realistically about the extraordinary and unanticipated cost of not just an atomic bomb but delivery systems."[114] As a result, as US-Indian relations remained cold in 1972, Doty and other CISAC members such as Franklin Long, Roger Revelle, and Jerome Wiesner wanted to meet key Indian scientists to prevent the "impact of this deterioration on relations between Indian and American scientists."[115] Yet Menon was candid in his meeting with Doty and others, in which he told his US interlocutors that there was "no conflict among Indian scientists between military and civilian research; certainly there is no moral conflict."[116] He added that atomic energy and space research, which "consume a large chunk of the Indian budget," were highly ranked "on the priority list of projects with access to foreign exchange."

After the American Academy meeting with Menon, CISAC considered the fall of 1973 to be an ideal time for a meeting in India. Such a meeting would be modeled on the June 1966 meeting, with eight scientists from each side, who would discuss behind closed doors critically important matters concerning science, technology, and politics. The main stumbling block from the US side was the lack of "readiness within government." In April 1973, the "general posture" of the Nixon administration toward India was "wait-and-see," where "[n]o initiatives are envisaged other than the oft-stated readiness to respond constructively to propositions of the Indian government."[117] The Nixon White House had directed the State Department to "follow a very cautious, carefully programmed strategy." As a result, the State Department remained "equivocal in its reactions" to the proposed 1973 CISAC meeting in India.[118]

During her visit to Ottawa in June 1973, Prime Minister Gandhi learned from the AECL director James L. Gray that the AECL would "no longer provide technology, heavy water fuel or any equipment specifically designed for use in power reactors" to the DAE.[119] The AECL's decision resulted from the DAE's opposition to participating in any new agreement that would subject its facilities to foreign inspections and safeguards.[120] The DAE's remaining options were to either build equipment related to the CANDU reactors on its own or purchase spare parts from countries that were still willing to sell without safeguards.[121] While Canada scaled down its cooperation with the DAE, the UKAEA sensed a business opportunity.[122]

Dr. Walter Marshall, director of the UK Atomic Energy Research Establishment at Harwell, visited key DAE sites and the ISRO headquarters in January 1974 to scout out British commercial possibilities. Based on Marshall's notes for the UKAEA, nonproliferation did not seem to be at the top of his agenda. He inquired about the status of the CANDU reactor development by the DAE, meticulously inspected various production lines, and collected brochures. Marshall was particularly impressed by the Electronics Corporation in Hyderabad. It had grown out of the Electronics Commission in Trombay created by Bhabha and expanded under Sarabhai.[123] He wrote in this note for the UKAEA: "Of all the technical activities I saw in India during this visit, this electronics factory impressed me more than anything else."[124]

Marshall observed: "They are building all the instrumentation and control consoles for India's Candu power stations. Each installation costs just under £1M apiece. They are manufacturing antennae systems for communications and defence and they also manufacture many microwave components."[125] The Electronics Corporation also had a computer division and television department. The DAE did not separate civilian-related activities from military-oriented ones. It exercised monopoly over all things nuclear. In theory, parts of the plutonium implosion device could be produced at the same site as television units.

The DAE's Nuclear Fuel Complex shared its campus with the Electronics Corporation. It was set up to develop both natural uranium fuel for the three CANDU reactors and low enriched uranium fuel for the Tarapur reactors.[126] Marshall visited the production line for the CANDU fuel, where "(t)he factory starts from crude yellow cake and ends up with assembled fuel elements."[127] The complex was built through a "sizeable 'diversification' exercise," he noted: "[T]he Indians had imported a vast range of capital equipment, some from England, some from Russia but most from the USA."[128]

The DAE's characteristic diversification strategy regarding fuel fabrication and heavy water also applied to plutonium supply. As the DAE began preparing for a nuclear explosion, it experienced a plutonium shortage because of malfunctions in the plutonium reprocessing plant in Trombay.[129] It therefore shut down the PURNIMA to conserve plutonium. Moreover, it embarked on the construction of an indigenously built heavy water reactor larger than the 40-MW CIRUS and completely without safeguards. This would be the 100-MW Dhruva reactor, also built at BARC in Trombay, which would reach criticality in 1985.

After several delays, the CISAC meeting between politically significant Indian and US scientists took place in January 1974 in Hyderabad. It was a joint meeting organized by Pugwash committees of the two countries. Officially held in the memory of Vikram Sarabhai, the gathering was hailed as "as a countervailing public gesture by the two scientific communities to reaffirm their traditional ties of friendship"[130] M. G. K. Menon of TIFR and Roger Revelle of Harvard University co-chaired the meeting. Atomic energy, originally considered as being part of the agenda, was carefully eschewed. Little substantive cooperation came out of the meeting since that would have required US and Indian government support. Neither government showed interest.

In February 1974, the two governments resolved one major outstanding issue related to US aid, namely the disposal of rupee funds under PL–480. The US government had accumulated roughly US\$3 billion in rupees from providing food aid to India under PL–480. The US rupee balance from PL–480 aid was required to be spent in India. On February 18, the two governments signed a bilateral agreement in a quiet ceremony in New Delhi, during which the US government paid its Indian counterpart a check of US\$2.05 billion for development purposes, notably agriculture. The other US\$1 billion was going to fund the maintenance of the US embassy in New Delhi.[131] A week later, US ambassador Daniel Patrick Moynihan cheekily wrote to the *Guinness Book of World Records*, reporting that he, by delivering the check to the Gandhi government, had created a new record "for the greatest amount paid by a single check in the history of banking."[132] US-Indian relations remained tepid.

India as a Nuclear Supplier in the Middle East

Desalination "could be a big business in a country like Libya," wrote Homi Taleyarkhan—Indian ambassador to Libya—to Prime Minister Gandhi's principal secretary P. N. Haksar in June 1972.[133] The DAE must conduct a "detailed feasibility study" at the government's expense to gauge Libyan interest in peaceful nuclear technologies, Taleyarkhan urged. It was "very much necessary" that the Indian government showed interest because it could help the

DAE gain a foothold in the global nuclear market as well as enhance India's standing with the oil-rich country.

The Libyan government, Taleyarkhan continued, seemed disaffected with Pakistan. Major Abdessalam Jalloud, the second-in-command in the government of Muammar Gaddafi, had expressed "apparent disenchantment" with Pakistan's "continued associations with imperialist organizations" and "affiliations with America and China." Even though Haksar himself doubted Libya's change in attitude, he recommended that the DAE and the Gandhi government "should certainly be forthcoming."[134] Such exploratory efforts to export nuclear technologies integrated technopolitics with geopolitics in the DAE's quest for freedom of action. They sought to sell nuclear technologies to countries that not only were less advanced in those technologies, but also expressed similar geopolitical preferences, such as opposition to the United States, China, and Pakistan.

There was a third motivating factor behind the DAE's exploratory nuclear exports: establishing its reputation as an "innovator," not a "proliferator."[135] The DAE enjoyed the reputation of leading one of the most advanced nuclear programs in the nonaligned world, while not being constrained by the NPT. In 1969, it had signed five-year nuclear cooperation agreements with Brazil and Argentina, neither of which had signed the NPT. By contrast, King Idris of Libya had signed the NPT when the treaty was first opened for signature. The king was later removed through a military coup that made way for Muammar Gaddafi to lead the country. The Gaddafi government started exploring a nuclear program in 1970 and set up a national committee for atomic energy in March 1972.[136] Taleyarkhan's letter to Haksar thus arrived at a time when the Libyan government was actively searching for technology partners for its fledgling nuclear program.

Even though the global atomic marketplace contracted because of unprecedented controls, new buyers emerged with shopping lists for nuclear technologies. After all, Article IV of the NPT promised its signatories the "inalienable right" to "develop, research, production and use of nuclear energy for peaceful purposes without discrimination."[137] Libya's pursuit of nuclear desalination was well within the parameters of the NPT. Desalination through nuclear energy involves the treatment of seawater to produce potable water in a facility that drew energy from a nuclear reactor.[138] In other words, it was a "ploughshare." Its stated goal was to provide drinkable water to the people. It could become a "sword" if fissile material were produced from that reactor for use in a nuclear explosive device.

Despite Libya's NPT membership and its interest in buying nuclear technologies, DAE secretary Homi Sethna showed measured enthusiasm. Sethna wrote back to Haksar that the DAE itself "cannot take any initiative" but "if the Libyans do so, we would certainly give the necessary cooperation."[139] He decided that his own institution would not send representatives to Tripoli. Instead, the DAE could welcome a Libyan delegation for talks in New Delhi followed by a visit to BARC facilities in Trombay. This tentativeness was not limited to Libya. Sethna adopted a similar approach to other potential recipients of Indian nuclear aid, especially after the 1973 oil price shock, when officials from Libya, Egypt, Yugoslavia, Iran, Argentina, Brazil, and elsewhere approached the DAE seeking nuclear cooperation of some sort. Sethna's response was controlled eagerness, followed by little actual help. When US policymakers would begin to scrutinize DAE's activities abroad, especially after the May 1974 nuclear explosion, Sethna would make the case that his organization had a clean track record of consistent export restraint.[140] In other words, he would argue that the DAE was a desirable and responsible nuclear supplier.

Tectonic shifts recast the global political order in the 1970s. The postwar economic system crafted at Bretton Woods unraveled, as exemplified by the New Economic Policy program of President Nixon, also called the "Nixon shock," announced in August 1971. A structural transformation unfolded, which the historian Daniel Sargent called the "Third World's new insurgency."[141] This first took the form of the 1973 oil price hike by OPEC and oil export embargo by OAPEC against those countries that had supported Israel in the Yom Kippur War, precipitating the oil crisis of 1973–74. It later manifested itself in the May 1974 UN General Assembly resolution calling for economic redistribution between countries of the Global North and those of the Global South through a New International Economic Order.[142] Leaders of oil-producing countries depicted their price hike and embargo as "an economic equivalent to decolonization," as historian Christopher Dietrich has masterfully shown, but it came at a steep price for countries of the Global South that did not have oil.[143]

Against this backdrop, there was renewed interest in new nuclear programs in many parts of the world. Oil-dependent countries rushed to find energy alternatives to reduce dependence on oil. Oil-rich countries like Iran, Iraq, and Libya used their petrodollars to embark on large nuclear programs. Technologically advanced countries like the United States, France, and West Germany offered to sell nuclear power reactors worth millions of dollars to oil-rich countries to alleviate their own balance-of-payments crises, compensate for declining domestic demand for nuclear power, and recycle the recipients' petrodollars.[144]

The oil price shock damaged India's already struggling economy, but Indian officials publicly applauded OAPEC's oil embargo as a much-needed corrective measure to address unequal terms of trade between the Global North and the Global South. The support for the Arab oil embargo among poor countries without oil, such as India, represented what Dietrich has termed the "economic culture of decolonization." The Gandhi government itself was at the forefront of the global advocacy for economic equality across nations through platforms such as the UN Conference on Trade and Development (UNCTAD) and the Group of 77 at the UN—economic analogs of the non-aligned movement. By the late 1960s, Afro-Asian solidarity of the late–1940s and the 1950s had fragmented, perhaps most acutely represented by General Idi Amin's expulsion of Asians from Uganda in August 1972.[145] Calls for South-South economic solidarity took its place. In her inaugural address at the first UNCTAD summit in New Delhi in 1968, Gandhi had called for economic solidarity of decolonized countries to fight against poverty. Chilean president Salvador Allende reiterated the call in his own opening speech at the 1972 UNCTAD summit in Santiago, when he demanded the replacement of the unequal trade order with a fair and just one.[146]

By January 1974, it was evident that India's food production was expected to "drop at least three million tons during the spring harvest because of the rising oil price and a shortage of petroleum-based fertilizer."[147] The sharp rise in petroleum prices created a fertilizer crisis for India because petroleum-based components like naphtha became inaccessible. This, in turn, led to the possibility of impending food shortages in the country.[148] The Gandhi government's response was to negotiate bilateral arrangements with notable oil-rich countries to purchase crude oil at below-market rates in exchange for Indian goods and technical services.

Prime Minister Gandhi's oil diplomacy necessitated subverting Cold War divides. She reached out to US and Soviet allies in the oil-rich Middle East adopting a conciliatory approach framed in North-South terms, instead of East-West blocs. Her government signed an agreement with pro-Soviet Iraq in January 1974 under which Iraq agreed to sell India two million tons of crude oil at below-market prices, half of which would be financed by a US$110 million concessional credit.[149] Vice President Saddam Hussein even paid a state visit to New Delhi in March that year to strengthen ties between the two countries. During this period, India helped to build Iraq's railways and other infrastructure and trained Iraqi Air Force pilots, who flew Soviet-supplied MiG-21 planes like the Indian Air Force.[150]

There was also a political dimension to the Indian government's reengagement with the Middle East. Several Middle Eastern countries had supported Pakistan in the 1971 war. The Nixon administration had provided military hardware to Pakistan for the war, rerouted through Jordan and Saudi Arabia to avoid congressional checks. During the oil crisis, as Indian policymakers wooed oil-rich countries of the Islamic world, they also hoped to counteract Pakistan's influence in the region. When Egyptian president Anwar al-Sadat visited New Delhi in February 1974, arriving directly from the second session of the Islamic Summit Conference held in Lahore, Pakistan, he publicly commended Pakistan's recent recognition of Bangladesh. During Sadat's visit, Prime Minister Gandhi reiterated her country's support for the "Arab cause," while her guest expressed his faith in nonalignment and the "brotherly support" between their two countries. Inattentive to the economic side of Gandhi's diplomacy, Ambassador Moynihan sarcastically noted that India "has got itself so ideologically committed to the political causes of the Arabs that it just can't deal with the economic consequences of Arab actions on India itself."[151]

Under its February 1974 agreement with the shah of Iran—a US ally—the Gandhi government obtained crude oil at US$8.50 a barrel, US$500 million in credit to purchase part of its oil imports, and Iranian assistance to expand its Madras oil refinery, among others.[152] India was expected to pay Iran through iron ore, aluminum, cement, and sugar. The two countries even agreed to set up a joint shipping company. Prime Minister Gandhi visited Tehran in late April 1974 for a five-day visit for further talks with the shah, which the *New York Times* dubbed as "détente" between the two countries. Iran and India had differences over Iran's good relations with Pakistan and the United States, and India's coziness with the Soviet Union.[153] Yet, they agreed on their mutual quest for autonomy and opposition to the militarization of the Indian Ocean region.[154] In the joint communiqué released at the end of Prime Minister Gandhi's visit, oil—the controversial issue of the hour—was conspicuous by its absence. When the shah would visit India later that fall, he would be very curious about India's newest technical expertise, namely, underground nuclear explosions.

Conclusion

Prime Minister Gandhi's decision to conduct an underground nuclear explosion came at a time when she was at the height of her political power. Sarabhai's death had removed a key impediment for the BARC explosions group. Institutional and technopolitical factors facilitated by political will, thus, created an ideal opportunity for those within the DAE, who had harbored desires to conduct a PNE for years.

The Gandhi government's geopolitical anxieties did not recede with India's military victory in the 1971 war. India's territorial threats were intermestic with China and Pakistan's support for insurgencies in India's borderlands and demands for increased autonomy by Sikkim's Chogyal. Bangladesh, after the jubilation of its independence in 1971, spiraled into a corrupt and inexperienced regime led by Mujibur Rahman himself. By the time the Bhutto government in Pakistan recognized it as a sovereign nation-state, the country faced hunger, poverty, and a crushing famine.[155]

US-Indian relations remained rife with tensions despite initial hopes of improved relations with the arrivals of Moynihan and Kaul as ambassadors in New Delhi and Washington, DC, respectively. Gandhi's own fears of a CIA conspiracy against her, especially after the 1973 coup against Allende in Chile, added another layer of complexity to US-Indian relations.[156] Moynihan confessed about US-Indian relations to the *New York Times* in March 1974: "Whether we've reached a dead end or started a new relationship, I just don't know."[157] He would resign from his post in New Delhi in early 1975, expressing his many frustrations with India in his controversial *Commentary* article. Titled, "The United States in Opposition," Moynihan would call the global North-South conflict the result of "tyranny of the UN's new majority."[158] President Ford would respond by appointing him as the US ambassador to the United Nations.

CHAPTER 7

Explosion and Fallout, 1974–1980s

Around 10 a.m. on May 18, 1974, Indian foreign secretary Kewal Singh telephoned the US embassy in New Delhi. Singh informed chargé d'affaires David Schneider that the Gandhi government had conducted a "peaceful nuclear explosion" at 8 o'clock that Saturday morning.[1] "[T]he experiment," Singh explained to Schneider, "had been carried out by the Indian Atomic Energy Commission in order to keep India abreast of the technology . . . for such purposes as mining and earth moving." The Indian government remained "absolutely committed against the use of nuclear energy for military purposes," continued Singh, adding that he was informing the US embassy ahead of all other diplomatic missions, under the instructions of the foreign minister. Taken aback, Schneider responded that "this news would be received with considerable shock in Washington" because the US government "did not believe it possible to distinguish between explosions for peaceful and military purposes."[2] Singh changed tack. It was his "devout hope," he said, that the "event will not interfere with improving US-India relations."[3]

What Schneider told Singh was already known to the Gandhi government. The USAEC's aide-mémoire to the DAE in November 1970 had underlined the Nixon administration's position that the test of a nuclear weapon and a PNE were indistinguishable. USAEC chairman Glenn Seaborg had communicated the same position of the Johnson administration to DAE secretary Vikram Sarabhai in January 1967 (both discussed in chapter 5). Even Indian ambassador V. C. Trivedi had stated at the ENDC that he did not deny that the technology for the two was the same. Yet, he had asserted that "the weapon has many characteristics which are not present in a peaceful device."[4] In other words, the Indian government was aware of the US position, but publicly disagreed with it.

The problem was of interpretation. The US government did not consider a nuclear explosion to be "peaceful" when conducted by a country for the very first time using its own resources. It was a nuclear weapon test and a "setback to nonproliferation," as US deputy secretary of state Kenneth Rush informed US diplomatic missions.[5] In definitional terms, to the DAE and the Gandhi government, if the United States and the Soviet Union could conduct PNEs, which they did for civil engineering projects such as creating artificial harbors in Alaska and lakes in Kazakhstan, then that category of underground nuclear explosions for civilian purposes also applied to India. The fact that the US government thought differently depicted to Indian leaders the intrinsic inequality of the US-led global nonproliferation regime.[6]

On the day of the explosion, Schneider wrote to Ambassador Moynihan, who was in London at the time, that the embassy found "no dissimulation" because Indian policymakers had repeatedly stated that "studies are underway" including Prime Minister Gandhi, who had mentioned in May 1973 that such studies included "ecological and geological aspects of nuclear explosives."[7] Schneider assessed that if the source of nuclear materials used in India's nuclear explosion was indeed plutonium reprocessed from the CIRUS reactor for which the USAEC had provided heavy water in 1956, then "[W]e have a problem with the GOI."[8]

The "Indian test," noted US deputy secretary Rush, came at a "particularly awkward time" when India-US relations were showing gradual signs of improvement.[9] Baffled State Department officials, therefore, agreed with the embassy in New Delhi that the "decision to test now was at least in good part an attempt on Mrs. Gandhi's part to distract Indian concerns from an increasingly depressing domestic scene, and to provide a morale booster to flagging spirits."[10] Popularized by Ambassador Moynihan, India's underground nuclear explosion became predominantly construed as a one-dimensional act for domestic political gains. As a good sociologist, Moynihan looked for explanations for India's nuclear explosion inside the society and found social and political disruption against Indira Gandhi as its root cause. The explosion became predominantly about the "20,000 Trade Union leaders she [Gandhi] threw into prison a month ago when they began talking of a rail strike," as Moynihan wrote to Winston Lord, director of policy planning staff at the State Department.[11] The railway strike's convergence with the nuclear explosion perpetuated the incomplete explanation that the Gandhi government conducted the nuclear explosion to serve its domestic political interests. This argument would be repeated in US policy memos, media accounts, and scholarly analyses for years. The full picture was much more complex.

The official US response was muted. Secretary of State Henry Kissinger's guidance to US diplomatic missions was to adopt a low-key approach to India's nuclear explosion for public and press inquiries.[12] As President Nixon experienced congressional and public backlash from the Watergate scandal, his administration had a lot on its plate in May 1974. Against the backdrop of the oil crisis, Kissinger had also been trying to mend US relations with India as part of his engagement with the "Third World." By May 22, 1974, the MEA concluded that "the official American reaction may be considered rather mild and restrained."[13] MEA officials observed that "[o]n May 18, the US Government through its official spokesman expressed 'disappointment' over India's peaceful nuclear explosion which it said was likely to have an adverse impact on world stability." However, "[a]part from that, there has been no other official statement nor has the matter been raised with our Embassy in Washington."[14]

Despite the inconspicuous official US reaction, India's underground nuclear explosion was a major event for the Nixon administration. US deputy secretary Rush noted that the most "unsettling effect" of India's PNE was going to be on Pakistan. The Bhutto government "will regard India's going nuclear as posing a new threat to Pakistani security," leading them to "intensify their efforts to get a change in our arms policy," "seek added security assurances from China and the US," and perhaps even "decide to launch their own crash [nuclear] program."[15] Rush informed US diplomatic missions that the new US policy challenge was going to be about "stabilizing a new nuclear 'power' within the international framework and trying to dissuade others from following suit," both near-nuclears, like Japan, Israel, and South Africa, and India's arch-rival, Pakistan.[16] US officials quietly began to take steps for nonproliferation in response.

On May 23, 1974, "in light of India's announcement of its underground nuclear test," the Nixon administration launched an interagency review of US policy on the NPT. Under National Security Study Memorandum 202, Kissinger directed a reassessment of whether the US government "should press for renewed support for the treaty by those now party to it and accession to the treaty by those not yet signatories, and if so how and to what extent."[17] Within weeks, the administration also decided, under National Security Decision Memorandum 255, to begin multilateral consultations to manage "the problems associated with the increased availability of weapons useable materials from the growth and dissemination of nuclear power industries."[18] These consultations would begin in early 1975 in London, building on the Zangger Committee, to form a multilateral export control group irrespective of the suppliers' NPT membership. Initially called the London Suppliers Conference, it would eventually be known as the Nuclear Suppliers Group (NSG).[19]

Congressional and media criticisms of India's nuclear explosion were sharp. Prime Minister Gandhi chastised the US media and politicians for making India "a favorite and convenient whipping boy" seen as a "soft state and a flabby democracy" as well as "ruthless and tough, cynical and power hungry."[20] In the midst of the media furor, Indian ambassador T. N. Kaul addressed the National Press Club in Washington, DC, to discuss what he claimed were the "fact, philosophy, rationale and thinking of India about the underground nuclear experiment."[21] The ever-so-eloquent Kaul reaffirmed the Gandhi government's public position on its nuclear explosion. He bemoaned that even though "India has had its first nuclear explosion underground, without any radioactive fallout," unlike China in 1964, countries have shown "all kinds of feelings ranging from shock and surprise to disappointment and distrust."

Kaul recited with rightful indignation: "(I) India has been declaring for the last 25 years that she would use nuclear technology exclusively for peaceful purposes and reaffirmed it again; (II) India has used hundred percent its own technology, material and personnel; (III) India said that she will publish all the relevant scientific data for the benefit of world science; (IV) India has not violated any bilateral or multilateral agreements she had signed." Kaul asked rhetorically, "Why then, it may be asked, is there adverse reaction in some countries and circles, favorable reaction in most countries of the developing world and muted criticism in a few?[22]

Kissinger in his conversation with Indian foreign secretary Singh and Ambassador Kaul provided an explanation, which he called an "intellectual distinction" between PNEs.[23] He argued that a PNE "had a different meaning and significance for a developing country than it has for an advanced country" because "we [the United States] can establish criteria with which we can control the nature of a peaceful nuclear explosion with precision." A developing country in "the early stages of nuclear explosion technology" could not "differentiate with this kind of precision." Kissinger's precision-driven distinction and its implications for intent behind a nuclear explosion—peaceful or military—logically contradicted the earlier US position that PNEs were technologically indistinguishable from nuclear weapon tests. It highlighted another marker of difference, namely, economic hierarchies among countries. Kissinger's remark thus gave credence to Indian assertions against global economic inequality, most prominently expressed in the UN General Assembly Resolution calling for the establishment of a New International Economic Order, just weeks before India's nuclear explosion.[24]

Oil and PNEs

Global protestations of economic rights in 1973–74 offered a rhetorical stage on which India's nuclear explosion could be reaffirmed as a "ploughshare" of a poor country in dire need of cost-effective national development projects, such as oil exploration. Days after the explosion, DAE secretary Sethna called it an experiment to ascertain the viability of such nuclear devices for oil and natural gas extraction.[25] Sethna even gestured at the possibility of conducting more nuclear explosions through larger hydrogen bombs with the goal to secure oil from shale rock.[26] On August 25, 1974, in the lower house of the Indian Parliament or Lok Sabha, two members of the Parliament asked whether the government-owned Oil and Natural Gas Commission was collecting information about nuclear explosions for oil exploration from foreign countries, including the superpowers. Minister of State for Petroleum and Chemicals Shahnawaz Khan responded that the commission was indeed studying its possibility through published literature, but that the technology remained at an experimental stage.[27]

The contextual correlation between oil and underground nuclear explosions went back to the very origin of PNEs itself. Project Plowshare, the US underground nuclear explosions program, had emerged in the wake of the 1956 Suez Crisis that had led to blockage of shipments including oil through the canal. In response, scientists at the Lawrence Radiation Laboratory in California (today, Lawrence Livermore National Laboratory) looked for a way to build sea-level canals by moving earth through nuclear explosives.[28] The Plowshare Program reflected the unbounded faith in the peaceful atom of the Atoms for Peace era. Indian policymakers remained attentive to US PNE developments.

The 1967 Arab oil embargo in the wake of the Six-Day War by Israel gave impetus to oil exploration through PNEs. On June 8, 1967, days after the oil embargo, Ambassador Trivedi told the ENDC that PNEs had several uses such as "extracting oil from deep deposits for which purposes certainly conventional methods are not at present available."[29] In September, the USAEC conducted its first US natural gas reservoir stimulation experiment using nuclear explosives. It exploded a twenty-nine-kiloton nuclear device in a sandstone formation at a depth of roughly 4,300 feet in northwestern New Mexico. Cannily called Project Gasbuggy and jointly sponsored by the US Department of Interior and the El Paso Natural Gas Company, it was the first government-industry PNE endeavor in the United States.[30] The USAEC shared technical data of its PNEs, including that of the Gasbuggy, at the IAEA.[31] It exploded its third and last underground nuclear device for gas stimulation in Colorado on May 17, 1973—a year and a day before India's nuclear explosion.

The history of PNEs is one of ambiguity and camouflage. India's PNE formed a part of that history. The most well-known proponent of PNEs in the United States was Edward Teller, the father of the hydrogen bomb. In 1961, Teller had argued that "real security" and "real peace" depended on the development of nuclear explosives "both for defence and for constructive peacetime purposes."[32] When the 1963 Limited Test Ban Treaty allowed only underground nuclear tests, subterranean nuclear explosions became, for Teller, a means to continue nuclear weapon testing with limited radioactive fallout and civilian support.[33] With the NPT close to being finalized, Teller coauthored a study on the Plowshare Program, hailing the use of nuclear explosives for mining and oil explorations as the "most promising industrial suggestions."[34] A PNE, Teller argued, was merely an engineering tool. He claimed, brimming with overoptimism, that "[t]here is no less expensive source of large quantities of energy and no less expensive way to move large quantities of earth than with nuclear explosives."[35]

Yet, PNEs were an "excellent way of justifying the pursuit of underground testing with military implications" as the French physicist Bertrand Goldschmidt bluntly stated in his 1982 book, *Atomic Complex*.[36] France itself began conducting its nuclear weapon tests underground in the South Pacific after 1974, in the face of environmental concerns raised by New Zealand and Australia at the International Court of Justice.[37] By its very nature, an underground nuclear explosion was a "sword" and a "ploughshare." It was what one made of it. The leaders of India's nuclear program knew that well.

Earth-Moving in Pokhran

India's first nuclear explosion in Pokhran on May 18, 1974, at 8:05 a.m. was not a predetermined outcome.[38] It was marked by contingencies and unintended consequences. The nuclear explosion was originally scheduled for February that year because the weather was expected to be cooler in the desert. It had to be postponed owing to a series of hurdles.

The DAE needed a dry and secure L-shaped shaft in the Thar Desert in the northwestern state of Rajasthan for emplacing the plutonium-filled implosion device. The 61 Engineer Regiment of the Indian Army based in Jodhpur was entrusted with digging the shaft in May 1973.[39] Formed soon after the 1965

India-Pakistan War, the regiment had built bunkers for Indian troops during the 1971 war. The army engineers initially refused. They were inexperienced in digging shafts as well as unwilling to get involved with civilian scientists interested in conducting a "seismic experiment," as BARC director Raja Ramanna had described the task to them.[40] The work finally began in October after the Chief of Army Staff General G. G. Bewoor personally informed Commanding Officer Lieutenant Colonel P. P. Subherwal, who was overseeing the regiment, that Prime Minister Gandhi herself had sent them the orders to dig the shaft.[41]

A dry well collapsed in November 1973 leading to one death and multiple injured personnel. In January 1974, the engineers accidentally struck an aquifer that filled the shaft with water, making it unusable for a nuclear explosion.[42] The military engineers then had to excavate a different site to develop a new dry shaft, delaying the explosion by several months. Meanwhile, the neutron trigger was being developed by the BARC radioisotope group. It was ready only in early May 1974.[43] On May 18, the explosion was scheduled for 8 a.m., but a Jeep engine's refusal to start and faulty reading on a voltage indicator caused a five-minute delay.

At 8:05 a.m. that day, P. R. Dastidar of BARC's electronics detonation team pressed the button that initiated the neutron trigger. It exploded the nuclear device emplaced about one hundred meters underground. The explosion released energy creating a mound of elevated earth visible from the control point (see figure 7.1). The dome of earth then fell, creating a crater on the surface

FIGURE 7.1. "Seconds after the nuclear test a sandy mound rises above the ground, somewhere in India, May 18, 1974, as India sets off its first nuclear explosion." Caption by Associated Press. Photo identifier: 7405180204. Published with permission.

of the desert. According to the DAE, the explosive yield of the nuclear device was "estimated at about 12 kilotons."[44] This made India's nuclear device similar to that of the "Little Boy" nuclear bomb dropped on Hiroshima on August 6, 1945, while its implosion-type design was modeled on the "Fat Man" or the Nagasaki bomb. Its actual explosive yield would become contentious and be estimated between eight to twelve kilotons.[45]

At the Fourth IAEA Technical Meeting on PNEs held in Vienna in January 1975, Ramanna and R. Chidambaram from BARC shared official Indian data on the nuclear explosion. The first three IAEA technical meetings on PNEs had been held in March 1970, January 1971, and November 1972.[46] In pursuit of Article V of the NPT, these meetings were intended to share on a global platform the technical data on underground nuclear explosions for civilian uses. The BARC study presented at the IAEA in 1975 claimed that the Indian nuclear explosion was of 12 kilotons, that the seismic data from the explosion read 5.0 on the Richter scale, and that it first created a dome of 170 meters in diameter and 34 meters in height and then, a crater of 47 meters in radius and 10 meters in depth.

Ramanna and Chidambaram were unequivocal about radioactivity, which was a particularly sensitive topic: "Extensive radiation monitoring of the site and analysis of air samples before and after the experiment showed that no radioactivity had been released to the atmosphere during the experiment."[47] The study claimed that "the mound remained essentially intact during its growth and fall," which meant that there was "no indication of any air blast due to escaping cavity gases," and consequently, no radioactive release. The Pokhran test site was close to the India-Pakistan border. Any radioactive release would transgress the territorial boundaries of the Indian nation-state. The BARC study firmly denied any atmospheric radioactivity from the explosion, but, of course, it was not to be independently verified.[48]

Oil exploration provided a multifaceted façade for India's nuclear explosion at home and abroad. While the 61 Engineer Regiment dug shaft for the DAE in the fall of 1973, the locals from neighboring villages were told that the government's Oil and National Gas Commission was looking for oil.[49] With the oil crisis underway, it was credible, not least to poor illiterate villagers accustomed to disruptive national development projects. Politicians eagerly inquired whether PNEs were being considered for gas stimulation, as in the case of the Lok Sabha session earlier discussed. In their BARC study, Ramanna and Chidambaram reaffirmed at the IAEA that oil extraction was a goal of future PNE experiments: "Applications like stimulation of oil reservoirs and mining of nonferrous metals are promising in the context of Indian conditions."[50] The leaders of India's nuclear program thus framed their act in terms of economic rights of developing countries, a key demand of the advocates for a New International Economic Order.[51]

When the earth moved in Pokhran in May 1974, "[a]ll types of political opinion, from the ultra-left communist to the extreme right," rallied behind the Indian prime minister in jubilation, noted French ambassador Daniel Jurgensen.[52] Coming at a time of acute economic and political crisis for India, the nuclear explosion in Pokhran became a consensus-enforcing device. Its intrinsic duality as a "ploughshare" and a "sword" made it hard to oppose by domestic political parties at home and those in favor of South-South solidarity abroad. The nuclear explosion—whether one accepted its peaceful character or not—thus functioned as an anti-dissent machine for the time being at least.

Throughout 1973, there were claims of corruption against Prime Minister Gandhi, her government, and her political party. Failed monsoons and the oil crisis led to rising food prices. Rural and urban poverty was pervasive. Against this backdrop, Gandhian socialist leader Jayaprakash Narayan, popularly known as J. P., became a formidable force against the government.[53] He inspired large antigovernment rallies and demanded the resignation of the prime minister. Railway workers' labor militancy seeking higher wages stopped the nation on May 8, 1974. "Better jail than rail," chanted George Fernandes, one of the prime minister's political opponents in the Parliament, who had led the strike and was imprisoned.[54] The railway strike, which resulted in a production loss of US$1.5 billion to US$2 billion, was called off by the striking railway workers themselves on May 28. It was hailed as a victory for the Gandhi government.[55]

The strident political opposition to her government in 1973–74 and the emergency beginning in June 1975, during which Prime Minister Gandhi suspended civil and political liberties in the entire country, have encouraged scholars and analysts to view the May 1974 nuclear explosion as a diversionary tactic of the Indian prime minister in the face of domestic political turmoil. However, Prime Minister Gandhi's decisions to conduct a nuclear explosion took place in 1972, when she was politically strong riding the high tide of India's 1971 military victory and her party's 1972 electoral victories in state assemblies. Her funding approvals for DRDO's missile programs, Projects Valiant and Devil, and her unsuccessful efforts to draw ISRO's activities closer to the DRDO went back to 1970. She was not politically weak at the time, but consolidating her political position (discussed in chapter 6).

India's nuclear explosion was deliberately ambiguous and polyvalent. As a plutonium device, it needed far less weapon-grade fissile material than a highly enriched uranium device. It was a poor country's atomic weapon backed by rudimentary deterrent options, such as three squadrons of British-supplied Canberra planes with a maximum flight radius of 1,100 miles, as one NATO report observed, and potential nuclear waste mining of the Himalayas, as discussed by Sarabhai (discussed in chapter 5).[56] The polyvalence of India's PNE was ironical. On May 28, 1974, Prime Minister Gandhi called India a "nuclear country, not a nuclear weapons country," assuring its neighbors of its peaceful intentions.[57] Editor of the journal *Gandhi Marg*, T. K. Mahadevan captured this irony the following day in the *Times of India* through the epithet, the "Swadeshi Bomb." Invoking *swadeshi* or the anticolonial movement for self-sufficiency that shook early twentieth-century British India, Mahadevan demystified the nuclear explosion: "The swadeshi bomb is the real thing. It wasn't a mirage in the Rajasthan desert. The bomb, like beauty, is in the eye of the beholder. If you are a hawk, you will know it is a bomb. If you are a dove, you will pretend it is a device."[58]

The Pokhran explosion's total cost was a nearly impossible estimate given the DAE/AECI's early investments in infrastructure, informal budgets, as in the case of the BARC explosion group during Sarabhai's tenure, and the amalgamation of a variety of technological artifacts concurrently serving civilian and military ends in the nuclear program.[59] Prime Minister Gandhi firmly maintained, "No new budgetary provision was made for it [nuclear explosion]; there is no foreign exchange expenditure, and there was no dependence on any other country."[60] Initial US government estimate of the cost of India's nuclear explosion was US$10 to US$20 million.[61] A US NATO mission report from June 1974 estimated the cost to be US$10 million—the same figure that Bhabha had given Wiesner in 1965. The report projected that "[w]ith relatively little extra expense, India could undertake the necessary work for a continuing nuclear test program."[62]

The ambiguity around the cost of the Pokhran explosion facilitated freedom of action for Indian policymakers. First, the opaqueness on cost prevented potential criticism of the nuclear explosion inside the country at a time of economic crisis. Instead, it generated support among India's middle classes, represented in editorials, recommending that the DAE use miniaturized PNEs to divert the course of rivers to prevent floods and alter rock formations to stall earthquakes.[63] Second, outside the country, the economic opacity helped to dodge questions about whether development aid was channeled into funding the underground nuclear explosion. Despite initial concerns of diversion of economic assistance, the Aid-India Consortium pledged US$1.4 billion in June 1974. The amount even exceeded the previous year's aid by US$200 million in light of India's economic woes owing to high oil prices.[64] Third, to countries embarking on new nuclear programs in the backdrop of the oil crisis, the Pokhran explosion made the DAE stand out among developing countries as a potential supplier of affordable nuclear know-how. During the shah of Iran's October 1974 visit to New Delhi, unsurprisingly, the monarch inquired about India's technological capabilities and willingness to share information and training in the nuclear domain.[65]

Prime Minister Gandhi visited the Pokhran test site on December 22, 1974, seven months after the explosion. DAE secretary Homi Sethna, Cabinet Minister K. C. Pant, Lieutenant Colonel Subherwal, and AECI member J. R. D. Tata accompanied her, among others (figure 7.2). The presence of J. R. D Tata, the chairman of Tata Sons, at the test site was logical but noteworthy. He was

FIGURE 7.2.   Prime Minister Indira Gandhi visited the Pokhran test site on December 22, 1974. She is seen here with her cabinet minister, K. C. Pant (left), DAE secretary Homi Sethna (center, gesticulating), and AECI member J. R. D. Tata (right corner). Lieutenant Colonel P. P. Subherwal is directly behind her, possibly showing a pulverized rock formation created by the underground nuclear explosion. Published with permission from Photo Division, Ministry of Information and Broadcasting, Government of India.

at the Pokhran test site as an AECI member, a position he had been in since 1962. He had also been a member of the Board for Research on Atomic Energy that first met in May 1946 in Bombay House, headquarters of Tata Industries, to discuss the organization of nuclear fission research in soon-to-be independent India. Tata's presence at India's nuclear test site depicted the persistence of an interlaced relationship between the government and a large corporation in India's nuclear program.

Sikkim's Annexation

The nuclear explosion of May 1974, conducted on *Buddha Purnima*, the auspicious day commemorating the birth of Buddha, is entrenched in Indian popular culture as the "Smiling Buddha," denoting its official characterization as a peaceful act.[66] BARC director Ramanna reportedly called Prime Minister Gandhi from an unsecured telephone line near the test site informing her of the successful detonation using the codeword, "The Buddha is smiling."[67] That month in the eastern Himalayas, the small Buddhist kingdom of Sikkim—a fraught borderland between India and China—was in the midst of becoming "Indian." It was against the wishes of its monarch, Chogyal Palden Thondup Namgyal, and the Buddhist ethnic minority groups of the Bhutias and the Lepchas, whom he represented. If Buddha smiled in Pokhran, he likely felt unsettled in Sikkim.

The Indian annexation of Sikkim (1973–75) was entangled with the geopolitical dimension of the nuclear explosion. Through R&AW's covert support for Kazi Lhendup Dorji, who led pro-Indian political forces composed of the Nepali ethnic majority, the Indian government slowly but deliberately incorporated Sikkim into its own territory over a period of roughly two years. India's actions in Sikkim encapsulated the intermestic character of India's national security threats. Sikkim's absorption into India to counter the Chogyal's demands for greater autonomy communicated the capability and willingness of the Gandhi government to suppress secessionist movements of the Mizos and Nagas demanding independence in the northeast. At the same time, India's absorption of Sikkim into its own territory was a geopolitical act to the Chinese government that had been claiming Sikkim to be one of its "five fingers" since the 1950s.[68]

The Chinese government sharply criticized Indian actions in Sikkim, unlike its tepid response to the nuclear explosion. The *People's Daily*, official mouthpiece of the Chinese Communist Party, called Indian merger of Sikkim "a monologue produced and performed by the Indian government."[69] By contrast, Chinese vice premier Deng Xiaoping had said that his government "would not rise to the bait" and make an issue of India's nuclear explosion, blaming the Soviet Union for encouraging it.[70]

India's absorption of Sikkim, like its PNE in Pokhran, remains largely misunderstood. The territorial annexation did not result from the nuclear explosion, but the two were concurrent and entangled. Prime Minister Gandhi's decisions in favor of the Chogyal's incapacitation and the nuclear explosion were taken around the same time in the latter half of 1972. Both resulted from India's geopolitical anxieties emerging from the 1971 war. Despite being a military victory for India, the war created new territorial challenges and exacerbated old ones. As the Chogyal sought greater autonomy, the Gandhi government offered "permanent association" for Sikkim to replace its "protectorate" status under the 1950 India-Sikkim Treaty.[71]

As the East Pakistan crisis and Sino-US rapprochement preoccupied Indian policymakers, the Chogyal called for a "more liberal and well-defined policy for Sikkim" in the kingdom's dealings with the Indian government.[72] His letter to Prime Minister Gandhi on August 30, 1971, indicated that he wanted greater autonomy and even independence: "[W]e hope that Protecting Power or the Guardian will look into our real needs and future prospects and *enable us to reach a self-reliant position in due course* so that both India and Sikkim can share the joys of such achievements."[73] After over three months of silence, Prime Minister Gandhi wrote back to the monarch on December 4, 1971, the day after declaring war on Pakistan. She told him that she had asked the MEA "to look into the matters" and that the ministry will write to him through the Indian political officer in Sikkim, K. Shankar Bajpai.[74] Gandhi's purposeful choice of writing to the Chogyal during the 1971 Bangladesh Liberation War was noteworthy. In the letter, she bemoaned, "[S]ometimes voices are heard in Sikkim about her 'economic strangulation' by India," advising the Chogyal to dispel "these wrong impressions."[75]

By the fall of 1972, when it was clear that the Chogyal would not settle for "permanent association," or greater autonomy solely in internal matters, Prime Minister Gandhi instructed R. N. Kao, the head of R&AW, to supplant the monarch of Sikkim. By then, she had already taken the final decisions to conduct the underground nuclear explosion. In December 1972, Prime Minister Gandhi asked Kao, "Can you do something about Sikkim?"[76] Gandhi was not politically weak at the time, but anxious about what the transformation of the global Cold War—the Sino-US rapprochement and the US-China-Pakistan alignment—meant for India's geopolitical threats, particularly in the disputed borderlands along China and Pakistan.[77]

Kao masterminded what a R&AW insider called the "happy denouement in Sikkim."[78] Sikkim was R&AW's major assignment after training the *Mukti*

Bahini in 1971 during the East Pakistan crisis. In early 1973, Indian policymakers decided on a calibrated approach on Sikkim.[79] The goal was to disempower the Chogyal, but while giving the public impression that it was the will of the people of Sikkim. R&AW agents in Sikkim began to cultivate ties with the Nepali ethnic majority in Sikkim, who did not have political representation commensurate to their size despite being over 70 percent of the population. The Sikkimese political system favored the Bhutia-Lepcha ethnic minority. The Nepalis had settled in Sikkim during the British colonial period to work in tea plantations and copper mines. The Nepali population further increased in size in Sikkim after India's independence. Sikkim National Congress leader Kazi Lhendup Dorji's opposition to the Chogyal and demands for rights of the Nepali majority became R&AW's point of leverage.

In March 1973, large prodemocracy demonstrations took place all over the kingdom incited by R&AW. On April 4, on the monarch's fiftieth birthday, protests against the monarchy reached new heights, compelling the Chogyal to make a formal request to Indian political officer Bajpai for Indian assistance to remain in power. Within twenty-four hours, the Indian Army restored order in Sikkim by reinstating the Chogyal while the Indian government appointed B. S. Das as the chief executive of Sikkim.[80] The Gandhi government thus got the opportunity it had sought in Sikkim. After several rounds of negotiations, a tripartite agreement was signed on May 8, 1973, by the Chogyal, Indian foreign secretary Kewal Singh, and the leaders of the political parties of Sikkim. This agreement would pave the way for democratization of the kingdom through universal adult suffrage under full Indian oversight.[81]

Even though the May 8, 1973, agreement called for elections based on universal adult suffrage, it was not until April 1974 that general elections were held in Sikkim. There were several interconnected reasons for the year-long gap. First, Prime Minister Gandhi and her advisors preferred that the anti-Chogyal political coalition in Sikkim appear to be a grassroots prodemocracy movement led by the Nepali majority. Indian policymakers waited for those pressures to emerge in their due course. Second, as was in the case of the 1971 war, the Gandhi government wanted to avoid stirring up too much trouble against the monarch, fearing that the Sikkim youth movement, the Naxalites, and the secessionist movements in the northeast might benefit from the political chaos that could ensue. Third, Soviet authorities advised the Indian government against a 1971-like swift military intervention in order to avoid international criticism.[82] Fourth, the Chinese government was harshly criticizing Indian moves in the spring of 1973.[83] China's official *Xinhua News Agency* repudiated the 1973 tripartite agreement for giving the Gandhi government "wider control over the Himalayan kingdom" far more than the 1950 "unequal treaty" between the Nehru government and the kingdom of Sikkim.[84] Beijing's position as a permanent member in the UN Security Council meant that the possibility of UN involvement in Sikkim could not be ruled out. The Indian government proceeded slowly.

There was another factor hidden in plain sight. Prime Minister Gandhi and her close group of trusted advisors, particularly P. N. Haksar, likely wanted Sikkim's first general elections to be roughly around the same time as the nuclear explosion. India's merger of Sikkim and the nuclear explosion were entangled over the course of 1973–74. The nearly one-year gap between R&AW-incited prodemocracy protests in Sikkim in spring 1973 and the general elections in April 1974 matched the timeline of the Indian Army's nuclear test preparations in Pokhran. A small group of trusted high-level policymakers close to the prime minister was aware of both developments, particularly P. N. Haksar, while different institutions were in charge on the ground: DAE with the help of the Indian Army in Rajasthan and R&AW with the help of Indian political, administrative, and paramilitary machineries in Sikkim. The success of both policy outcomes was far from predetermined. There were stumbling blocks for both.

Preparations for the PNE in Rajasthan had just started in May 1973 with the digging of a suitable shaft by the 61 Engineer Regiment. After initial opposition by army engineers, they began their work to construct a dry L-shaped shaft for the PNE in September–October 1973. The Election Commissioner of India was originally expected to visit Gangtok, Sikkim's capital, in August–September 1973 to set up the election machinery for elections in February–March 1974.[85] This was when the PNE itself was anticipated to be in February 1974. Army engineers encountered several challenges through the end of 1973. In early December 1973, when a journalist asked Foreign Secretary Singh after his two-day trip to Gangtok when elections were going to be held in Sikkim, he vaguely responded that they could be held "as early as possible."[86] The underground shaft in Pokhran for the PNE device was still not ready.

Indian authorities publicly announced the dates of the elections on April 3, 1974, through a gazette notification, giving voters in Sikkim less than a two-week notice for their first general elections based on universal adult suffrage.[87] Four battalions of the Indian Central Reserve Police Force remained on guard while widespread rigging was feared by the pro-Indian Sikkim Congress led by Dorji, which eventually won thirty-one out of thirty-two seats in the Sikkim Assembly.[88] By the time the newly elected Sikkim Assembly passed its resolution on May 11 for closer ties with India, and reduced the Chogyal to a figurehead, the BARC radioisotope team had readied the neutron trigger that would explode the nuclear device in Pokhran.

After the underground nuclear explosion in Pokhran, Indian political moves in Sikkim were swift. The Government of Sikkim Bill of June 1974 urged "immediate steps to insure fuller participation of Sikkim in the economic and social institutions of India."[89] The Chogyal boycotted the assembly, Indian police forces tear-gassed pro Chogyal protestors, and the Indian Army remained on high alert.[90] The *New York Times* noted that the "Chogyal appears to have only two choices: to yield or to abdicate and leave Sikkim."[91] Under pressure from Indian government representatives, the Chogyal finally assented to the bill on July 4, leading to the Government of Sikkim Act. The Indian Parliament swiftly passed the Thirty-Fifth Constitutional Amendment Bill on September 4, 1974, which transformed Sikkim from India's "protectorate" country to an "associate" of the Indian Union, with political representation in both houses of the Indian Parliament.[92]

The PNE ensured that preplanned actions by R&AW to overthrow Sikkim's monarch could be swiftly executed without the risk of opposition within Sikkim or from the PLA on the Tibet-Sikkim border. Moreover, the Gandhi government likely anticipated that after the nuclear explosion, the national and international media would be focused on Pokhran, not Gangtok. They would be preoccupied wondering whether India's nuclear explosion was peaceful or not, and thereby neglect Indian actions in Sikkim.

The Chinese government did not miss the connection between the two. When Sikkim's associate status was confirmed in September 1974, the *People's Daily* published an editorial denouncing Prime Minister Gandhi and her government for exploding "a nuclear device to make nuclear blackmail and nuclear menace in the South Asia region" while trying to "set up a so-called South Asian countries' group with itself as the overlord."[93] China officially announced that it did not recognize India's authority over Sikkim, pledging to support the "Sikkimese people's struggle in nationalist independence" against India.[94] A CIA research study noted that Chinese authorities also undertook "some limited but unmistakable military gestures" in the area, but those were defensive. They "moved to strengthen its strategic position in Tibet by stepping up programs for highway improvement and the construction of a pipeline, and eventually a railroad, into the area."[95]

On October 2, 1974, Chinese foreign minister Qiao Guanhua criticized India's actions in Sikkim at the UN General Assembly, calling it an "annexation"—a designation that the Gandhi government wanted to avoid. In response, the Indian permanent representative Rikhi Jaipal defended that it was "a natural and free political evolution of the people of Sikkim in the direction of internal democracy and closer link with neighboring India."[96] In his UN statement, Jaipal called Sikkim a former princely state, which the Chogyal himself had lobbied

against in 1946, when he was crown prince. In response, the monarch of Sikkim wrote a strongly worded letter to Indian political officer Gurbachan Singh
informing him that Sikkim had never signed an instrument of accession relin-
quishing its sovereignty to the Indian Union as other princely states had, nor did
the 1950 treaty involve an abnegation of "Sikkim's territorial integrity and her
international personality."[97] The Chogyal's demand that Sikkim's actual status
be clarified at the UN remained unfulfilled.

India's annexation of Sikkim elicited silence from the superpowers just like
their muted responses to the underground nuclear explosion in Pokhran. The
Soviet government considered Sikkim an internal matter of the Gandhi government. Officials within the Ford administration adopted a "no comment" approach. The State Department memo to Kissinger advised that "[t]he Indian
absorption of Sikkim does not directly involve the US," and Sikkim's "new status raises no question of direct American legal obligation to an existing sovereign
state."[98]

On March 1, 1975, as the constitutional amendment making Sikkim an associate state entered into force, Sikkim's monarch declared at a press conference in
Kathmandu, Nepal, that he would leave "no stone unturned" for Sikkim's separate identity to be preserved.[99] Indian authorities acted rapidly in response. On
April 7, Chief Minister Dorji requested the Indian government for the immediate removal of the Chogyal and the disarming of the Sikkim Guards, the monarch's decorative bodyguards, for obstructing Sikkim's "march to democracy."[100]
Then, on April 9, the Sikkim cabinet adopted a resolution calling for the abolition of the monarchy while the Indian Army arrived at the palace, disarmed the
Sikkim Guards, and placed the Chogyal under house arrest.[101] The following
day, the Sikkim assembly unanimously passed the resolution for the monarchy's
abolition and called for a referendum on Sikkim's merger with India.[102] The
monarch broadcast a message through ham radio about a coup against him.
Even though the message was picked up in Tehran, Ford administration officials
decided to stick to their position of nonintervention.[103]

On April 15, the Sikkimese people overwhelmingly voted in favor of a
merger with India in the referendum—59,637 in favor with 1,496 against.[104]
The promerger Nepali majority easily outnumbered the largely indigenous minority groups of the Bhutias and the Lepchas. On April 26, the upper house
of the Indian Parliament or Rajya Sabha passed with an overwhelming majority of 157 to 3 the Thirty-Sixth Amendment to the Constitution Bill to make
Sikkim the twenty-second state of India. The Indian president gave his assent
on May 16, 1975, completing the process.[105] Within a year of India's nuclear
explosion, Sikkim became a part of India. The 333-year-old monarchy was thus
abolished. Its former monarch, Mr. Palden Thondup Namgyal, remained a

"virtual prisoner" in his palace.[106] He refused to sign the instrument of accession to India until he died. Like Sir C. P., the last dewan of Travancore, had done in 1947, the former Chogyal spent his last days in obscurity.[107]

Soviet acquiescence of Indian political moves in Sikkim was likely not the only reason for China's inaction during the crisis.[108] Nuclear devices without long-range missiles and planes could offer a rudimentary deterrent if several of those were emplaced on the Himalayas. The leaders of the Indian nuclear program had considered such an option at various times, at least theoretically, and communicated that to scientific experts close to the US government. Jerome Wiesner had learned in January 1965 during his visit to India and meetings with Homi Bhabha and high-level Indian policymakers that they were contemplating a "nuclear minefield" along the India-China border as a cost-effective approach to nuclear weapons development. Vikram Sarabhai had discussed the deterrent effects of installing radioactive waste units in the Himalayan passes against the PLA during his meeting with the American Academy's CISAC delegation in June 1966 (both discussed in chapter 5). A British-origin NATO assessment dated May 28, 1974, asserted that one could not "discount the possibility, however, that the Indians may consider installing nuclear devices at strategic points near their border with China in order to be able to block the approaches to India."[109]

Could it be possible that US officials had warned the Chinese government about the potential for Indian emplacement of nuclear devices on the Tibet-Sikkim border in 1974–75? There were three Himalayan passes on the border that connected Sikkim with Tibet's Chumbi Valley: Jelep La, Nathu La, and Cho La. These passes have been the site of Indian Army-PLA clashes in 1962 and 1967 and the turf of frequent tensions between the two militaries. The American Academy's notes from its 1966 CISAC meeting in New Delhi were shared with members of the Soviet-American Disarmament Study Group, also based at the American Academy, of which Kissinger himself was an active member.[110] The meeting notes reached the State Department's Bureau of Near Eastern and South Asian Affairs, arms control experts Spurgeon Keeny and Harold Brown, and Alastair Buchan, the founding director of the London-based think tank International Institute for Strategic Studies.[111] In other words, high-level policymakers in the United States and the United Kingdom were aware of the rudimentary deterrent options that the DAE and top Indian policymakers were considering.[112] They might have informally communicated to the Chinese government to prevent a major conflict between the two countries during the Sikkim crisis.[113]

With Sikkim's territorial absorption, the Gandhi government exuded confidence about future Chinese actions along the eastern Himalayas. In a Cabinet Secretariat paper titled, "Threats to India's Security" dated April 25, 1975, Indian policymakers noted that it was "very unlikely that China will resort to any attack on India through the independent neighboring countries of Nepal, Bhutan and Burma."[114] The Chinese military would neither "use her Air Force against Indian ground forces holding positions, Indian airbases and installations deep inside our territory nor bomb the civilian population." This was in sharp contrast to the MEA paper from November 1964 written immediately after the first Chinese nuclear test (discussed in chapter 5). In that document, MEA officials had worried that the Chinese bomb was a "strategic instrument" that was "bound to have an impact on the entire strategy, political and military, surrounding the border question."[115] The 1964 paper had warned that the Chinese government could "indulge with impunity in infiltration and subversion, particularly in NEFA [North-East Frontier Agency] and the Himalayan kingdoms." The changed Indian outlook in April 1975 had much to do with Chinese military inaction during the Sikkim crisis, under the shadow of India's nuclear capability.

The Iron Fist of Legality

India's nuclear explosion was a "sword" and a "ploughshare," garbed in legality. Having been conducted underground, the nuclear explosion did not violate the 1963 Partial Test Ban Treaty, that India had signed and ratified, a point that Indian policymakers continued to remind the world. Never having signed the NPT, the Indian government was not in violation of that treaty either. The 1975 NPT Review Conference in Geneva—the first of its kind—held from May 5 to 30, 1975, was attended by ninety-one signatories while the Gandhi government completed Sikkim's merger with India. The Final Document of the Conference tacitly admitted that India had got away with conducting its PNE before any regulation could be in place: "[T]he technology of nuclear explosions for peaceful purposes is still at the stage of development and study and that there are a number of interrelated international legal and other aspects of such explosions which still need to be investigated." The conference assigned the central role to administer PNEs to the IAEA with safeguards and verifications owing to their "arms control implications."[116]

Sikkim's merger was a "ploughshare" and a "sword," also masked in legality. The largest democracy in the world led by a woman brought universal adult suffrage through resolutions and bills to a kingdom, whose monarch was repressing the rights of the majority. The Gandhi government justified its actions in Sikkim as promoting democracy and development in a backward theocracy.

Much like the nuclear explosion, the kingdom's absorption into the Indian Union was politically ambiguous—was it an annexation or an integration? Yet, it was legal, achieved through elections and constitutional amendments. It was even moralistic, conducted in the name of spreading democracy.

The official Indian positions of bringing democracy to the people of Sikkim and exploring for oil during the oil crisis made it hard for domestic and international audiences to fully discredit the peaceful character of the nuclear explosion and the defensive nature of India's foreign policy. The geopolitical reality was that the Gandhi government seized a fraught borderland and battlefield under the shadow of its nuclear capability. The geopolitical implications of Pokhran and Sikkim were clear to India's adversaries, but it elicited different responses. China criticized Sikkim. Pakistan criticized the nuclear explosion. The two superpowers remained quiet about both.

The territorial annexation of Sikkim through constitutional amendments became the prelude to the dark era of the Emergency (June 1975–March 1977). In response to the Allahabad Court's decision on June 12, 1975, challenging her 1971 electoral victory on grounds of electoral malpractice, Prime Minister Gandhi directed President Fakhruddin Ali Ahmed to declare a "National Emergency" under Article 352 (1) of the Indian Constitution on June 25.[117] India was already under emergency since the 1971 war on grounds of "external aggression." Under the legal advice of Siddhartha Sankar Ray, West Bengal's chief minister adept at curbing Naxalite violence in his own state, the Indian prime minister proclaimed national emergency anew, claiming that this time it was because "the security of India is threatened by internal disturbances."[118] The fundamental rights of citizens under Article 19 of the Indian Constitution were immediately suspended.[119]

The following day, about six hundred political opponents were behind bars, including J. P. Narayan. Gandhi delivered an unscheduled radio broadcast that morning in which she blamed widespread conspiracy against her progressive reforms to justify the proclamation. On June 27, the president declared another proclamation under Article 359 that suspended the right of citizens to move to court to enforce their rights under Article 14, 21, and 22 of the constitution.[120] The infamous 1971 Maintenance of Internal Security Act was amended on June 29 to quell political dissent, suppress freedom of the press, and upend fundamental rights of citizens. The act was used throughout the Emergency against Gandhi's opponents. Under the Defence of India Rules, critical reporting on Sikkim landed journalists in jail.[121]

The twenty-one-month Emergency was not merely authoritarianism, just as Sikkim was not simply annexation. Prime Minister Gandhi's "paradoxical suspension of the law by law" created a constitutional autocracy with "shadow powers and shadow laws" as historian Gyan Prakash has masterfully narrated.[122] The iron fist of legality hid its own incongruities in plain sight. Promoting democracy in Sikkim served as a prelude to the suspension of democracy in India.

Pokhran and the World

Immediately after the nuclear explosion in Pokhran, André Giraud, the CEA's administrator-general, had sent a personal telegram to DAE secretary Sethna congratulating him. To a *Le Monde* reporter, Giraud justified his telegram on grounds of the long history of nuclear cooperation between the two atomic energy commissions: the CEA's cooperation with the DAE/AECI went back to a time when no other country was sharing information in nuclear technologies with France.[123] Giraud added that the congratulatory message was merely protocol between friendly organizations.[124] Sethna also sent a congratulatory telegram to France in May 1974. His was to the recently elected French president Valéry Giscard d'Estaing, who had secured a narrow margin of victory against François Mitterrand on May 19, a day after the Pokhran explosion.[125]

The two telegrams put top-ranking officials within the French Foreign Ministry in a fix. They worried that the international media might allege that the CEA had helped the DAE to conduct the nuclear explosion. Neither India nor France had signed the NPT. Both opposed IAEA safeguards and were in direct communication only days before the nuclear explosion. On May 7, the CEA and the DAE had signed a bilateral safeguards agreement on French-supplied highly enriched uranium for the breeder reactor under construction in Kalpakkam. The reactor was also based on French designs. The CEA-DAE negotiations continued until May 16—two days prior to the PNE.

In June 1974, the *Office de Radiodiffusion-Télévision Française* did a special segment on India's nuclear program for which they interviewed Prime Minister Gandhi and Sethna. The Indian prime minister spoke in fluent French defending India's nuclear explosion as peaceful, adding that it was intended for exploration for oil and natural gas. She emphasized that India was not imitating China because its own nuclear program was a peaceful one, unlike the Chinese program. The Gandhi government even permitted the French national media agency to visit BARC, at a time when no other foreign press was allowed.[126] French Foreign Ministry officials pressured Giraud to retract his telegram and decided that the French embassy in New Delhi should only verbally thank Sethna for his telegram to the French president, mentioning that the French president had followed with interest the DAE's recent "technological success."[127]

An article in the *Economist* published in August 1974 was likely the last straw in convincing the French Foreign Ministry that the CEA-DAE proximity needed to be revisited and their contracts renegotiated. The first line of the article read: "Access to the latest French nuclear technology was a key factor behind India's successful nuclear test."[128] Citing "Asian intelligence sources," it claimed that "much of the highly sophisticated testing and measuring equipment used by the Indians were designed in France."[129] That the DAE had invited CEA's Bertrand Goldschmidt and André Giraud to travel to India in September 1974 to visit several Indian nuclear facilities, including the Pokhran test site, horrified the French Foreign Ministry officials.[130] They compelled Goldschmidt and Giraud to postpone their trip to India.

The leaders of India's nuclear program did not expect the CEA to request a renegotiation of its contracts, but it did. French president Giscard d'Estaing together with Foreign Minister Jean Sauvagnargues and top-ranking foreign policy officials like Geoffroy Chodron de Courcel and Xavier de Nazelle wanted to increase French commitment to nonproliferation without signing the NPT. The newly elected French president and his advisors believed that the CEA had been enjoying too much autonomy in its international cooperation since its founding in 1945. With nonproliferation and nuclear export controls ranking high on the Ford administration's agenda, the French government decided to improve Franco-American relations through increased cooperation on nonproliferation.[131] They thus decided to try and tame the CEA to toe the French Foreign Ministry's line of enhancing nonproliferation commitments in nuclear exports. CEA, under the instructions of the French Foreign Ministry requested renegotiation of its contracts with DAE. The DAE refused to both commit to not using French-supplied fissile materials in any future nuclear explosion and accepting new bilateral safeguards on fissile materials related to the Kalpakkam reactor. Nevertheless, Goldschmidt and Sethna continued their renegotiation talks for several years.[132]

The Pakistan Atomic Energy Commission began negotiating with the CEA for a plutonium reprocessing plant to separate weapon-grade plutonium from its CANDU-type reactor in Karachi. In June 1974, Pakistan prime minister Zulfikar Ali Bhutto had stated at the National Assembly that India's nuclear explosion was anything but peaceful: "All the roads led to the conclusion that India is brandishing the nuclear sword to extract political concessions from Pakistan and to establish New Delhi's hegemony in the subcontinent."[133] India's nuclear explosion gave further impetus to Pakistan's nuclear weapons program that Bhutto had already initiated after the 1971 war.[134] The two atomic energy commissions signed a contract in December 1974. French firm *Saint Gobain Nouvelle Technique* was going to construct the plant in Pakistan. Owing to pressures from the US government and the French Foreign Ministry, the CEA would abrogate the agreement four years later.

The leaders of India's nuclear program were eager to leverage the DAE's position as a nuclear supplier as countries from the nonaligned world and oil-rich nations sought nuclear know-how and technologies after the nuclear explosion. Not only did Yugoslav president Josip Broz Tito endorse the official Indian position that the nuclear explosion was a peaceful experiment, but he also dispatched a scientific delegation to New Delhi to discuss bilateral nuclear cooperation.[135] As more countries requested know-how, they endorsed, tacitly or explicitly, India's official stance that the explosion was peaceful.

DAE secretary Sethna intentionally kept US policymakers aware of the DAE's rising demand as a nuclear supplier, to reinforce that the DAE was not a "proliferator" but a responsible "innovator."[136] After a meeting with Sethna in August 1974, US ambassador Moynihan wrote to Kissinger, "Evidently Egypt has approached them asking India, in return for various considerations, to provide the technology that would enable them to produce nuclear weapons. . . . He [Homi Sethna] added that they [sic] Libyans had been to see them for the same purpose. He was emphatic, however, that India has no intention of providing Egypt or Libya with any such potential. I hope so."[137]

The outreach by Arab countries worried Israeli officials. Yehoshua Trigor, chief of the Israeli consulate in Bombay, sent several anxious reports to Israel's Ministry of Foreign Affairs in Jerusalem. In his August 1974 report, Trigor observed that the "Arab states are interested in nuclear knowledge" while the Indian government is "interested in cash and oil," and that "the potential cooperation is not unsympathetic."[138] Tying the question of Indian nuclear assistance to Arab countries with its global advocacy for a New International Economic Order, the Israeli official noted that perhaps the DAE saw itself as "a sort of a new Robin Hood" wanting "to make the poor states as powerful as the rich states." Through nuclear know-how and direct technological assistance to military programs of Israel's enemies—Iraq, Egypt, and Syria—the DAE could become a "hired sword in the nuclear field."[139]

DAE secretary Sethna had other plans. He wanted US policymakers to recognize the DAE's export potential as well as its restraint in selling nuclear technologies and know-how. After seven major nuclear supplier countries from the Global North met in London to determine common nuclear export controls in 1975, which became the NSG, Sethna told US embassy official David

Schneider that "India had earlier turned down Brazilian request for nuclear fuel fabrication and reprocessing technology as it had turned down similar Argentine and Egyptian requests as well."[140] Sethna, however, warned US officials that "he did not know how long this position would last."[141] As news of the 1975 West German-Brazil "deal of the century" involving uranium enrichment, plutonium reprocessing, and power reactors became public knowledge, Sethna told Schneider that "pressure would inevitably mount in India and in Parliament particularly to sell nuclear technology as well" and he did not know "who is going to discipline the sort of thing."[142] Kissinger instructed Schneider to communicate to Sethna that the US government "continue[d] to have strong interest in India['s] nuclear export restraint, particularly in supply of nuclear explosive and reprocessing technology."[143]

Despite signing oil-for-services agreements with Iraq and Iran in early 1974 (discussed in chapter 6), the Gandhi government was wary of oil-rich Middle Eastern countries. Prime Minister Gandhi's five-day visit to Tehran in April to May 1974, just before the nuclear explosion, was described in the *New York Times* as a détente between the two countries.[144] Nevertheless, Indian policymakers worried about what "the political use of oil weapon and the economic power of accumulated petrodollars" in the Middle East meant for Indian interests in the long run.[145] They were anxious about how the Middle East would react, emboldened with oil money, in future India-Pakistan conflicts. A 1975 Cabinet Secretariat assessment observed, "It is not inconceivable that in any future Indo-Pak conflict, the Arab states and even Iran may in sympathy for Pakistan and to put pressure on us, [impose] sanction and oil embargo against us."[146] The DAE's offer of nuclear aid to these countries was thus economic statecraft in the short run as well as a part of a long-term diplomatic engagement strategy.

The shah of Iran's ambitions to build a large nuclear energy program in the 1970s was the direct result of the oil crisis and Iran's accumulation of petrodollars.[147] The monarch had launched a twenty-year program for importing twenty power reactors with a capacity of twenty-three million kilowatts.[148] The shah's visit to New Delhi in October 1974 thus generated speculation of nuclear cooperation between the two countries.[149] Cooperation between the DAE and the Atomic Energy Organization of Iran (AEOI) materialized over the course of 1975. Ali Akbar Etemad, AEOI's founding director, visited Bombay and New Delhi several times that year. In January 1975, at a press conference in New Delhi, Etemad said, "Iran has not yet considered peaceful nuclear explosions but will not rule them out altogether."[150]

Etemad's visit to India was reciprocated by Sethna, who visited Iran to discuss the areas of future DAE-AEOI cooperation. Etemad, who was also Iran's deputy prime minister, wanted the DAE's help to develop an indigenous Iranian nuclear program with the eventual mastery of the full nuclear fuel cycle. In December 1975, six months into the Emergency, when Etemad returned to India for further talks with Sethna, the *Hindu* reported that "[t]hough it is too early for India to think in terms of building nuclear power plants in third countries on a turn-key basis, it is certainly in a position to assist friendly countries like Iran in the construction of experimental reactors for research and development purposes."[151]

The "economic culture of decolonization," to quote historian Christopher Dietrich, influenced the rhetoric around India-Iran cooperation.[152] Both Prime Minister Gandhi and the shah of Iran advocated for a New International Economic Order at the UN General Assembly and South-South solidarity. The shah's oil revenues, however, made it harder for him to be a genuine champion for the poor countries suffering from the oil crisis.[153] From India, Iran wanted technical skills to manage large infrastructure projects from nuclear power reactors to petroleum engineering. An article in the *Hindu* in December 1975 claimed that solely India could help Iran "without any political strings or economic dominance." It was a match made in heaven: Iran's "unlimited financial resources" with India's "immense reservoir of technical skills." [154]

Etemad himself invoked civilizational and cultural associations when discussing DAE-AEOI cooperation.[155] He recalled in his biography: "I had very good relations with Homi Sethna, the head of India's nuclear energy organization, who was a Parsi, very powerful, and worked directly under the PM."[156] The Parsi or Zoroastrian community in India originally hails from what is present-day Iran. They fled religious persecution and took refuge in western India in the eighth century A.D.[157] The word "Parsi" means Persian. Homi Bhabha, J. R. D. Tata, Homi Sethna, and Homi Taleyarkhan—characters that have already appeared in this book—were all Parsi.[158] Etemad reminisced in his biography about attending a Parsi event in Bombay in the mid-1970s, from which he was whisked away to meet J. R. D. Tata in the middle of the night. Etemad recounted meeting J. R. D. at Bombay House, the headquarters of Tata Industries.[159] According to Etemad's recollections, J. R. D. Tata expressed a strong desire to develop Iran—the home of the Parsis. The business magnate told the AEOI director that "all Indian Parsis consider themselves, in some ways, Iranian since their roots lie in Iran."[160] The next morning, Etemad met Prime Minister Gandhi in New Delhi, who expressed her support for Tata's interest in "putting his expertise in the service of Iran."

The AEOI sought power reactors, uranium enrichment, and plutonium reprocessing plants from industrially advanced countries. It signed contracts with the CEA and West German firm Kraftwerk Union, subsidiary of Siemens.

It would also sign an initial contract for purchasing eight US reactors in 1978. From the DAE, the AEOI wanted know-how to develop its own nuclear program. It however remains unclear the extent to which the DAE provided nuclear know-how until the cooperation was disrupted by the Iranian revolution.

Owing to the implication of plutonium procured from the Canadian-supplied CIRUS reactor in India's nuclear explosion, Canada had immediately suspended its nuclear cooperation with India. The two governments, however, began negotiating since March 1975 for the resumption of AECL's assistance to DAE for the Rajasthan Atomic Power Station in Kota.[161] The two sides initialed an agreement in March 1976 in New Delhi. Two months later, the Canadian government unilaterally decided to terminate AECL's cooperation with DAE.[162] MEA officials found the Canadian decision "sudden and unexpected" and "all the more surprising."[163]

The Indian foreign secretary J. S. Mehta sent an indignant note to Indian embassies blaming the Canadian government for a "breach of faith" by breaking off negotiations when they were nearly complete. Mehta concluded that political opposition to the Trudeau government, the government's obligations as a founding member of the NSG, and criticisms in the Canadian press about AECL's nuclear export offers to autocratic governments in Argentina and South Korea were the actual causes because "we were willing to accept stronger safeguards on the Rajasthan Atomic Power Project even though there was no need for such safeguards in the agreement with the IAEA."[164] The Canadian government's documents indicate that the Canadian media also opposed the autocratic nature of India's government since the country was under Emergency at the time. Mehta added in his note another key reason for Canada's termination: "It has been our position that since PNE is an internationally recognized concept, we had every right to conduct such an experiment. We do not accept the Canadian view that there is no difference between a PNE and a bomb."[165]

In the summer of 1976, the US heavy water supply to India became suspect. Senator Abraham Ribicoff "raised the issue of use of American supplied heavy water in our PNE" in the US Congress, leading to delays in the NRC's granting export licenses for exports related to the two US-supplied reactors in Tarapur.[166] After the NRC granted the export license, US civil society groups filed a petition in the US Court of Appeals for the District of Columbia Circuit opposing the commission's decision. The ongoing public hearings on Capitol Hill against US nuclear exports to India gave little hope to those at the helm of India's nuclear program.

The Gandhi government turned to the Soviet Union. A contract was initialed in Moscow on June 4, 1976, only days before Indira Gandhi's six-day official visit to Moscow.[167] The contract was signed on June 11 in New Delhi between the DAE secretary and the Soviet trade representative for the purchase of two hundred tons of heavy water from the Soviet Union.[168] The Soviet government sought IAEA safeguards and a statement from the Indian government within thirty days of signing the agreement that it "will not use fissionable nuclear material, produced or used in plants for which heavy water is delivered, for the production of nuclear weapons or any other nuclear explosive mechanism."[169] Soviet provision of heavy water for the DAE arrived in December 1976.[170]

Old Wine, New Bottle

In January 1977, Prime Minister Gandhi ordered fresh elections in March, ending the Emergency. She lost to her longtime opponent and former deputy prime minister Morarji Desai. Desai, from the Janata Party, became India's first non-Congress prime minister on March 24, 1977. That same day, President Jimmy Carter announced Presidential Directive-8, which contained the blueprint of a stringent US nonproliferation policy.[171] Although Desai made a public statement that India would not conduct any further nuclear explosions, not much changed beyond that. His government retained its predecessor's position against the nonproliferation regime as a contravention of India's sovereignty.[172] Nevertheless, the Carter administration and the Trudeau government hoped for fresh start in their dealings with the DAE.

In July 1977, the Indian High Commission in London learned that the NSG would take a formal decision in September to invite India to join the export control group. Indian officials learned that from John Edmonds, head of the Arms Control and Disarmament Department at the British Foreign Office. The anticipated expansion of the NSG was to "seek acceptance by India and other invitees of safeguards envisaged by the Suppliers Group."[173] M. A. Vellodi, secretary (east) at the MEA, expressed reservations. He wrote to Indian foreign minister Atal Behari Vajpayee that the "London Club [NSG] was essentially an extension of the Non-Proliferation Treaty," to which India was being invited "less as potential supplier than as potential customer."[174] The "special interest some of the members of the Club have shown of late in inviting India to join the Club was to ensure our acceptance of a safeguards system which would be commonly acceptable to supplier countries as a condition of sale of nuclear material and nuclear components."[175] Indian policymakers, thereby, judged that any invitation to join the NSG was NPT through the backdoor and decided to decline if the matter were formally raised.

Vellodi was concerned about the future of US supply of low-enriched uranium fuel for the Tarapur reactors. He directed Vajpayee to oppose any renegotiation of contracts: "During the talks, United States will certainly refer to the question of renegotiation of the Tarapur contract. I feel that we should take the line that apart possibly from the widening of the scope of bilateral safeguards on Tarapur, other provisions in the contract . . . cannot be renegotiated at least as far as the substance of the relevant provisions are concerned.[176] In August 1977, the US Congress passed the Glenn Amendment to the 1961 US Foreign Assistance Act. Along with the 1976 Symington Amendment, the new amendment prohibited all US economic and military aid to any country exporting or importing reprocessing and enrichment facilities and related materials and technology without full-scope IAEA safeguards. Full-scope safeguards applied to all nuclear material and facilities in a country, which were far more stringent than previous IAEA safeguards.[177]

The Desai government continued to oppose Carter administration officials' demand for full-scope safeguards on the Tarapur reactors as the condition for obtaining US reactor fuel. Even President Carter's visit to New Delhi in January 1978 did not result in any policy change within the Indian government. Two months later, President Jimmy Carter signed into act the Nuclear Nonproliferation Act, which stipulated that US nuclear assistance could only be provided to countries that were NPT signatories and had accepted full-scope IAEA safeguards. By fall 1978, rumors circulated within the Carter administration that the Soviet Union could replace the United States as the reactor fuel supplier for the Tarapur reactors.

In response, the Carter administration began to look for a third-party fuel supplier for Tarapur. By January 1979, the CEA emerged as the preferred choice of US officials.[178] The French Foreign Ministry was not opposed to it, but the ongoing impasse in the CEA-DAE renegotiation talks made them less enthusiastic. Indian newspapers compared the Carter administration's demands for full-scope safeguards on the Tarapur reactors with those by the Giscard d'Estaing government on the Kalpakkam reactor. Both, they claimed, were examples of Western obstacles to India's national sovereignty.[179] In the Indian Parliament, legislators questioned how the CEA's reactor supplier, *Framatome*, could conduct business with China but place conditions on India.[180]

In March 1979, Klaus Goldschlag, Canadian undersecretary of state for external affairs, met MEA officials in India to "not look at what had happened in the past but try and make a new beginning."[181] Goldschlag had represented Canada at the NSG negotiations in London. He blamed "strong opinion both in public, parliament, and the press on nuclear exchanges after 1974" for the

Trudeau government's unilateral decision in May 1976 to terminate AECL's contracts with the DAE. The Canadian delegation did not arrive in New Delhi with lower demands on safeguards, but higher expectations. Owing to the DAE's ongoing challenges to complete the CANDU-type reactors in Rajasthan, they hoped for a change in the Indian government's policy against full-scope safeguards. The talks did not result in a fresh start, but MEA official Vellodi reminded the Canadian officials of DAE's export restraint. He argued that being a restrained nuclear exporter should suffice for DAE's reputation as a responsible actor: "In spite of the fact that there were many demands for it, we had deliberately avoided parting with any sensitive technology and where we had cooperation with certain countries, it was confined to non-sensitive areas."[182]

The rest of 1979 was characterized by events that redefined US nonproliferation efforts, India's nuclear procurement, and the global Cold War in South Asia. The Three Mile Island accident in Pennsylvania in March, the revolution in Iran, and the Soviet invasion of Afghanistan in December were transformative. They united probusiness coalitions opposing President Carter's restrictions on US nuclear exports, while making nonproliferation far less important to the US administration at a time of revived superpower hostilities. The revolution in Iran jeopardized US, French, and West German business interests that had expected to build several reactors in Iran. The partial meltdown of the reactor core at Three Mile Island worried DAE officials about the safety of US-supplied reactors in Tarapur. Major US companies like General Electric involved in reactor construction and smaller ones like Edlow International in charge of fuel transportation got the opportunity to make reactor safety–based arguments to export spare parts and fuel to Tarapur.[183] Nonproliferation was swept aside for business interests and Cold War geopolitics.

Tarapur Fuel for No-Test Understanding

Indira Gandhi's landslide victory in the January 1980 and a hot war of the Cold War at India's doorstep led the Carter administration to warm up to the Indian government. President Carter's special envoy Clark Clifford visited New Delhi in late January to allay the Gandhi government's fears about increased US military assistance to Pakistan to support the *mujahideens* fighting Soviet troops in Afghanistan. Prime Minister Gandhi's well-known pro-Soviet stance worried Carter administration officials. In an interview published in French newspaper *Le Matin*, she compared Soviet invasion of Afghanistan to US interventions in Latin America.[184] She told the reporter that based on her recent talks in New

Delhi with Soviet foreign minister Andrei Gromyko, it was evident that the Soviet government was "forced to intervene," just as the US government did in its own backyard. In one stroke, Gandhi called both superpowers imperialist.

In March 1980, in her first parliamentary statement on nuclear policy since being reelected, Prime Minister Gandhi declared that India "remain[ed] committed to the use of atomic energy for peaceful purposes" but that did not preclude "carrying out nuclear explosions . . . or whatever is necessary in the national interests."[185] Geopolitics overruled nonproliferation for US policymakers. Carter used his presidential authority in June 1980 to override the Nuclear Nonproliferation Act to send two US fuel shipments for the Tarapur reactors. Congressional opposition on grounds of nonproliferation and Gandhi's pro-Soviet position caused delays to the shipment.[186]

With public knowledge that Pakistan was procuring gas centrifuge equipment for uranium enrichment through nuclear smuggling networks from Switzerland, France, Canada, and elsewhere, Gandhi faced pressures to expand India's nuclear explosions program.[187] Pressures from the DAE and BARC to conduct further nuclear tests had never completely disappeared, despite tensions between Sethna and Ramanna after May 1974.[188] Conducting more nuclear explosions could help the DAE test miniaturized nuclear devices, improve their designs, and test the more sophisticated lithium-tritium trigger, unlike the beryllium-polonium initiator used in 1974.[189]

Preparations in Pokhran to conduct underground nuclear tests began in February 1981.[190] That April, Prime Minister Gandhi stated in the Lok Sabha that India would respond to Pakistan's nuclear weapons acquisition in "an appropriate manner."[191] The economic crisis had made nuclear weapons acquisition hard to justify to India's domestic political audience in 1974. By contrast, in 1981, political momentum was building up in favor of nuclear weapons to counter Pakistan. K. Subrahmanyam, strategist and director of the New Delhi–based think tank Institute for Defence Studies and Analyses, even published a front-page essay in the *Times of India* titled "BOMB: The Only Answer."[192] The following day, Senator Alan Cranston raised alarm on the US Senate floor about an imminent Indian nuclear test citing "excavations for burial of a nuclear warhead for an underground test" in the Rajasthan desert.[193]

Israel's airstrike on Iraq's Osirak reactor on June 7, 1981, raised the specter of a similar military attack by the Pakistan Air Force on BARC in Bombay.[194] That the Israel Air Force had used US-supplied F-16 jetfighters to conduct the raid made the Gandhi government even more alarmed when the Reagan administration decided to provide Pakistan with F-16 planes on June 12.[195] It was not a one-sided anxiety. Both Pakistan and Indian governments began to fear counterproliferation airstrikes on their nuclear facilities by each other. As the

Pakistan government increased security at Kahuta—the uranium enrichment facility led by A. Q. Khan—an MEA spokesperson publicly criticized Pakistan's claims of Indian plans for an airstrike as "fantastic, tendentious and utterly baseless."[196] Such fears would persist on both sides for most of the 1980s.

The Gandhi government used nuclear test preparations to garner the attention of US policymakers, who were preoccupied with countering the Soviet military in Afghanistan. Unlike in 1974, when test preparations were kept extremely secret, in May to June 1981, Indian and US media reported that another nuclear test in Pokhran could take place any day.[197] US military assistance to Pakistan to fight the Soviet troops in Afghanistan, Chinese nuclear weapons assistance to Pakistan, and US neglect of Pakistan's nuclear weapons program created a precarious geopolitical position for India.[198] Pressure was building up for nuclear weapons from political leaders from the Bharatiya Janata Party (BJP), formerly the Janata Party, and even military officials.[199]

Upon entering the White House, President Ronald Reagan had sought a "virtual 180-degree reversal of the Carter administration policy" on nonproliferation to get the "U.S. nuclear industry back on its feet," based on recommendations from Bechtel whose top executives were part of his Energy Policy Task Force.[200] The recommendations were to make US nonproliferation policy business friendly because "[t]he influence of the U.S. on international nonproliferation policies [was] in direct proportion to its role as a leading supplier." This shift in favor of nuclear exports was evident in Reagan's statement on nonproliferation on July 16, 1981.[201] Business calculations made Reagan administration officials interested in resolving US-Indian differences over Tarapur, while Indian policymakers remained intransigent in their opposition to full-scope safeguards on the reactors.

President Reagan and Prime Minister Gandhi first met on the outskirts of the two-day North-South Summit in Cancun, Mexico, in October 1981, laying the groundwork to resolve bilateral issues. The spirit of the New International Economic Order became a thing of the past in Cancun as Reagan talked of private capital and open markets as the solution to unequal development among countries while Gandhi reasoned that developed and developing nations could "survive in harmony only in conditions of true interdependence."[202] The two leaders reportedly developed a personal rapport despite opposing positions. She also held meetings with French president François Mitterrand and Chinese premier Zhao Ziyang in Cancun.

Building shafts for exploding underground nuclear devices, as the Gandhi government did in 1981 and the first half of 1982, served the dual purpose of keeping the option to test nearly ready and use the test preparations as a bargaining chip in talks with US officials on Tarapur. Despite the Reagan administration being in favor of increasing US nuclear exports, US-Indian talks made little progress in 1981. DAE secretary Homi Sethna and MEA secretary (east) Eric Gonçalves met US assistant secretary of state James Malone, the chief US negotiator on Tarapur, on several occasions, but the 1963 US-India agreement on Tarapur seemed impossible to save.[203] US officials wanted to abrogate the agreement. Indian officials demanded that the US government adhere to its original 1963 commitments instead of asking retroactively for full-scope IAEA safeguards under the 1978 Nuclear Nonproliferation Act. US policymakers also opposed the DAE's plans to reprocess spent fuel from the Tarapur reactors, which Sethna and Gonçalves refused to accept. The DAE had started reprocessing spent fuel from the CIRUS in its PREFRE facility built at the Tarapur reactor site. The PREFRE was India's second plutonium reprocessing plant commissioned in 1977.[204]

In May 1982, Prime Minister Gandhi dispatched Indian foreign secretary Maharajakrishna Rasgotra to discuss matters related to Tarapur with the Reagan administration prior to her July visit to the United States.[205] US officials informed Rasgotra that they would not oppose if the Mitterrand government of France took over US fuel supply commitments for the Tarapur reactors.[206] They thus offered to make the French the third-party fuel supplier, as the Carter administration officials had considered in 1978–79. Rasgotra also met US undersecretary of state for political affairs Lawrence Eagleburger, who asked him directly about the ongoing test preparations in Pokhran: "I'm talking to you man to man. . . . [W]hat are you doing in Pokhran?"[207] The Eagleburger-Rasgotra meeting was high level, though informal.[208] Eagleburger held the highest-ranking position for a career diplomat in the State Department at the time.[209] He had also served as Kissinger's top aide in the Nixon administration. Rasgotra himself was a veteran career diplomat, who had joined the Indian Foreign Service in 1949, becoming the foreign secretary in late 1981. The Reagan administration thus signaled through the high-level informal conversation their desire for an Indian commitment to not conduct nuclear tests in return for a resolution of the Tarapur issue.

The Reagan administration had already conducted informal "no-test bargains" with South Africa and Pakistan. President Reagan reached an understanding in May 1981 with South African foreign minister Pik Botha that South Africa would not conduct nuclear tests in return for US authorization of nuclear fuel shipments for the Koeberg reactor. Secretary of State Alexander Haig had a similar understanding with Pakistan foreign minister Agha Shahi and General Khalid Mahmud Arif in April 1981 that Pakistan would not conduct nuclear tests in return for US security assurances against Soviet and Indian aggression.[210] The two informal deals were modeled on an earlier one: President Nixon's understanding with Israeli prime minister Golda Meir in September 1969 that the US would drop requests to inspect the Dimona reactor if the Israelis did not conduct nuclear tests.[211]

When US policymakers could not prevent nuclear proliferation, they often sought to prevent nuclear tests both to avoid embarrassment and curtail further advancement of nuclear programs that they could not stop.[212] Israel, South Africa, and Pakistan were US allies in geopolitically fraught regions, whose cooperation the US government needed and who needed US military assistance, among other things. India was different. It was neither an ally nor an adversary. With Soviet troops in Afghanistan, Reagan administration officials wanted a more constructive relationship with India. The Carter administration had wanted the same in 1980 for the same reasons. Moreover, fresh Indian nuclear tests could lead other countries to follow suit, particularly, Pakistan and South Africa.[213]

The Nixon-Meir and Reagan-Botha deals became public knowledge through media reports in 1991 and 1995, respectively, but the Reagan administration's understanding with the Zia ul-Haq government surfaced in the news soon after.[214] At the Senate Foreign Relations Committee, US undersecretary of state for arms control and international security affairs James L. Buckley stated in November 1981, "Given the premises of U.S. relationship with Pakistan, it was hard to believe that assistance would go forward if Pakistan exploded a nuclear device. . . . I do not think anyone in Pakistan expects U.S. assistance to continue in the aftermath of an explosion."[215]

Like the other three no-test bargains, the Eagleburger-Rasgotra understanding is hard to trace in the primary sources.[216] Nevertheless, public statements by Gandhi were along the lines of what US policymakers wanted to hear. On May 13, 1982, when a reporter asked her whether a nuclear test was likely, she answered in the negative.[217] She was responding to BJP leader and former foreign minister Vajpayee's remarks that India would imminently explode a nuclear device. She said, "[W]hy not wait and see. Has anything they [the opposition] said come true?"

The longstanding dispute over Tarapur was resolved when Rasgotra revisited Washington, DC, in July 1982 to hold talks with US undersecretary of management Richard Thomas Kennedy, who was also the US representative to the IAEA at the time. Kennedy had served as NRC commissioner during the Ford and Carter administrations, during which he had encouraged US nuclear exports to India. Rasgotra and Kennedy met on July 23, days before Prime Minister Gandhi's official visit. US officials had submitted a paper to the Gandhi government on December 17, 1981, discussing the modalities of the agreement on Tarapur whereby France would take over US fuel supply commitments.[218]

Most of the details were worked out based on Indian responses to US proposals contained in that paper. After Rasgotra met Kennedy in Washington, US ambassador Harry G. Barnes Jr. held talks with Indian officials in New Delhi. They decided that the details of the agreement's implementation would be finalized during DAE secretary Sethna's visit to the United States later that year.

When Prime Minister Gandhi arrived to the United States on July 27, 1982, to meet President Reagan—her first visit since 1971—the Tarapur agreement was nearly ready.[219] On July 29, the two leaders signed and announced the agreement, making France the third-party fuel supplier until 1993, when the original 1963 U.S.-India agreement was set to expire.[220] The following day, Gandhi reaffirmed at the National Press Club that India had no nuclear weapons.[221]

George Shultz, former Bechtel president and advocate for increased US nuclear exports, was sworn in as the US secretary of state only weeks before Gandhi's visit. He had advocated to Reagan for a constructive engagement with Gandhi "at a time of major change" in the South Asian subcontinent.[222] Bechtel itself had constructed the Tarapur reactors, which would make Shultz take a strong interest in resolving the DAE's need for spare parts later on.[223] In November 1982, Indian and French governments signed the agreement confirming that *Framatome* would supply low-enriched uranium fuel for the Tarapur reactors but buy back the spent fuel to prevent its reprocessing. India committed to use the reactor fuel "only for peaceful purposes."[224]

The Gandhi government did not conduct further nuclear tests. Instead, it undertook several steps to develop delivery systems for nuclear weapons, building on earlier efforts. After ISRO's SLV-3 project proved to be successful with the launch of the Rohini satellite in July 1980, a new ballistic missile program was conceived at the DRDO—the Integrated Guided Missile Development Program. It was officially launched in 1983. The earlier DRDO-based missile development programs, Projects Valiant and Devil, were canceled. The Indian government even bought forty Mirage 2000 nuclear-capable planes from France, only months before the India-France agreement on Tarapur. Prime Minister Gandhi also began to show interest in Soviet assistance for a nuclear submarine development program.[225]

Nuclear, space, and defense technologies became more closely integrated in India during the 1980s than ever before. A part of this process had begun during the Desai government, which had also bought forty Jaguar nuclear-capable planes in 1978. The Indian Air Force deployed the Jaguars in 1981. Raja Ramanna's leadership of the DRDO (1978–82), his successful efforts to draw A. P. J. Abdul Kalam back from ISRO to DRDO in 1981 to work on ballistic missiles, and

Ramanna's own return to BARC in 1981 while continuing to work with DRDO ensured integration across laboratories through overlapping leadership, expertise, and personnel.[226] In 1985, when the Dhruva reactor in Trombay attained criticality, it became India's largest source of weapon-grade plutonium.

Conclusion

The public conversation in the 1980s about whether India should develop its own nuclear weapons in response to Pakistan's nuclear weapons reinforced the official position of the Indian government that what had happened in May 1974 in Pokhran was a peaceful nuclear experiment. The annexation of Sikkim was lost first amidst the horrors of the Emergency and then in the violent territoriality of intermestic security threats in Assam and Punjab that gripped the national imagination through the 1980s. The narrative of the peaceful explosion would become further entrenched after the BJP government led by Vajpayee would conduct five nuclear weapon tests in Pokhran in May 1998. India's first nuclear explosion would thus be relegated to a less significant place in history.

Owing to Canadian exit from India's nuclear program in 1976, the DAE's large power development endeavor based on the CANDU-type pressurized heavy water reactor suffered. In the absence of the AECL's nuclear assistance, the DAE fell back on its own know-how gathered through its past cooperation with the AECL. Indian scientists, engineers, and workers were able to complete the second reactor in Kota, Rajasthan, and the first reactor in Madras, connecting them to the power grid in October 1980 and July 1983, respectively.[227] DAE secretary Sethna recalled years later, "No foreigner would come and give us know-how. . . . That was what helped us. Nobody was willing to help."[228] The Canadian-origin reactor thus became *Indian* as "a kind of writing upon writing," to quote Sudipta Kaviraj on non-Western modernity.[229]

Plutonium, the by-product from these reactors, became a technopolitical artifact in the name of the nation. Being useful for both nuclear weapons and breeder reactors when reprocessed, plutonium encapsulated the "ploughshare" and the "sword" that made up India's nuclear program. The right to reprocess plutonium, the opposition to full-scope IAEA safeguards, and the resistance to complete separation of military and civilian facilities became the program's chief characteristics. Freedom of action became insubordination to the global nonproliferation regime.

Epilogue

The Anti-Dissent Machine

Throughout the 1990s and the early 2000s, nonproliferation became a dirty word in Indian political culture. It reached its climax after the 1998 nuclear tests and during the contestations over the US-India civil nuclear agreement. The Indian media interpreted the 2008 NSG waiver, which allowed the DAE to reengage in civil nuclear trade without signing the NPT, as the regime's concession to the Indian nuclear program.[1] The prevalent narrative was that scientists and engineers at the helm of the nuclear program had fought a righteous battle in which the other side—the nonproliferation regime—had capitulated. The reality was much more complex.[2]

The NSG waiver materialized through the efforts of the George W. Bush administration to help cash-strapped US companies such as Westinghouse and General Electric to sell power reactors to the DAE. Hopes of a "nuclear renaissance" remained unfulfilled. First, the 2010 Indian nuclear liability law gave foreign companies cold feet even though the legislation did not allow victims to sue companies in case of a nuclear accident caused by design flaw.[3] Then, the 2011 Fukushima Daiichi accident in Japan reignited India's anti-nuclear movement.[4] Civil society groups such as the People's Movement Against Nuclear Energy agitated at sites where the DAE had allocated lands for the construction of power reactors.

The spectacular state violence against anti-nuclear activists, particularly in Kudankulam, showed how India's nuclear program was a disciplining device of the state. It rewarded good citizens, who supported nuclear energy, but punished mischievous ones with legal charges of sedition.[5]

Freedom of action of the leaders of India's nuclear program has transformed it into an anti-dissent machine. The nuclear program is a vast technopolitical enterprise containing myriad objects that could concurrently serve national goals of development and security. Opposing nuclear energy is, therefore, resisting economic modernity. Disputing nuclear weapons is helping India's geopolitical adversaries. Defying both is rebelling against the nation itself. The coproduction of India's nuclear program and Indian society as an opaque, inegalitarian, and hierarchical order creates and reinforces an antidemocratic culture.[6] This culture abhors oversight and is perpetually suspicious of independent inquiries.[7]

India's nuclear program is made up of dreams, hopes, and promises. It is largely a program of potential. Nuclear energy officially meets only 3.2 percent of the country's share of electricity production—a figure that has remained largely static over several decades.[8] The DAE has twenty-three power reactors under operation and is constructing six more. It produces fissile material in the forms of plutonium from the Dhruva reactor and highly enriched uranium from the Rattehalli plant.[9] Its prototype fast breeder program continues to encounter delays leading to cost overruns worth billions of dollars.[10] The DAE blames the nonproliferation regime for not letting it live up to its full capacity. Citizens' inquiries and independent media reporting of its activities are, thus, often framed as "pro-nonproliferation" and even "unpatriotic."[11]

The two sets of Indian nuclear tests in May 1974 and May 1998 were largely similar, despite differences in their rhetorical justifications. Both skirted nonproliferation controls to showcase the technological prowess of the DAE. Both were partly India's response to geopolitical insecurities vis-à-vis China and Pakistan.[12] Both rounds of tests brought similar results to the villagers of Khetolai, the nearest human habitation, from the Pokhran test site in the Thar Desert. The explosions cracked the walls of their mud houses and split open the underground water tanks. Humans and animals suffered deformities, tumors, blindness, and other maladies. When novelist Amitav Ghosh visited Khetolai after the 1998 nuclear tests, he witnessed the effects of radiation from the 1974 nuclear explosion. [13] Both times the DAE guaranteed that the air, soil, and water of the village were completely safe, despite evidence to the contrary.[14]

Territorial notions of state power are manifest in uranium mining in indigenous lands in Jharkhand, Meghalaya, Andhra Pradesh, and elsewhere. Politically fraught resource-rich geographic spaces are being tamed to conform to the sociotechnical imaginaries of "self-sufficiency" of the leaders of India's nuclear program.[15] Signs of the Anthropocene abound in the sites of nuclear infrastructure. Continuous monazite extraction in Kerala (formerly, Travancore) has shrunk its coastline. Over the last fifty years, the DAE's mining of rare earths has diminished the village of Alappad in Kerala from 33.8 square miles to just 3.6 square miles.[16] Territoriality is thus leading to the disappearance of territory itself.

Nuclear deterrence in South Asia balances on a knife edge. India is estimated to have 150 nuclear warheads, which is lower than that of China, but not much more than that of Pakistan.[17] News of fisticuffs between the Indian Army and the PLA in Sikkim, and Indian surgical strikes on Pakistan's territory fill social media timelines.[18] The opacity around India's no-first-use policy, the threat of terrorism in Kashmir, and the ongoing nuclear arms race in South Asia raise concerns for the region's geopolitical stability.[19]

It might be tempting to think that today, India's nuclear program is no longer a collection of ploughshares and swords, but is merely more swords. That would be a mistake. The deliberate ambiguity in the nuclear program is both the source of its leaders' freedom of action as well as the key to the anti-dissent machine that the program is. Ploughshares and swords, thus, sustain an antidemocratic culture in the largest democracy in the world in the name of freedom.

NOTES

Acknowledgments

1. Jayita Sarkar, "From the Dependable to the Demanding Partner: The Renegotiation of French Nuclear Cooperation with India, 1974-1980," *Cold War History* 21, no. 3 (2021): 301–318; "U.S. Policy to Curb West European Nuclear Exports, 1974-1978," *Journal of Cold War Studies* 21, no. 2 (Spring 2019): 110–149; "The Making of a Nonaligned Nuclear Power: India's Proliferation Drift, 1964-1968," *International History Review* 37, no. 5 (2015): 933–950; "'Wean them away from French tutelage': Franco-Indian nuclear relations and Anglo-American anxieties in the early Cold War, 1948-1952," *Cold War History* 15, no. 3 (2015): 375–394; "The Making of a 'Ship-to-Mouth' Nuclear Power: The Johnson Administration and India's Nuclear Tilt, 1964–1968," *Jadavpur Journal of International Relations* 18, no. 1 (2014): 1–29; "India's Nuclear Limbo and the Fatalism of the Nuclear Non-Proliferation Regime, 1974-1983," *Strategic Analysis* 37, no. 3 (2013): 322–337; With Nicolas Blarel, "Sub-State Organizations as Foreign Policy Agents: New Evidence and Theory from India, Israel and France," *Foreign Policy Analysis* 15, no. 2 (2019): 413–431; With John Krige, "U.S. Technological Collaboration for Nonproliferation: Key Evidence from the Cold War," *Nonproliferation Review* 25, no. 3–4 (2018): 249–262; With Or Rabinowitz, "'It Isn't Over Until the Fuel Cell Sings': A Reassessment of the US and French Pledges of Nuclear Assistance in the 1970s," *Journal of Strategic Studies* 41, no. 1–2 (2018): 275–300.

Introduction

1. Jawaharlal Nehru's speech at Lahore, August 25, 1945, SWJN, vol. 14, series 1, Nehru Memorial and Museum Library, New Delhi (hereafter, NMML), 162.

2. I adopt Jasanoff's definition of sociotechnical imaginaries, which she defines as "collectively imagined forms of social life and social order reflected in the design and fulfillment of nation-specific scientific and/or technological projects." See Sheila Jasanoff and Kim Sang-Hyun, "Containing the Atom: Sociotechnical Imaginaries and Nuclear Power in the United States and South Korea," *Minerva* 47, no. 2 (2009): 120.

3. Jawaharlal Nehru's presidential address at the Indian Science Congress, January 3, 1947, "The Architects of Nuclear India," *Nuclear India* 26, no. 10 (1989), Homi J. Bhabha Papers, NMML.

4. Charles S. Maier, "Consigning the Twentieth Century to History: Alternative Narratives for the Modern Era," *American Historical Review* 105, no. 3 (June 2000): 808.

5. I adopt Fredrik Logevall's definition of "intermestic" to mean a dynamic and intertwined relationship between the international and the domestic spheres. See Craig

Campbell and Fredrik Logevall, *America's Cold War: The Politics of Insecurity* (Cambridge, MA: Belknap Press of Harvard University Press, 2009); Fredrik Logevall, "Domestic Politics," in *Explaining the History of American Foreign Relations*, eds. Frank Costigliola and Michael J. Hogan (New York: Cambridge University Press, 2016), 151–67.

6. Srinath Raghavan, *War and Peace in Modern India* (Ranikhet, India: Permanent Black, 2010), chapters 2, 3, 4.

7. I adopt Gabrielle Hecht's definition of technopolitics as the use of technology to enact political goals. Gabrielle Hecht, *The Radiance of France: Nuclear Power and National Identity after World War II* (Cambridge, MA: MIT Press, 1998), 15–16, and Gabrielle Hecht, *Entangled Geographies: Empire and Technopolitics in the Global Cold War* (Cambridge, MA: MIT Press, 2011), 3. See also Nick Cullather, "Development and Technopolitics," in *Explaining the History of American Foreign Relations*, eds. Frank Costigliola and Michael J. Hogan (New York: Cambridge University Press, 2016), 102–18.

8. Langdon Winner, "Do Artifacts Have Politics?," *Daedalus* 109, no. 1 (Winter 1980): 131, 134.

9. Freedom of action is more capacious than the notion of "strategic autonomy" commonly used by political scientists to explain foreign policies of countries that did not toe the line of the powerful. A key difference is that the leaders of India's nuclear program sought freedom of action at home as well as abroad. See, for example, C. Raja Mohan, "India: Between 'Strategic Autonomy' and 'Geopolitical Opportunity,'" *Asia Policy*, no. 15 (January 2013): 21–25.

10. Swords and ploughshares as metaphors for nuclear weapons and nuclear energy, respectively, were used during the Cold War by defense intellectuals such as Albert Wohlstetter. Albert Wohlstetter et al., *Swords from Ploughshares: The Military Potential of Civilian Nuclear Energy* (Chicago: University of Chicago Press, 1977). The metaphors themselves were derived from the biblical verse, "(A)nd they shall beat their swords into ploughshares, and their spears into pruning hooks: nation shall not lift up sword against nation, neither shall they learn war anymore" (Isaiah 2:3–4).

11. Tata Institute of Fundamental Research, *Homi Jehangir Bhabha on Indian Science and the Atomic Energy Programme: A Selection* (Mumbai, India: TIFR, 2009), 14–15. See also Indira Chowdhury, *Growing the Tree of Science: Homi Bhabha and the Tata Institute of Fundamental Research* (Oxford, UK: Oxford University Press, 2016).

12. Homi Bhabha was related to the Tata family on his mother's side through marriage. His maternal aunt, Meherbai Bhabha, was married to Sir Dorabji Tata, who was the elder son of Jamsetji Nusserwanji Tata, the founder of the Tata Group. Jahnavi Phalkey, *Atomic State: Big Science in Twentieth-Century India* (Ranikhet and Bangalore, India: Permanent Black, 2013), 153; Sir Dorabji Tata, "Tata Titans," accessed May 12, 2021, https://www.tata.com/about-us/tata-group-our-heritage/tata-titans/sir-dorabji-tata.

13. Robert Anderson, *Nucleus and Nation: Scientists, International Networks and Power in India* (Chicago: University of Chicago Press, 2010), chapters 2, 3.

14. On the significance of Nehru and Gandhi's differences, see Partha Chatterjee, *Nationalist Thought and the Colonial World: A Derivative Discourse?* (London: Zed Books, 1986), chapters 4, 5.

15. Jawaharlal Nehru to Mahatma Gandhi, October 4, 1945, Allahabad, SWJN, vol. 14, series 1, NMML, 555.

16. Dipesh Chakrabarty, "The Legacies of Bandung: Decolonization and the Politics of Culture," in *Making a World after Empire: The Bandung Moment and Its Political Afterlives*, ed. Christopher J. Lee (Athens, OH: Ohio University Press, 2010), 54. On Nehru's notion of the "scientific temper," see Jawaharlal Nehru, *The Discovery of India* (New Delhi: Oxford University Press, 1946, 1985), 512.

17. Message to the Royal Institute of Science in Bombay on the occasion of its silver jubilee, November 21, 1945, SWJN, vol. 14, series 1, NMML, 558.

18. Ibid.

19. See Abha Sur, "Scientism and Social Justice: Meghnad Saha's Critique of the State of Science in India," *Historical Studies in the Physical and Biological Sciences* 33, no. 1 (2002): 87–105; Pratik Chakrabarti, *Western Science in Modern India: Metropolitan Methods, Colonial Practices* (New Delhi: Permanent Black, 2004), 290–91.

20. Phalkey, *Atomic State*, 183.

21. Mircea Raianu, "The Incorporation of India: The Tata Business Firm between Empire and Nation, ca. 1860–1970," *Enterprise & Society* 19, no. 4 (December 2018): 820. See also Mircea Raianu, *Tata: The Global Corporation That Built Indian Capitalism* (Cambridge, MA: Harvard University Press, 2021).

22. Indira Chowdhury and Ananya Dasgupta, *Masterful Spirit: Homi J. Bhabha, 1909–1966* (New Delhi: Penguin, 2010), 132.

23. I have solely used "AECI" in chapters 1 and 2 and the "DAE" in chapters 4 through 7 to denote the Indian government's institution for atomic energy research and development. When making general points about India's nuclear program in this introduction, I have used "AECI/DAE." In chapter 3, where I discuss the institutional expansion from the AECI to the DAE, I have used the two acronyms interchangeably in the way the actors used them.

24. Gyan Prakash, *Another Reason: Science and the Imagination of Modern India*. (Princeton, NJ: Princeton University Press, 1999), 199.

25. Sudipta Kaviraj, "An Outline of a Revisionist Theory of Modernity," *European Journal of Sociology* 46, no. 3 (2005): 504.

26. Ibid., 522.

27. Scott D. Sagan, "Why Do States Build Nuclear Weapons? Three Models in Search of a Bomb," *International Security* 21, no. 3 (Winter 1996–1997): 65–69; Jacques E. Hymans, *The Psychology of Nuclear Proliferation* (Cambridge, UK: Cambridge University Press, 2006), 171–203.

28. For a critique of histories of nuclear programs that privilege the development of nuclear weapons or "going nuclear" as the end goal, see Itty Abraham, "The Ambivalence of Nuclear Histories," *Osiris* 21, no. 1 (2006): 49–65.

29. Jaswant Singh, "Against Nuclear Apartheid," *Foreign Affairs* 77, no. 5 (September–October 1998): 41–52.

30. For representative texts of the strategic culture debate, see Jaswant Singh, *Defending India* (London: Palgrave Macmillan, 1999); Kanti Bajpai, "Indian Strategic Culture," in *South Asia in 2020: Future Strategic Balances and Alliances*, ed. Michael R. Chambers (Carlisle, PA: US Army War College, 2002), 245–304; Kanti Bajpai, "BJP and the Bomb," in *Inside Nuclear South Asia*, ed. Scott D. Sagan (Palo Alto, CA: Stanford University Press, 2009), 25–67; Anit Mukherjee, "K. Subrahmanyam and Indian Strategic Thought,"

Strategic Analysis 35, no. 4 (2011): 710–3; Rajesh Basrur, "Nuclear Weapons and Indian Strategic Culture," *Journal of Peace Research* 38, no. 2 (March 2001): 181–98.

31. Sankaran Krishna, "Cartographic Anxiety: Mapping the Body Politic in India," *Alternatives* 19, no. 4 (1994): 507–21.

32. Balveer Arora, "Les établissements français de l'Inde", *Revue française de science politique* 18, no. 2 (1968): 362–75; Jessica Namakkal, "The Terror of Decolonization: Exploring French India's 'Goonda Raj,'" *Interventions* 19, no. 3 (2016): 338–57.

33. Sanket Upadhyay, "Was Nehru Communal? PM Modi Rebuts Congress on CAA Attacks," *NDTV*, February 6, 2020; Shekhar Gupta, "Why Modi Is Using Nehru to Try and Demolish the Gandhi Dynasty and Congress," *Print*, February 8, 2020; Manoj Joshi, "The BJP Wants to Erase Nehru: Let's See What India Would Have Been without Him," *Wire*, May 24, 2016.

34. See, for example, Albert Wohlstetter, "Nuclear Sharing: NATO and the N + 1 Country," *Foreign Affairs* 39 (April 1961): 355–87. On the intellectual limitations imposed by the term "proliferation," see Benoît Pelopidas, "The Oracles of Proliferation: How Experts Maintain a Biased Historical Reading That Limits Policy Innovation," *Nonproliferation Review* 18, no. 1 (2011): 297–314. See also Abraham, "Ambivalence of Nuclear Histories."

35. "India Will Not Sign Nuclear Pact Even If Aid Is Stopped," *Times of India*, April 13, 1968; "India Will Not Sign NPT, Says PM," *Hindu*, April 13, 1968; "Development of Know-How at BARC," *Times of India*, October 21, 1968.

36. Quoted in Itty Abraham, *The Making of the Indian Atomic Bomb: Science, Secrecy and the Postcolonial State* (London and New York: Zed Books, 1998), 140.

37. Shane J. Maddock, *Nuclear Apartheid: The Quest for American Atomic Supremacy from World War II to the Present* (Chapel Hill, NC: University of North Carolina Press, 2010), 2.

38. Vineet Thakur, "An Asian Drama: The Asian Relations Conference," *International History Review* 41, no. 3 (2019): 673–95.

39. Prime Minister Jawaharlal Nehru's speech to the Political Committee of the Asian-African Conference, Bandung, April 23, 1955, *Proceedings of the Political Committee of the Asian-African Conference*, April 20–24, 1955.

40. See, for example, George Perkovich, *India's Nuclear Bomb: The Impact on Global Proliferation* (Berkeley, CA, Los Angeles, and London: University of California Press, 1999); Rohan Mukherjee, "Nuclear Ambiguity and International Status: India in the Eighteen-Nation Committee on Disarmament, 1962–1969," in *India and the Cold War*, ed. Manu Bhagavan (Chapel Hill, NC: University of North Carolina Press, 2019), 126–50. A related argument is that a sense of victimhood and trauma from colonialism has led to India's ideological foreign policy including its opposition to the nonproliferation regime. See Manjari Chatterjee Miller, *Wronged by Empire: Post-Imperial Ideology and Foreign Policy in India and China* (Palo Alto, CA: Stanford University Press, 2013), 82–105.

41. Lorenz M. Lüthi, *Cold Wars: Asia, Middle East, Europe* (Cambridge, UK: Cambridge University Press, 2020), chapters 7, 11, 12.

42. David Engerman, *The Price of Aid: The Economic Cold War in India* (Cambridge, MA: Harvard University Press, 2018).

43. Abraham, *Making of the Indian Atomic Bomb*; Perkovich, *India's Nuclear Bomb*; Anderson, *Nucleus and Nation*; Phalkey, *Atomic State*.

44. Raj Chengappa, *Weapons of Peace Weapons of Peace: Secret Story of India's Quest to Be a Nuclear Power* (New Delhi: Harper Collins, 2000); M. V. Ramana, *The Power of Promise: Examining Nuclear Energy in India* (New Delhi: Viking, 2012).

45. On recent political and diplomatic histories of South Asia, see, for example, Raghavan, *War and Peace*, Engerman, *Price of Aid*; Paul McGarr, *The Cold War in South Asia: Britain, the United States and the Indian Subcontinent, 1945–1965* (Cambridge, UK, and New York: Cambridge University Press, 2013); Elisabeth Leake, *The Defiant Border: The Afghan-Pakistan Borderlands in the Era of Decolonization, 1936–1965* (Cambridge, UK: Cambridge University Press, 2016); Bérénice Guyot-Réchard, *Shadow States: India, China and the Himalayas, 1910–1962* (Cambridge, UK: University of Cambridge Press, 2016); Pallavi Raghavan, *Animosity at Bay: An Alternative History of the India-Pakistan Relationship, 1947–1952* (New York: Oxford University Press, 2020).

46. See, for example, Gaurav Kampani, "New Delhi's Long Nuclear Journey: How Secrecy and Institutional Roadblocks Delayed India's Weaponization," *International Security* 38, no. 4 (Spring 2014): 79–114; Yogesh Joshi, "The Imagined Arsenal: India's Nuclear Decision-Making, 1973–76," NPIHP working paper no. 6, 2015; Vipin Narang, "Strategies of Nuclear Proliferation: How States Pursue the Bomb," *International Security* 41, no. 3 (Winter 2016 / 2017): 110–50.

47. Abraham, *Making of the Indian Atomic Bomb*; Abraham, "Ambivalence of Nuclear Histories"; Itty Abraham, "Contra-Proliferation: Interpreting the Meaning of India's Nuclear Tests in 1974 and 1998," in *Inside Nuclear South Asia*, ed. Scott D. Sagan (Stanford, CA: Stanford University Press, 1999), 110–11; Itty Abraham, "India's 'Strategic Enclave': Civilian Scientists and Military Technologies," *Armed Forces & Society* 18, no. 2 (1992): 231–52.

48. See, for example, A. Vinod Kumar, *India and the Nuclear Non-proliferation Regime: The Perennial Outlier* (Cambridge, UK: Cambridge University Press, 2014). See also earlier footnote about prestige and ideology.

49. By coproduction, I mean science and society as a joint enterprise, "each underwriting the other's existence." Sheila Jasanoff, "Ordering Knowledge, Ordering Society," in *States of Knowledge: The Co-Production of Science and Social Order*, ed., Sheila Jasanoff (London and New York: Routledge, 2004), 17.

50. On political science scholarship that foregrounds geopolitics as the driving factor behind India's nuclear program, see Šumit Ganguly, "India's Pathway to Pokhran II: The Prospects and Sources of New Delhi's Nuclear Weapons Program," *International Security* 23, no. 4 (Spring 1999): 148–77; Šumit Ganguly, "Why India Joined the Nuclear Club," *The Bulletin of the Atomic Scientists* (April 1983): 30–33; Andrew Kennedy, "India's Nuclear Odyssey: Implicit Umbrellas, Diplomatic Disappointments, and the Bomb," *International Security* 36, no. 2 (Fall 2011): 120–53; Nicholas L. Miller, "Nuclear Dominoes: A Self-Defeating Prophecy?," *Security Studies* 23, no. 1 (2014): 33–73.

1. Atomic Earths and State-Making, 1940s–1948

1. "Travancore Monazite," *The Mining Journal*, April 1, 1916, 219.

2. "Appendix I: Notes as to the Consumption and Supplies of Certain Commodities in the British Empire," *Dominions Royal Commission Final Report* (London: His Majesty's Stationary Office, 1918), 446–47.

3. "Travancore: A Lively Lesson for Great Britain on the Perils of German Trade Penetration," in *Russia: A Journal of Russian-American Trade* 1, nos. 1–8, May to December 1916 (New York: R. Martens & Co., Inc., 1916), 5.

4. Glenn T. Seaborg, who was awarded the Nobel Prize in Chemistry in 1951 and appointed chairman of the US Atomic Energy Commission (1961–71), is most famous as the codiscoverer of plutonium, the artificial radioactive element used in implosion-type nuclear bombs, such as the one dropped on Nagasaki on August 9, 1945. He appears in chapter 5 of this book.

5. "Atomic earths" is used in chapter 1 and in this book as a shorthand for the entire gamut of metals, minerals, and rare earths found in the Earth's crust and are useful for any part of the production of atomic energy for civilian and military ends.

6. Itty Abraham, "Rare Earths: The Cold War in the Annals of Travancore," in *Entangled Geographies: Empire and Technopolitics in the Global Cold War*, ed. Gabrielle Hecht (Cambridge, MA: MIT Press, 2011), 101–24.

7. H. D. McCaskey, "Mineral Resources of the United States, 1916, US Department of Interior, Part II: Nonmetals," (Washington, DC: Government Printing Office, 1919), 229.

8. C. W. Schomberg's last name appears also as Schomburg. "Nationality of C. W. Schomburg," Proceedings July 1918, no. 11, Delhi Records, Government of India, Home Department, Confidential, Identifier: PR_000003000089, National Archives of India, New Delhi (hereafter, NAI).

9. Even though the British government removed from the Travancore Minerals Company all German financial influence, they were not completely successful. As late as July 1918, the British authorities in London and Delhi were unsure how to legally prevent C. W. Schomburg from holding shares in the Travancore Minerals Company because he was both a German citizen and a naturalized Indian subject operating in a princely state. "Nationality of C. W. Schomburg," Proceedings July 1918, no. 11, Delhi Records, Government of India, Home Department, Confidential, Identifier: PR_000003000089, NAI.

10. Julie Michelle Klinger, *Rare Earth Frontiers: From Terrestrial Subsoils to Lunar Landscapes* (Ithaca, NY: Cornell University Press, 2017), 47.

11. Dietrich Stoltzenberg, *Fritz Haber: Chemist, Nobel Laureate, German, Jew* (Philadelphia: Chemical Heritage Press, 2004), 180; See also Jehuda Reinharz, "Science in the Service of Politics: The Case of Chaim Weizmann during the First World War," *The English Historical Review* 100, no. 396 (July 1985): 572–603.

12. Fred Aftalion, *A History of the International Chemical Industry* (Philadelphia: Chemical Heritage Press, 2001), 193.

13. Peter Hayes, *From Cooperation to Complicity: Degussa in the Third Reich* (Cambridge, UK: Cambridge University Press, 2007), 80–82; oral history interview of Nikolaus Riehl by Mark Walker on December 13, 1984, Niels Bohr Library & Archives, American Institute of Physics.

14. Annie LaCroix-Riz, *Industriels et Banquiers Français Sous l'Occupation: La Collaboration Economique entre le Reich et Vichy* (Paris: Armand Colin, 1999), 170.

15. Samuel A. Goudsmit, *Alsos* (Woodbury, NY: American Institute of Physics, 1947), 56; Vince Houghton, *The Nuclear Spies: America's Atomic Intelligence Operation Against Hitler and Stalin* (Ithaca, NY: Cornell University Press, 2019), chapter 3.

16. *Auergesellschaft* also sold radioactive thorium toothpaste during the Second World War, called the *Doramad Radioaktive Zahncreme*. The thorium came from STR in Paris from the monazite sands it extracted.

17. Jean Matricon and Georges Waysand, *The Cold Wars: A History of Superconductivity* (New Brunswick, NJ: Rutgers University Press), 113; Philip Morrison, "Alsos: The Story of German Science," *The Bulletin of the Atomic Scientists* (December 1947): 354, 365; Diana Preston, *Before the Fallout: From Marie Curie to Hiroshima* (New York: Walker & Company, 2005), 267.

18. *Auergesellschaft*'s association with the Nazi bomb project came to light through the Alsos Mission, the US intelligence-gathering operation (1943–45) to uncover wartime German advancement in nuclear weapons development. German knowledge in nuclear fission was eventually found to be far less advanced than that of the Allies. As Glenn Seaborg and others in the Manhattan Project had originally believed, German scientists adopted the thorium route to develop the atomic bomb. At the end of the war, with the partition of Germany and Berlin, *Auergessellschaft*'s extraction plant in Oranienburg came to the possession of the Soviet Union while its chemical plant in Berlin went to the United Kingdom. On this subject, see Roger F. Robinson, *Mining and Selling Radium and Uranium* (Heidelberg, Germany: Springer, 2015), 238; on thorium and nuclear fission, see Eva C. Uribe, "Thorium power has a protactinium problem," *The Bulletin of the Atomic Scientists*, August 6, 2018. Kirk Frederick-Sorensen, "Thorium Research in the Manhattan Project Era," (MA thesis, University of Tennessee, Knoxville, 2014), 67. See also footnote 15 of this chapter.

19. "US Strategic and Critical Materials Stockpiling Act," Act of June 7, 1939, ch. 190, §2, 53 Stat. 811, accessed May 17, 2021, https://uscode.house.gov/statviewer .htm?volume=53&page=811.

20. On the US Department of Interior's global stockpiling efforts during the Second World War and the early Cold War, see Megan Black, *The Global Interior: Mineral Frontiers and American Power* (Cambridge, MA: Harvard University Press, 2018), chapters 2, 3.

21. The Atlantic Charter, August 14, 1941, accessed May 17, 2021, http://avalon.law .yale.edu/wwii/atlantic.asp.

22. See "The Quebec Conference—Agreement Relating to Atomic Energy," August 19, 1943, The Avalon Project, accessed May 17, 2021, http://avalon.law.yale.edu /wwii/q002.asp.

23. Ibid.

24. Michael Gordin, *Red Cloud at Dawn: Truman, Stalin, and the End of the Atomic Monopoly* (New York: Farrar, Straus and Giroux, 2009), 73.

25. Ibid.

26. Quoted in Robert Bothwell, *Eldorado: Canada's National Uranium Company* (Toronto: University of Toronto Press, 1984), 162–63.

27. Itty Abraham, "Rare Earths," 107.

28. Srinath Raghavan, *India's War: World War II and the Making of Modern South Asia* (New York: Basic Books, 2016), 214.

29. Ibid., 219.

30. Jugantar, vol. 6, no. 85 (December 19, 1942), EAP262/1/2/1369, Credit for Archives: Centre for Studies in Social Sciences, Calcutta. See also "Calcutta Bombed Anew by Japanese," *New York Times*, December 28, 1942, 3.

31. Max Holland, "Private Sources of US Foreign Policy: William Pawley and the 1954 Coup d'État in Guatemala," *Journal of Cold War Studies* 7, no. 4 (Fall 2005): 41; Max Holland, "A Luce Connection: Senator Keating, William Pawley, and the Cuban Missile Crisis," *Journal of Cold War Studies* 1, no. 3 (Fall 1999): 157–58.

32. Anthony R. Carrozza, *William D. Pawley: The Extraordinary Life of the Adventurer, Entrepreneur and Diplomat who Cofounded the Flying Tigers* (Washington, DC: Potomac Books, 2012), 111–13. See also his obituary: Murray Illson, "A Lone and Varied Career," *The New York Times*, January 8, 1977, 22; Rachel Lee, "Constructing A Shared Vision: Otto Koenigsberger and Tata & Sons," *ABE Journal* (online), no. 2, 2012.

33. The global and transnational connections in independent India's aeronautical project did not only involve William D. Pawley's initial contribution. In 1961, the HF-24 or Marut conducted its flight as the first Indian-built fighter bomber produced by the Hindustan Aeronautics Limited. The HF-24 was designed by German aeronautical engineer and aircraft designer Kurt Tank. After the fall of Nazi Germany, Tank had first moved to Argentina, where he designed military aircraft and later moved to India after the fall of Juan Perón's government in 1955. See Jahnavi Phalkey, "German Émigré Scientists and Engineers and Aeronautics in India," unpublished manuscript, cited with author's permission.

34. On this subject, see Mircea Raianu, *Tata: The Global Corporation That Built Indian Capitalism* (Cambridge, MA: Harvard University Press, 2021), chapter 3.

35. Vivekananda was traveling to the World Parliament of Religions in Chicago where his speech on religious tolerance made him famous in the United States. See "Swami Vivekananda and His 1893 Speech," accessed October 15, 2020, The Art Institute of Chicago, https://www.artic.edu/swami-vivekananda-and-his-1893-speech.

36. Letter from H. J. Bhabha to Sorab Saklatvala, March 12, 1944, DTT/PHIL/TIFR/FP/1, box 194, Tata Central Archives, Pune (hereafter TCA).

37. A note trust policy by R. Choksi, April 10, 1944, DTT/PHIL/TIFR/FP/1, box 194, TCA.

38. Ibid.

39. Note by R. Choksi to the trustees for their consideration at the meeting on 14-4-44 in connection with Dr. H .J. Bhabha's Scheme, DTT/PHIL/TIFR/FP/1, box 194, TCA.

40. Ibid. One lac is equal to one hundred thousand. The currency conversion is based on the foreign exchange rate of June 1944, where 1 Indian rupee was valued at 0.3037 of the US dollar. Foreign Exchange, *Wall Street Journal*, June 30, 1944, 9.

41. Historical note on Tata Institute of Fundamental Research, prepared by Dr. H. J. Bhabha for the prime minister on the occasion of the laying of the foundation stone of the institute's new building on January 1, 1954, Archives of the Tata Institute of Fundamental Research, Mumbai (hereafter TIFR).

42. Government of Bombay, Education Department Resolution No. 7793, Bombay Castle, January 3, 1947, DTT/PHIL/TIFR/FP/1, box 194, TCA. The currency conversion is based on the foreign exchange rate of January 1947, where 1 rupee was valued at 0.3025 of the US dollar. Foreign exchange rates, *Wall Street Journal*, January 31, 1947, 9.

43. Letter from Homi J. Bhabha to Irène Joliot-Curie, April 28, 1947, ref: TFR/36/2148, D-2004-00003-TIFR-ARCH-DIR-HJB-CORRESP-GEN-3, TIFR.

44. Letter from Irène Joliot-Curie to Homi Bhabha, May 30, 1947, enclosed with note about sending error by airmail dated June 20, 1947, D-2004-00003-TIFR-ARCH-DIR-HJB-CORRESP-GEN-3, TIFR.

45. Letter from Homi Bhabha to Sir Frederick S. James, November 20, 1947, D-2004-00003-TIFR-ARCH-DIR-HJB-CORRESP-GEN-3, TIFR.

46. Letter from Homi Bhabha to Jamshed N. Duggan, superintendent of Tata Memorial Hospital, November 20, 1947, D-2004-00003-TIFR-ARCH-DIR-HJB-CORRESP-GEN-3, TIFR.

47. The apparatus included an electrometer, electroscope, quartz piezo electric crystal, ionization chambers, and the "lame" of quartz, among others. The company that provided the quote was Charles Baudouin of Paris. The currency conversion is based on the foreign exchange rate of June 1944, where 1 French franc was valued at 0.8425 of the US dollar. Foreign exchange, *Wall Street Journal*, November 28, 1947, 13.

48. On this subject, see V. P. Menon, *The Story of the Integration of Indian States* (Bombay, Calcutta, Madras: Orient Longmans, 1956); Ian Copland, *The Princes of India in the Endgame of Empire, 1917–1947* (Cambridge, UK: Cambridge University Press, 1997).

49. Through treaties signed with the British East India Company, these kingdoms had accepted the "paramount" power first of the company and, later on, of the British Crown. After the 1857 mutiny in India, the Government of India Act of August 2, 1858, transferred paramountcy from the East India Company to the British Crown. After the British Government dissolved the East India Company by an act of Parliament in 1874, British direct imperial rule of India was formalized. "East India Company and Raj 1785–1858," UK Parliament, Parliament and Empire: Overview, accessed April 14, 2021, https://www.parliament.uk/about/living-heritage/evolutionofparliament/legislativescrutiny/parliament-and-empire/parliament-and-the-american-colonies-before-1765/east-india-company-and-raj-1785–1858/.

50. Memorandum in regard to states treaties and paramountcy, Cabinet Mission, Simla, May 12, 1946, appendix III, 44–45, White Paper on Indian States, Government of India, 1950.

51. Ibid.

52. Ibid.

53. On the territorialization of national space after 1857, see Manu Goswami, *Producing India: From Colonial Economy to National Space* (Chicago: University of Chicago Press, 2004).

54. Raghavan, *War and Peace*, chapters 2–4.

55. For Sir C. P.'s life and work, see Shakunthala Jagannathan, *Sir C.P. Remembered: To Thatha With Love: A Granddaughter's Reminiscences* (Mumbai: Vakils, Feffer & Simmons Ltd., 1999).

56. Sir C. P. Ramaswamy Aiyar represented India at the Seventh and Eighth Ordinary Sessions of the League of Nations General Assembly held in September 1926 and 1927, respectively. His last name also appears as Iyer in the League of Nations documents. See League of Nations search engine record: http://www.lonsea.de/pub/person/11859 (accessed May 17, 2021).

57. For an authoritative study of Travancore's monazite during Indian independence, see Abraham, "Rare Earths."

58. G. A. Roush and Allison Butts, *The Mineral Industry: Its Statistics, Technology and Trade during 1920* (New York: McGraw Hill, 1921), 471.

59. Lindsay Light and Chemical Company discarded radioactive thorium waste from processing monazite in its Rare Earths Facility in West Chicago, attracting public scrutiny in the 1970s. Erin Meyer, "40 years later, toxic waste still haunts pockets of DuPage County," *Chicago Tribune*, January 21, 2012; Nuclear Regulatory Commission Issuances, April 1986, vol. 23, issues 4–6, NUREG 0750, (Washington, DC: US Government Printing Office), 815–16.

60. P. Priya, "Malabar Famine of 1943: A Critique of War Situation in Malabar (1939–45)," *Proceedings of the Indian History Congress*, vol. 75, Platinum Jubilee (2014), 628–38; Mark B. Tauger, "Indian Famine Crises of World War II," *British Scholar* 1, no. 2 (March 2009): 166–96.

61. On famines in Second World War India, see Yasmin Khan, *India at War: The Subcontinent and the Second World War* (New York: Oxford University Press, 2015), chapter 15, Scorched Earth; Madhushree Mukherjee, *Churchill's Secret War: The British Empire and the Ravaging of India during World War II* (New York: Basic Books, 2010).

62. William D. Pawley, "India: Its Future Bright For Post-War Jobs—Pawley sees Vast Trade if Britain, United States Cooperate," *Miami Daily News*, February 11, 1945, published in Congressional Record: Proceedings and Debates of the Seventy-Ninth Congress, First Session, appendix, vol. 91, part II, March 23–June 8, 1945 (Washington, DC: Government Printing Office, 1945), A1808–09.

63. Abraham, "Rare Earths," 108.

64. Dewan's statement on the budget for 1121 ME (1945–46), Proceediigs of the Sri Mulam Popular Assembly, 1945–46, 35, quoted in K. T. Ram Mohan, "'Captains of the Sands': Metropolitan Hegemony in Mining in Tiruvitamkur, 1900–50," *Economic and Political Weekly* 30, no. 52 (December 30, 1995): 3365–72.

65. CIA information report, "Monazite Sand and Rare Earth Metals," September 13, 1948, 3, distributed November 4, 1948, CIA-RDP 80-00926A000600020025–8, CIA FOIA Reading Room.

66. Jahnavi Phalkey, "Science, State-Formation and Development: The Organisation of Nuclear Research in India, 1938–1959" (PhD diss., Georgia Institute of Technology, 2007), 121; Phalkey, *Atomic State*, 183.

67. The centralization of nuclear physics in the TIFR precipitated tensions between Homi Bhabha and Meghnad Saha of the Palit Laboratory in Calcutta. On the nature of the dispute, see Phalkey, *Atomic State*, 183–205.

68. "State Control of Monazite and Thorium Nitrate," February 27, 1947, file no. 17 (4) 47-PMS, from *Selected Works of Jawaharlal Nehru* (New Delhi: Jawaharlal Nehru Memorial Fund), volume 2, 604–07, quoted in Itty Abraham, "Rare Earths," op. cit., 111.

69. Ramachandra Guha, "The strange case of Sir C.P. Ramaswamy Iyer," *The Hindu*, May 25, 2008, last updated October 10, 2016; Ajit Bhattacharjea, "Notional Divide: Countdown to Partition," *Outlook Magazine*, July 30, 1997.

70. A. G. Noorani, "C.P. and Independent Travancore," *Frontline*, July 4, 2003.

71. Abraham, "Rare Earths," 106.

72. Ibid., 116.

73. Noorani, "C.P. and Independent Travancore."

74. Ibid.

75. Letter from J. P. Gibson to D. E. H. Peirson, April 7, 1948, AB 16/515, Commonwealth Relations: India Research and Supplies 1947–53, UK National Archives, Kew (hereafter UKNA).

76. The Atomic Energy Research Committee and the Board for Research on Atomic Energy, both lasting from 1946–48, had placed an embargo on beryl and monazite in 1946 prior to India's independence, which the 1948 Indian Atomic Energy Act reaffirmed.

77. Andrew Rotter, *Comrades at Odds: The United States and India, 1947–1964* (Ithaca, NY: Cornell University Press, 2000), 98–99.

2. Radium to Reactors, 1948–1953

1. Marie Curie, "Radium and the New Concepts in Chemistry," Nobel lecture, Nobel Prize in Chemistry, December 11, 1911, accessed October 16, 2020, https://www.nobelprize.org/prizes/chemistry/1911/marie-curie/lecture/.

2. Radium and Cancer," *New York Times*, December 31, 1903, 8; "Radium: From Wonder Drug to Hazard," *New York Times*, October 4, 1987, 47.

3. Radium's use in cancer treatment was well underway in British India in Bengal and Bihar during and since the First World War at the Ranchi Radium Institute and the Bengal Cancer Institute and Hospital. After Sir Dorabji Tata's wife, Lady Meherbai Tata, died of leukemia in 1931, he began to provide philanthropic support for cancer research. For an institutional history of the Tata Memorial Hospital, see Shirish N. Kavadi, "The founding of the Tata Memorial Hospital, 1932–1941," *Indian Journal of Cancer* 56, no. 3 (2019): 282–84.

4. Naidu had conducted research at the Radium Institute in Paris until Madame Curie's death in 1934 due to radiation poisoning. This was followed by his postdoctoral research at the University of London with renowned British experimental physicist P. M. S. Blackett.

5. Homi Bhabha's correspondence with Irène Joliot-Curie has been discussed at the end of chapter 1.

6. On this subject, see Alex Wellerstein, *Restricted Data: The History of Nuclear Secrecy in the United States* (Chicago: University of Chicago Press, 2021).

7. This meant that knowledge in nuclear things was secret as soon as it was produced, and it remained so until declassified. US Atomic Energy Act of 1946, public law 585, Seventy-Nine Congress, accessed March 15, 2019, http://www.sc.doe.gov/bes/Atomic_Energy_Act_of_1946.doc.

8. The McMahon Act took legal inspiration from the 1917 US Espionage Act that had crafted a complicated classification system to control scientific communication and practices. On this subject, see Wellerstein, *Restricted Data*, chapter 4; Mario Daniels and John Krige, "Beyond the Reach of Regulation? 'Basic' and 'Applied' Research in the Early Cold War United States," *Technology & Culture* 59, o. 2 (April 2018): 231–32; Michael Dennis, "Our Monsters, Ourselves: Reimagining the Problem of Knowledge in Cold War America," in *Dreamscapes of Modernity: Sociotechnical Imaginaries and the Fabrication of Power*, eds. Sheila Jasanoff and Sang-Hyung Kim (Chicago: University of Chicago Press, 2014), 56–78.

9. Vannevar Bush, *Science: The Endless Frontier* (Washington, DC: US Government Printing Office, 1945); Henry DeWolf Smyth, *Atomic Energy for Military Purposes* (Princeton, NJ: Princeton University Press, 1945).

10. Appendix A to the Secret Minutes of a Special Meeting of the Atomic Energy Commission (Homi J. Bhabha, S. S. Bhatnagar, and K. S. Krishnan), Prime Minister Jawaharlal Nehru and CEA Hight commissioner Frédéric Joliot-Curic, January 16, 1950, New Delhi, CEA: Relations Internationals: Relations avec l'Inde (1948–50), F-86, Joliot-Curie Papers, Institut Curie, Bibliothèque Nationale de France, Paris (hereafter, BnF-FJC).

11. The policy also mentioned that the cyclotron in Calcutta should be used for training purposes (a priority for Meghnad Saha) and that fundamental research in physics should concern cosmic rays (a specialization of Homi Bhabha). Ibid.

12. Text of letter from Sir Roger Makins at the UK Foreign Office to Mr. Lewis L. Strauss, chairman of the US Atomic Energy Commission, April 21, 1954, AB 16/565, UKNA.

13. Secret letter from Homi J. Bhabha to Jawaharlal Nehru, no. TFR/A/4-K, December 1, 1948, folder: Monazite Factory Scheme (Mr. Dandekar's note), papers of Sardar Patel, 1948, PP_000000006114, NAI.

14. Report on the establishment of a factory for treating Indian Monazite, appendix to secret letter from Homi J. Bhabha to Jawaharlal Nehru, no. TFR/A/4-K, December 1, 1948, PP_000000006114, NAI.

15. Ibid.

16. Ibid.

17. Ibid.

18. Ibid.

19. The currency conversion is based on the foreign exchange rate of December 1948, where 1 Indian rupee was valued at 0.3583 of the US dollar. Foreign exchange rates, *Christian Science Monitor*, December 10, 1948, 26.

20. Letter from Joseph M. Blumenfeld to Homi J. Bhabha, November 20, 1948, no. J. M. B./MLM, folder: Monazite Factory Scheme (Mr. Dandekar's note), papers of Sardar Patel, 1948, identifier: PP_000000006114, NAI.

21. Confidential letter ref. no. TFR/A/4/ from Homi J. Bhabha to Frédéric Joliot-Curie, February 11, 1949, F-86, BnF-FJC.

22. Secret letter no. AEC/5(10)-49/1201 from S. S. Bhatnagar to Frédéric Joliot-Curie, June 21, 1949, F-86, BnF-FJC.

23. Balveer Arora, "Les établissements français de l'Inde," *Revue française de science politique* 18 (1968): 364. On this subject, see also Patrick Pitoëff, "L'Inde française en suris, 1947–1954," *Outre Mers. Revue d'histoire* 290 (1991): 105–31; Jessica Namakkal, *Unsettling Utopia: The Making and Unmaking of French India* (New York: Columbia University Press, 2021).

24. Quoted in Russell H. Fifield, "The Future of French India," *Far Eastern Survey* 19, no. 6 (1950): 62.

25. Akhila Yechury, "Imagining India, Decolonizing *L'Inde Française*, c. 1947–1954," *The Historical Journal* 58, no. 4 (2015): 1150.

26. On the role of thugs to create violence in French India during this period, see Jessica Namakkal, "The Terror of Decolonization: Exploring French India's 'Goonda Raj,'" *Interventions* 19, no. 3 (2017): 338–57.

27. "Treaty establishing De Jure Cession of French Establishments in India," May 28, 1956, Ministry of External Affairs, Government of India, accessed October 15, 2020, https://mea.gov.in/bilateral-documents.htm?dtl/5302/Treaty+establishing+De+Jure +Cession+of+French+Establishments+in+India.

28. On the notion of co-subalterns, see Kris Manjapra, *Age of Entanglement: German and Indian Intellectuals Across Empire* (Cambridge, MA: Harvard University Press, 2014); Kris Manjapra, "Transnational Approaches to Global History: A View from the Study of German-Indian Entanglement," *German History* 32, no. 2 (2014): 274–93.

29. On the French contribution to the Manhattan Project, see Bertrand Gold-schmidt, *The Atomic Complex: A Worldwide Political History of Nuclear Energy* (La Grange, IL: American Nuclear Society, 1982), 56–65.

30. Jayita Sarkar, "'Wean them away from French Tutelage': Franco-Indian Nuclear Relations and Anglo-American Anxieties during the Early Cold War, 1948–1952," *Cold War History* 15, no. 3 (2015): 381–83.

31. Goldschmidt, *Atomic Complex*, 60.

32. The United States had already secured priority access to the uranium in Belgian Congo during the Second World War through Union Minière. Canada, a member of the Common Development Trust, was thought to have the next largest deposits of uranium. It was not known how abundant uranium would be in nature. This drove the French quest for nuclear fuel alternatives like thorium. The extraction of uranium in Madagascar, Niger, and elsewhere in the 1960s and 1970s would reduce French and global interest in thorium.

33. Secret letter no. AEC/5(10)-49/1201 from S. S. Bhatnagar to Frédéric Joliot-Curie, June 21, 1949, F-86, BnF-FJC.

34. Zoé was called so because it was zero powered, used uranium oxide, and was moderated by heavy water or *eau lourde*. Note prepared by Francis Perrin titled, "La pile atomique de Chatillon," 1949, Carton F-76 (300), FJC-BnF. See also CEA, Département des Relations Publiques, *Zoé: The atomic pile which has been the first French reactor to diverge in December 1948*, INIS-FR—16-0797, France, accessed April 21, 2021, https:// inis.iaea.org/search/search.aspx?orig_q=RN:47082623.

35. "A Mineral Policy for India," by D. N. Wadia, advisor on mineral development, Department of Minerals, Works and Power, folder: Central Control of certain minerals; establishment of a Directorate General of mineral Development; Conference on national mineral policy acquisition of mineral rights by the State; file no. 1(6)-IE/46, Political Department 9E Branch, nos. 1–77, NAI.

36. This reactor cooperation agreement has been fully examined here: Sarkar, "Wean them away from French Tutelage."

37. Telegram from the Commonwealth Relations Office's Trade and Transport Department to the UK high commissioner in India, May 17, 1949, AB 16/515, UKNA.

38. Telegram from Commonwealth Relations Office to UK high commissioner in India, November 30, 1949, AB 16/515, Commonwealth Relations, India: Research and Supplies, 1947–53, UKNA.

39. Secret minutes of a special meeting of the Atomic Energy Commission (Jawaharlal Nehru, Homi J. Bhabha, S. S. Bhatnagar, and K. S. Krishnan), January 16, 1950, prime minister's room at the Ministry of External Affairs, New Delhi, F-86, BnF-FJC.

40. Ibid.

41. Ibid.

42. Secret minutes of a special meeting of the Atomic Energy Commission (Homi J. Bhabha, S. S. Bhatnagar, and K. S. Krishnan) with Frédéric Joliot-Curie, January 17, 1950, F-86, BnF-FJC.

43. Letter from Raoul Dautry, administrator-general of the CEA to René Lescop, secretary-general of the CEA, September 14, 1950, 307 AP 203, Raoul Dautry Papers, Archives Nationales de France, Paris (hereafter, ANF).

44. Letter from Oliver Harvey, British Embassy in Paris to the British Government, October 30, 1951, AB16/565, UKNA.

45. Letter from F. C. How to Roger Makins, August 18, 1951, AB 16/565, UKNA.

46. Report by F. W. Marten in Washington, DC, to W. Harpham at the Foreign Office in London, on debates at the US Senate and at the House of Representatives on loaning wheat to India, May 31, 1951, AB 16/565, UKNA.

47. Secret envelope from Jules Guéron to Raoul Dautry containing resumé of discussions with Homi J. Bhabha in London, July 2, 1950, 307 AP 225, Dautry Papers, ANF.

48. Article 1 of draft contract from July 1950, secret envelope from Jules Guéron to Raoul Dautry containing resumé of discussions with Homi J. Bhabha in London, July 2, 1950, 307 AP 225, Dautry Papers, ANF.

49. Secret note 1241 from A. H. Waterfield to Meiklereid, head of Chancery, September 11, 1951, AB16/565, UKNA.

50. Secret letter 1241/18/51 no. 492 from Ambassador Oliver Harvey at the UK Embassy in Paris to Foreign Secretary Anthony Eden, October, 30 1951, AB16/565, UKNA.

51. High-purity beryllium metal continues to be classified as a critical and strategic material by the Strategic Materials Protection Board of the US Department of Defense as of this writing. On this subject, see N. K. Foley et al., "Beryllium," chapter E of K. J. Schulz, ed., *Critical mineral resources of the United States—Economic and environmental geology and prospects for future supply*, US Geological Survey Professional Paper 1802, E1–E32.

52. Jonathan E. Helmreich, *Gathering Rare Ores: The Diplomacy of Uranium Acquisition, 1943–1954* (Princeton, NJ: Princeton University Press, 1986), 170.

53. Secret cypher telegram no. 1626 from Commonwealth Relations Office to the UK high commissioner in India, May 17, 1949, AB16/515, UKNA.

54. Secret letter DLH/22(3)-52/2837 from Santi Swarup Bhatnagar to John D. Cockcroft, May 30, 1952, AB16/565, UKNA.

55. Inaugural address of President Harry S. Truman, January 20, 1949, accessed May 18, 2021, https://avalon.law.yale.edu/20th_century/truman.asp.

56. Black, *Global Interior*, 118–19.

57. Ibid., 125.

58. Ibid., 126.

59. *Resources for Freedom, A Report to the President by the President's Materials Policy Commission, 1952: Vol. I, Foundations for Growth and Security by The President's Materials Policy Commission* (Washington, DC: US Government Printing Office, 1952); see also Glenn H. Snyder, "Stockpiling Strategic Materials: Politics and National Defense" (San Francisco: Chandler Pub. Co., 1966), 146–54; Mats Ingulstad, "The Interdependent Hegemon: The United States and the Quest for Strategic Raw Materials During the Early Cold War," *International History Review* 37, no. 1 (2014): 59–79.

60. Throughout this book, "China" has been used to refer to the People's Republic of China.

61. On this food-for-monazite episode, see Sarkar, "'Wean Them away from French Tutelage,'" 389–92; Engerman, *Price of Aid*, 55; Dennis Kux, *India and the United States: Estranged Democracies, 1941–1991* (Washington, DC: National Defense University Press, 2002), 78–82.

62. Report by F. W. Marten in Washington, DC, to W. Harpham at the Foreign Office in London, on debates at the US Senate and at the House of Representatives on loaning wheat to India, May 31, 1951, AB 16/565, UKNA.

63. Sermon on the Mount" by Herblock, *Washington Post*, April 5, 1951.

64. "China Raises Rice Offer to India; Would 'Sell' Second 50,000 Tons," *New York Times*, March 31, 1951, 9.

65. Ibid.

66. Engerman, *Price of Aid*, 52–55.

67. Secret letter from Roger Makins at the UK Foreign Office to M.W. Perrin at the Ministry of Supply, June 5, 1951, AB16/565, UKNA.

68. On Chester Bowles's role in US technical assistance to India, see Engerman, *Price of Aid*, chapter 2.

69. Minutes of the meeting of the United States Members of the Combined Policy Committee, Washington, April 15, 1952, FRUS, 1952–54, vol. 2, part 2, National Security Affairs, document 14.

70. NIE-61: Consequences of Communist Control over the Indian Subcontinent, July 28, 1952, Secret Security Information, CIA-RDP79S01011A000800010001-0.

71. Confidential memo for Mr. Pawley from US secretary of defense Robert A. Lovett, September 16, 1952, Pawley Official Correspondence, 1948–52, box 4, accession no. 42; 82–46, William D. Pawley Papers, George C. Marshall Foundation, Lexington, VA.

72. Memorandum: Notes on the Discussion I of Questions Related to the Establishing and Operating Joint Indo-American Monazite-Processing Plant in India, and Related Matters, October 18, 1952, Secret Security Information, Pawley Official Correspondence, 1948–52, box 4, Pawley Papers.

73. Memorandum: Notes on the Discussion II of Questions Related to the Establishing and Operating Joint Indo-American Monazite-Processing Plant in India, and Related Matters, October 20, 1952, Secret Security Information, Pawley Official Correspondence, 1948–52, box 4, Pawley Papers.

74. Ibid.

75. Information from Foreign Documents or Radio Broadcasts, CIA Secretly Secure Information, December 24–27, 1952, distributed March 18, 1953, "Indian Atomic Energy Production," CIA-RDP 80-00809A000700210219-1

76. Secret telegram from US ambassador George V. Allen to US secretary of state John Foster Dulles, July 21, 1953, Foreign Relations of the United States (hereafter FRUS), 1952–54, vol. XI, part 2, Africa and South Asia, document 1040.

77. Mutual Defense Assistance Control Act, October 26, 1951 [H. R. 4550], statute 65, public law 213, chapter 575, 644–47, accessed May 18, 2021, https://www.govinfo.gov/content/pkg/STATUTE-65/pdf/STATUTE-65-Pg644-2.pdf#page=1.

78. Secret cypher inward telegram no. 865 to Commonwealth Relations Office from acting UK high commissioner in New Delhi, July 31, 1953, AB 16/565, UKNA.

79. Secret cypher inward telegram no. 871 to Commonwealth Relations Office from acting UK high commissioner in New Delhi, August 1, 1953, AB 16/565, UKNA.

80. Ibid.

81. Secret letter M 344/23G from the UK Foreign Office to the Commonwealth Relations Office, August 14, 1953, AB 16/565, UKNA.

82. Secret telegram from George V. Allen to US State Department, August 25, 1953, FRUS, 1952–54, vol. 11, part 2, Africa and South Asia, document 1057.

83. Ibid.

84. Secret telegram from George V. Allen to John Foster Dulles, August 1, 1953, FRUS, 1952–54, vol. 11, part 2, Africa and South Asia, document 1048.

85. Rotter, *Comrades at Odds*, 103.

86. Secret CIA information report, Chinese-Polish shipping, September 3, 1954, CIA-RDP80-00809A000600060301-1, CIA FOIA Reading Room. On the history of Chipolbrok, see Margaret K. Gnoinska, "Chipolbrok—Continuity in Times of Change: Sino-Polish Relations during the Cold War, 1949–1969," in *Europe and China in the Cold War: Exchanges Beyond the Bloc Logic and the Sino-Soviet Split*, eds. Janick Marina Schaufelbuehl, Marco Wyss, and Valeria Zanier (Leiden and Boston: Brill, 2019), 192–211.

87. Helmreich, *Gathering Rare Ores*, 234.

88. Dispatch 1436 from US embassy in India, March 12, 1953, FRUS, 1952–54, Africa and South Asia, vol. 11, part 2, document 1078.

89. Memorandum by the president to the director of the Foreign Operations Administration, June 29, 1954, FRUS, 1952–54, vol. 11, part 2, Africa and South Asia, document 1089.

3. Nuclear Marketplace Opens for Business, 1953–1962

1. Press release, "Atoms for Peace" speech, December 8, 1953, Dwight D. Eisenhower Papers as President, Speech Series, box 5, United Nations Speech 12/8/53, Dwight D. Eisenhower Presidential Library, Abilene, KS (hereafter DDEL).

2. Ibid.

3. The AECI and the DAE have been used interchangeably in this chapter based on how the actors referred to India's nuclear program. From chapter 4 onward, DAE has been used to replace the AECI in the text.

4. Confidential letter from Meghnad Saha to Jawaharlal Nehru, November 11, 1953, letter enclosed with report prepared by Saha on the activities of the Atomic Energy Commission of India, NEH/J-53-28(E), Meghnad Saha Papers, Saha Institute of Nuclear Physics, Kolkata, India (hereafter, SINP).

5. Speech by S. S. Bhatnagar, January 1, 1954, TIFR Foundation Stone-Laying Ceremony, DTT/PHIL/TIFR/Mis/12, box 196, TCA.

6. On Atoms for Peace as part of the Eisenhower administration's psychological warfare, see Kenneth Osgood. *Total Cold War: Eisenhower's Secret Propaganda Battle at Home and Abroad* (Lawrence, KS: University Press of Kansas, 2006); Shane J. Maddock, *Nuclear Apartheid: The Quest for American Atomic Supremacy from World War II to the Present* (Chapel Hill, NC: University of North Carolina Press, 2010), 87–92; see also Martin Medhurst, "Atoms for Peace and Nuclear Hegemony: The Rhetorical Structure of a Cold War Campaign," *Armed Forces & Society* 23, no. 4 (Summer 1997): 571–93.

7. Secret Security Information, Project "Candor," July 22, 1953, White House Office, National Security Council Papers, PSB Central Files Series, box 17, PSB 091.4 US (2), NAID no. 12021612, DDEL.

8. Robbert S. Norris & Hans M. Kristensen. "Global nuclear weapons inventories, 1945–2010," *Bulletin of the Atomic Scientists*, 66, no. 4 (2010): 8.

9. Mara Drogan, "The Nuclear Imperative: Atoms for Peace and the Development of US Policy on Exporting Nuclear Power, 1953–1955," *Diplomatic History* 40, no. 5 (2015): 948–74; John Krige. "Atoms for Peace, Scientific Internationalism, and Scientific Intelligence." *Osiris* 21, no. 1 (2006): 161–81; Elisabeth Roehrlich, "The Cold War, the developing world, and the creation of the International Atomic Energy Agency (IAEA), 1953–1957," *Cold War History* 16, no. 2 (2016): 195–212.

10. "Text Statement of Atom Bill," *New York Times*, August 31, 1954, 19.

11. By February 1956, twenty-five thousand technical reports on atomic energy were reviewed, out of which one-third were entirely declassified and about a quarter were reclassified to a lower level of classification. See John Krige. "Atoms for Peace, Scientific Internationalism, and Scientific Intelligence," *Osiris* 21, no. 1 (2006): 165.

12. Remarks prepared by Lewis L. Strauss, chairman of USAEC for delivery at the Founders' Day Dinner, National Association of Science Writers, September 16,1954, US Nuclear Regulatory Commission online documents, accessed March 18, 2019, https://www.nrc.gov/docs/ML1613/ML16131A120.pdf; on the history of the role of US reactor businesses in the United States since Atoms for Peace, see Mark Hertsgaard, *Nuclear Inc.: The Men and Money Behind Nuclear Energy* (New York: Pantheon Books, 1983); Irving C. Bupp and Jean-Claude Derian, *Light Water: How the Nuclear Dream Dissolved* (New York: Basic Books, 1978).

13. Hertsgaard, *Nuclear Inc.*, 27.

14. NSC 5507/2, Peaceful Uses of Atomic Energy (1), March 12, 1955, box 14, NSC Series, Policy Papers Subseries, White House Office, Office of the Special Assistant for National Security Affairs: Records, 1952–61, DDEL.

15. Ibid.

16. Ibid.

17. Press release, "Atoms for Peace" speech, December 8, 1953, DDEL.

18. Drogan, "The Nuclear Imperative," 949.

19. Geoff Fraga, "Prof. Bhabha's Address Stirs Scientists of the World," *Times of India*, October 3, 1954, TIFR.

20. Abraham, *Making of the Indian Atomic Bomb*, 84.

21. Confidential letter from Meghnad Saha to Jawaharlal Nehru, November 11, 1953, NEH/J-53-28(E), SINP.

22. "Several Nations Open Exhibits at Geneva Conference to Show Peaceful Uses of Atomic Energy," *New York Times*, August 9, 1955, 8, accessed March 18, 2019, https://timesmachine.nytimes.com/timesmachine/1955/08/09/83367080.pdf.

23. Krige, "Atoms for Peace," 174.

24. Ibid.

25. Conference on the Peaceful Uses of Atomic Energy presidential address by Homi J. Bhabha, August 8, 1955, MPUAE/34/55, Department of Public Information, Press and Publications Division Geneva, UN.

26. Ibid.

27. Letter from Meghnad Saha to Jawaharlal Nehru, circa late July 1955, NEH/J-55-54(E)-1, Meghnad Saha Papers, SINP.

28. Letter from Homi J. Bhabha to Meghnad Saha, August 1, 1955, ref. DAE/Per-MNS /4735, Meghnad Saha Papers, Correspondence with Homi J. Bhabha, First Installment, NMML.

29. Letter no. 11(3)/1429 from Meghnad Saha to Jawaharlal Nehru, July 18, 1955, NEH/J-55-50(E)-1, Meghnad Saha Papers, SINP.

30. Joliot-Curie's removal in April 1950 did not throw a wrench in AECI-CEA negotiation for reactor cooperation because his successor Francis Perrin continued and concluded the agreement.

31. Letter no. 11(1)(a)/2739 from Meghnad Saha to Jawaharlal Nehru, November 24, 1954, NEH/J-54-39(E)-1, SINP.

32. This was written by Betrand Goldschmidt when he had to explain to the French foreign ministry after India's 1974 nuclear explosion why the CEA had worked so closely with the DAE. The French quote is: "L'Inde—premier champ de bataille des rivalités nucléaires occidentales dans le Tiers Monde . . ." Chronologie des Relations Nucleaires Franco-Indiennes," signed by Bertrand Goldschmidt, Confidentiel, Commissariat a l'energie atomique, circa November 1978, Carton 2254, Inde, Direction Asie-Oceanie, no. 15-11-5, January 1978–June 1980, ADF.

33. When a reactor is said to become "critical" it means that it has become operational. The US Nuclear Regulatory Commission defines "criticality" as follows: "The normal operating condition of a reactor, in which nuclear fuel sustains a fission chain reaction. A reactor achieves criticality (and is said to be critical) when each fission event releases a sufficient number of neutrons to sustain an ongoing series of reactions." https://www .nrc.gov/reading-rm/basic-ref/glossary/criticality.html (accessed March 19, 2019).

34. Kaviraj, "Outline of a Revisionist Theory of Modernity," 518.

35. Jawaharlal Nehru's speech at the inauguration of the APSARA Swimming Pool Reactor at Trombay, January 20, 1957, *Jawaharlal Nehru's Speeches Vol. 3, 1953–1957* (New Delhi: Publications Division of the Government of India); also cited in Itty Abraham, "Contra-proliferation: Interpreting the Meanings of India's Nuclear Tests in 1974 and 1998," in *Inside Nuclear South Asia*, ed. Scott D. Sagan (Palo Alto, CA: Stanford University Press), 110.

36. Bertrand Goldschmidt, *Atomic Complex*, 65. On the patent-related controversy, see "Relations with France on Atomic Energy Work, Covering the Years 1942–45, 1947, 1967," James Chadwick Papers, CHAD IV 5, Churchill Archives Centre, University of Cambridge.

37. Robert Bothwell, *Nucleus: The History of the Atomic Energy of Canada Limited* (Toronto: University of Toronto Press, 1988), 246.

38. Ibid., 206.

39. The other fissile material is enriched uranium. Both enriched uranium and reprocessed plutonium must be at weapon-grade level in order to be used in a nuclear weapon. Weapon-grade uranium is more 90 percent enriched uranium (U-235) and weapon-grade plutonium is more than 93 percent of plutonium (Pu-239).

40. It was so named because "Kell" stood for Kellogg (the parent company) and "X" stood for secret because of its participation in the Manhattan Project.

41. William Kupp, *A Nuclear Engineer in the Twentieth Century* (Victoria, BC: Trafford, 2005), 84; KLX-1134 Completion Report Purex and Redox Phase II Expansion Jobs 1063 and 1063R, volume I, contract AT(45-1) 628, May 1, 1955, USAEC.

42. On plutonium contamination at the Hanford site leading to plant closures in the 1960s, see Kate Brown, *Plutopia: Nuclear Families, Atomic Cities, and the Great Soviet and American Plutonium Disasters* (New York: Oxford University Press, 2013), 271–81; General Electric held the technical responsibility over Vitro Engineering's USAEC contract for the Hanford plant, which was not their only interfirm connection. George White, the director and executive vice president of Vitro / Kellex Corporation, joined General Electric's Atomic Power Division as its director in 1956 just as the reactor business was taking off. Stephen Schwartz, "Obituary: George White," *SF Gate*, October 11, 1995.

43. Stuart W. Leslie and Indira Chowdhury, "Homi Bhabha, Master Builder of Nuclear India," *Physics Today* 71, no. 9 (September 2018): 53–54. Stone was also the architect for the Pakistan Institute for Nuclear Science and Technology. See Stuart W. Leslie, "Atomic structures: the architecture of nuclear nationalism in India and Pakistan," *History and Technology* 31, no. 3 (2015): 229; see also "Edward Durell Stone Dead at 76; Designed Major Works Worldwide," *New York Times*, August 7, 1978, section A, 1.

44. Kaviraj, "Outline of a Revisionist Theory of Modernity," 504.

45. Homi Bhabha's speech delivered at the inauguration of the plutonium plant, January 22, 1965, Tata Institute of Fundamental Research, *Homi Jehangir Bhabha on Indian Science and the Atomic Energy Programme: A Selection* (Mumbai: TIFR, 2009), 176.

46. USAEC memo from Chairman Lewis Strauss to President Dwight Eisenhower, August 30, 1956, DNSA.

47. Memo from USAEC chairman Lewis Strauss to President Eisenhower with a release report, "India to Purchase Heavy Water for Research Reactor near Bombay," February 11, 1955, DNSA; memo from Allen J. Vander Weyden, acting director of the USAEC Division of International Affairs, "Commission Decision on Sale of Heavy Water to India," October 10, 1956, DNSA.

48. Memo from USAEC chairman Lewis Strauss to President Eisenhower with a release report, "India to Purchase Heavy Water for Research Reactor near Bombay," February 11, 1955, DNSA. On the negotiation of the IAEA statute, see Bernhard Bechhoefer, "Negotiating the Statute of the International Atomic Energy Agency," *International Organization* 13, no. 1 (1959): 38–59.

49. Conference on the Statute of the International Atomic Energy Agency, Verbatim Record of the Twenty-Fourth Meeting of the Main Committee, October 22, 1956 at 02:45 p.m., IAEA/CS/OR.38, IAEA Archives, Vienna.

50. After the IAEA was established in 1957, Goldschmidt served as the French representative at the IAEA Board of Governors (a position he held well into the 1980s). Bhabha served as the Indian representative on the IAEA Board of Governors until his death in January 1966.

51. The underlying logic was that the industrial capacity to produce special fissionable materials (namely, to enrich uranium and reprocess plutonium) was limited to only a handful of technologically advanced countries, unlike raw materials for nuclear fission that were more widely available as natural resources in the Earth's crust.

52. Conference on the Statute of the International Atomic Energy Agency, Verbatim Record of the Eleventh Meeting of the Main Committee, October 10, 1956, at 02:45 p.m., IAEA/CS/OR.24, IAEA, Vienna.

53. On the role of raw materials in the negotiation of the IAEA statute, see Gabrielle Hecht, "Negotiating Global Nuclearities: Apartheid, Decolonization, and the Cold War in the Making of the IAEA." *Osiris* 21 (2006): 25–48.

54. Letter ref. no. DIR/C/30/Per-ELP/ from Homi J. Bhabha, chairman of Atomic Energy Commission, to Sir Edwin Plowden, chairman of UK Atomic Energy Authority, June 18, 1954, AB 16/565, UKNA.

55. Secret memorandum of conference with the President, November 11, 1959, others present: Secretary Herter, Chairman McCone, General Goodpaster, prepared on November 13, 1959, DNSA.

56. Ibid.

57. Secret letter from USAEC chairman Lewis Strauss to Elmer B. Staats, executive officer of the Operation Coordinating Board, July 1, 1954, OCB 000.9, Atomic Energy, file no. 1, 8, October 1953–August 1954, box 8, OCB Central Files Series, NSC, DDEL.

58. Anna-Mart van Wyk, "South African Nuclear Development in the 1970s: A Non-Proliferation Conundrum?," *International History Review*, 40, no. 5 (2018): 1154. On the US offer of power reactor for Berlin, see Mara Drogan, "The nuclear nation and the German question: an American reactor in West Berlin," *Cold War History* 15, no. 3 (2015): 301–19; on the US-Belgian agreements on uranium and its impact on reactor cooperation under the EURATOM, see Jonathan E. Helmreich, "The United States and the Formation of the EURATOM," *Diplomatic History* 15, no. 3 (July 1991): 387–410.

59. Homi J. Bhabha and N. B. Prasad, "A study of the contribution of atomic energy to a power programme in India," Proceedings of the Second UN Conference on the Peaceful Uses of Atomic Energy, Geneva, 1958, 89–101; see also M. V. Ramana, "India and Fast Breeder Reactors," *Science and Global Security* 17 (2009).

60. Robert McMahon, "U.S. Policy toward South Asia and Tibet during the Early Cold War," *Journal of Cold War Studies* 8, no. 3 (2006): 131–44. See also Sergey Radchenko, "The Rise and Fall of Hindi Chini Bhai Bhai," *Foreign Policy*, September 18, 2014, accessed January 15, 2019, https://foreignpolicy.com/2014/09/18/the-rise-and-fall-of-hindi-chini-bhai-bhai/.

61. Memorandum of a conversation Between President Eisenhower and Prime Minister Nehru, New Delhi, December 13, 1959, 8:30 p.m., FRUS, volume 15, 1958–60, South and Southeast Asia, document 164.

62. Memorandum for Chairman McCone, subject: Toner Report, "Visit of USAEC Mission to India (OUO)," February 12, 1960, John McCone Papers, box 2, 79-9, O&M 8-reports, DDEL.

63. Engerman, *Price of Aid*, 152.

64. Dwight D. Eisenhower, "Joint Statement Following Discussions With Prime Minister Nehru," December 14, 1959, online by Gerhard Peters and John T. Woolley, The American Presidency Project, accessed March 19, 2019, https://www.presidency.ucsb.edu/documents/joint-statement-following-discussions-with-prime-minister-nehru-0.

65. National Intelligence Estimate Number 13-2-60, "The Chinese Communist Atomic Energy Program," December 13, 1960, Papers of President Kennedy, NSF, Robert W. Komer, box 410, China (CPR), Nuclear Explosion, 1961–63, folder 2, JFKL.

66. Ibid. See also "Secret outgoing airgram from Secretary of State Dean Rusk to various US embassies," May 22, 1961, Papers of President Kennedy, NSF, Komer, box 410, JFKL.

67. White House memorandum from Ted Clifton to McGeorge Bundy, February 27, 1961, Papers of President Kennedy, NSF, Komer, box 410, JFKL.

68. Memo from NSC staffer Robert Komer to McGeorge Bundy, special assistant to the president for national security, with draft memo attached entitled, "Anticipating the First ChiCom Nuclear Explosion," March 7, 1961, Papers of President Kennedy, NSF, Komer, box 410, JFKL.

69. Ibid.

70. Secret memorandum from Joseph O. Hanson Jr. to Robert W. Komer, titled "Blunting Expected ChiCom A-bomb Propaganda," March 3 1961, Papers of President Kennedy, NSF, Komer, box 410, JFKL.

71. Memo to Secretary of State Robert McNamara from the Joint Chiefs of Staff signed by L. L. Lemnitzer, June 26, 1961, Papers of President Kennedy, NSF, Komer, box 410, JFKL.

72. The long-term goals for 1968–70 and much of the 1970s were to establish a cohesive anti-Chinese alliance or alliances and to strengthen US bases in the area. The medium- and short-term goals consisted of two notable elements. Ibid.

73. Perkovich, *India's Nuclear Bomb*, 52.

74. Raghavan, *War and Peace*, 275-76.

75. Krishna Menon had also publicly opposed India's development of nuclear weapons on multiple occasions, but his anti-US attitude was legendary, which might have led US officials to suspect his intentions.

76. Secret telegram 2937 from the US embassy in New Delhi to Secretary of State Dean Rusk, June 1961, Papers of President Kennedy, NSF, Komer, box 410, JFKL.

77. Ibid.

78. "Early Action To Free Goa Urged," *Times of India*, 26 November 1961, 1.

79. "Declaration on the Granting of Independence to Colonial Countries and Peoples," United Nations General Assembly resolution 1514 (XV) of 14 December 1960, accessed October 3, 2021, https://www.ohchr.org/EN/ProfessionalInterest/Pages/Independence.aspx.

80. Quincy Wright, "The Goa Incident," *The American Journal of International Law* 56, no. 3 (July 1962): 619.

81. Letter from Homi J. Bhabha to R. Choksi, December 16, 1961, DTT.PHIL. TMH.FP.3, box 207, TCA.

82. Ibid.

83. J. R. D. Tata's speech at the inauguration of the Tata Institute of Fundamental Research, January 15, 1962, TIFR.

84. Ashok Maharaj, "An Overview of NASA-India Relations," in *NASA in the World: Fifty Years of International Collaboration*, eds. John Krige, Angelina Long Callahan, and Ashok Maharaj (New York: Palgrave MacMillan, 2013), 217.

85. Reconstitution of the Governing Board of the Tata Memorial Hospital, from V. M. Parulekar (joint secretary to the government of India, DAE) to the superintendent of Tata Memorial Hospital, No.2/1/62-Tech.II, March 19, 1961, DTT.PHIL. TMH.FP.3, box 207, TCA.

86. Apart from J. R. D. Tata, the other AECI members were Homi Bhabha (chairman), S. Jagannathan (as a member of finance), and S. S. Khera (cabinet secretary). Annual report of the Department of Atomic Energy of India for 1962, obtained from the library of the DAE, Mumbai.

87. "Indian Atomic Energy Budget to Be Increased," Current Support Brief, Office of Research and Reports, April 15, 1963, CIA/RR CB 63-37, CIA-RDP79T01003A001 600080001-5.

88. The Atomic Energy Act of 1962, Department of Atomic Energy, Government of India, accessed July 11, 2019, https://dae.nic.in/?q=node/153.

89. Abraham, *The Making of the Indian Atomic Bomb*, 114–20.

90. On recent studies of the 1962 Sino-Indian Border War, see Amit R. Das Gupta and Lorenz M. Lüthi, *The Sino-Indian War of 1962: New Perspectives* (New York: Routledge, 2016). See also Lorenz M. Lüthi, "Sino-Indian Relations, 1954–1962," *Eurasia Border Review* 3 (2012): 95–119; Rudra Chaudhuri, "Why Culture Matters: Revisiting the Sino-Indian Border War of 1962," *Journal of Strategic Studies* 32, no. 6 (2009): 841–69.

91. Guyot-Réchard, *Shadow States*, 241.

92. Letter from Jawaharlal Nehru to John F. Kennedy, November 19, 1962, NSF Files of Robert Komer, box 23, LBJL.

93. Protocol of the presidium session, October 14, 1962, in *Arkhivy Kremlia: Prezidium TsK KPSS*, 1954–64, 616, cited in Jeremy Friedman, *Shadow Cold War: The Sino-Soviet Competition for the Third World* (Chapel Hill, NC: University of North Carolina, 2015), 96.

94. Ibid.

95. Letter from Prime Minister Jawaharlal Nehru to the Soviet leader Nikita S. Khrushchev, October 22, 1962, document No. 1879, India-China Relations 1947–2000: A Documentary Study, vol. 4, introduced and edited by Avtar Singh Bhasin (published in cooperation with the Policy Planning and Research Division, MEA, New Delhi: Geetika Publishers, 2018), 3929.

96. Ibid.

97. See Kux, *Estranged Democracies*, 206–7; Rotter, *Comrades at Odds*, 75; Robert J. McMahon, *The Cold War on the Periphery: The United States, India, and Pakistan* (New York: Columbia University Press, 1994), 287–89.

98. Letter from Jawaharlal Nehru to Homi J. Bhabha, November 8, 1962, published under collected letters between Jawaharlal Nehru and Homi J. Bhabha, "The Architects of Nuclear India," *Nuclear India*, vol. 26/10/1989, Homi J. Bhabha Papers, NMML.

99. See the video clip without audio where Bhabha is clearly visible: "India's New National Defence Council meets for First Time," *British Pathe/Reuters*, November 25, 1962, reference BGY504250347, accessed January 15, 2019, https://www.britishpathe .com/video/VLVACKVZTCIV54O8BXAFKLGA43SGH-INDIAS-NEW-NATIONAL -DEFENCE-COUNCIL-MEETS-FOR-FIRST-TIME/query/FOR+FIRST+TIME.

100. "Indian Atomic Energy Budget to Be Increased," Current Support Brief, Office of Research and Reports, April 15, 1963, CIA/RR CB 63-37, CIA-RDP79T01003A001 600080001-5.

4. Plutonium, Power Reactors, and Space Projects, 1962–1964

1. Current Intelligence Weekly Summary, *India Expanding Atomic Energy Program*, April 5, 1963, Papers of President Kennedy, NSF, Komer, box 422, JFKL.

2. Confidential memorandum of conversation at the US State Department, "Tarapur Nuclear Power Plant," May 31, 1962, Papers of President Kennedy, NSF, Komer, box 422, JFKL.

3. "Survey of Indian Nuclear Energy Program," September 6, 1961, with classification markings of "SECRET" and "NOFORN" (No Foreign Nationals), Papers of President Kennedy, NSF, Komer, box 422, JFKL.

4. Ibid.

5. Bertrand Goldschmidt, "Les Problèmes Nucléaires Indiens," *Politique étrangère* 47, no. 3 (1982): 620.

6. Memorandum for the president from Robert W. Komer, "Indian Power Reactor Project," June 5, 1962, Papers of President Kennedy, NSF, Komer, box 422, JFKL.

7. For Homi Bhabha's shopping for nuclear power reactors prior to the DAE's tender in 1960, see Engerman, *Price of Aid*, 148–54; "G. E. Receives Big Contract For Indian Atomic Plant," *New York Times*, September 26, 1962, 60.

8. Ibid.

9. Letter from Homi J. Bhabha to US ambassador to India Kenneth Galbraith, September 24, 1962, quoted in confidential telegram 1062 from New Delhi to Secretary of State Dean Rusk, telegram dated September 29, 1962, Papers of President Kennedy, NSF, Komer, box 422, JFKL.

10. Ibid.

11. Confidential telegram 2783 from US Ambassador to India Kenneth Galbraith to Secretary of State Dean Rusk, January 16, 1963, Papers of President Kennedy, NSF, Komer, box 422, JFKL.

12. Ibid.

13. Letter from Homi J. Bhabha to US Ambassador to the IAEA Henry D. Smyth, February 15, 1963, quoted in confidential telegram 1453 from the US Permanent Mission in Vienna to Secretary of State Dean Rusk, telegram dated February 20, 1963, Papers of President Kennedy, NSF, Komer, box 422, JFKL.

14. Ibid.

15. "Indian Atomic Energy Budget to be Increased," Current Support Brief, Office of Research and Reports, April 15, 1963, CIA/RR CB 63-37, CIA-RDP79T01003A001 600080001-5.

16. Engerman, *Price of Aid*, 152–53.

17. National Security Action Memorandum 223, "Appraisal of Sino-Indian Relations," February 26, 1963, Papers of President Kennedy, NSF, Meetings and Memoranda Series, National Security Action Memoranda, JFKL.

18. Ibid.

19. "Memorandum from Robert W. Komer of the National Security Council Staff to President Kennedy," document 268, FRUS, 1961–63, volume 19, South Asia, 1517–18.

20. Confidential research memorandum from Roger Hilsman of US State Department's Bureau of Intelligence and Research, INR-77, subject entitled, "Probable

Soviet Attitude toward Tarapur Power Reactor Project," August 8, 1962, Papers of President Kennedy, NSF, Komer, box 422, JFKL.

21. Ibid.

22. Engerman argues that a meeting in Paris led to all potential reactor sellers agreeing to sell reactors to DAE only with safeguards. This might be related to Charles de Gaulle's efforts to make the CEA toe his line because of the French nuclear weapon assistance to Israel, which de Gaulle did not support. Engerman, *Price of Aid*, 156.

23. Confidential NSC memorandum from Charles E. Johnson to Carl Kaysen, April 8, 1963, Papers of President Kennedy, NSF, Komer, box 422, JFKL.

24. Goldschmidt, "Les Problèmes Nucléaires Indiens," 620.

25. "India Agrees to Inspection of Atomic Plant," *New York Times*, June 26, 1963, 8.

26. Secret memo from Harold Saunders to Robert Komer, June 20, 1963, NLK-16-125, Papers of President Kennedy, NSF, Komer, box 422, JFKL.

27. "United States: Agreements for Cooperation concerning the Civil Uses of Atomic Energy, with India and Certain Other Countries," *International Legal Materials* 2, no. 5 (1963): 892–901; "Agreement on Civil Uses of Atomic Energy," Ministry of External Affairs of India, August 8, 1963, accessed October 28, 2020, https://mea .gov.in/bilateral-documents.htm?dtl/6460/Agreement+on+Civil+Uses+of+Atomic +Energy.

28. A turnkey project is often used for a major construction project such as the building of a dam, a power station, or similar large endeavor, usually in a different country where the contracted foreign firm designs and constructs the facility, such that the operator then only has to "turn the key" to run it. Turnkey projects, as a result, offer very limited amount of technology transfer to the recipient.

29. Confidential memorandum from Charles E. Johnson to Carl Kaysen, April 8, 1963, Papers of President Kennedy, NSF, Komer, box 422, JFKL; see also "India Asks $60,000,000 From U.S. for Atom Plant," *New York Times*, December 19, 1962, 8.

30. "U.S. and India Sign Atomic Plant Pact," *New York Times*, December 16, 1963, 33.

31. One of the first reports was on August 30, 1963. "Congressional Panel Sets Hearings on Atomic Pacts," *New York Times*, August 30, 1963, 21.

32. Prime Minister Jawaharlal Nehru's statement in the Lok Sabha, titled, "Standstill Agreement," 2 April 1954, http://meaindia.nic.in/cdgeneva/?pdf0601 ?000, last accessed October 3, 2021.

33. Maddock, *Nuclear Apartheid*, 1.

34. The term "fourth power problem" was used to mean that France would soon become the fourth country to get its own nuclear weapons (after the United States, the Soviet Union, and the United Kingdom) and that it was a policy problem. In $n+1$, "n" was the number of countries with indigenous nuclear weapons and "+1" the new country that wanted to enter the so-called nuclear club. Albert Wohlstetter, "Nuclear sharing: NATO and the $N+1$ country," *Foreign Affairs* 39 (April 1961): 355–87.

35. Perkovich, *India's Nuclear Bomb*, 57

36. Abraham, *Making of the Indian Atomic Bomb*, 93–94.

37. Engerman, *Price of Aid*, 152–56.

38. On the India-China proliferation cascade, see Nicholas L. Miller, "Nuclear Dominoes: A Self-Defeating Prophecy?," *Security Studies* 23, no. 1 (2014): 42–52.

39. Gordon Chang, "JFK, China and the Bomb," *The Journal of American History* 74, no. 4 (March 1988): 1300; William Burr and Jeffrey T. Richelson, "Whether to 'Strangle the Baby in the Cradle': The United States and the Chinese Nuclear Program, 1960–1964," *International Security* 25, no. 3 (Winter 2000/1): 70–72.

40. Secret memo from Policy Planning Council Chairman Walt W. Rostow to planning group members with paper, "A Chinese Communist Nuclear Detonation and Nuclear Capability," October 18, 1963, Papers of President Kennedy, NSF, Komer, box 410, JFKL.

41. Veteran Indian diplomat Maharajakrishna Rasgotra claimed in his biography that President Kennedy had made an offer to Prime Minister Nehru to install US nuclear weapons on Indian soil, but the latter turned it down. Although Rasgotra's claims cannot be confirmed from the existing pool of US declassified documents, any US nuclear weapon on Indian territory would have been under US control and, therefore, a compromise of India's national sovereignty—a principle Nehru regularly upheld in his public diplomacy. See M. Rasgotra, *A Life in Diplomacy* (Gurgaon, India: Penguin, Viking, 2016), 186-88. See also "Nehru Should Have Accepted Kennedy Offer for N-Device: Former Foreign Secy," *Times of India*, July 14, 2016. In the past, there have been claims that President Kennedy was willing to use nuclear weapons to defend India against China based on a statement by the president in a tape recording from May 1963. See Andrew Buncombe, "JFK Was Ready to Use Nuclear Bomb on China, Tapes Reveal," *Independent* 26, August 2005.

42. According to physicist P. K. Iyengar's account, the plutonium plant began operating in 1965. This is likely a reference to the inauguration of the plutonium plant that took place in January 1965. Bhabha's speech at the inauguration mentioned that plant was completed in February 1964 and the first active fuel element was loaded in June 1964, when the plant began fully operating. This is also corroborated with evidence from US intelligence accounts from the time. See P. K. Iyengar, *Briefings on Nuclear Technology in India*, 2009, 38; speech delivered at the inauguration of the plutonium plant, Homi Bhabha, Trombay, January 22, 1965 in TIFR, *Homi Jehangir Bhabha on Indian Science and the Atomic Energy Programme: A Selection* (Mumbai: TIFR, 2009), 175.

43. Memo by George C. Denney Jr., Bureau of Intelligence and Research, Department of State, to Secretary of State Dean Rusk, February 24, 1964, NSF Robert Komer Files, box 25, LBJL.

44. Ibid.

45. Memo by Thomas L. Hughes, Bureau of Intelligence and Research, Department of State to Secretary of State Dean Rusk, May 14, 1964, NSF Robert Komer Files, box 25, LBJL.

46. "1.5 Million View Rites for Nehru; Procession Route Jammed as Indians and Foreigners Pay Last Respects," *New York Times,* May 29, 1964, 1; see also "India Mourning Nehru, 74, Dead of a Heart Attack; World Leaders Honor Him; Funeral is Today; Party Members Meet Tomorrow Try to Pick Leader," *New York Times*, May 28, 1964, 1; "Prime Minister Succumbs to a Stroke—Cabinet Is Called to His Home," *New York Times*, May 27, 1964, 1.

47. On Shastri's ascent as Nehru's successor, see Paul M. McGarr, "After Nehru, What? Britain, the United States, and the Other Transfer of Power in India, 1960–64,"

International History Review 33, no. 1 (2011):115–42; Rakesh Ankit, "Lal Bahadur Shastri, 1964–1966: Leader at a Glance," *Studies in Indian Politics* 8, no. 1 (2020): 39–57.

48. Memo by Thomas L. Hughes, Bureau of Intelligence and Research, Department of State, to Secretary of State Dean Rusk, May 14, 1964, NSF Robert Komer Files, box 25, LBJL.

49. Ibid.

50. Ibid.

51. Homi J. Bhabha, "The Implications of a Wider Dispersal of Military Power for World Security and the Problem of Safeguards," *Proceedings of the Twelfth Pugwash Conference*, Udaipur, India, February 1964.

52. "India Agrees to Inspection of Atomic Plant," *New York Times*, June 26, 1963, 8.

53. Letter from Chester Bowles to McGeorge Bundy, September 16, 1964, NSF Robert Komer Files, box 25, LBJL.

54. "Subject: The Indian Nuclear Problem: Proposed Course of Action," September 29, 1964, NSF Robert Komer Files, box 25, LBJL.

55. Ibid. The Turner Cameron report identified four policy options: first, to assist India to develop a nuclear weapons capability; second, to be prepared to impose economic and other sanctions in an effort to prevent India from going the nuclear weapons route; third, to provide technical assistance to reinforce India's peaceful nuclear program; and fourth, to do nothing on a bilateral basis.

56. Ibid.

57. Ibid.

58. Ashok Maharaj, "An Overview of NASA-India Relations," in *NASA in the World: Fifty Years of International Collaboration*, eds. John Krige, Angelina Long Callahan, and Ashok Maharaj (New York: Palgrave MacMillan, 2013), 217.

59. Asif Siddiqi, "Another global history of science: making space for India and China," *British Journal for the History of Science* (2016): 120–21.

60. Robert Anderson, *Nucleus and Nation: Scientists, International Networks and Power in India* (Chicago: University of Chicago Press, 2010), 285; Asif Siddiqi, "Another global history of science," 120.

61. I am grateful to Douglas Haynes for drawing my attention to Vikram Sarabhai's role in the establishment of the Indian Institute of Management in Ahmedabad.

62. Maharaj, "Overview of NASA-India Relations," 217.

63. "Explorer-11," NASA, accessed November 3, 2020, https://heasarc.gsfc.nasa.gov/docs/heasarc/missions/explorer11.html.

64. Maharaj, "Overview of NASA-India Relations," 219.

65. "What is a Sounding Rocket?," *NASA*, April 12, 2004, https://www.nasa.gov/missions/research/f_sounding.html, accessed July 21, 2019.

66. Maharaj, "Overview of NASA-India Relations," 217.

67. Ibid., 221.

68. Ibid., 220.

69. Asif A. Siddiqi, "Spaceflight in the National Imagination," in *Remembering the Space Age*, ed. Steven J. Dick (Washington, DC: National Aeronautics and Space Administration, 2008), 18.

70. Shreya Biswas, "Transported on a bicycle, launched from a church: The fascinating story of India's first rocket launch," *India Today*, June 2, 2016.

71. On this subject see, for example: Dinshaw Mistry & Bharath Gopalaswamy "Ballistic Missiles and Space Launch Vehicles in Regional Powers," *Astropolitics*, 10, no. 2 (2012): 126–151.

72. Lal Bahadur Shastri's speech at Nonaligned Nations Conference, Cairo, October 7, 1964, Indian National Congress, accessed November 1, 2020, https://www.inc.in/en/media/speech/speech-at-non-aligned-nations-conference-cairo-october-7-1964.

73. Homi J. Bhabha's UN Day speech on nuclear disarmament, October 24, 1964, accessed October 31, 2020, http://digitalarchive.wilsoncenter.org/document/114195.

74. Ibid. One crore is equal to ten million. The currency conversion is based on the foreign exchange rate of October 1964, where 1 Indian rupee was valued at 0.2089 of the US dollar. Foreign exchange rates, *Wall Street Journal*, October 30, 1964, 19.

75. Ibid.

76. "AICC and the Bomb," *Economic Weekly*, November 14, 1964.

77. Thomas F. Brady, "Indians Split on Building Bomb," *New York Times*, November 8, 1964, 7.

78. Ibid.

79. Thomas F. Brady, "Shastri's Party Rejects A-Bombs," *New York Times*, November 9, 1964, 5.

80. Ibid.

81. Perkovich, *India's Nuclear Bomb*, 82.

82. Lok Sabha Debates, Tenth Session, Third Series, vol. 35, no. 10, November 27, 1964, Lok Sabha Secretariat, New Delhi, 2286–99.

83. Ibid., 2274.

84. Ibid.

85. Ibid., 2266.

86. Ibid., 2290.

87. Ibid., 2295.

88. Ibid., 2288. Author's translation from the original text in Hindi; see also Perkovich, *India's Nuclear Bomb*, 182.

89. "PM Rejects Plea for Bomb: 'Peaceful Use' Policy Reiterated," *Times of India*, November 28, 1964.

90. Bhabha's UN Day speech, October 24, 1964.

91. Current Intelligence Digest, South Asia, "India's Plans Regarding Development of Nuclear Weapons," January 22, 1965, RAC, NLJ-032-025-3-2-7, LBJL; see also Perkovich, *India's Nuclear Bomb*, 82.

92. Maharaj, "Overview of NASA-India Relations," 226.

93. "Subject: The Indian Nuclear Problem: Proposed Course of Action," September 29, 1964, NSF Robert Komer Files, box 25, LBJL.

94. Ashok Maharaj, "Space for Development: US-Indian Space Relations, 1955–1976" (PhD diss., Georgia Institute of Technology, 2011), 81; Jacques Blamont, *L'action soeur du rêve: Souvenirs de voyages* (Paris: Editions Edite, 2011), 207.

95. Blamont recounts fondly of his friendship with Sarabhai in his biography. I am grateful to Asif Siddiqi for bringing this to my attention. See Blamont, *L'action soeur du rêve*.

96. John Krige and Jayita Sarkar, "U.S. Technological Collaboration for Nonproliferation: Key Evidence from the Cold War," *Nonproliferation Review* 25 (no. 3–4): 249–62.

97. John Krige, *Sharing Knowledge, Shaping Europe: U.S. Technological Collaboration and Nonproliferation* (Cambridge, MA: MIT Press, 2016).

98. "U.S. and India Sign Atomic Plant Pact," *New York Times*, December 16, 1963, 33.

99. R. J. Graham and J. E. S. Stevens, "Experience with CANDU Reactors outside of Canada: KANUPP, Karachi, Pakistan, and RAPP, Rajasthan, India," CAN-74-203, accessed October 31, 2020, https://inis.iaea.org/collection/NCLCollectionStore/_Public/06/160/6160925.pdf.

5. The Plowshare Loophole, 1964–1970

1. Airgram (A-650) from US embassy in New Delhi sent by L. Douglas Heck to US State Department, "Transmittal of MEA Working Paper Advocating GOI Development of the Nuclear Bomb," December 30, 1964, NSF Committee File, RAC, NLJ-009R-6-3-1-3, LBJL.

2. This was according to L. Douglas Heck's note accompanying his airgram to the State Department. Ibid.

3. Ibid.

4. The MEA paper discussed four alternatives for India: "(1) to agree to coexist with China on Chinese terms, (2) to seek alliance and nuclear protection from the United States, (3) to organize world public opinion against China and to work for disarmament, and (4) to make our own nuclear weapons." It recommended the fourth option. "India and the Chinese Bomb," Ministry of External Affairs of India, November 25, 1964, enclosure with airgram A-650, December 30, 1964, RAC, NLJ-009R-6-3-1-3, LBJL.

5. Airgram (A-650) from US embassy to US State Department, December 30, 1964, RAC, NLJ-009R-6-3-1-3, LBJL.

6. Ibid.

7. "India and the Chinese Bomb," MEA, November 25, 1964, 2.

8. Ibid.

9. Ibid.

10. Thomas F. Brady, "Shastri's Party Rejects A-Bombs," *New York Times*, November 9, 1964, 5.

11. "India and the Chinese Bomb," MEA Paper, November 25, 1964, 11.

12. Ibid.

13. "Statement by President," *New York Times*, October 17, 1964, 10.

14. President Lyndon Johnson's speech, "Report to the Nation on Events in China and the USSR," October 18, 1964, LBJL; also available at https://millercenter.org/the-presidency/presidential-speeches/october-18-1964-report-nation-events-china-and-ussr (accessed March 19, 2021).

15. Author's emphasis. "Nuclear Guarantee is Urged by Shastri," *New York Times*, December 5, 1964, 9.

16. A. G. Noorani, "India's Quest for a Nuclear Guarantee," *Asian Survey* 7, no. 7 (July 1967): 490–502.

17. The ENDC was the UN body on disarmament formed in Geneva in 1961 to address nuclear disarmament at the multilateral level. It comprised five countries from the Western bloc, five from the Eastern bloc, and eight from nonaligned and neutral coun-

tries. Its earlier iteration was the Ten Nations Disarmament Committee of 1960 that constituted five countries from the Western bloc and five from the Eastern bloc.

18. The Soviet Union acted as the mediator of the conflict after the UN ceasefire, leading to the Tashkent Declaration in January 1966.

19. Paul M. McGarr, *The Cold War in South Asia: Britain, the United States and the Indian subcontinent, 1945–1965* (Cambridge, MA: Cambridge University Press, 2013), 316.

20. Ibid., 316–17.

21. Ibid., 317.

22. Ibid., 329.

23. Kux, *Estranged Democracies,* 235–40.

24. On the origins of the Sino-Pakistan strategic partnership, see Rudra Chaudhuri, "The Making of an 'All Weather Friendship' Pakistan, China and the History of a Border Agreement: 1949–1963," *International History Review* 40, no. 1 (2018): 41–64.

25. Khan wrote in *Foreign Affairs*: "We are profoundly concerned over this new development. We consider that this continued arming of India, in which the Soviet Union has also, for reasons of its own, joined, poses a serious threat to Pakistan's security." Ayub Khan, "The Pakistan-American Alliance," *Foreign Affairs* (January 1964).

26. These were the Southeast Asia Treaty Organization (SEATO) and the Central Treaty Organization (CENTO).

27. Robert McMahon, "The Lyndon Johnson administration and its Asian Allies," in *The Foreign Policies of Lyndon Johnson Beyond Vietnam,* ed. H. W. Brands (College Station, TX: Texas A&M University Press, 1999), 172.

28. Note for McGeorge Bundy prepared by Robert W. Komer, October 5, 1965, NSF Komer Files, box 23, LBJL.

29. Special National Intelligence Estimate (SNIE) 31-1-65, October 21, 1965, NSF, National Intelligence Estimates, box 6, LBJL.

30. Quoted in Feroz H. Khan, *Eating Grass: The Making of the Pakistani Bomb* (Stanford, CA, Stanford University Press, 2013), 59.

31. "DF-2/ CSS-1," *Federation of American Scientists*, June 10 1998, accessed January 15, 2019, https://fas.org/nuke/guide/china/theater/df-2.htm.

32. The Indiagram, Information Service of India, Office of the High Commissioner for India, Ottawa, August 3, 1966, Candu Nuclear Power Reactor for India, Department of Trade and Commerce, folder 3-51-1, part 2, box 1672, Library and Archives of Canada, Ottawa (hereafter, LAC).

33. Memorandum from Myron B Kratzer, director of the Division of International Affairs at USAEC, "Discussion between Chairman Seaborg and Dr. Vikram Sarabhai on October 17, 1966," October 25, 1966, microfilm reel 3, Glenn T. Seaborg Papers, Library of Congress (hereafter, LOC).

34. Rajya Sabha starred question no. 463 for 16.08.66 regarding Pakistan memo to UNO on alleged atom blast by India, U.IV/125/66/1966, Ministry of External Affairs Files (1914–71), NAI.

35. Note for supplementary questions, Rajya Sabha starred question no. 463 for 16.08.66 regarding Pakistan memo to UNO on alleged atom blast by India, U.IV/125/66/1966, Ministry of External Affairs Files (1914–71), NAI.

36. The panel study group consisted of Sir Michael Right (chairman), Hon. Alastair Buchan, Mr. Leonard Beaton, and Dr. R. Press. Their meetings were held on May 17,

May 21, June 13, and July 11. The Panel Study Group on India, the Bomb and Proliferation, July 1966, Chalfont Advisory Panel on Disarmament, CKFT 18/2, John Cockcroft Papers, Churchill Archives Centre, University of Cambridge.

37. Ibid.

38. Ibid.

39. The currency conversion is based on the US Treasury's foreign exchange rate
at the time, when 1 US dollar was valued at 0.3583 of the British pounds sterling.
US Treasury Reporting Rates of Exchange as of June 30, 1966, Treasury Department,
Fiscal Service, Bureau of Accounts (Washington, DC: Government Printing Office), 4.

40. Incoming telegram 2054 US State Department from Jerome Wiesner for John
Palfrey through US Embassy in New Delhi, January 21, 1965, NSF Files, Robert Komer,
box 25, LBJL.

41. Ibid.

42. Ibid.

43. Paul Doty, "Report of the Committee on International Studies of Arms Control,"
Records of the Academy (American Academy of Arts and Sciences), no. 1966/1967 (1966–67):
16–19. This Committee on International Studies of Arms Control or CISAC, based at the
American Academy of Arts and Sciences, was closely related to the Soviet-American
Disarmament Studies Group or SADS (1965–75) led by Paul Doty. See box 5, AMACAD
Archives. In 1980, Doty formed another CISAC (Committee on International Security
and Arms Control) at the National Academy of Sciences. This is different from CISAC
(Center for International Security and Cooperation) at Stanford University established in
1983.

44. I am grateful to Maggie Boyd, associate archivist at the American Academy of
the Arts and Sciences in Cambridge, Massachusetts, for bringing this to my attention.

45. Record of Indian meeting, June 3–6, 1966, folder 1, box 5, AMACAD Archives,
Cambridge, MA.

46. The Multilateral Force proposal concerned an integrated European nuclear
force under NATO command. Since such an arrangement would give West Germany
access to nuclear weapons, it was unacceptable to the Soviet government. NATO countries like France were also against the MLF fearing that it might provide West Germany the know-how to develop and operate nuclear weapons.

47. Glenn T. Seaborg, *Stemming the Tide: Arms Control in the Johnson Years* (Lexington, MA: Lexington, 1987), 180–82.

48. Letter from Chester Bowles to McGeorge Bundy, September 16, 1964, NSF
Komer Files, box 25, LBJL.

49. Confidential notes on meetings in India, June 3–6, 1966, American Academy of
Arts and Sciences, Committee on International Studies of Arms Control, box 353, part 7,
series 3, July 1963–May 1969, group no. 628, series 3, Special Subjects, India, Chester
Bowles Papers, Yale University Library. I have used the confidential notes of the meeting
from the Chester Bowles papers because those were more detailed than the minutes of
the meeting I found at the AMACAD archives.

50. Ibid.

51. Ibid.

52. Secret memorandum from Joseph O. Hanson Jr. to Robert W. Komer titled "Blunting Expected ChiCom A-Bomb Propaganda," March 3, 1961, Papers of President Kennedy, NSF, Komer, box 410, JFKL.

53. Confidential notes on meetings in India, June 3–6, 1966, Chester Bowles Papers, Yale University Library.

54. Ibid.

55. Ibid.

56. On the nuclear security guarantees in the context of India's nuclear diplomacy, see Andrew B. Kennedy, "India's Nuclear Odyssey: Implicit Umbrellas, Diplomatic Disappointments, and the Bomb," *International Security* 36, no. 2 (2011): 120–53; A. G. Noorani, "India's Quest for a Nuclear Guarantee," op. cit.

57. Trivedi argued that this was because the nuclear powers "would go on proliferating anyway" while the "non-nuclear powers will not jump to produce nuclear weapons." Confidential notes on meetings in India, June 3–6, 1966, Chester Bowles Papers, Yale University Library.

58. National Security Action Memorandum 351, June 10, 1966, NSF Files, National Security Action Memoranda, LBJL.

59. National Security Action Memorandum 355, August 1, 1966, NSF NSAM Files, LBJL; see also memoranda for Walt W. Rostow by Benjamin Read, October 31, 1966, and August 31, 1966, NSF NSAM Files, NSAM 355, LBJL.

60. Author's emphasis. Ibid. For more on this subject, see Sarkar, "The Making of a Nonaligned Nuclear Power," 940–41.

61. Seaborg, *Stemming the Tide*, 185.

62. Historians disagree over the influence of the Gilpatric Committee on nonproliferation policy outcomes. Gavin claims that the Gilpatric Committee had a lasting impact on US nonproliferation policy. Maddock argues that while the US Arms Control and Disarmament Agency was sympathetic to the Gilpatric Committee Report, key policymakers such as Dean Rusk were not. As a result, according to Maddock, several of the proposals of the agency were eventually rejected by the Johnson administration. See Francis J. Gavin, "Blasts from the Past: Proliferation from the 1960s," *International Security* 29, no. 3 (Winter 2004/5): 100–135; Maddock, *Nuclear Apartheid*, 243–44, 250.

63. A report to the president by the Committee on Nuclear Proliferation, January 21, 1965, FRUS, Arms Control and Disarmament, 1964–68, vol. 11.

64. Telegram 1393 from the US State Department to the US Embassy in New Delhi, January 12, 1965, NSF Files, Robert Komer, box 25, LBJL.

65. Letter from Jerome Wiesner to President Lyndon Johnson, February 24, 1965, NSF Files, Robert Komer, box 25, LBJL.

66. Incoming telegram 2054 US State Department from Jerome Wiesner for John Palfrey through US Embassy in New Delhi, January 21, 1965, NSF Files, Robert Komer, box 25, LBJL.

67. On the use of technology for nonproliferation, see John Krige and Jayita Sarkar, "US Technological Collaboration for Nonproliferation: Key Evidence from the Cold War," *Nonproliferation Review* 25, no. 3–4 (2018): 249–62.

68. Secret memorandum for the president by Robert Komer, January 19, 1966, NSF Files, Robert Komer, box 25, LBJL.

69. Ibid.

70. US State Department airgram A-546 from the US embassy in New Delhi, December 23, 1965; note for Mr. Komer by Charles E. Johnson, January 17, 1966, NSF Files, Robert Komer, box 25, LBJL. See also secret memorandum from Charles E. Johnson to Walt W. Rostow, April 8, 1966, NSF Files, Charles E. Johnson, box 34, LBJL.

71. Memorandum for president by Robert Komer, March 18, 1966, NSF Files, Robert Komer, box 25, LBJL.

72. Ibid.

73. Šumit Ganguly, "Of Great Expectations and Bitter Disappointments: Indo-U.S. Relations under the Johnson Administration," *Asian Affairs* 15, no. 4, Symposium: India and America: Toward a Realistic Relationship? (Winter, 1988/89): 212–19; Kristin Ahlberg, "'Machiavelli with a Heart': The Johnson Administration's Food for Peace Program in India, 1965–1966," *Diplomatic History* 31, no. 4 (September 2007): 665–701.

74. Pronab Sen, "The 1966 Devaluation in India: A Reappraisal," *Economic and Political Weekly* 21, no. 30 (July 26, 1986): 1322–29; Engerman, *Price of Aid,* 260.

75. Kux, *Estranged Democracies,* 260–61; Engerman, *Price of Aid,* 262–67.

76. On Indian policymakers' support for Chinese entry into the UN, see Sarkar, "The Making of a Nonaligned Nuclear Power," 942–44.

77. "Indian Food Squeeze," *New York Times,* November 29, 1966; see also Jack Anderson, "Mrs. Gandhi's Dilemma: President Johnson Is Holding up Grain in a Peeve over India's Vietnam Stand," *Bell-McClure Syndicate, Inc.,* 1966; "Food for Peace, Food for Freedom, Food for Politics," *Amrita Bazaar Patrika,* November 29, 1966, box 353, part 7, series 3, July 1963–May 1969, group no. 628, series 3, Special Subjects, India, Chester Bowles Papers, Yale University Library.

78. "Indian Food Squeeze," *New York Times,* November 29, 1966, 42.

79. Ibid.

80. Warren Unna, "India to Allow check at A-Power Station," *Washington Post,* December 23, 1966, Candu Nuclear Power Reactor for India, Department of Trade and Commerce, folder 3-51-1, part 2, box 1672, LAC.

81. Memorandum from the Office of the High Commissioner for Canada in New Delhi to the undersecretary of state for external affairs in Ottawa, "Rapp Safeguards Agreement-Public Reaction," January 31, 1967, 65-3-1-INDIA, Candu Nuclear Power Reactor for India, Department of Trade and Commerce, folder 3-51-1, part 2, box 1672, LAC.

82. "Nuclear Self-Reliance?," *Indian Express,* January 25, 1967; "Dr. Sarabhai Must Go, Says Dange," *Indian Express,* January 12, 1967, Candu Nuclear Power Reactor for India, Department of Trade and Commerce, folder 3-51-1, part 2, box 1672, LAC.

83. This 1965 safeguards system was codified in INFCIRC/66, which was the pre-NPT safeguards system of the IAEA. For the first time, reactors of all sizes and, later on, all reprocessing plants (INFCIRC/66/Rev.1) and fuel fabrication facilities (INFCIRC/66/Rev.2) were subject to IAEA safeguards. Prior to this, under the 1961 safeguards system (INFCIRC/26), only reactors of 100 MW or more were subject to IAEA safeguards. In 1971, in order to enforce Article 3 of the NPT, the IAEA adjusted its safeguards system as codified in INFCIRC/153. See *The Evolution of IAEA Safeguards* (Vienna: IAEA, 1998), accessed April 14, 2021, https://www-pub.iaea.org/MTCD /Publications/PDF/NVS2_web.pdf.

84. Report of Glenn T. Seaborg on his trip to Australia, Thailand, India, and Pakistan, January 3–14, 1967, NSF Files, Harold Saunders, box 14, LBJL.

85. Memorandum from the State Department, "Security Assurances for India," April 20, 1967, with attached memorandum of conversation, "Rough Translation of the Revised Russian Draft," and memorandum for the president, 1967–69, Central Files of the Department of State, record group 59, NARA.

86. Memorandum for the president from Walt Rostow, April 19, 1967, NSF Files, Harold Saunders, box 14, LBJL.

87. Lettre Mme. Gandhi, premier ministre de l'Inde, au General De Gaulle, Président de la République, April 19, 1967, document 147, 1967, vol. 2, Documents Diplomatiques Français.

88. Télégramme de M. Couve de Murville, ministere des affaires étrangères a M Daridan, Ambassadeur de France a New Delhi, "Texte de la réponse du géneral de Gaulle à Madame Indira Gandhi," May 12, 1967, document 177, 1967, vol. 2, Documents Diplomatiques Français.

89. Top-secret note by L. K. Jha to prime minister's secretariat entitled "Nuclear Policy," May 3, 1967, P. N. Haksar Papers (III), no. 111, April–May 1967, NMML.

90. Ibid.

91. Ibid.

92. Ibid.

93. "17 June 1967: China's first thermonuclear test," *CTBTO*, accessed April 9, 2021, https://www.ctbto.org/specials/testing-times/17-june-1967-chinas-first-thermonuclear-test.

94. "China says it fires H-Bomb," *United Press International*, June 17, 1967, accessed July 24, 2019, https://www.upi.com/Archives/1967/06/17/China-says-it-fires-H-bomb/5458453012585/.

95. Dinesh Lal, *Indo-Tibet-China Conflict* (New Delhi: Kalpaz Publications, 2008), 201; Srinath Raghavan, *1971: A Global History of the Creation of Bangladesh* (Cambridge, MA: Harvard University Press, 2013), 194.

96. Swati Chawla, "How Bhutan Came to Not Be a Part of India," *The Wire*, February 8, 2019.

97. Zorawar Daulet Singh, *Power & Diplomacy: India's Foreign Policies During the Cold War* (Delhi: Oxford University Press, 2019), 311.

98. N. Ram, "Sikkim Story: Protection to Absorption," *Social Scientist* 3, no. 2 (September 1974): 67.

99. Singh, *Power & Diplomacy*, 318.

100. Guyot-Réchard, *Shadow States*, 185.

101. Top-secret minutes of the meeting held at the Residency, Gangtok, on the December 28, 1959. Attendees included two members each from political office, army, and Sikkim durbar, Sikkim Palace Archives (hereafter with SPA and EAP codes), SPA/MA/ML/001, EAP880/1/6/1.

102. George N. Patterson, "Recent Chinese Policies in Tibet and towards the Himalayan Border States," *The China Quarterly* (October–December 1962): 191–202; on Naga nationalist claims making, see Lydia Walker, "Decolonization in the 1960s? On Legitimate and Illegitimate Nationalist Claims-Making," *Past & Present* 242 (February 2019): 227–64.

103. Secret note from Palden Thondup Namgyal, Maharajkumar of Sikkim, to Baleshwar Prasad, Dewan of Sikkim, March 2, 1962, SPA/MA/ML/006, EAP880/1/6/6.

104. Report from Sikkim forest ranger, December 11, 1962, note sheets regarding illicit felling of trees by the Indian Army, SPA/MA/ML/006, EAP880/1/6/6; letter no. 260/PE from Chief Secretary Government of Sikkim D. Dahdul to Indian political officer, July 16, 1963, SPA/MA/ML/006, EAP880/1/6/6.

105. Copy of letter no. F.4 (60)-NS/63 dated August 28, 1963, from Shri R. K. Manchua, the first secretary to the political officer, Gangtok, to Shri D. Dahdul, the chief secretary, Government of Sikkim, Gangtok, SPA/MA/ML/006, EAP880/1/6/6.

106. Folder: Clearance of Artillery Range "A," SPA/MA/ML/002, EAP880/1/6/2.

107. Sunaina Kumar, "Kingdom," *Fifty Two*, October 15, 2020, accessed May 2, 2021, https://fiftytwo.in/story/kingdom/.

108. Letter no. 5/CL/67 from Chogyal of Sikkim Palden Thondup Namgyal to prime minister of India, June 30, 1967, correspondence between Chogyal and Prime Minister Indira Gandhi, SPA/FA/IN/013, EAP880/1/2/24.

109. Note GAN/C/463/3/67 from N. B. Menon, political officer in Sikkim to the Chogyal, September 17, 1967, correspondence with N. B. Menon, SPA/CO/OF/022, EAP880/1/7/22/14.

110. Leo E. Rose, "India and Sikkim: Redefining the Relationship," *Pacific Affairs* 42, no. 1 (Spring 1969): 32–46.

111. Raj Chengappa, *Weapons of Peace: The Secret Story of India's Quest to Be a Nuclear Power* (New Delhi: Harper Collins), 112; Sarkar, "Making of a Non-Aligned Nuclear Power," 945.

112. Note no. 42/AS, June 6, 1974, "Audience accordee par le Secretaire Generale a l'Ambassadeur de l'Inde," carton 2253, no. 15-11-5, 206INVA, log 1648, ADF. Author's translation.

113. Instructions to India's representative to UN on nonproliferation treaty, April 20, 1968, P. N. Haksar Files (I-II), sub. file 35, NMML.

114. Ibid.

115. Ibid.

116. Ibid.

117. Juan de Onis, "Nuclear Treaty Endorsed in UN by 92-to-4 vote," *New York Times*, June 11, 1968, 1, 2.

118. Quoted in Ashok Maharaj, "An Overview of NASA-India Relations," in *NASA in the World: Fifty Years of International Collaboration*, eds. John Krige, Angelina Long Callahan, and Ashok Maharaj (New York: Palgrave MacMillan, 2013), 222.

119. Ramabhadran Aravamudan, "How India's Late President Learned About Rocket Science With NASA," *Time*, July 28, 2015, accessed April 12, 2021, https://time.com/3974888/apj-abdul-kalam-nasa/.

120. A. P. J. Abdul Kalam, *Wings of Fire: An Autobiography* (Hyderabad: Universities Press, 1999), 51–52; Amrita Shah, *Vikram Sarabhai: A Life* (New Delhi: Penguin India, (2007), 203.

121. "India and the USSR Sign Protocol for Collaboration in the Peaceful Uses of Atomic Energy of 30 April 1968," DAE, Government of India press release, PR-18, November 30, 1968, signed by Y. S. Das, accessed April 12, 2021, http://www.idsa.in/npihp/documents/IDSA-DAE-01051968.pdf.

122. George Ginsburg and Robert M. Slusser, *A Calendar of Soviet Treaties, 1958–73* (Alphen aan den Rijn, the Netherlands: Sijthoff & Noordhoff International Publishers, 1981), 383.

123. "India and the USSR Sign Protocol for Collaboration in the Peaceful Uses of Atomic Energy of 30 April 1968," DAE, Government of India press release, PR-18.

124. Ibid.

125. Secret telegram 13839 from New Delhi to US State Department, May 7, 1968, DNSA.

126. TIFR report by Yash Pal and B. M. Udgaokar, "Possibilities of Collaborating with USSR in the Field of Experimental High Energy Physics," circa late 1968, accessed April 12, 2021, https://idsa.in/npihp/documents/IDSA-DAE-01051968.pdf.

127. Chengappa, *Weapons of Peace*, 121–22; Perkovich, *India's Nuclear Bomb*, 150.

128. P. K. Iyengar et al. "PURNIMA—A PuO$_2$-Fueled Zero-Energy Fast Reactor at Trombay," *Nuclear Science and Engineering* 70, no. 1 (1979): 37–52.

129. M. V. Ramana, *The Power of Promise: Examining Nuclear Energy in India* (New Delhi, Viking, 2013), 27.

130. Ibid.

131. Odd Arne Westad, *The Cold War: A World History* (New York: Basic Books, 2017), 255.

132. Vojtech Mastny, "The Soviet Union's Partnership with India," *Journal of Cold War Studies* 12, no. 3 (2010): 67.

133. Secret MEA note signed by C. B. Muthamma, joint secretary (ENA), "Brezhnev Proposals," July 25, 1969, WII/121/31/69, folder marked with "Record C-Destroy in 1985," NAI.

134. Ibid.

135. Ibid.

136. Secret MEA note, "Indian Response to the Kosygin/Brezhnev Proposals," unsigned and undated, circa July 1969, WII/121/31/69, NAI.

137. Ibid.

138. Secret savingram, CCB no. 6905-Sav, from MEA New Delhi to all heads of Indian Missions, President Nixon's visit to Delhi, August 14, 1969, signed by superintendent, WII/121/31/69, vol. 2, NAI.

139. Ibid.

140. Secret MEA record of conversation, "US-India talks held at the Panel Room of the Rashtrapati Bhavan (Presidential Palace) during 1500–1700 hours," July 31, 1969, WII/121/31/69, vol. 2, NAI.

141. Handwritten note from D. P. Dhar, Indian ambassador in Moscow to T. N. Kaul in New Delhi, October 9, 1969, T. N. Kaul Papers (I, II, III), correspondence with D. P. Dhar, NMML.

142. Handwritten note from D. P. Dhar to T. N. Kaul, undated, circa pre-August 1971, T. N. Kaul Papers (I, II, III), correspondence with D. P. Dhar, NMML.

143. Breeder reactors were called so because, in theory, they could generate more plutonium than they consumed as fuel (i.e., they "bred" plutonium and therefore could become an additional source of plutonium for the DAE). This was one reason why the French military took interest in the CEA's breeder program. See Mycle Schneider, "Fast Breeder Reactors in France," *Science Band Global Security* 17 (2009): 44.

144. Gopal Raj, *Reach for the Stars: The Evolution of India's Rocket Program* (New Delhi: Viking, 2000), 32.

145. Agreement between the government of Brazil and the government of India for cooperation regarding the utilization of atomic energy for peaceful purposes, March/April 1969, WII-110(1)/69, MEA, Nuclear Agreement with Argentina—proposal regarding, NAI.

146. Ibid.

147. Letter from Vikram Sarabhai to Oscar A. Quihillalt, May 19, 1969, ref. 13/38/68-69-ER, WII-110(1)/69, MEA, Nuclear Agreement with Argentina—proposal regarding, NAI.

148. Argentina and Brazil did not sign the NPT until 1995 and 1998, respectively. They both pursued nuclear weapons programs in the 1970s and 1980s.

149. On the Ottawa Group, see Isabelle Anstey, "Negotiating Nuclear Control: The Zangger Committee and the Nuclear Suppliers' Group in the 1970s," *International History Review* 40, no. 5 (2018): 975–95.

150. Fritz W. Schmidt, "The Zangger Committee: Its History and Future," *Nonproliferation Review* (Fall 1994): 38–44.

151. Perkovich, *India's Nuclear Bomb*, 122–23; Anderson, *Nucleus and Nation*, 441.

152. On Sarabhai's conflict with BARC scientists who favored nuclear explosions, see also Amrita Shah, *Vikram Sarabhai*, 205.

153. Perkovich, *India's Nuclear Bomb*, 150.

154. P. K. Iyengar, "Twenty Years after Pokhran," *Indian Express*, May 18, 1994, 11. Cited in Perkovich, *India's Nuclear Bomb*, 149.

155. Ibid.

156. Atomic Energy Commission, Government of India, *Atomic Energy and Space Research: A Profile for the Decade 1970–1980* (Bombay: Atomic Energy Commission, 1970), accessed April 12, 2021, https://inis.iaea.org/collection/NCLCollectionStore/_Public/02/006/2006423.pdf; also cited in Raj, *Reach for the Stars*, 21.

157. Maharaj, "An Overview of NASA-India Relations," 231.

158. Handwritten notes on "India-Soviet Study Group Meeting on Problems of Security, Arms Control, Disarmament, and Economic Development," India International Center, New Delhi, February 12–13, 1968, Pitambar Pant Papers (III), Diaries/Notebooks, file no. 14, December 1967–68, NMML.

159. Telex message from Vikram Sarabhai to Indira Gandhi forward by P. N. Haksar, April 28, 1970, 56/69/70-Parl., PMO, "Secret Manufacture of Atom Bomb by India—Use of nuclear engineering technology for peaceful purposes—launching of earth satellite by China—Discussions in Parliament," 1970, NAI.

160. Siddiqi, "Another global history of science," 127.

161. On the prehistory of DAE-NASA cooperation on communication satellites, see Asif A. Siddiqi, "Whose India? SITE and the origins of satellite television in India," *History and Technology* 36, nos. 3–4 (2020): 452–74.

162. Asif A. Siddiqi, "Making Space for the Nation: Satellite Television, Indian Scientific Elites, and the Cold War," *Comparative Studies of South Asia, Africa and the Middle East* 35, no. 1 (2015): 45.

163. The secret note stated: "This is costlier than the cost of generation from a coal based thermal station in the region. With the investment contemplated U.P. State Elec-

tricity Board would be able to obtain considerably cheaper power from hydro sources available in the Himalayan region." Secret note prepared by Planning Commission (Power Division), "Nuclear-Powered Agro-Industrial Complex," September 14, 1970, file no. 85 (1968–72), Ashok Mitra Papers, Planning/Planning Commission, NMML.

164. Ibid.

165. Secret summary record of the meeting of the Planning Commission with the members of the Electronics Committee held at 12 p.m. on December 3, 1969, prepared by Planning Commission (S. R. Section), file no. 80 (1968 and 1970), Ashok Mitra Papers, Planning/Planning Commission, NMML.

166. USAEC Aide-Mémoire to the Indian Atomic Energy Commission, November 16, 1970, http://www.nci.org/06nci/04/Historic_Documents_India_Nuclear_Test.htm, accessed August 9, 2019, cited in Sharon Squassoni, "India's Nuclear Separation Plan: Issues and Views," *CRS Report for Congress*, December 22, 2006, footnote 22; Jayita Sarkar, "India's Nuclear Limbo and the Fatalism of the Nuclear Non-Proliferation Regime, 1974–1983," *Strategic Analysis* 37, no. 3 (2013): 324 and footnote 13. See also: A. G. Noorani, "Indo-U.S. Nuclear Relations." *Asian Survey* 21, no. 4 (1981): 403.

167. Sarabhai died in December 1971 and so did not actually witness the French nuclear tests to which he was invited. Shah, *Vikram Sarabhai*, 207. See also Shivanand Kanavi, "How Indian PMs reacted to nuclear ambitions: Interview with K. Subrahmanyam," *Rediff News*, February 10, 2011, https://www.rediff.com/news/report/slide-show-1-an-interview-with-k-subrahmanyam/20110210.htm, accessed January 15, 2019.

168. Shah, *Vikram Sarabhai*, 206.

169. Anderson, *Nucleus and Nation*, 469.

170. Anderson, *Nucleus and Nation*, 470; Chengappa, *Weapons of Peace*, 157.

171. On the often-arbitrary distinction in history between "proliferator" and "innovator," see Asif A. Siddiqi, "Spaceflight in the National Imagination," in *Remembering the Space Age*, ed. Steven J. Dick (Washington, DC: National Aeronautics and Space Administration, 2008), 23; see also Itty Abraham, "The Ambivalence of Nuclear Histories," *Osiris* 21 (2006): 49–65; Hugh Gusterson, "Nuclear Weapons and the Other in the Western Imagination," *Cultural Anthropology* 14 (1999): 111–43.

6. Fractured Worlds, 1970–1974

1. The cyclone was named after the largest island in the Bay of Bengal, Bhola, which was directly hit and completely devastated by the storm.

2. Walter Sullivan, "Disaster. East Pakistan: Cyclone May be the Worst Catastrophe of Century," *New York Times*, November 22, 1970, 169.

3. Ibid.

4. See, for example, "Toll in Pakistan is put at 16,000, Expected to Rise," *New York Times*, November 16, 1970, 1; "Pakistan Death Toll 55,000, May Rise to 300,000," *New York Times*, November 17, 1970, 1; Walter Sullivan, "Disaster. East Pakistan."

5. Floods in East Pakistan in the summer of 1970 had originally led General Yahya Khan to postpone the elections to December 7, 1970. For electoral history of Pakistan prior to the December 1970 elections, see Craig Baxter, "Pakistan Votes—1970," *Asian Survey* 11, no. 3 (March 1971): 198–202.

6. James M. Naughton, "Nixon Pledges $10-Million Aid for Storm Victims in Pakistan," *New York Times*, November 18, 1970, 16; "World Bank offers Plan to Reconstruct East Pakistan," *New York Times*, December 3, 1970, 4.

7. On this subject, see, for example, Sravani Biswas, "'Cyclone Not Above Politics': East Pakistan, disaster politics, and the 1970 Bhola Cyclone," *Modern Asian Studies* (2020), advance access.

8. Willem van Schendel, *A History of Bangladesh* (Cambridge, UK: Cambridge University Press, 2009, 125); Baxter, "Pakistan Votes–1970," 212.

9. Baxter, "Pakistan Votes," 212.

10. Ralph Blumenthal, "Bengali and Leftist Parties Lead in Pakistani Elections," *New York Times*, December 8, 1970, 3. Ibid.

11. The Six Points that the Awami League of East Pakistan adopted on March 18, 1966, called for a federation governed by a parliamentary democracy based on universal adult suffrage, where the federal government would only be in charge of foreign affairs and defense, with freely convertible currencies for the two federated wings to prevent capital flight from East Pakistan, powers of taxation and revenue collection vested in the federated units, separate foreign exchange accounts of the federated units, and a separate paramilitary force for East Pakistan. See, "June 7, 1966: Six-Points were Bengalis' charter for freedom," *Dhaka Tribune*, June 6, 2020.

12. On the controversies surrounding the number of dead in the 1971 genocide and war, see David Bergman, "The Politics of Bangladesh's Genocide Debate," *New York Times*, April 5, 2016.

13. Letter from Chogyal of Sikkim to Prime Minister Gandhi, February 20, 1969, Correspondence between Chogyal and Prime Minister, SPA/FA/IN/013, EAP880/1/2/24.

14. The first and second waves were in the mid-1940s and the 1960s, respectively. Jan C. Jansen and Jürgen Osterhammel, *Decolonization: A Short History* (Princeton, NJ: Princeton University Press, 2017), 2.

15. Ibid.

16. On the economic rights discourse of decolonization during this period, see Giuliano Garavini, "Completing Decolonization: The 1973 'Oil Shock' and the Struggle for Economic Rights," *The International History Review* 33, no. 3 (2011): 473–87.

17. Robert Alden, "China's First U. N. Veto Bars Bangladesh," *New York Times*, August 26, 1972, 1.

18. "Limited Detention Law for West Bengal: Prime Minister's announcement," *Jugantar*, November 12, 1970, 1, vol. 34, no. 39 (October 28 1970), EAP262/1/2/10975, BL. Author's translation.

19. "Bill to prevent violent activities in West Bengal being discussed at Parliamentary Advisory Council," *Jugantar*, November 17, 1970, 1, vol. 34, no. 44 (November 2, 1970), EAP262/1/2/10989, BL. Author's translation. On Naxalite-era violence, see, for example, Ashoke Kumar Mukhopadhyay, "Through the Eyes of the Police: Naxalites in Calcutta in the 1970s," *Economic and Political Weekly* 41, no. 29 (July 22–28, 2006): 3227–33; see also Dom Moraes, "The Naxalites, whose extremism knows no extremes, are Indian Revolutionaries with a Chinese accent," *New York Times*, November 8, 1970, 232, 281–84, 288–89.

20. The West Bengal (Prevention of Violent Activities) Act, 1970, President's Act No. 19 of 1970, Government of India, Ministry of Law, Legislative Department, November 22, 1970, WBGP-70/71-3269A-6M.

21. Gyan Prakash, *Emergency Chronicles: Indira Gandhi and Democracy's Turning Point* (Princeton, NJ: Princeton University Press, 2019), 136; see also Robert L. Hardgrave Jr., "The Congress in India—Crisis and Split," *Asian Survey* 10, no. 3 (March 1970): 256–62.

22. Morarji Desai opposed the nationalization of banks. He would succeed Indira Gandhi as the country's prime minister in 1977 after the Emergency.

23. Prakash, *Emergency Chronicles*, 146.

24. "Mrs. Gandhi Orders Elections, Dissolving India's Parliament," *New York Times*, December 28, 1970, 1.

25. Sydney H. Schanberg, "Mrs. Gandhi Wins Parliament Majority," *New York Times*, March 12, 1971, 1.

26. van Schendel, *History of Bangladesh*, 125.

27. Ibid., 129.

28. Ibid., 161–62.

29. David Ludden, "Forgotten Heroes," *Frontline* 20, no. 15 (August 1, 2003), accessed March 28, 2021, https://www.sas.upenn.edu/~dludden/LuddenFrontline-Heroes.htm.

30. "'Suppression' in Pakistan deplored by Mrs. Gandhi," *New York Times*, March 28, 1971, 3.

31. James P. Sterba, "India, Backing Bengalis, Wary of Meddling Charge," *New York Times*, April 9, 1971, 3.

32. Jairam Ramesh, "Behind the Scenes of India's Response to the East Pakistan Crisis of 1971," *The Wire*, June 18 2018; see also Jairam Ramesh, *Intertwined Lives: P.N. Haksar and Indira Gandhi* (New York, NY: Simon & Schuster, 2018).

33. Sterba, "India, Backing Bengalis."

34. In the March 1971 elections, Indira Gandhi's party did not win a majority in West Bengal, which still remained a communist stronghold at the level of the state government. The communist state government was violently repressing the far-left anti-state "Naxalite" groups. See "No Party Victor in West Bengal," *New York Times*, March 14, 1971.

35. Confidential telegram Dacca 01138, Subject: Dissent from US policy toward East Pakistan, April 6, 1971, FRUS, 1969–76, vol. 11, South Asia Crisis, 1971.

36. Ibid.

37. Memorandum for the president, policy options toward Pakistan, April 28, 1971, NSC Files, Country Files: Middle East, box 625, Richard Nixon Presidential Library, DNSA.

38. On Indian covert military support for Mukti Bahini, see Gary Bass, *The Blood Telegram: Nixon, Kissinger, and a Forgotten Genocide* (New York: Alfred A. Knopf, 2013), 99–101; See also Chapter 12: Mukti Bahini in Bass, *The Blood Telegram*.

39. James P. Sterba, "Indian Volunteers Sought to Go to Aid East Pakistanis," *New York Times*, March 30, 1971, 10.

40. van Schendel, *A History of Bangladesh*, 164.

41. Anthony Mascarenas, "Genocide," *The Sunday Times,* June 13, 1971; "Pakistani Charges Massacres by Army," *New York Times,* June 13 1971; see also Mark Dumett, "Bangladesh war: The article that changed history," *BBC News,* December 16, 2011, accessed January 15, 2019, https://www.bbc.com/news/world-asia-16207201.

42. "Mrs. Gandhi Says Pakistan Solution Grows Remote," *New York Times,* June 16, 1971, 12.

43. Sydney H. Schanberg, "India Seeks to Halt in Refugee Flow," *New York Times,* May 23, 1971, 11; "Three Million Links in a Chain of Misery," *New York Times,* May 23, 1971, section E, 3.

44. Ibid.

45. "Mrs. Gandhi Says Pakistan Solution Grows Remote," *New York Times*

46. MemCon, July 7, 1971, FRUS, 1969–76, vol. E-7, document 139.

47. Memorandum from Director of Central Intelligence Helms to the president's assistant for national security affairs (Kissinger), July 29, 1971, FRUS, 1969–76, vol. 11, document 110; see also editorial note in document 93 of the same volume.

48. Srinath Raghavan, *1971: A Global History of the Creation of Bangladesh* (Cambridge, MA: Harvard University Press), 199.

49. P. N. Haksar to Indira Gandhi, July 16, 1971, enclosing draft letter to Zhou En-lai (sent on July 18, 1971), subject file 169, P. N. Haksar (III Installment), NMML. Cited in Raghavan, *1971,* 199.

50. Treaty of Peace, Friendship, and Cooperation between the government of India and the government of the Union of Soviet Socialist Republics, August 9, 1971, accessed March 23, 2019, https://mea.gov.in/bilateral-documents.htm?dtl/5139/Treaty+of+.

51. "Mrs. Gandhi's Statement," *New York Times,* December 4, 1971, 10.

52. On Kissinger's overtures to China to involve itself in the 1971 war, see Gary Bass, *The Blood Telegram,* 291–92; Srinath Raghavan, *1971,* chapter 8; see also Zorawar Daulet Singh, "Calling the US's Bluff in 1971," *The Hindu,* December 19, 2019.

53. T. N. Kaul, *The Kissinger Years: Indo American Relations* (New Delhi: Arnold Heinman, 1980), 62.

54. Indira Gandhi, "India and the World," *Foreign Affairs* 51, no. 1 (October 1972).

55. The Instrument of Surrender was signed on December 16, 1971, by General Jagjit Singh Aurora of the Indian Eastern Forces and Lieutenant-General A. A. K Niazi of the Pakistan Army. See https://www.mea.gov.in/bilateral-documents.htm?dtl/5312/Instrument, last accessed October 3, 2021; see also "Surrender Document," *New York Times,* December 17, 1971, 1.

56. Secret MEA (AMS) note, "Impact of Sino-American, India-Soviet and Indo-Pakistan relations on India-US relations", undated, circa March/April 1972, Ministry of External Affairs, Americas Division, file no. WII/103/17/72: Indo-US Relations, NAI.

57. "Saigon Bars Indian on Control Team," *New York Times,* January 9, 1972, 20.

58. Secret MEA note prepared by V. V. Paranjpe, joint secretary (EA), "Sino-US relations and implications," April 6, 1972, WII/103/17/72: Indo-US Relations, NAI.

59. The Constitution (Twenty-Sixth Amendment) Act, December 28, 1971, accessed March 29, 1971, https://www.india.gov.in/my-government/constitution-india/amendments/constitution-india-twenty-sixth-amendment-act-1971.

60. William L. Richter, "Princes in Indian Politics," *Economic & Political Weekly* 6, no. 9 (February 1971): 535, 537–42.

61. "Mrs. Gandhi Orders Elections, Dissolving India's Parliament," *New York Times*.

62. Prakash, *Emergency Chronicles*, 139.

63. Ibid.

64. The Northeastern Areas (Reorganization) Act of 1971, December 30, 1971, accessed April 1, 2021, https://www.indiacode.nic.in/bitstream/123456789/1534/1/197181.pdf.

65. "Indira ushers in Meghalaya & Arunachal Pradesh," *Times of India*, January 21, 1972.

66. See also V. Venkata Rao, "Reorganization of Northeast India," *The Indian Journal of Political Science* 33, no. 2 (April–June 1972): 123–44; Lorenz Lüthi, *Cold Wars. Asia. The Middle East. Europe* (Cambridge, UK: Cambridge University Press), 180; Sanjib Baruah, *In the Name of the Nation: India and Its Northeast* (Palo Alto, CA: Stanford University Press, 2020), chapter 1; for pre-1970s political history of the eastern Himalayas, see Bérénice Guyot-Réchard, *Shadow States: India, China and the Himalayas, 1910–1962* (Cambridge, UK: University of Cambridge Press, 2016).

67. On Mizo rebels' role in the 1971 war, see Willem Van Schendel, "A War Within a War: Mizo rebels and the Bangladesh liberation struggle," *Modern Asian Studies* 50, no. 1 (2016): 99–103; on the Special Frontier Force composed of Tibetan exiles established in the 1960s by India's Intelligence Bureau and the CIA, see Kallol Bhattacharjee, "They came, they fought, they stayed," *Hindu*, March 11 2017; Amit S. Upadhye, "On the road to victory, they soldiered on," *New Indian Express*, December 17, 2020.

68. van Schendel, *History of Bangladesh*, 172–73.

69. On "intermestic," see Campbell Craig and Fredrik Logevall, *America's Cold War*; Fredrik Logevall, "Domestic Politics."

70. Secret MEA (Bangladesh Division) note prepared by K. P. S. Menon, JS (Bangladesh Division) MEA for the Indian ambassador in Pakistan, "Bangladesh—Talking Points for our Ambassador in the United States," March 30, 1972, WII/103/17/72: Indo-US Relations, NAI.

71. "Dr. Vikram A. Sarabhai Dead: Led India's Atom Energy Body," *New York Times*, December 31, 1971.

72. Asif Siddiqi, "Another global history of science: making space for India and China," *British Journal for the History of Science* (2016): 140.

73. Tiki Rajwai, "How did a scientific talent like Vikram Sarabhai meet with an unnatural death?," *New Indian Express*, October 27, 2017, https://www.newindianexpress.com/states/kerala/2017/oct/27/how-did-a-scientific-talent-like-vikram-sarabhai-meet-with-an-unnatural-death-1684227.html, accessed July 28, 2019; "Mystery behind Vikram Sarabhai's death," *Times of India*, December 29, 2008, https://timesofindia.indiatimes.com/city/ahmedabad/mystery-behind-vikram-sarabhais-death/articleshow/3910516.cms, accessed July 28, 2019.

74. Anderson, *Nucleus and Nation*, 288.

75. The uranium metal plant was constructed by the DAE to produce pure uranium metal for the fuel rods of the Canadian-supplied CIRUS.

76. Chengappa, *Weapons of Peace*, 154.

77. Internal memo of the prime minister's secretariat prepared by P. N. Haksar, January 4, 1972, 17/39/72-PMS, vol. 1, SECRET, Prime Minister's Office, Subject: Atomic Energy, NAI.

78. Chengappa, *Weapons of Peace*, 154.

79. Letter from Prime Minister Indira Gandhi to M. G. K. Menon (secretary of Department of Electronics), No. 14-PMH/72, January 14, 1972, 17/39/72-PMS, vol. 1, SECRET, Prime Minister's Office, Subject: Atomic Energy, NAI.

80. Anderson, *Nucleus and Nation*, 469.

81. Chengappa, *Weapons of Peace*, 158.

82. A. P. J. Abdul Kalam was nicknamed the "Missile Man" while he worked at the DRDO in the 1980s, where he led the ballistic missile program of India. India's first ballistic missile was the intermediate-range Agni that used technological aspects of the SLV-3. He became the president of India from 2002 to 2007.

83. Chengappa, *Weapons of Peace*, 159; Anderson, *Nucleus and Nation*, 468.

84. Anderson, *Nucleus and Nation*, 469. The currency conversion is based on the foreign exchange rate of June 1970, where 1 Indian rupee was valued at 0.1330 of the US dollar. Foreign exchange rates, *Wall Street Journal*, June 30 1970, 28.

85. Perkovich, *India's Nuclear Bomb*, 172; Anderson, *Nucleus and Nation*, 479.

86. Tanvi Madan, *The Fateful Triangle: How China Shaped U.S.-India Relations during the Cold War* (Washington, DC: Brookings Institution, 2020), 256–57.

87. Chengappa, *Weapons of Peace*, 131–32.

88. Perkovich, *India's Nuclear Bomb*, 159.

89. Chengappa, *Weapons of Peace*, 180–81.

90. Ibid., 183.

91. Quoted in Feroz Hassan Khan, *Eating Grass: The Making of the Pakistani Bomb* (Palo Alto, CA: Stanford University Press, 2013), 59.

92. Ibid., chapter 5.

93. "India and the Chinese Bomb," Ministry of External Affairs of India, November 25, 1964, enclosure with airgram A-650, December 30, 1964, RAC, NLJ-009R-6-3-1-3, LBJL.

94. U.S. Embassy Canada cable 391 from Ottawa to State Department, "India's Nuclear Intentions," March 7, 1972, RG 59, SN 70–73, AE 1 India, NARA, DNSA.

95. U.S. Mission Geneva cable 2755 to State Department, "Japanese-Pakistani Conversations Regarding Indian Nuclear Plans," June 26, 1972, RG 59, SN 70–73, AE 1 India, NARA, DNSA.

96. Henry Kissinger to President Nixon, "Proposed NSSM on the Implications of an Indian Nuclear Test," with cover memorandum from Richard T. Kennedy, July 4, 1972, Nixon Presidential Library, National Security Council Institutional Files, box H-192, NSSM-156, DNSA.

97. National Security Study Memorandum 156, July 5, 1972, FRUS, vol. E-7, Documents on South Asia, 1969–97.

98. Special National Intelligence Estimate 31–72, "Indian Nuclear Developments and Their Likely Implications," August 3, 1972, FRUS, 1969–76, volume E-7, Documents on South Asia, 1969–72.

99. H. Daniel Brewster to Herman Pollack, "Indian Nuclear Developments," January 16, 1973, enclosing "Summary," September 1, 1972, RG 59, SN 70–73, AE 6 India, NARA, DNSA.

100. Note on collaborative programmes between ISRO and foreign countries, PMS, undated, circa early 1972, 17/39/72-PMS, vol. 1, SECRET, Prime Minister's Office, Subject: Atomic Energy, NAI.

101. Letter from M. A. Vellodi, JS of Space/DAE in Bombay to A. P. Venkateswaran, JS, MEA, May 16, 1972, WI/239/30/72 (EE), vol. 1: Indo-Soviet Agreement on Space Research, NAI.

102. Agreement between Academy Sciences of the USSR and the Indian Space Research Organization, signed by M. V. Kaldysh (AS-USSR) and M. G. K Menon (ISRO), May 10, 1972, WI/239/30/72 (EE), vol. 1: Indo-Soviet Agreement on Space Research, NAI.

103. Asif Siddiqi, "Another global history of science," 141.

104. Satish Dhawan's remarks were to Walter Marshall, the director of UK's Harwell. Confidential note for the record, discussion with Professor Dhawan, chairman of the Space Commission of India and director of the Indian Institute of Science at Bangalore on Saturday, January 19, 1974, prepared on February 8, 1974, by Dr. W. Marshall, India: Basic Information on Nuclear Activities, AB48/1613, UKNA.

105. M. V. Ramana, *Power of Promise*, 27. See also chapter 3.

106. P. K. Iyengar, M. Srinivasan, V. R. Nargundkar, K. Chandramoleswar, K. Subba Rao, C. S. Pasupathy, T. K. Basu, P. K. Job, "Purnima fast critical facility: experiments and results," Proceedings of the Indo-Soviet Seminar on Fast Reactors, Reactor Research Centre, Kalpakkam, December 6–8, 1972.

107. Indo-Soviet Seminar on Fast Reactor in Kalpakkam, WI/62/47/72 EE, NAI.

108. Bombay consulate cable 705 to Department of State, "India's Nuclear Position," April 4, 1973, RG 59, SN 70–73, Def 1 India, NARA, DNSA.

109. The DAE was building three CANDU-type pressurized heavy water reactors at the time. These were in Rajasthan and Kalpakkam near Madras with Canadian help and in Narora in Uttar Pradesh without a foreign supplier.

110. Anstey, "Negotiating Nuclear Control," 985.

111. Telegram from Ambassador Jean-Claude Winckler, French embassy in New Delhi to French Foreign Ministry (no. 1027/29), Objet: Inde-URSS, December 11, 1976, carton 2253, 206INVA, Direction Asie-Oceanie, Inde, 1973–80, ADF.

112. Notes on meeting with Dr. M. G. K. Menon, September 25, 1972, prepared by John Voss, executive officer of the American Academy of the Arts and Sciences, November 15, 1972, box 4, Possible Visits to India, 1972–73, AMACAD.

113. Engerman, *Price of Aid*, 328–32.

114. Letter from John Voss of the American Academy to Daniel Patrick Moynihan, December 13, 1972, box 4, AMACAD.

115. Notes on meeting with Dr. M. G. K. Menon, September 25, 1972, box 4, AMACAD.

116. Ibid.

117. Memorandum from Julien Engel at the National Academy of Science to Roger Revelle and John Voss at the American Academy, April 13, 1973, box 4, AMACAD.

118. Ibid.

119. Nuclear Setback, CIA Weekly Summary, July 20, 1973, CIA-RDP79-00927A 010400 3001-5.

120. Telegram number 491–92 from Ambassador Jean-Daniel Jurgensen in New Delhi to Directors of Asia Section, Ministry of External Affairs in Paris, June 20, 1973, Folder: Questions Atomiques, 15-11-5, January 1975 to February 1974, carton 206INVA /2252, ADF.

121. Ibid.

122. West European exports of heavy water plants to the DAE created concerns of potential patent violations for the UKAEA. Policymakers in London worried that *Uhde* and *Gelpra* were infringing patents that the UK institution held in the European continent. Inquiries with the DAE, however, did not elicit any information. Letter from B. D. MacLean at the UKAEA's Commercial Policy and Overseas Relations to S. Staveley at the UK High Commission, December 21, 1973, AB48/1613, UKNA.

123. The Electronics Division of Trombay was moved and expanded into the Electronics Corporation in Hyderabad in 1967.

124. Note for the record, "Visit to the Electronics Corporation of India Limited in Hyderabad on Monday," January 24, 1974, prepared on February 11, 1974, by Dr. W. Marshall, AB48/1613, UKNA.

125. Ibid.

126. Ibid.

127. Note for the record, "Commercial: In Confidence, Visit to the Nuclear Fuel Complex at Hyderabad on Monday, January 24, 1974," prepared on February 11, 1974, by Dr. W. Marshall, AB48/1613, UKNA.

128. Ibid.

129. Chengappa, *Weapons of Peace*, 185.

130. Julien Engel, "Indian-American Scientific Cooperation," *Bulletin of the American Academy of Arts and Sciences* 27, no. 7 (April 1974): 8.

131. Engerman, *The Price of Aid*, 335.

132. Moynihan to Norris and Ross McWhirter, February 25, 1974, India Correspondence, Part 1: India File, 1965–75, box 361, Moynihan Papers, LOC.

133. Secret letter no. TRIP/110/1/70 from Amb. Homi J. H. Taleyarkhan in Tripoli, Libya, to P. N. Haksar, principal secretary to prime minister, June 5, 1972, 17/39/72-PMS, vol. 2, NAI.

134. Secret note from P. N. Haksar to F. S., Shri S. K. Banerji, copy to Homi Sethna, chairman, AEC, June 12, 1972, 17/39/72-PMS, vol. 2, NAI.

135. Asif A. Siddiqi, "Spaceflight in the National Imagination," 23.

136. Målfrid Braut-Hegghammer, *Unclear Physics: Why Iraq and Libya Failed to Build Nuclear Weapons* (Ithaca, NY: Cornell University Press, 2016), 139.

137. For the text of the NPT, see https://www.un.org/disarmament/wmd/nuclear/npt/text/ (accessed August 3, 2019).

138. Mohamed M. Megahed, "Nuclear desalination: history and prospects," *Desalination* 135 (2001): 172.

139. Secret letter no. TRIP/110/1/70 from Amb. Homi J. H. Taleyarkhan in Tripoli, Libya, to P. N. Haksar, principal secretary to prime minister, June 5, 1972, 17/39/72-PMS, vol. 2, 1972, NAI.

140. Confidential telegram from the US Embassy in New Delhi to secretary of state, EXDIS, August 26, 1974, Presidential Country Files, box 12, Country File: India (3), Folder: India-State Department Telegrams, Gerald R. Ford Presidential Library (hereafter GRFL).

141. Daniel J. Sargent, *A Superpower Transformed: The Remaking of American Foreign Relations in the 1970s* (Oxford, UK: Oxford University Press, 2015), 176.

142. "UN General Assembly Resolution 3202 (S-VI): Programme of Action on the Establishment of a New International Economic Order," *Official Records of the General Assembly: Sixth Special Session, May 1974* (New York: United Nations, 1974), 3–12. See also Nils Gilman, "The New International Economic Order: A Reintroduction," *Humanity Journal* (Spring 2015): 1–16.

143. Christopher R. W. Dietrich. *Oil Revolution: Anticolonial Elites, Sovereign Rights, and the Economic Culture of Decolonization* (New York: Cambridge University Press, 2017), 264.

144. On this subject, see Jacob D. Hamblin, *The Wretched Atom: America's Global Gamble with Peaceful Nuclear Technology* (Oxford, UK: Oxford University Press, 2021); Jacob D. Hamblin, "The Nuclearization of Iran in the Seventies," *Diplomatic History* 38, no. 5 (2014): 1114–35.

145. Hasu H. Patel, "General Amin and the Indian Exodus from Uganda," *Issue: A Journal of Opinion* 2, no. 4 (Winter 1972), 12–22.

146. Dietrich, *Oil Revolution*, 270–71.

147. Bernard Weinraub, "India, Slow to Grasp Oil Crisis, Now Fears Severe Economic Loss," *New York Times*, January 20, 1974, 2.

148. "Lag in Fertilizer Threatens India," *New York Times*, April 4, 1974, 47.

149. Paul F. Power, "The Energy Crisis and Indian Development," *Asian Survey* 15, no. 4 (April 1975): 331.

150. Ashok Parthsarathi, "Oil Shock and Surprise," *Frontline*, February 16, 2018.

151. "Sadat hails India's stand on West Asia," *National Herald*, February 25, 1974. Enclosed with private correspondence from Daniel P. Moynihan to Nathan Glazer, February 26, 1974, part 1, box 361, Moynihan Papers, LOC.

152. Power, "The Energy Crisis and Indian Development," 330–31.

153. James F. Clarity, "Détente pushed by India and Iran," *New York Times*, May 6, 1974, 9.

154. Ibid.

155. Van Schendel, *History of Bangladesh*, 180.

156. Seymour M. Hersch, "Concern by India on CIA Related," *New York Times*, September 13, 1974, 11.

157. Bernard Weinraub, "Daniel Moynihan's passage to India," *New York Times*, March 31, 1974, 16.

158. Daniel Patrick Moynihan, "The United States in Opposition," *Commentary*, March 1975.

7. Explosion and Fallout, 1974–1980s

1. Telegram 6591 signed by David T. Schneider from US Embassy India to State Department and US Embassy in the UK, May 18, 1974, FRUS, 1969–76, vol. E-14, part 2, document 47; also in vol. E-8, document 161.

2. Ibid.

3. Ibid.

4. Appendix 1: Some Indian Statements on Peaceful Nuclear Explosive Devices, NATO Unclassified, carton 2253, ADF.

5. Telegram TOSEC 794/104621 from Rush at State Department to US Mission to the IAEA, May 18, 1974, FRUS, 1969–76, vol. E-8, document 162.

6. Article 5 of the NPT called upon state parties to make available PNEs on a "nondiscriminatory basis" to nonnuclear weapon states "under appropriate international observation and through appropriate international procedures." The treaty did not permit countries to develop their own PNEs devices as India had done.

7. Telegram 6602 signed by David T. Schneider from US Embassy in India to US Embassy in the UK, May 19, 1974, FRUS, 1969–76, vol. E-8, document 163.

8. Ibid.

9. Telegram TOSEC 794/104621 from Rush at State Department to US Mission to the IAEA, May 18, 1974, FRUS, 1969–76, vol. E-8, document 162.

10. Ibid.

11. Moynihan to Winston Lord, May 30, 1974, India Correspondence, Part I: India File, 1965–75, box 361, Moynihan Papers, LOC.

12. Telegram TOSEC 794/104621 from Kenneth Rush at the State Department to the US Mission to IAEA, May 18, 1974, FRUS, 1969–76, vol. E-8, document 162.

13. Secret MEA note prepared by J. S. Teja (joint secretary, Americans Division) at MEA, New Delhi, "India's Peaceful Nuclear Experiment: American Reaction," May 22, 1974, WII/103(18)74, NAI.

14. Ibid.

15. Telegram TOSEC 794/104621 from Kenneth Rush at the US State Department to the US Mission to the International Atomic Energy Agency, May 18, 1974, FRUS, 1969–76, vol. E-8, document 162.

16. Ibid.

17. "National Security Study Memorandum (NSSM) 202," May 23 1974, accessed April 26, 2021, https://www.nixonlibrary.gov/sites/default/files/virtuallibrary/documents/nssm/nssm_202.pdf. See also Joseph O'Mahoney, "The Smiling Buddha effect: Canadian and US policy after India's 1974 nuclear test," *Nonproliferation Review* (2020, advance access).

18. "National Security Decision Memorandum (NSDM) 255," June 3, 1974, accessed October 30, 2020, https://www.nixonlibrary.gov/sites/default/files/virtuallibrary/documents/nsdm/nsdm_255.pdf.

19. On the history of the NSG, see William Burr, "A Scheme of 'Control': The United States and the Origins of the Nuclear Suppliers' Group, 1974–1976," *International History Review* 36, no. 2 (2014): 252–76.

20. "Mrs. Gandhi terms India Whipping Boy," *New York Times*, May 28, 1974, 8.

21. Text of Ambassador Kaul's address at the National Press Club, June 1974, FS-8, NESA-7 USIS Wireless Files, box 373, India: Subject File, T. N. Kaul, 1973–75, Moynihan Papers, LOC.

22. Ibid.

23. US Department of State MemCon, August 2, 1974, FRUS, 1969–76, vol. E-8, document 171.

24. UN General Assembly Resolution 3202 (S-VI), May 1, 1974. On decolonization and NIEO, see Adom Getachew, *Worldmaking after Empire: The Rise and Fall of Self-Determination* (Princeton, NJ: Princeton University Press, 2019), chapter 5; Giuliano Garavini, *The Rise and Fall of OPEC in the Twentieth Century* (Oxford, UK: Oxford Uni-

versity Press, 2019), chapter 5; Michael Franczak, "Losing the Battle, Winning the War: Neoconservatives versus the New International Economic Order, 1974–82," *Diplomatic History* 43, no. 5 (November 2019): 867–89.

25. "J. R. D. Fowell from Canadian Delegation to George Andrews at Supreme Headquarters Allied Powers Europe NATO, Brussels, Indian Statements Concerning the Test," June 5 1974, NATO Confidential, carton 2253, ADF.

26. Power, "The Energy Crisis and Indian Development," 336.

27. "Lok Sabha Debates," Session 11, August 27, 1974, 153–54.

28. Scott Kaufman, *Project Plowshare: The Peaceful Use of Nuclear Explosives in Cold War America* (Ithaca, NY: Cornell University Press, 2012), 13–14.

29. J. R. D. Fowell to George Andrews, June 5, 1974, Appendix 1: Some Indian Statements on Peaceful Nuclear Explosive Devices, NATO Unclassified, carton 2253, ADF.

30. Gasbuggy Site Factsheet, Office of Legacy Management, US DOE.

31. See, for example, C. H. Atkinson and Don C. Ward (Bureau of Mines, Department of Interior) and R. F. Lemon (El Paso Natural Gas Company), "Gasbuggy Reservoir Evaluation—1969 Report," 1970.

32. Edward Teller, "The Case for Continuing Nuclear Tests," *Headline Series* 145 (1961): 57.

33. Peter Goodchild, *Edward Teller: The Real Dr. Strangelove* (Cambridge, MA: Harvard University Press, 2004), 284–95.

34. Edward Teller et al., *The Constructive Uses of Nuclear Explosives* (New York: McGraw-Hill, 1968), preface, vii.

35. Ibid., i.

36. Bertrand Goldschmidt, *Atomic Complex*, 175.

37. Nuclear Tests (Australia v. France) ICJ 253; Nuclear Tests (New Zealand v. France) ICJ 457, December 20 1974.

38. Chengappa, *Weapons of Peace*, 198, 201.

39. Ibid., 188.

40. Ibid.

41. Perkovich claims that preparations for the PNE test began in September 1973, citing an unattributable interview conducted in 1996. Perkovich, *India's Nuclear Bomb*, 172, footnote 81.

42. Chengappa, *Weapons of Peace*, 190.

43. Ibid., 194.

44. R. Chidambaram and R. Ramanna, "Some Studies on India's Peaceful Nuclear Explosion Experiment," IAEA-TC-1-4/19, in *Proceedings of a Technical Committee, Vienna, 20–24 January 1975, Peaceful Nuclear Explosions IV* (Vienna: IAEA, August 1975), 421–36.

45. Anderson, *Nucleus and Nation*, 488; Perkovich, *India's Nuclear Bomb*, 181–82.

46. The March 1970 and November 1972 IAEA technical meetings were to review the phenomenology of both contained and cratering explosions. The January 1971 meeting was to review the practical applications of PNE for industrial purposes.

47. Chidambaram and Ramanna, "Some Studies on India's Peaceful Nuclear Explosion Experiment, op. cit.

48. Indian media reported elation and puzzlement of scientists that a shallow nuclear explosion of a plutonium device like that in Pokhran did not lead to any radiation.

The Pakistan Atomic Energy Commission claimed to have detected radioactivity. See "Fall-out absence elates scientists," *Times of India*, May 20, 1974, 5; "Pakistan detects fall-out," *New York Times*, June 17, 1974, 8. Decades later, claims would surface of radiation release from India's 1974 explosion. Perkovich cites such claims by US government officials in 1996, likely made in the context of the Comprehensive Test Ban Treaty. Perkovich, *India's Nuclear Bomb*, 180, footnote 139.

49. Chengappa, *Weapons of Peace*, 190.

50. Chidambaram and Ramanna, "Some Studies on India's Peaceful Nuclear Explosion Experiment," op. cit.

51. General Assembly resolution 3281 (XXIX) of December 12, 1974, Charter of Economic Rights and Duties of States.

52. Confidential note number 505 AS from French ambassador to India Jean-Daniel Jurgensen to Foreign Minister Jean Sauvagnargues, June 5, 1974, carton 2253, no. 15-11-5, ADF.

53. Jayaprakash Narayan returned from political retirement to lead a student and youth movement against the Gandhi government. J. P., a Gandhian freedom fighter who had fought the British and used to be close to Jawaharlal Nehru, enjoyed social and political legitimacy. This facilitated the J. P. movement's popularity. Prakash, *Emergency Chronicles*, 1.

54. Ironically, Fernandes was India's defense minister during the five nuclear weapon tests in May 1998. His opposition to the 1974 explosion was more political than the result of any moral opposition to nuclear weapons; Amitav Ghosh, "Countdown," *The New Yorker*, October 26, 1998, 190.

55. Bernard Weinraub, "India's Rail Strike Ends in Collapse," *New York Times*, May 28, 1974, 1.

56. "India: Explosion of Nuclear Device," Sitcen Series no. 3307, May 28, 1974, NATO Situation Centre, carton 2252, no. 15-11-5, ADF.

57. "Nuclear power not for attack: PM," *Times of India*, May 28, 1974, 5.

58. T. K. Mahadevan, "Swadeshi Bomb," *Times of India*, May 29, 1974, 4.

59. On India's multifaceted nuclear program as reported in the US media, see Victor McElhany, "Dozen Projects Mark India's Drive For Self-Sufficiency in Nuclear Power," *New York Times*, November 29, 1974, 63, 65.

60. "Nuclear power not for attack: PM," *Times of India*, May 28, 1974, 5.

61. Telegram TOSEC 794/104621, May 18, 1974, FRUS, 1969–76, vol. E-8, document 162.

62. "US Mission to NATO, Assessment of Indian Nuclear Test," June 5 1974, carton 2253, no. 15-11-5, ADF. Perkovich offers a few other cost estimates from interviews with Indian scientists, but those are vague and unverifiable. Perkovich, *India's Nuclear Bomb*, 181.

63. S. C. Mody, "Atomic Blast: To the Editor," *Times of India*, May 28, 1974, 4.

64. Clyde H. Farnsworth, "1.4-Billion Pledged to India by West," *New York Times*, June 15, 1974; see also Edward Cowan, "Blast by India Prompts High-Level U.S. Review of Aid," *New York Times*, May 28, 1974; Bernard Weinraub, "Increases in Aid to India in Doubt," *New York Times*, May 21, 1974.

65. "India, Badly Needing Aid, Hails Visiting Shah of Iran," *New York Times*, October 3, 1974, 3.

66. The May 1998 Indian nuclear weapon tests are known by their codename, "Operation Shakti," as well as their MEA designation, "Pokhran-II."

67. It remains unclear whether the Ramanna-Gandhi telephone call ever happened because the epithet, "Smiling Buddha," emerged in popular discussions in the Indian media nearly two decades after the 1974 nuclear explosion, in the context of the Clinton administration's unsuccessful efforts to get India to sign the NPT and the CTBT. See "Twenty Years After Pokhran: Scientists oppose US bullying, Scientists not in favour of capping N-programme," *Times of India*, May 18, 1994.

68. China had been claiming Sikkim, Bhutan, Nepal, North-East Frontier Agency (renamed Arunachal Pradesh in 1972 by India), and Tibet as its "five fingers" in its foreign policy propaganda since the 1950s.

69. Quoted in "Annexation move, says China," *Times of India*, September 4, 1974, 7.

70. "Blast: China not to make issue," *Times of India*, June 7, 1974, 1.

71. Permanent association meant greater autonomy for the monarch over the kingdom's internal matters like post and telegraph services with the possibility of accession to the United Nations with Indian support, like neighboring Bhutan had done in September 1971. It did not mean full sovereignty, as the monarch seemed to have wanted. Andrew Duff, *Sikkim: Requiem for a Himalayan Kingdom* (Edinburgh: Birlinn, 2015), 175–76.

72. Letter from Chogyal of Sikkim to Prime Minister Gandhi, August 30, 1971, SPA/FA/IN/013, EAP880/1/2/24.

73. Ibid. Author's emphasis.

74. Letter from Prime Minister Indira Gandhi to the Chogyal of Sikkim, December 4, 1971, SPA/FA/IN/013, EAP880/1/2/24.

75. Ibid.

76. G. B. S. Sidhu, *Sikkim: Dawn of Democracy* (New Delhi: Viking, 2018), 2, 16; Zorawar Daulet Singh, *Power & Diplomacy: India's Foreign Policies During the Cold War* (Delhi: Oxford University Press, 2019), 325.

77. The separatist Khalistan movement in Punjab, bordering Pakistan, that demanded a sovereign nation-state for the Sikhs grew violent in the late 1970s and 1980s with Pakistan's support.

78. B. Raman, *The Kaoboys of R&AW* (New Delhi: Lancer Publishers, 2007), 26.

79. Singh, *Power & Diplomacy*, 327.

80. Kasturi Rangan, "In Sikkim, Only the First Phase of the Crisis Seems to Be Over," *New York Times*, April 16, 1973, 3.

81. The Tripartite Agreement, May 8, 1973, SPA/FA/TR/002, EAP880/1/2/52.

82. Singh, *Power & Diplomacy*, 331.

83. "China attacks Indian take-over in Sikkim," *Times of India*, April 13, 1973, 7.

84. "China hits out at India-Sikkim pact," *Times of India*, May 14, 1973, 7.

85. "Sikkim council by week-end," *Times of India*, July 25, 1973, 7. Sidhu, who oversaw R&AW's operations in Gangtok during this period, claims that April 1974 was the earliest that elections could have been held in Sikkim because of winter weather conditions. That timeline still aligns with that of the Pokhran explosion, which was originally anticipated in February 1974, prior to elections in April. Sidhu, *Sikkim*, 172.

86. "Early Sikkim poll: Kewal Singh's hope," *Times of India*, December 4, 1973, 5.

87. "Sikkim Cong for electoral reform," *Times of India*, April 7, 1974, 7.

88. N. Ram, "Sikkim Story: Protection to Absorption," *Social Scientist* 3, no. 2 (September 1974): 57; Kasturi Rangan, "Sikkim Holds an Election, But India Will Still Rule," *New York Times*, April 21, 1974, 2.

89. "Assembly in Sikkim Approves Move to Closer Tie with India," *New York Times*, June 22, 1974, 6.

90. "Violence Reported by Ruler of Sikkim," *New York Times*, June 23, 1974, 6.

91. "Assembly in Sikkim Approves Move to Closer Tie with India," *New York Times*.

92. "Sikkim's protectorate status to go," *Times of India*, September 5, 1974.

93. Quoted in "Annexation move, says China," *Times of India*, September 4, 1974, 7.

94. Telegram 10183 from the consulate general in Hong Kong to State Department, September 13, 1974, FRUS 1969–76, volume E-8, document 254.

95. "Top-Secret CIA Research Study, Chinese-Indian Relations: 1972–1975," OPR 206, September 1975, CIA-RDP86T00608R000600170014-4.

96. Statement made on October 2, 1974, by Indian permanent representative in the UN in reply to statement of representative of People's Republic of China, SPA/FA/IN/012, EAP880/1/2/23.

97. Note on statement made on October 2, 1974 on Sikkim by permanent representative of India in the United Nations in reply to the statement of representative of People's Republic of China, October 24, 1974; letter no. 82/CL/74 from Chogyal of Sikkim to Gurbachan Singh, political officer of Sikkim, October 24, 1974, SPA/FA/IN/012, EAP880/1/2/23.

98. Briefing memorandum from the acting assistant secretary of state for Near Eastern and South Asian affairs (Sober) to Secretary of State Kissinger, September 7, 1974, FRUS 1969–76, volume E-8, document 253.

99. Marvin Kurve, "Chogyal to fight for free Sikkim," *Times of India*, March 2, 1971, 1.

100. "Sikkim CMs SOS to PM," *Times of India*, April 7, 1975, 1.

101. "Chogyal must go," *Times of India*, April 10, 1975, 1.

102. "Special Sikkim poll," *Times of India*, April 11, 1975, 1.

103. Briefing memorandum from acting assistant secretary of state for Near Eastern and South Asian affairs (Saunders) to the undersecretary of state for political affairs (Sisco), April 10, 1975, FRUS 1969–76, volume E-8, document 258.

104. "Sikkimese vote for merger with India," *Times of India*, April 16, 1975, 1; "Sikkim Votes to End Monarchy, Merge with India," *New York Times*, April 16, 1975, 3.

105. The three dissenting votes were from members of the Communist Party of India (Marxist), who were criticized for toeing the Chinese government line on Sikkim. "Parliament approves Sikkim's statehood," *Times of India*, April 27, 1975, 1.

106. "Sikkim's ex-king Virtual Prisoner," *New York Times*, December 14, 1975, 8. Hope Cooke left Sikkim in April 1973, when anti-Chogyal protests first began. Her US citizenship was reinstated by an act of Congress since she had renounced it in 1965 to become the queen of Sikkim.

107. Hope Cooke, the Chogyal's wife, left Sikkim in 1973 and published her account seven years later. Hope Cooke, *Time Change: An Autobiography* (New York: Simon & Schuster, 1980).

108. "Radio Moscow blasts Peking stand on Sikkim," *Times of India*, April 25, 1975, 7.

109. "India: Explosion of Nuclear Device," Sitcen Series no. 3307, May 28, 1974, NATO Situation Centre, carton 2252, no. 15-11-5, ADF.

110. Yellow handwritten note of Benjamin H. Brown about sending copies of the notes of the 1966 meeting, "Sent July 5 to: SADS comm.: Doty, Kaysen, Kissinger, Long, Rathjens, Schulman, Sohn, Wiesner," box 5, AMACAD.

111. Barbara Wollison (secretary to Benjamin H. Brown, Harvard University) to Carol C. Laise (deputy director of the Office of South Asian Affairs at the State Department), July 5, 1966; Barbara Wollison to Spurgeon Keeny (Executive Office of the President), July 19, 1966; Benjamin H. Brown to Alastair Buchan, July 19, 1966, box 5, AMACAD.

112. Kissinger, then a professor of government at Harvard University, met Vikram Sarabhai along with other CISAC members in October 1967 in Cambridge, Massachusetts, to informally discuss the agenda for the 1968 India-US meeting. He attended the first day of that meeting held on June 3–5, 1968, in Cambridge on "Strategic Interests and Problems of the United States and India in Asia." Months later, he was appointed advisor to President-Elect Nixon. MemCon, American Academy of Arts and Sciences, October 10, 1967; Indian-US Meeting, June 3–6, 1968, box 5, AMACAD.

113. It is impossible to confirm whether India implemented a nuclear minefield in Sikkim. However, in the 1980s, Indian scientists close to the DAE, BARC, and the Department of Space published research papers about "Chinese nuclear debris" in the Changme Khangpu glacier in northern Sikkim. In the paper, their inference that the nuclear debris was Chinese was based on the DAE's claim that there was no radioactivity from India's PNE. Alternatively, the nuclear debris could be the result of an Indian nuclear minefield. See N. Bhandari et al., "Deposition of Chinese nuclear debris in Changme Khangpu Glacier, Sikkim," *Current Science* 51, no. 8 (April 20, 1982): 416–18; V. N. Nijampurkar, N. Bhandari, and D. V. Borole, "Radiometric Chronology of Changme-Khangpu Glacier, Sikkim," *Journal of Glaciology* 31, no. 107 (1985): 28–33.

114. "Threat to India's Security," Cabinet Secretariat, Department of Cabinet Affairs (Military Wing), April 24, 1975, P. N. Haksar Papers, III, NMML.

115. "India and the Chinese Bomb," MEA, November 25, 1964, enclosure with airgram A-650, December 30, 1964, RAC, NLJ-009R-6-3-1-3, LBJL.

116. Review Conference of the Parties to the Treaty on the Nonproliferation of Nuclear weapons, Final Document, part 1, Geneva, 1975, NPT/CONF/35/I.

117. Prakash, *Emergency Chronicles*, 166–67.

118. Ibid., 165; Ray likely also knew about R&AW's operations in Sikkim as they were taking place. Sidhu, *Sikkim*, 184–85.

119. The day after the Allahabad Court's decision, Sikkim's Council of Ministers expressed their "fullest confidence" in Prime Minister Gandhi. "Sikkim has 'full confidence' in PM," *Times of India*, June 14, 1975, 7.

120. Prakash, *Emergency Chronicles*, 165.

121. Sunanda K. Datta-Ray, "One More Anniversary: Was the Emergency a Good Thing for Everyone?," *Telegraph*, June 20, 2015.

122. Prakash, *Emergency Chronicles*, 163, 167.

123. "Nos voisins et les autres pays n'ont rien à craindre de l'Inde déclare Mme Gandhi," *Le Monde*, May 28, 1974, carton 2252, no. 15-11-5, ADF.

124. Support for India's PNE also came from General Pierre-Marie Gallois. See Pierre M. Gallois, "L'Inde et le droit à la Sécurité," *Politique étrangère* 40, no. 3 (1975): 293–306.

125. Telegram from Homi Sethna to Valery Giscard d'Estaing, May 20, 1974, carton 2253, no. 15-11-5, ADF.

126. Incoming telegram no. 450/51 from French Embassy in New Delhi to French Foreign Ministry in Paris, "Interview accordee a l'ORTF," signed by Cadol, June 21, 1974, carton 2253, no. 15-11-5, ADF.

127. Outgoing telegram no. 231 from French Foreign Ministry in Paris to French Embassy in New Delhi, signed by Angles, "Protocole/ Remerciement aux felicitations addressées à M. Giscard d'Estaing," June 12, 1974, carton 2253, no. 15-11-5, ADF.

128. "France backs India's nuclear project," *The Economist*, August 22, 1974, carton 2253, no. 15-11-5, ADF.

129. Vasudev Iya and T. S. Murthy of the BARC radioisotope team that developed the trigger for the nuclear device were trained at the University of Paris in the 1950s. Anderson, *Nucleus and Nation*, 487.

130. Note pour le secretaire general, "Objet: Invitation addressee par le President de la Comission de l'energie atomique indienne a M. Giraud et Goldschmidt," Services des Affaires Scientifiques, September 2, 1974, carton 2253, no. 15-11-5, ADF.

131. On this subject, see Jayita Sarkar, "U.S. Policy to Curb West European Nuclear Exports, 1974–1978," *Journal of Cold War Studies* 21, no. 2 (Spring 2019): 110–49.

132. For the details of the renegotiation talks, see Jayita Sarkar, "From the Dependable to the Demanding Partner: The Renegotiation of French Nuclear Cooperation with India, 1974–1980," *Cold War History* 21, no. 3 (2021), advance access.

133. Kathleen Telsch, "Pakistan Disputes India on A-Arms," *New York Times*, June 8, 1974, 13.

134. Khan, *Eating Grass*, chapter 5.

135. Dragomir Bondžić, "India's Nuclear Test 1974: Reverberations in Yugoslavia," Istorija 20, veka, no. 1 (2016). Document furnished by Jovan Cavoski.

136. Siddiqi, "Spaceflight in the National Imagination," 23.

137. Confidential telegram 11304 from Ambassador Daniel P. Moynihan to Secretary of State Henry Kissinger, EXDIS, August 26, 1974, Presidential Country Files, box 12, Country File: India (3), GRFL. In 1978 and 1980, there were further Libyan attempts at seeking nuclear assistance from the DAE in return for foreign debt relief and oil, but the DAE did not provide anything substantive. Malfrid Braut-Hegghammer, *Unclear Physics: Why Iraq and Libya Failed to Build Nuclear Weapons* (Ithaca, NY: Cornell University Press, 2016); Chengappa, *Weapons of Peace*, 224–25, 289–90.

138. Ref. 103.1/1129, "Subject: the Indian nuclear explosion and its consequences," report from Yehoshua Trigor, head of the Israel Consulate in Bombay to Israel Foreign Office, August 21, 1974, 93.42.1.32, Foreign Office Files, ISA.

139. Urgent cable from Yehoshua Trigor to Mr. Veron, October 23, 1974; ref. 103.1/1793, "Subject: Discussion on India," report from Yehoshua Trigor, head of Israel Consulate in Bombay, to Mr. Veron to Israel Foreign Office, December 19, 1974, 93.42.1.32, ISA.

140. Confidential telegram from David T. Schneider at US Embassy in New Delhi to Secretary of State Henry Kissinger, NODIS, June 20, 1975, Presidential Country Files, box 12, Country File: India (3), GRFL.

141. Ibid.

142. Ibid.; on the West German-Brazil nuclear cooperation agreement, see William Glenn Gray, "Commercial Liberties and Nuclear Anxieties," *International History Review* (2012): 449–74; Dennis Romberg, "How to Further Develop the Nonproliferation Regime? West German Nuclear Exports to Brazil and Iran in Context of US Criticism," *International History Review* 40, no. 5 (2018): 1094–114.

143. Secret State Department telegram to US Embassy in New Delhi, EXDIS, July 22, 1975, Presidential Country Files, box 11, Folder: India (1), GRFL.

144. James F. Clarity, "Détente Pushed by India and Iran," *New York Times*, May 6, 1974, 9.

145. Top Secret Most Immediate, Threat Assessment, World Strategic Situation, "Threat to India's Security," Cabinet Secretariat, Department of Cabinet Affairs (Military Wing), April 24 1975, P. N. Haksar Papers, III, NMML.

146. Ibid.

147. Jacob D. Hamblin, "The Nuclearization of Iran in the Seventies," *Diplomatic History* 38, no. 5 (2014): 1117.

148. "Arab oil nations to buy N-reactors," *Times of India*, April 21, 1976, 7.

149. "India, Badly Needing Aid, Hails Visiting Shah of Iran," *New York Times*, October 3, 1974, 3.

150. Quoted in Roham Alvandi, *Nixon, Kissinger, and the Shah: The United States and Iran in the Cold War* (New York: Oxford University Press, 2014), 156.

151. G. K. Reddy, "Indo-Iranian Efforts: Nuclear Energy for Peaceful Purposes," *The Hindu* (International Edition) 1, no. 3 (December 20, 1975).

152. Christopher R. W. Dietrich, *Oil Revolution: Anticolonial Elites, Sovereign Rights, and the Economic Culture of Decolonization* (Cambridge, UK: Cambridge University Press, 2017), 264.

153. Roham Alvandi, "Introduction: Iran in the Age of Aryamehr," in *The Age of Aryamehr: Late Pahlavi Iran and Its Global Entanglements*, ed. Roham Alvandi (London: Gingko Library, 2018), 19.

154. "Iran's Move for Closer Co-operation with India," *The Hindu* (International Edition) 1, no. 3 (December 20, 1975).

155. On Iran's civilizational developmentalism, see Cyrus Schayegh, "Iran's Global Long 1970s: An Empire Project, Civilizational Developmentalism, and the Crisis of the Global North," in *Age of Aryamehr: Late Pahlavi Iran and its Global Entanglements*, ed. Roham Alvandi (London: Gingko Library, 2018), 262–91.

156. Mohammad-Hoseyn Yazdani Rad, *Dar Partgah-e Hadeseh: Zendeginameh-ye Akbar-e E'temad, bonyangozar-e sazeman-e enerzhi-ye atomi-ye Iran* (Tehran: Nashr-e Akhtaran, 2017), 313; translation by Houchang Chehabi.

157. Secular Iranian nationalism under the Shah reserved a special place for Zoroastrians in the national narrative, generating sympathy among Iranians for the Parsis of India. On the Parsi community in India, see: John R. Hinnells, "The Parsis," in *The Wiley Blackwell Companion to Zoroastrianism*, edited by Michael Stausberg and Yuhan-Sohrab-Dinshaw Vevaina (Hoboken, NJ: Wiley Blackwell, 2015), 157–172. On Parsi diaspora networks, see Afshin Marashi, *Exile and the Nation: The Parsi Community of India and the Making of Modern Iran* (Austin, TX: University of Texas, 2020).

158. Indira Gandhi's late husband, Feroze Gandhi, was a Parsi.

159. Rad, *Dar Partgah-e Hadeseh*, 315–18; see also Majid Karimi. *Salha-ye E'temad: Khaterat-e Doktor Akbar E'temad, nakhostin ra'is-e Sazeman-e Enerzhi-ye Atomi-ye Iran* (Tehran: Arvan, 2018), 162–63.

160. Rad, *Dar Partgah-e Hadeseh*, 317. Translated from Persian by Houchang Chehabi.

161. Confidential memorandum from T. K. Shoyama to minister, May 10, 1976, no. 9116-05/I3, Nuclear Cooperation with India Cab. Doc., Nuclear Power-Foreign Relations, India: General, File 4830/I 39-1, LAC.

162. Secret record of cabinet decision, meeting of May 13, 1976, Privy Council Office, serial no. 235-76RD, Nuclear Power-Foreign Relations, India: General, file 4830/I 39-1, LAC.

163. Secret circular no. 25223 marked "Immediate" from foreign secretary at MEA to Indian embassies in Vienna, Washington, United Nations, New York, Paris, London, and Moscow, May 27, 1976, Folder: Canada's termination of nuclear cooperation agreement with India, WII/110/4/76, NAI.

164. Ibid.

165. Ibid.

166. "Import of Enriched UF6 from USA—A Position Paper 13.7.76, Atomic Power Authority Note by J. C. Shah, Chairman and Chief Executive," P. N. Haksar Papers III, Subject File 316, 1976, NMML; Don Oberdofer, "US concedes probable US blast in Indian A-blast," *Washington Post*, August 9, 1976.

167. William Borders, "Mrs. Gandhi set for Soviet Visit," *New York Times*, June 6, 1976, 25.

168. "Secret/Most Immediate Memo of Ministry of External Affairs by M.A. Vellodi, Secretary (East) to AEC Chairman Homi Sethna," July 31, 1976, P. N. Haksar Papers III, Subject File 316, 1976, NMML.

169. Ibid.

170. "Soviet to Sell India Heavy Water for Use In Nuclear Program," *New York Times*, December 9, 1976, 7.

171. "Presidential Directive/NSC-8, Nuclear Nonproliferation Policy," March 24, 1977, JCPL.

172. On Sikkim, Desai publicly said that the annexation was undesirable but that he could not undo it. "Desai Defends Criticism of Sikkim's Annexation," *New York Times*, March 11, 1978, 7.

173. "Secret MEA Note prepared by M.A. Vellodi, Secretary (East), MEA for Foreign Minister with copies sent to Principal Secretary to Prime Minister, For Secretary and Chairman of AEC," July 5, 1977, WII/504/3/77, vol. 3, NAI.

174. Ibid.

175. Ibid.

176. Ibid.

177. Comprehensive or full-scope safeguards are based on the IAEA's 1972 safeguards system, explained in INFCIRC/153.

178. NSC memo for Ben Evans, executive secretary at CIA, "Enriched Uranium for India," January 24, 1979, RAC, NLC-24-93-4-1-8, JCPL.

179. Telegram no. 523/24 from French Embassy in New Delhi to French Foreign Ministry, "Surregenerateur de Kalpakkam: Fourniture d'uranium enrichi," May 7, 1979, signed by Ambassador Andre Ross, carton 2254, no. 15-11-5, ADF.

180. Telegram 1248–49 from French Embassy in Washington, DC, to French Foreign Ministry in Paris, "Objet: Relations Americano-Indiennes dans le domaine nucleaire," signed by Pierre Boyer, carton 2254, no. 15-11-5, ADF.

181. Record of discussions for the meeting of Canadian and Indian delegations on 20.3.1979 (second day), Folder: Visit to India, Mr. Klaus Goldschlag, Under Secretary of State for External Affairs, Govt. of Canada and Mr. Tom Delworth, Director General, WII/121/20/79, NAI.

182. Ibid.

183. Ben D. Wilson, manager, Government Relations and Export Licensing, General Electric, to James R. Shea, director, Office of International Programs, NRC, October 1, 1979, "Request for expedited processing -XCOM-250," Richard T. Kennedy Papers, box 33, folder 1, HIA.

184. "Indira defends Soviet action," *Times of India*, March 4, 1980, 7.

185. "Indian-Nuclear," AP news item, March 1980, AP-WX-0313 1316EST, Kennedy Papers, box 33, folder 1, HIA; "PM: N-test if needed," *Times of India*, March 14, 1980, 1.

186. Memorandum from Acting Secretary of State Christopher to President Carter, June 19, 1980, FRUS, 1977–80, volume 19, South Asia, document 189; secret memo for the president from Secretary of State Edward Muskie, September 3, 1980, RAC, NLC-7-23-7-4-8, JCPL; separate opinion of Commissioner Gilinsky, June 16, 1980, Kennedy Papers, box 33, folder 2, HIA.

187. Leonard Downie Jr., "Swiss Send Nuclear Aid to Pakistan," *Washington Post*, September 21, 1980; "Indian among N-smugglers to Pakistan," *Times of India*, December 13, 1980, 1. Confidential memo from Swiss ambassador P. Stauffer in Islamabad to the Swiss Federal Office of Foreign Trade and Payments in Bern, January 21, 1980; memo by Commissioner A. Schuwey of Swiss Federal Police in Bern, January 8, 1980; confidential memo by Monsieur Mädory at BAWI, Exportations nucléaires vers le Pakistan, December 3, 1980; Nuklear-Technologie, 1980, dossier E7115A#1990/142#2666*, SBA.

188. On Sethna-Ramanna rivalry, see Anderson, *Nucleus and Nation*, 493; Chengappa, *Weapons of Peace*, 208–12; Prime Minister Gandhi had reportedly considered conducting a nuclear test in 1976, but Kissinger dissuaded it. Chengappa, *Weapons of Peace*, 204.

189. Ibid., 207.

190. Ibid., 246.

191. Ibid., 247; "Pak N-intentions a threat, says PM," *Times of India*, April 10, 1981, 1.

192. K. Subrahmanyam, "BOMB -The Only Answer," *Times of India*, April 26, 1981, A1.

193. Judith Miller, "Cranston says India and Pakistan are preparing for nuclear testing," *New York Times*, April 28, 1981, A1.

194. "Lok Sabha questions Govt. aware of F-16 danger to BARC," *Times of India*, August 20, 1981, 19.

195. "Pakistan is being offered the F-16 as part of US military aid plan," *New York Times*, June 13, 1981, 1.

196. B. K. Joshi, "Security at Pak reactor tightened," *Times of India*, June 22, 1981, 9; "Delhi denies Pak report on N-plants," *Times of India*, July 30, 1981, 1.

197. "Unclassified Cables from US Embassy in New Delhi to State Department: Indian Press Reports Preparation for Nuclear Explosion and U.S. Attitudes Towards

It," May 5, 1981; "Indian Magazine Speculates About Nuclear Blast at Pokhran Test Site," May 12, 1982, DNSA.

198. "Pak A-blast site near Indian border," *Times of India*, January 21, 1981, 1.

199. Chengappa, *Weapons of Peace*, 253–55; "Krishan Kant for India going nuclear," August 22, 1981, 13; "N-bomb if security needs it: Janata," *Times of India*, May 3, 1981, 1.

200. Subcommittee on Nuclear Power and Electric Utilities, "Recommended Action Plan for the New Administration," sent as enclosure by F. M. Staszesky Jr. at Bechtel Power Corporation (on behalf of W. Kenneth Davis) to Michel T. Halbouty, November 4, 1980, box 91, Kennedy Papers, HIA.

201. Statement on United States Nuclear Nonproliferation Policy, July 16, 1981, Ronald Reagan Presidential Library.

202. J. N. Parimoo, "Cancun consensus on vital issues likely," *Times of India*, October 24, 1981, 1.

203. "Tarapur pact finally off," *Times of India*, November 17, 1981, 1; "India not scrapping Tarapur treaty: Lok, Sabha questions," *Times of India*, December 3, 1981, 6; "India's reported 'no' to Russia: fuel for Tarapur," *Times of India*, December 4, 1981, 9.

204. Ramanna, *Power of Promise*, 124. In 1982, the PREFRE reprocessed fuel from the CANDU reactor in Rajasthan.

205. Chengappa, *Weapons of Peace*, 255.

206. Prime Minister Indira Gandhi's state visit to France in November 1981 had facilitated the bilateral understanding needed for French fuel supply for the Tarapur reactors.

207. Chengappa, *Weapons of Peace*, 256–57. Chengappa writes that Rasgotra was shocked to hear about Pokhran test preparations. However, the test preparations were reported in the US and Indian media, and even raised on the US Senate floor in April 1981. This creates some doubt whether Rasgotra was really shocked.

208. According to Rasgotra's autobiography, Prime Minister Indira Gandhi communicated to him "three or four weeks before" her state visit to the United States that she wanted the Tarapur issue to be resolved ahead of her visit. His autobiography does not provide clear timelines of his meetings with Eagleburger and Richard Kennedy, except that those took place prior to Gandhi's visit in July 1982. Maharajakrishna Rasgotra, *A Life in Diplomacy* (New Delhi: Penguin, 2016), 327–329.

209. Bernard Gwertzman, "Lawrence Eagleburger, a Top Diplomat, Dies at 80," *New York Times*, June 4, 2011.

210. Or Rabinowitz, *Bargaining Nuclear Tests: Washington and its Cold War Deals* (New York, NY: Oxford University Press, 2014), 120–21, 146, 180. Rabinowitz finds no clear evidence for a no-test bargain in the case of India in the 1980s. She quotes Perkovich who, based on unattributable interviews, claims the test preparations took place in 1982–83 and that it was unclear why Prime Minister Gandhi canceled the test. Perkovich, *India's Nuclear Bomb*, 242.

211. Rabinowitz, *Bargaining Nuclear Tests*, 88; Lawrence Eagleburger was Kissinger's top aide in early 1969, months before the Nixon-Meir deal. He then served at the US NATO Mission, only to return as Kissinger's executive assistant from 1973 when Kissinger was appointed secretary of state.

212. Or Rabinowitz and Nicholas L. Miller, "Keeping the Bombs in the Basement: U.S. Nonproliferation Policy toward Israel, South Africa, and Pakistan," *International Security* 40, no. 1 (Summer 2015): 47–86.

213. Preventing future South African nuclear tests was important to US policymakers in light of the 1979 Vela incident. See "Blast from the Past," *Foreign Policy* (September 2019).

214. Rabinowitz, *Bargaining Nuclear Tests*, 88, 120.

215. "Aid will stop if Pindi explodes A-bomb: Buckley," *Times of India*, November 14, 1981, 9.

216. Both FRUS documents on South Asia and Reagan Library documents on India remain classified as of May 2021.

217. "Another N-blast ruled out by PM," *Times of India*, May 13, 1982, 1.

218. Secret State Department memo to Richard Kennedy, "Tarapur: Your Meeting With Foreign Secretary Rasgotra, 10:30 a.m., Friday, July 23," dated July 23, 1982, DNSA.

219. Briefing memorandum to Kennedy from Nicholas Veliotes and James L. Malone, "Your Meeting with Prime Minister Indira Gandhi's Principal Secretary P.C. Alexander and Indian Foreign Secretary M.K. Rasgotra, Thursday, July 29, at 8:15 a.m.," dated July 25, 1982, DNSA.

220. Bernard Weinraub, "Reagan and Mrs. Gandhi resolve dispute for nuclear fuel for India," *New York Times*, July 30, 1982.

221. "India has no N-arms, asserts PM," *Times of India*, July 31, 1982, 1.

222. Memo from Secretary of State George Shultz to President Ronald Reagan, July 19, 1982, visit of Indira Gandhi, July 29, DNSA.

223. Philip Taubman, "Shultz tells India that U.S. will drop reactor-parts ban," *New York Times*, July 1, 1983.

224. Sanjoy Hazarika, "French sign an accord with India to fuel US-built nuclear plant," *New York Times*, November 28, 1982.

225. Chengappa, *Weapons of Peace*, 248–53.

226. Ibid., chapter 17.

227. Ramana, *Power of Promise*, 57, 62.

228. Homi N. Sethna, oral history, NMML.

229. Kaviraj, "An Outline of a Revisionist Theory of Modernity," 518.

Epilogue

1. Indrani Bagchi, "India enters nuclear club after high voltage diplomacy," *Times of India*, September 7, 2008; "Welcome to the nuclear club, India," *Financial Times*, September 22, 2008; Somini Sengupta and Mark Mazetti, "Atomic Club Votes to End Restrictions on India," *New York Times*, September 6, 2008.

2. See for example: Prerna Gupta and M.V. Ramana, "A Decade After the Nuclear Deal," *India Forum*, 26 May 2019.

3. M. V. Ramana and Suvrat Raju, "Nuclear safety before vendor interests," *Hindu*, October 30, 2012.

4. Monamie Bhadra, "Fighting Nuclear Energy, Fighting for India's Democracy," *Science as Culture* 22, no. 2 (2013): 238–46.

5. Arun Janardhanan, "8,856 'enemies of state': An entire village in Tamil Nadu lives under shadow of sedition," *Indian Express*, September 12, 2016.

6. Sheila Jasanoff, "Ordering knowledge, Ordering society," in *States of Knowledge: The Co-Production of Science and Social Order*, ed. Sheila Jasanoff (New York: Routledge, 2004), 17.

7. A. Gopalakrishnan, "Issues of Nuclear Safety," *Frontline*, March 13, 1999.

8. Country profile: India, IAEA, PRIS, accessed May 11, 2021, https://pris.iaea.org/PRIS/CountryStatistics/CountryDetails.aspx?current=IN.

9. Country profile: India, International Panel on Fissile Materials, accessed May 11, 2021, http://fissilematerials.org/countries/india.html.

10. "India's prototype breeder reactor is delayed again," International Panel on Fissile Materials Blog, 12 March 2020, http://fissilematerials.org/blog/2020/03/indias_prototype_breeder.html (last accessed September 24, 2021).

11. M. V. Ramana, *The Power of Promise: Examining Nuclear Energy in India* (New Delhi: Viking, 2012), 249.

12. The uniqueness of the 1998 tests lay in the fact that they brought Pakistan's nuclear weapons out into the open.

13. Amitav Ghosh, "Countdown," *The New Yorker*, October 26, 1998, 188.

14. Chinky Shukla, "Life at Ground Zero," Photo Essay, *Caravan*, 1 May 2019.

15. Shelia Jasanoff and Sang-Hyun Kim, "Containing the Atom: Sociotechnical Imaginaries and Nuclear Power in the United States and South Korea," *Minerva* 47, no. 2 (2009): 120.

16. V. M. Abijith, "Why is Kerala's Alappad village getting eaten up by the sea?," *Times of India*, January 17, 2019.

17. Hans M. Kristensen and Matt Korda, "Indian nuclear forces," *Bulletin of the Atomic Scientists* 76, no. 4 (2020): 217–25.

18. Karthika Sasikumar, "India's Surgical Strikes: Response to Strategic Imperatives," *The Round Table* 108, no. 2 (2019): 159–74; "Sikkim: Chinese and Indian troops 'in new border clash'" *BBC*, January 25, 2021.

19. Shivshankar Menon, *Choices: Inside the Making of India's Foreign Policy* (Washington, DC: Brookings Institution Press, 2016), chapter 5; Toby Dalton, "Much Ado About India's No-first-use Nuke Policy," *India Global Business*, September 26, 2019.

Bibliography

Archives Cited with Source Abbreviations

Onsite Repositories

Austria

IAEA: International Atomic Energy Agency Archives, Vienna

Canada

LAC: Library and Archives of Canada, Ottawa

France

ADF: Centre des Archives Diplomatiques de la Courneuve
   Direction Asie-Océanie
ANF: Archives Nationales Françaises, Paris
   Fonds Raoul Dautry
BnF-FJC: Bibliothèque Nationale de France, Paris
   Fonds Frédéric Joliot-Curie, Institut Curie

India

NAI: National Archives of India, New Delhi
   Ministry of External Affairs Files
   Prime Minister's Secretariat Files
   Sardar Vallabhbhai Patel Papers
NMML: Nehru Memorial Museum and Library, New Delhi
   Homi J. Bhabha Papers
   T. N. Kaul Papers
   Ashok Mitra Papers
   Pitambar Pant Papers
   P. N. Haksar Papers
   P. N. Dhar Papers
TCA: Tata Central Archives, Pune
TIFR: Tata Institute of Fundamental Research Archives, Mumbai
SINP: Saha Institute of Nuclear Physics Archives, Kolkata
   Meghnad Saha Papers

Israel
ISA: Israel State Archives, Jerusalem

Switzerland
SBA: Schweizerische Bundesarchiv

United Kingdom
UKNA: United Kingdom National Archives, Kew
—: Churchill Archives Centre, University of Cambridge (not abbreviated)
    James Chadwick Papers
    John D. Cockcroft Papers

United States
AMACAD: American Academy of Arts and Sciences, Cambridge, Massachusetts
DDEL: Dwight D. Eisenhower Presidential Library, Abilene, Kansas
—: George C. Marshall Foundation, Lexington, Virginia (not abbreviated)
    William Douglas Pawley Papers
GRFL: Gerald R. Ford Presidential Library, Ann Arbor, Michigan
HIA: Hoover Institution Archives, Palo Alto, California
    Richard T. Kennedy Papers
JCPL: Jimmy Carter Presidential Library, Atlanta, Georgia
JFKL: John F. Kennedy Presidential Library, Boston, Massachusetts
LBJL: Lyndon B. Johnson Presidential Library, Austin, Texas
LOC: Library of Congress, Washington, DC
    Daniel P. Moynihan Papers
    Glenn T. Seaborg Papers
NARA: National Archives and Records Administration, College Park, Maryland
—: Yale University Library, Manuscript Collections (not abbreviated)
    Chester Bowles Papers

Digitized Collections

CIA-RDP: CIA Records Search Tool
DNSA: Digital National Security Archive
FRUS: Foreign Relations of the United States
Lok Sabha Debates, Lok Sabha Secretariat, New Delhi (not abbreviated)
NYT: *New York Times*, Times Machine
NPIHP: Nuclear Proliferation International History Project
SPA/EAP: Sikkim Palace Archives, Endangered Archives Programme, British
    Library
SWJN: Selected Works of Jawaharlal Nehru, NMML
TOI: *Times of India*, ProQuest
WaPo: *Washington Post*

Published Collections in Print

Bhasin, Avtar Singh. *India-China Relations 1947–2000: A Documentary Study*. New Delhi: Geetika Publishers, 2018.

Maurice Vaïsse. *Documents Diplomatiques Français—Depuis 1954*. Bern: Peter Lang, 2009.

Secondary Sources

Books and Monographs

Abraham, Itty. *The Making of the Indian Atomic Bomb: Science, Secrecy and the Postcolonial State*. New York: Zed Books, 1998.

Akhtar, Rabia. *The Blind Eye: U.S. Non-Proliferation Policy towards Pakistan from Ford to Clinton*. Lahore, Pakistan: University of Lahore Press, 2018.

Alvandi, Roham. *Nixon, Kissinger, and the Shah: The United States and Iran in the Cold War*. Oxford, UK: Oxford University Press, 2014.

Anderson, Robert S. *Nucleus and Nation: Scientists, International Networks and Power in India*. Chicago: University of Chicago Press, 2010

Bass, Gary. *The Blood Telegram: Nixon, Kissinger and a Forgotten Genocide*. New York: Alfred A. Knopf, 2013.

Black, Megan. *The Global Interior: Mineral Frontiers and American Power*. Cambridge, MA: Harvard University Press, 2018.

Bothwell, Robert. *Nucleus: The History of Atomic Energy of Canada Limited*. Toronto: University of Toronto Press, 1989.

Braut-Hegghammer, Malfrid. *Unclear Physics: Why Iraq and Libya Failed to Build Nuclear Weapons*. Ithaca, NY: Cornell University Press, 2016.

Chatterjee, Partha. *Nationalist Thought and the Colonial World: A Derivative Discourse?*. London: Zed Books, 1986.

Chatterjee, Partha. *The Truths and Lies of Nationalism as Narrated by Charvak*. New Delhi: Orient Black Swan, 2021.

Chaudhuri, Rudra. *Forged in Crisis: India and the United States since 1947*. New York: Oxford University Press, 2014.

Chowdhury, Indira. *Growing the Tree of Science: Homi Bhabha and the Tata Institute of Fundamental Research*. Oxford, UK: Oxford University Press, 2016.

Chowdhury, Indira, and Ananya Dasgupta. *Masterful Spirit: Homi J. Bhabha, 1909–1966*. New Delhi: Penguin, 2010.

Chengappa, Raj. *Weapons of Peace: Secret Story of India's Quest to Be a Nuclear Power*. New Delhi: Harper Collins, 2000.

Cohen, Stephen P. *India: Emerging Power*. Oxford, UK: Oxford University Press, 2001.

Craig, Campbell, and Fredrik Logevall. *America's Cold War: The Politics of Insecurity*. Cambridge, MA: Belknap Press of Harvard University Press, 2009; rev. ed., 2020.

Craig, Malcolm M. *America, Britain and Pakistan's Nuclear Weapons Programme, 1974–1980*. London: Palgrave Macmillan, 2017.

Cullather, Nick. *Hungry World: America's Cold War Battle Against Poverty in Asia*. Cambridge, MA: Harvard University Press, 2010.

Datta-Ray, Sunanda. *Smash and Grab: Annexation of Sikkim*. New Delhi: Vikas, 1984.

Debs, Alexandre, and Nuno Monteiro. *Nuclear Politics: The Strategic Causes of Proliferation*. Cambridge, UK: Cambridge University Press, 2016.

Dietrich, Christopher R. W. *Oil Revolution: Anticolonial Elites, Sovereign Rights, and the Economic Culture of Decolonization*. Cambridge, UK: Cambridge University Press, 2017.

Dixit, J. N. *My South Block Years: Memoirs of a Foreign Secretary*. New Delhi: UBS Publishers' Distributors, 1996.

Duff, Andrew. *Sikkim: Requiem for a Himalayan Kingdom*. Edinburgh: Birlinn, 2017.

Engerman, David. *The Price of Aid: The Economic Cold War in India*. Cambridge, MA: Harvard University Press, 2018.

Friedman. Jeremy. *Shadow Cold War: The Sino-Soviet Competition for the Third World*. Chapel Hill, NC: University of North Carolina, 2015.

Garavini, Giuliano. *The Rise and Fall of OPEC in the Twentieth Century*. Oxford, UK: Oxford University Press, 2019.

Gavin, Francis J. *Nuclear Statecraft: History and Strategy in America's Atomic Age*. Ithaca, NY: Cornell University Press, 2012.

Getachew, Adom. *Worldmaking after Empire: The Rise and Fall of Self-Determination*. Princeton, NJ: Princeton University Press, 2019.

Goldschmidt, Bertrand. *The Atomic Complex: A Worldwide Political History of Nuclear Energy*. La Grange, IL: American Nuclear Society, 1982.

Gordin, Michael. *Red Cloud at Dawn: Truman, Stalin, and the End of the Atomic Monopoly*. New York: Farrar, Straus and Giroux, 2009.

Goswami, Manu. *Producing India. From Colonial Economy to National Space*. Chicago, IL: University of Chicago Press, 2004.

Goudsmit, Samuel A. *Alsos*. Woodbury, NY: American Institute of Physics, 1947.

Guyot-Réchard, Bérénice. *Shadow States: India, China and the Himalayas, 1910–1962*. Cambridge, UK: University of Cambridge Press, 2016.

Guha, Ramchandra. *India After Gandhi: The History of the World's Largest Democracy*. New Delhi: Harper Collins, 2007.

Hamblin, Jacob D. *The Wretched Atom: America's Global Gamble with Peaceful Nuclear Technology*. New York: Oxford University Press, 2021.

Hecht, Gabrielle. *Being Nuclear. Africans and the Global Uranium Trade*. Cambridge, MA: MIT Press, 2014.

Hecht, Gabrielle. *The Radiance of France: Nuclear Power and National Identity after World War II*. Cambridge, MA: MIT Press, 1998.

Helmreich, Jonathan E. *Gathering Rare Ores: The Diplomacy of Uranium Acquisition, 1943–1954*. Princeton, NJ: Princeton University Press, 1986.

Holloway, David. *Stalin and the Bomb: The Soviet Union and Atomic Energy, 1939–1956*. New Haven, CT: Yale University Press, 1994.

Hymans, Jacques E. *The Psychology of Nuclear Proliferation*. Cambridge, UK: Cambridge University Press, 2006.

Jansen, Jan C., and Jürgen Osterhammel. *Decolonization: A Short History*. Princeton, NJ: Princeton University Press, 2017.

Jervis, Robert. *The Meaning of the Nuclear Revolution: Statecraft and the Prospect of Armageddon*. Ithaca, NY: Cornell University Press, 1989.

Kaufman, Scott. *Project Plowshare: The Peaceful Use of Nuclear Explosives in Cold War America*. Ithaca, NY: Cornell University Press, 2012.

Kaul, Triloki Nath. *The Kissinger Years: Indo-American Relations*. New Delhi: Arnold-Heinemann, 1980.

Khan, Feroz Hassan. *Eating Grass: The Making of the Pakistani Bomb*. Palo Alto, CA: Stanford University Press, 2013.

Khilnani, Sunil. *The Idea of India*. New Delhi: Penguin, 1997.

Klinger, Julie Michelle. *Rare Earth Frontiers: From Terrestrial Subsoils to Lunar Landscapes*. Ithaca, NY: Cornell University Press, 2017.

Krige, John. *Sharing Knowledge, Shaping Europe: U.S. Technological Collaboration and Nonproliferation*. Cambridge, MA: MIT Press, 2016.

Kumar, A. Vinod. *India and the Nuclear Non-proliferation Regime: The Perennial Outlier*. Cambridge, UK: Cambridge University Press, 2014.

Kux, Dennis. *India and the United States: Estranged Democracies, 1941–1991*. Washington, DC: National Defense University Press, 1993.

Leake, Elisabeth. *The Afghan Crucible. The Soviet Invasion and the Making of Modern Afghanistan*. Oxford, UK: Oxford University Press, 2022.

Leake, Elisabeth. *The Defiant Border: The Afghan-Pakistan Borderlands in the Era of Decolonization, 1936–1965*. Cambridge, UK: Cambridge University Press, 2016.

Lüthi, Lorenz M. *Cold Wars: Asia, Middle East, Europe*. Cambridge, UK: Cambridge University Press, 2020.

Lüthi, Lorenz M. *The Sino-Soviet Split. Cold War in the Communist World*. Princeton, NJ: Princeton University Press, 2008.

Madan, Tanvi. *The Fateful Triangle: How China Shaped U.S.-India Relations during the Cold War*. Washington, DC: Brookings Institution, 2020.

Maddock, Shane J. *Nuclear Apartheid: The Quest for American Atomic Supremacy from World War II to the Present*. Chapel Hill, NC: University of North Carolina Press, 2010.

McGarr, Paul. *The Cold War in South Asia: Britain, the United States and the Indian Subcontinent, 1945–1965*. Cambridge, UK: Cambridge University Press, 2013.

McMahon, Robert J. *The Cold War on the Periphery: The United States, India, and Pakistan*. New York: Columbia University Press, 1994.

Menon, Shivshankar. *Choices: Inside the Making of India's Foreign Policy*. Washington, DC: Brookings Institution Press, 2016.

Miller, Manjari Chatterjee. *Wronged by Empire: Post-Imperial Ideology and Foreign Policy in India and China*. Palo Alto, CA: Stanford University Press, 2013.

Miller, Nicholas. *Stopping the Bomb: The Sources and Effectiveness of US Nonproliferation Policy*. Ithaca, NY: Cornell University Press, 2018.

Mukherjee, Anit. *The Absent Dialogue. Politicians, Bureaucrats, and the Military in India*. Oxford, UK: Oxford University Press, 2019.

Namakkal, Jessica. *Unsettling Utopia: The Making and Unmaking of French India*. New York: Columbia University Press, 2021.

Nehru, Jawaharlal. *The Discovery of India*. New Delhi: Oxford University Press, 1985, 1946.

Paliwal, Avinash. *My Enemy's Enemy: India in Afghanistan from the Soviet Invasion to the US Withdrawal*. Oxford, UK: Oxford University Press, 2017.

Phalkey, Jahnavi. *Atomic State: Big Science in Twentieth-Century India*. New Delhi: Permanent Black, 2013.

Perkovich, George. *India's Nuclear Bomb: The Impact on Global Proliferation*. Los Angeles: University of California Press, 1999.

Prakash, Gyan. *Another Reason: Science and the Imagination of Modern India*. Princeton, NJ: Princeton University Press, 1999.

Prakash, Gyan. *Emergency Chronicles: Indira Gandhi and Democracy's Turning Point*. Princeton, NJ: Princeton University Press, 2019.

Rabinowitz, Or. *Bargaining Nuclear Tests: Washington and Its Cold War Deals*. New York: Oxford University Press, 2014.

Raghavan, Pallavi. *Animosity at Bay: An Alternative History of the India-Pakistan Relationship, 1947–1952*. New York: Oxford University Press, 2020.

Raghavan, Srinath. *1971: A Global History*. Cambridge, MA: Harvard University Press, 2013.

Raghavan, Srinath. *Fierce Enigmas: A History of the United States in South Asia*. New York: Basic Books, 2018.

Raghavan, Srinath. *India's War: World War II and the Making of Modern South Asia*. New York: Basic Books, 2016.

Raghavan, Srinath. *War and Peace in Modern India*. Ranikhet, India: Permanent Black, 2010.

Raianu, Mircea. *Tata: The Global Corporation that Built Indian Capitalism*. Cambridge, MA: Harvard University Press, 2021.

Raj, Gopal. *Reach for the Stars: The Evolution of India's Rocket Program*. New Delhi: Viking, 2000.

Ramana, M. V. *The Power of Promise: Examining Nuclear Energy in India*. New Delhi: Viking, 2012.

Ramanna, Raja. *Years of Pilgrimage, an Autobiography*. New York: Viking, 1991.

Rasgotra, M. *A Life in Diplomacy*. Gurgaon: Penguin, 2016.

Rotter, Andrew. *Comrades at Odds: The United States and India, 1947–1964*. Ithaca, NY: Cornell University Press, 2000.

Sargent, Daniel J. *A Superpower Transformed: The Remaking of American Foreign Relations in the 1970s*. Oxford, UK: Oxford University Press, 2015.

Seaborg, Glenn T. *Stemming the Tide: Arms Control in the Johnson Years*. Toronto: Lexington, 1987.

Shah, Amrita. *Vikram Sarabhai: A Life*. New Delhi: Penguin, 2007.

Sidhu, G. B. S. *Sikkim: Dawn of Democracy*. New Delhi: Viking, 2018.

Singh, Zorawar Daulet. *Power and Diplomacy: India's Foreign Policies During the Cold War*. New Delhi: Oxford University Press, 2019.

Tata Institute of Fundamental Research. *Homi Jehangir Bhabha on Indian Science and the Atomic Energy Programme: A Selection*. Mumbai: TIFR, 2009.

Tellis, Ashley. *India's Emerging Nuclear Posture: Between Recessed Deterrent and Ready Arsenal*. Washington, DC: RAND, 2001.

van Schendel, Willem. *A History of Bangladesh*. Cambridge, UK: Cambridge University Press, 2009.

Wellerstein, Alex. *Restricted Data: The History of Nuclear Secrecy in the United States*. Chicago: University of Chicago Press, 2021.

Westad, Odd Arne. *The Cold War: A World History*. New York: Basic Books, 2017.

Westad, Odd Arne. *The Global Cold War: Third World Interventions and the Making of Our Times*. Cambridge, UK: Cambridge University Press, 2012.

Wohlstetter, Albert, T. A. Brown, G. Jones, D. C. McGarvey, H. Rowen, and R. Wohlstetter. *Swords from Ploughshares: The Military Potential of Civilian Nuclear Energy*. Chicago: University of Chicago Press, 1977.

Edited Volumes

Abraham, Itty. *South Asian Cultures of the Bomb: Atomic Publics and the State in India and Pakistan*. Bloomington, IN: Indiana University Press, 2009.

Alvandi, Roham. *The Age of Aryamehr: Late Pahlavi Iran and Its Global Entanglements*. London: Gingko Library, 2018.

Bhagavan, Manu. *India and the Cold War*. Chapel Hill, NC: University of North Carolina Press, 2019.

Mian, Zia, and Ashis Nandy. *The Nuclear Debate: Ironies and Immoralities*. Colombo, Sri Lanka: Regional Centre for Strategic Studies, 1998.

Ramana, M. V., and C. Rammanohar Reddy. *Prisoners of the Nuclear Dream*. Hyderabad: Orient Longman, 2003.

Sagan, Scott D. *Inside Nuclear South Asia*. Palo Alto, CA: Stanford University Press, 1999.

Articles and Book Chapters

Abraham, Itty. "Contra-proliferation: Interpreting the meaning of India's nuclear tests in 1974 and 1998." In *Inside Nuclear South Asia*, edited by Scott D. Sagan, 110–111. Stanford, CA: Stanford University Press, 1999.

Abraham, Itty. "India's 'Strategic Enclave': Civilian Scientists and Military Technologies." *Armed Forces & Society* 18, no. 2 (1992): 231–52.

Abraham, Itty. "Rare Earths: The Cold War in the annals of Travancore." In *Entangled Geographies: Empire and Technopolitics in the Global Cold War*, edited by Gabrielle Hecht, 101–24. Cambridge, MA: MIT Press, 2011.

Abraham, Itty. "The Ambivalence of Nuclear Histories." *Osiris* 21 (2006): 49–65.

Ahlberg, Kristin. "'Machiavelli with a Heart': The Johnson Administration's Food for Peace Program in India, 1965–1966." *Diplomatic History* 31, no. 4 (September 2007): 665–701.

Anstey, Isabelle. "Negotiating Nuclear Control: The Zangger Committee and the Nuclear Suppliers' Group in the 1970s." *International History Review* 40, no. 5 (2018): 975–95.

Bajpai, Kanti. "BJP and the Bomb." In *Inside Nuclear South Asia*, edited by Scott D. Sagan, 25–67. Palo Alto, CA: Stanford University Press, 2009.

Bajpai, Kanti. "Indian Strategic Culture." In *South Asia in 2020: Future Strategic Balances and Alliances*, edited by Michael R. Chambers, 245–304 Carlisle, PA: US Army War College, 2002.

Basrur, Rajesh. "Nuclear Weapons and Indian Strategic Culture." *Journal of Peace Research* 38, no. 2 (March 2001): 181–98.

Bhabha, Homi J. "Science and the problems of development." *Science* 15 (1966): 541–48.

Burr, William. "A Scheme of 'Control': The United States and the Origins of the Nuclear Suppliers' Group, 1974–1976." *International History Review* 36, no. 2 (2014): 252276.

Burr, William, and Jeffrey T. Richelson. "Whether to 'Strangle the Baby in the Cradle': The United States and the Chinese Nuclear Program, 1960–1964." *International Security* 25, no. 3 (Winter 2000/2001): 54–99.

Chakrabarty, Dipesh. "The Legacies of Bandung: Decolonization and the Politics of Culture." In *Making a World After Empire: The Bandung Moment and its Political Afterlives*, edited by Christopher J. Lee, 43–68 Athens, OH: Ohio University Press, 2010.

Chaudhuri, Rudra. "The Making of an 'All Weather Friendship': Pakistan, China and the History of a Border Agreement: 1949–1963." *The International History Review* 40, no. 1 (2018): 41–64.

Chidambaram, R., and Raja Ramanna. "Some Studies on India's Peaceful Nuclear Explosion Experiment." In *Proceedings of a Technical Committee, Vienna, 20–24 January 1975, Peaceful Nuclear Explosions IV*. Vienna: IAEA, August 1975.

Cullather, Nick. "Development and Technopolitics." In *Explaining the History of American Foreign Relations*, edited by Frank Costigliola and Michael J. Hogan, 102–18. New York: Cambridge University Press, 2016.

Drogan, Mara. "The Nuclear Imperative: Atoms for Peace and the Development of US Policy on Exporting Nuclear Power, 1953–1955." *Diplomatic History* 40 no. 5 (2015): 948–74.

Fifield, Russell H. "The Future of French India." *Far Eastern Survey* 19, no. 6 (1950): 62–64.

Franczak, Michael. "Losing the Battle, Winning the War: Neoconservatives versus the New International Economic Order, 1974–82." *Diplomatic History* 43, no. 5 (November 2019): 867–89.

Gallois, Pierre M. "L'Inde et le droit à la sécurité." *Politique étrangère* 40, no. 3 (1975): 293–306.

Ganguly, Šumit. "India's Pathway to Pokhran II: The Prospects and Sources of New Delhi's Nuclear Weapons Program." *International Security* 23, no. 4 (Spring 1999): 148–77.

Ganguly, Šumit. "Of Great Expectations and Bitter Disappointments: Indo-U.S. Relations under the Johnson Administration." *Asian Affairs* 15, no. 4 (Winter, 1988/1989): 212–19.

Ganguly, Šumit. "Why India Joined the Nuclear Club." *Bulletin of the Atomic Scientists* (April 1983): 30–33.

Garavini, Giuliano. "Completing Decolonization: The 1973 'Oil Shock' and the Struggle for Economic Rights." *The International History Review* 33, no. 3 (2011): 473–87.

Gavin, Francis J. "Blasts from the Past: Proliferation from the 1960s." *International Security* 29, no. 3 (Winter 2004/2005): 100–135.

Ghosh, Amitav. "Countdown." *The New Yorker*, October 26, 1998.

Goldschmidt, Bertrand. "Les Problèmes Nucléaires Indiens." *Politique étrangère* 47, no. 3 (1982): 617–31.

Hamblin, Jacob D. "The Nuclearization of Iran in the Seventies." *Diplomatic History* 38, no. 5 (2014): 1114–35.

Hecht, Gabrielle, and Paul N. Edwards. "'The Technopolitics of Cold War': Towards a Transregional Perspective." In *Essays on Twentieth Century History*, edited by Michael Adas, 271–314. Philadelphia: Temple University Press, 2010.

Jasanoff, Sheila, and Sang-Hyun Kim. "Containing the Atom: Sociotechnical Imaginaries and Nuclear Power in the United States and South Korea." *Minerva* 47, no. 2 (2009): 119–46.

Jasanoff, Sheila. "Ordering knowledge, Ordering society." In *States of Knowledge: The Co-Production of Science and Social Order*, edited by Sheila Jasanoff, 13–45. New York: Routledge, 2004.

Joshi, Yogesh. "Between Principles and Pragmatism: India and the Nuclear Non-Proliferation Regime in the Post-PNE Era, 1974–1980." *International History Review* 40, no. 5 (2018): 1073–93.

Joshi, Yogesh. "The Imagined Arsenal: India's Nuclear Decision-Making, 1973–76." *Nuclear Proliferation International History Project Working Paper #6.* Woodrow Wilson Center, 2015.

Kampani, Gaurav. "New Delhi's Long Nuclear Journey: How Secrecy and Institutional Roadblocks Delayed India's Weaponization." *International Security* 38, no. 4 (Spring 2014): 79–114.

Kaviraj, Sudipta. "An Outline of a Revisionist Theory of Modernity." *European Journal of Sociology* 46, no. 3 (2005): 497–526.

Kennedy, Andrew. "India's Nuclear Odyssey: Implicit Umbrellas, Diplomatic Disappointments, and the Bomb." *International Security* 36, no. 2 (Fall 2011): 120–53.

Krige, John. "Atoms for Peace, Scientific Internationalism, and Scientific Intelligence." *Osiris* 21 no. 1 (2006): 161–81.

Krige, John, and Jayita Sarkar. "US Technological Collaboration for Nonproliferation: Key Evidence from the Cold War." *Nonproliferation Review* 25, no. 3–4 (2018): 249–62.

Krishna, Sankaran. "Cartographic anxiety: Mapping the body politic in India." *Alternatives* 19, no. 4 (1994): 507–21.

Leake, Elisabeth. "Where National and International Meet: Borders and Border Regions in Postcolonial India," *International History Review*, 2021, advance access.

Leslie, Stuart W. "Atomic structures: the architecture of nuclear nationalism in India and Pakistan." *History and Technology* 31, no. 3 (2015): 220–42.

Logevall, Fredrik. "Domestic Politics." In *Explaining the History of American Foreign Relations*, edited by Frank Costigliola and Michael J. Hogan, 151–67. New York: Cambridge University Press, 2016.

Maharaj, Ashok. "An Overview of NASA-India Relations." In *NASA in the World: Fifty Years of International Collaboration*, edited by John Krige, Angelina Long Callahan, and Ashok Maharaj, 211–34. New York: Palgrave MacMillan, 2013.

Maier, Charles S. "Consigning the Twentieth Century to History: Alternative Narratives for the Modern Era." *American Historical Review* 105, no. 3 (June 2000): 807–31.

Mastny, Vojtech. "The Soviet Union's Partnership with India." *Journal of Cold War Studies* 12, no. 3 (2010): 67.

Miller, Nicholas L. "Nuclear Dominoes: A Self-Defeating Prophecy?" *Security Studies* 23, no. 1 (2014): 33–73.

Mistry, Dinshaw & Bharath Gopalaswamy. "Ballistic Missiles and Space Launch Vehicles in Regional Powers," *Astropolitics* 10, no. 2 (2012): 126–51.

Moynihan, Daniel Patrick. "The United States in Opposition," *Commentary*, March 1975.

Mukherjee, Rohan. "Nuclear Ambiguity and International Status: India in the Eighteen-Nation Committee on Disarmament, 1962–1969." In *India and the Cold War*, edited by Manu Bhagavan, 126–50. Chapel Hill, NC: University of North Carolina Press, 2019.

Namakkal, Jessica. "The Terror of Decolonization: Exploring French India's 'Goonda Raj.'" *Interventions* 19, no. 3 (2017): 338–57.

Narang, Vipin. "Strategies of Nuclear Proliferation: How States Pursue the Bomb." *International Security* 41, no. 3 (Winter 2016/2017): 110–50.

Noorani, A. G. "India's Quest for a Nuclear Guarantee." *Asian Survey* 7, no. 7 (1967): 490–502.

Pelopidas, Benoît. "The Oracles of Proliferation: How Experts Maintain a Biased Historical Reading that Limits Policy Innovation." *Nonproliferation Review* 18, no. 1 (2011): 297–314.

Rabinowitz, Or, and Nicholas L. Miller. "Keeping the Bombs in the Basement: U.S. Nonproliferation Policy toward Israel, South Africa, and Pakistan." *International Security* 40, no. 1 (Summer 2015): 47–86.

Raianu, Mircea. "The Incorporation of India: The Tata Business Firm Between Empire and Nation, ca. 1860–1970." *Enterprise & Society* 19, no. 4 (December 2018): 816–25.

Raja Mohan, C. "India: Between 'Strategic Autonomy' and 'Geopolitical Opportunity.'" *Asia Policy* no. 15 (January 2013): 21–25.

Sagan, Scott D. "Why Do States Build Nuclear Weapons? Three Models in Search of a Bomb." *International Security* 21, no. 3 (Winter 1996–1997): 65–69.

Sarkar, Jayita. "From the Dependable to the Demanding Partner: The Renegotiation of French Nuclear Cooperation with India, 1974–1980." *Cold War History* 21, no. 3 (2021): 301–18.

Sarkar, Jayita. "The Making of a Non-Aligned Nuclear Power: India's Proliferation Drift, 1964–8." *The International History Review* 37, no. 5 (2015): 933–50.

Sarkar, Jayita. "U.S. Policy to Curb West European Nuclear Exports, 1974–1978." *Journal of Cold War Studies* 21, no. 2 (Spring 2019): 110–49.

Sarkar, Jayita. "'Wean them away from French Tutelage': Franco-Indian Nuclear Relations and Anglo-American Anxieties during the Early Cold War, 1948–1952." *Cold War History* 15, no. 3 (2015): 389–92.

Sasikumar, Karthika. "India's Surgical Strikes: Response to Strategic Imperatives." *The Round Table* 108, no. 2 (2019): 159–74.

Schayegh, Cyrus. "Iran's Global Long 1970s: An Empire Project, Civilizational Developmentalism, and the Crisis of the Global North." In *Age of Aryamehr: Late Pahlavi Iran and its Global Entanglements*, edited by Roham Alvandi, 262–91. London: Gingko Library, 2018.

Siddiqi, Asif A. "Another global history of science: making space for India and China." *British Journal for the History of Science* 1 (2016): 115–43.

Siddiqi, Asif A. "Making Space for the Nation: Satellite Television, Indian Scientific Elites, and the Cold War." *Comparative Studies of South Asia, Africa and the Middle East* 35, no. 1 (2015): 35–49.

Siddiqi, Asif A. "Spaceflight in the National Imagination." In *Remembering the Space Age*, edited by Steven J. Dick, 17–35. Washington, DC: National Aeronautics and Space Administration, 2008.

Siddiqi, Asif A. "Whose India? SITE and the origins of satellite television in India." *History and Technology* 36, no. 3–4 (2020): 452–74.

Szalontai, Balázs. "The Elephant in the Room: The Soviet Union and India's Nuclear Program, 1967–1989." *Nuclear Proliferation International History Project Working Paper #1.* Woodrow Wilson Center, 2011.

van Schendel, Willem. "A War Within a War: Mizo rebels and the Bangladesh liberation struggle." *Modern Asian Studies* 50, no. 1 (2016): 99–103.

Walker, Lydia. "Decolonization in the 1960s? On Legitimate and Illegitimate Nationalist Claims-Making." *Past & Present* 242, no. 1 (February 2019): 227–64.

Winner, Langdon. "Do Artifacts Have Politics?" *Daedalus* 109, no. 1 (Winter 1980): 121–36.

Wohlstetter, Albert. "Nuclear sharing: NATO and the N+1 country." *Foreign Affairs* 39 (April 1961): 355–87.

Wright, Quincy. "The Goa Incident," *The American Journal of International Law* 56, no. 3 (July 1962): 617–32.

INDEX

AECI. *See* Atomic Energy Commission of India (AECI)

AECI / DAE. *See* Atomic Energy Commission of India (AECI); Department of Atomic Energy of India (DAE)

AECL. *See* Atomic Energy of Canada Limited (AECL)

aeronautics industry, Indian, 25, 30, 212n33

All-India Congress Committee, 94–95, 101

American Academy of Arts and Sciences, 108–9, 111, 136, 158–59, 184, 234n43. *See also* Committee on International Studies of Arms Control (CISAC)

Argentina, 130–31, 162, 240n148

atomic earths, 210n5; Anglo-American stockpiling, 22–23; beryllium, 44–47; Indian, 34, 45, 47–54, 215n76; monazite, 19–20, 30–34, 38–40, 43, 48–52, 54, 130, 204; plutonium, 66–67, 80–81, 87–89, 107, 160–61, 201; radium, 28, 36, 213n47, 215n3; scarcity, 44; technopolitics, 31–32, 38, 54; thorium, 19–20, 69; Travancore monazite and thorium resources, 19–20, 31–34, 38–40, 204; uranium, 22–23, 69, 76–77, 196–97, 217n32, 222n39

Atomic Energy Commission of India (AECI): atomic earth export embargoes, 45, 47; Bhabha, Homi Jehangir, 8, 38–40, 58, 76; creation, 8, 34; DAE integration, 58, 220n3; foreign partnerships, 37–40, 43–47, 52, 222n30; mandate, 38, 216n11; members, 76, 226n86; monazite processing plant goals, 38–39, 50–51

Atomic Energy of Canada Limited (AECL), 63–64, 66–67, 70, 81, 88, 99, 107, 125, 158, 160, 192, 194–95, 201, 245n75

Atomic Energy Research Committee (India), 7, 31–33, 215n76

Auergesellschaft (German company), 19–21, 39, 211n16, 211n18

A. V. Hill Report, 7, 26

Ayub Khan, Muhammad, 102–3, 233n25

Bangladesh, 143, 146–47, 165–66. *See also* Bangladesh Liberation War; East Pakistan

Bangladesh Liberation War, 149–52, 164–65, 179–80, 244n55

BARC. *See* Bhabha Atomic Research Centre (BARC)

beryllium, 44–47

Bhabha, Homi Jehangir, 2; at AECI, 8, 38–40, 58, 76; atomic earths sales, 69; career overview, 5–6; at CSIR, 7, 32; at DAE, 63, 75, 84, 131–32; death, 104, 152; Himalayan deterrent plans, 184; IAEA service, 223n50; Indian National Committee for Space Research, 8; National Defence Council, 78; nuclear weapons development cost estimates, 94–95, 97, 108; and Palfrey, John, 112; Parsi heritage, 191; plutonium processing plant design purchase, 67; power reactor negotiations (Tarapur), 82–83; relation to Tata family, 6, 206n12; safeguards positions, 68, 81–82, 84, 88, 115; and Saha, Meghnad, 62–63, 214n67; and Sethna, Homi, 152–53; space program, 90–91, 97–98; three-stage program, 70, 89, 130; at TIFR, 6, 8, 26–28, 36, 59; Travancore's monazite sands, 32; underground nuclear explosions, 113, 122

Bhabha Atomic Research Centre (BARC), 8, 64, 131–35, 152, 155, 157–58, 161, 176, 187, 201, 256n129

Bhatnagar, Santi Swarup (S. S.), 8, 38–39, 44, 49–52

Blumenfeld, Joseph, 21, 39–40

Lightning Source UK Ltd.
Milton Keynes UK
UKHW012158150622
404478UK00003B/376